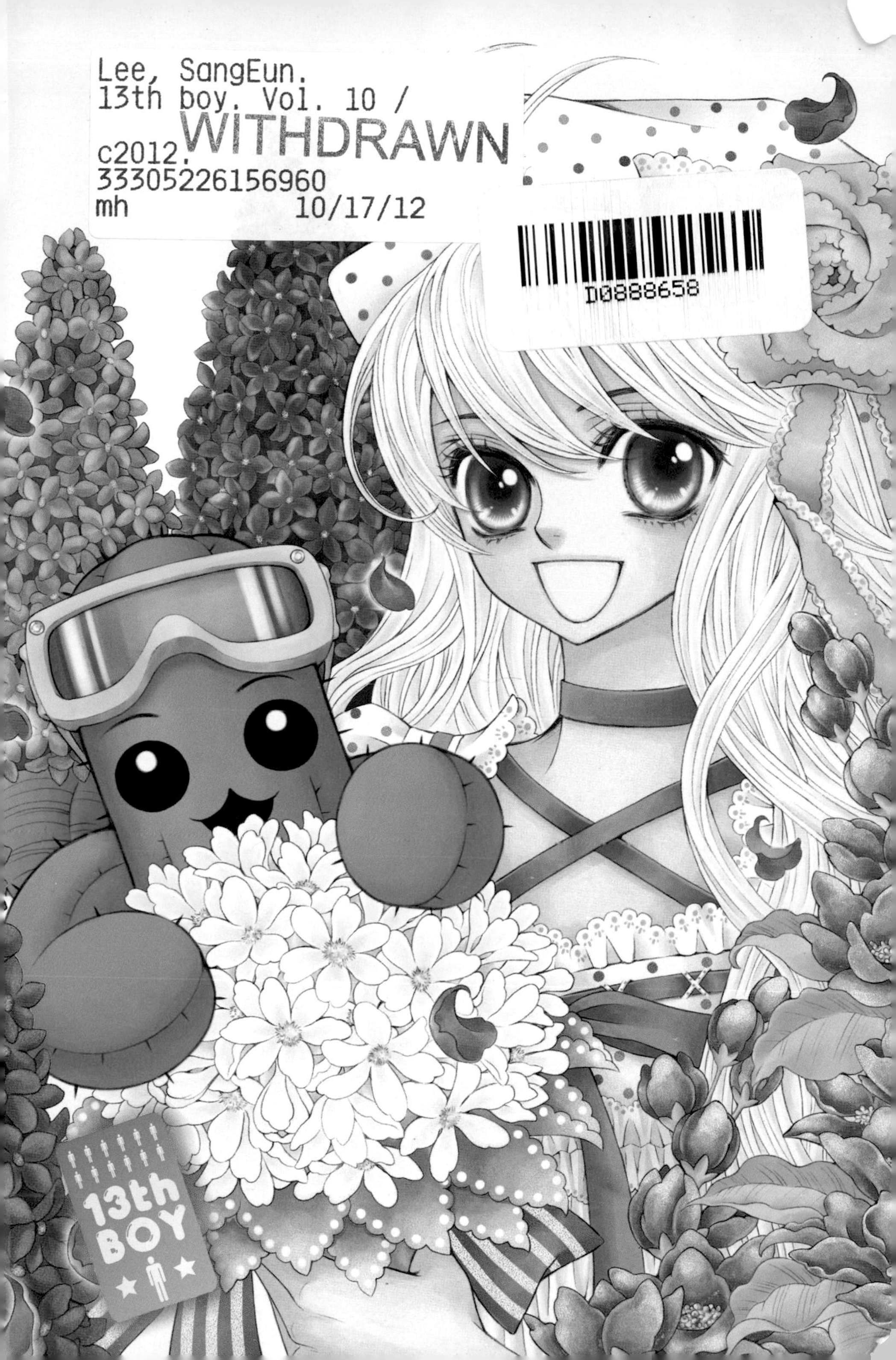
13th
BOY

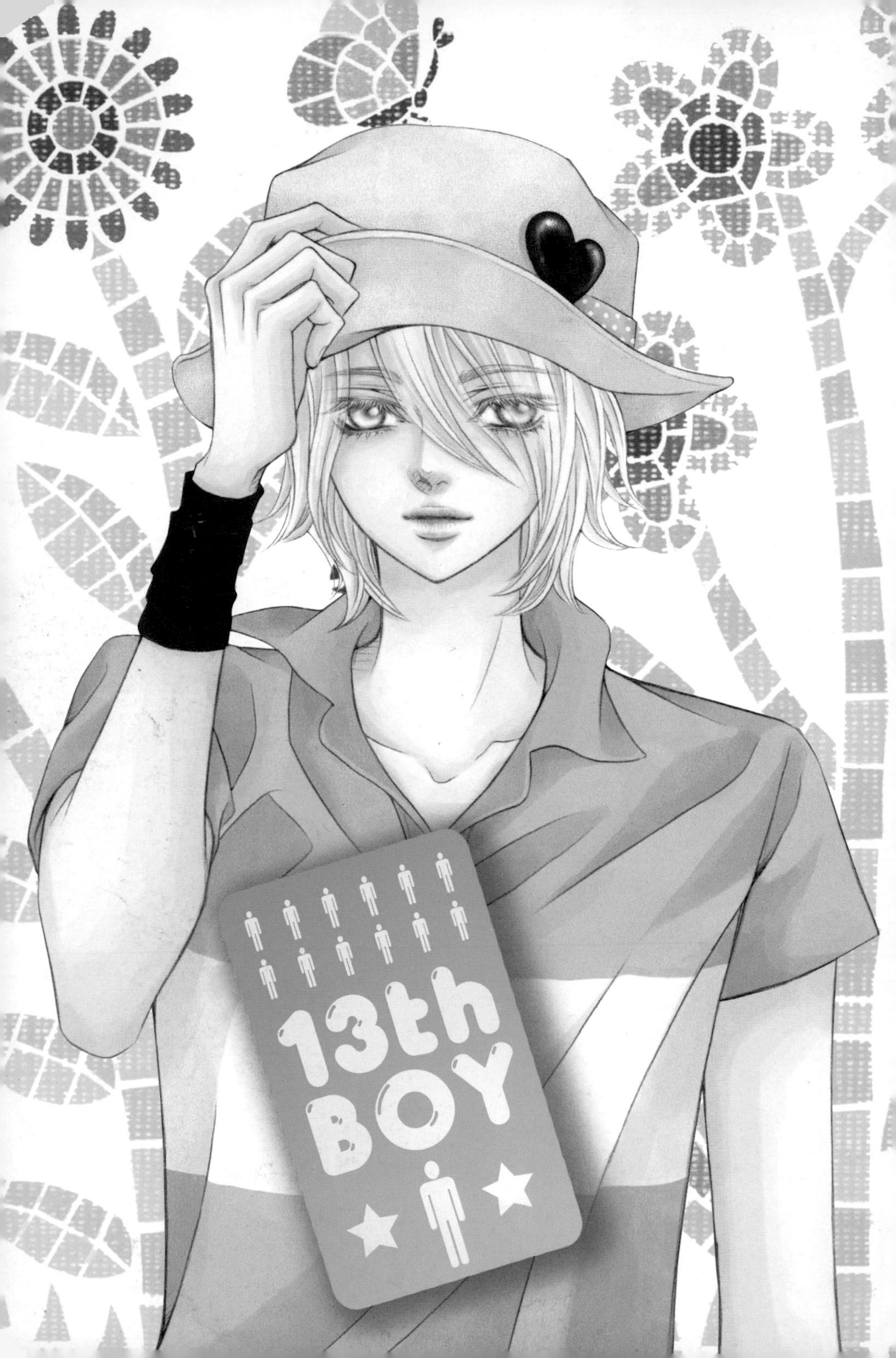
13th
BOY

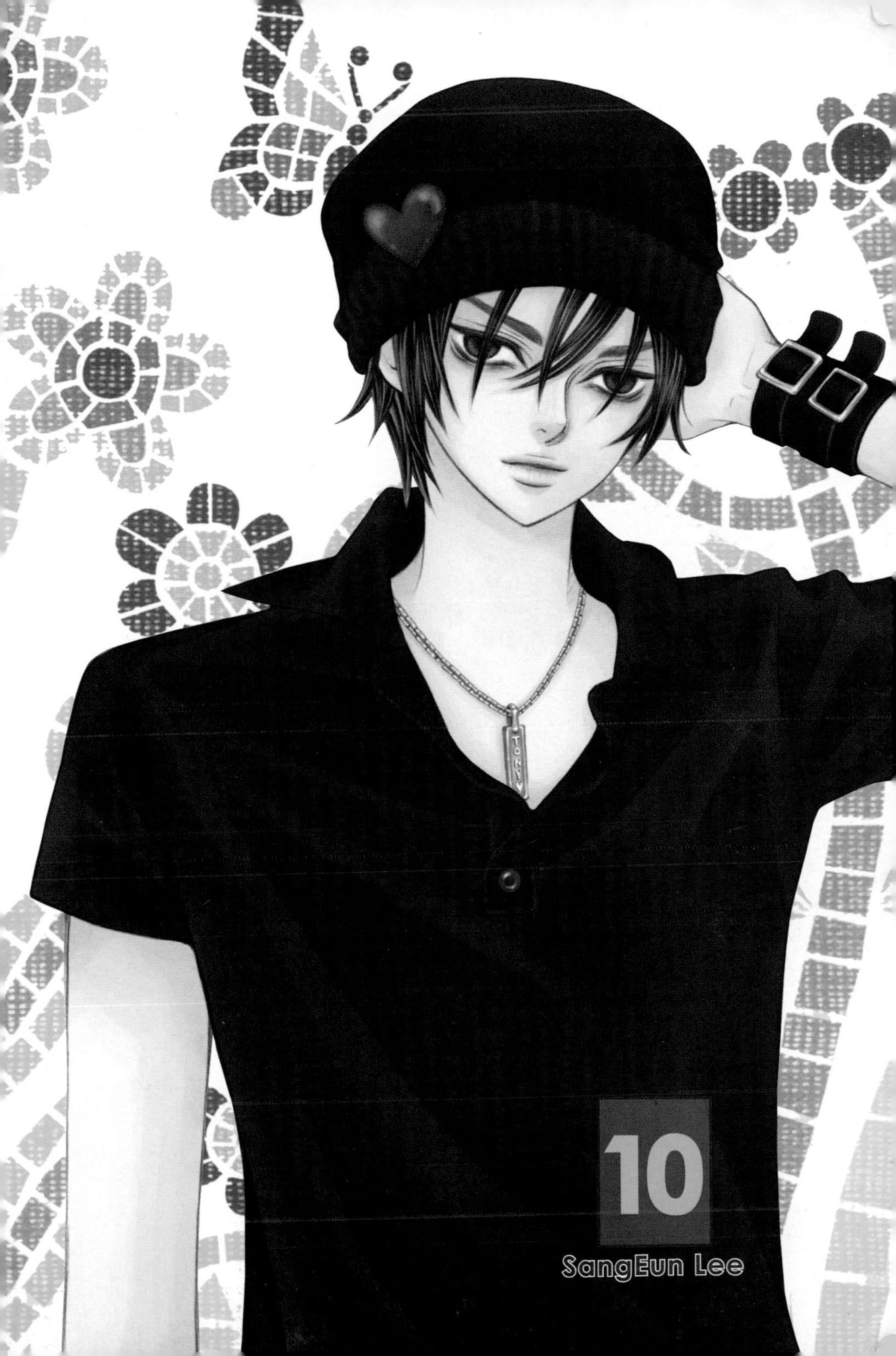
10
SangEun Lee

13th BOY♥ CONTENTS

STEP 36. *THE TRUTH ABOUT THE RED VELVET RIBBON* 10

STEP 37. *WHIE-YOUNG JANG'S DREAM* 50

STEP 38. *A HEART WITH ROOM FOR ONE* 118

STEP 39. *MY MASTER* 182

BONUS STEP *BEHIND THE SCENES OF <13TH BOY>! LET'S TAKE A LOOK~! ♥ ~SPECIAL EPISODE~* 188

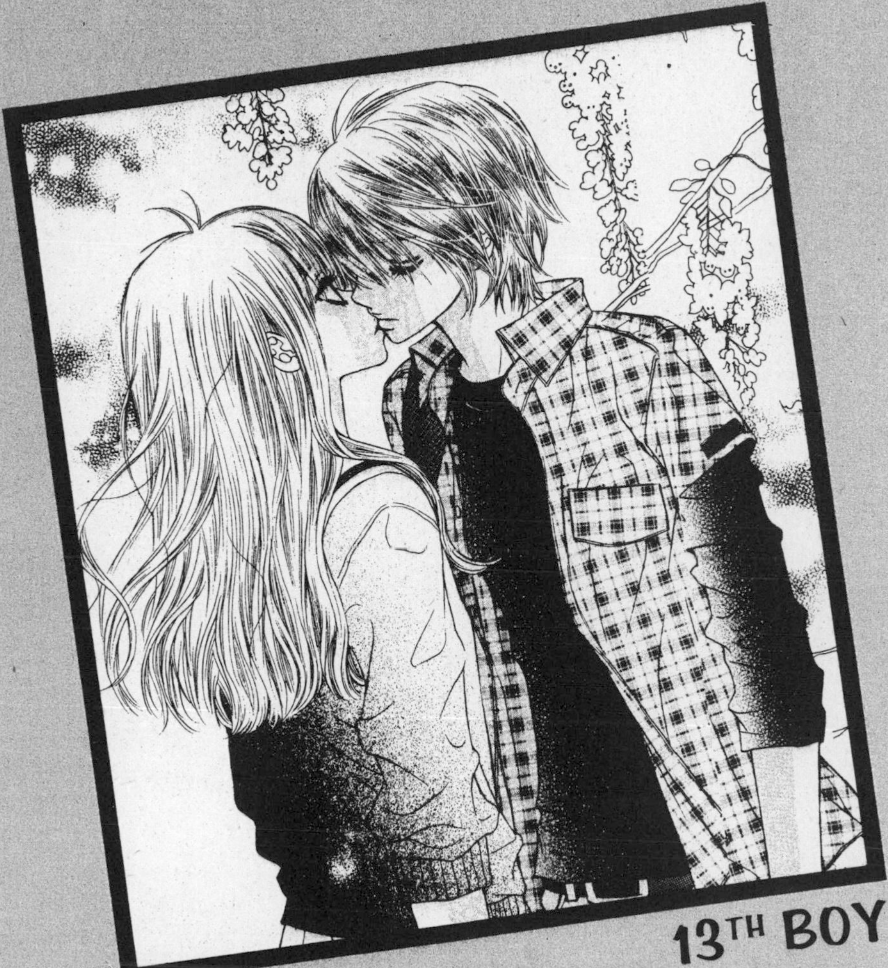

13TH BOY

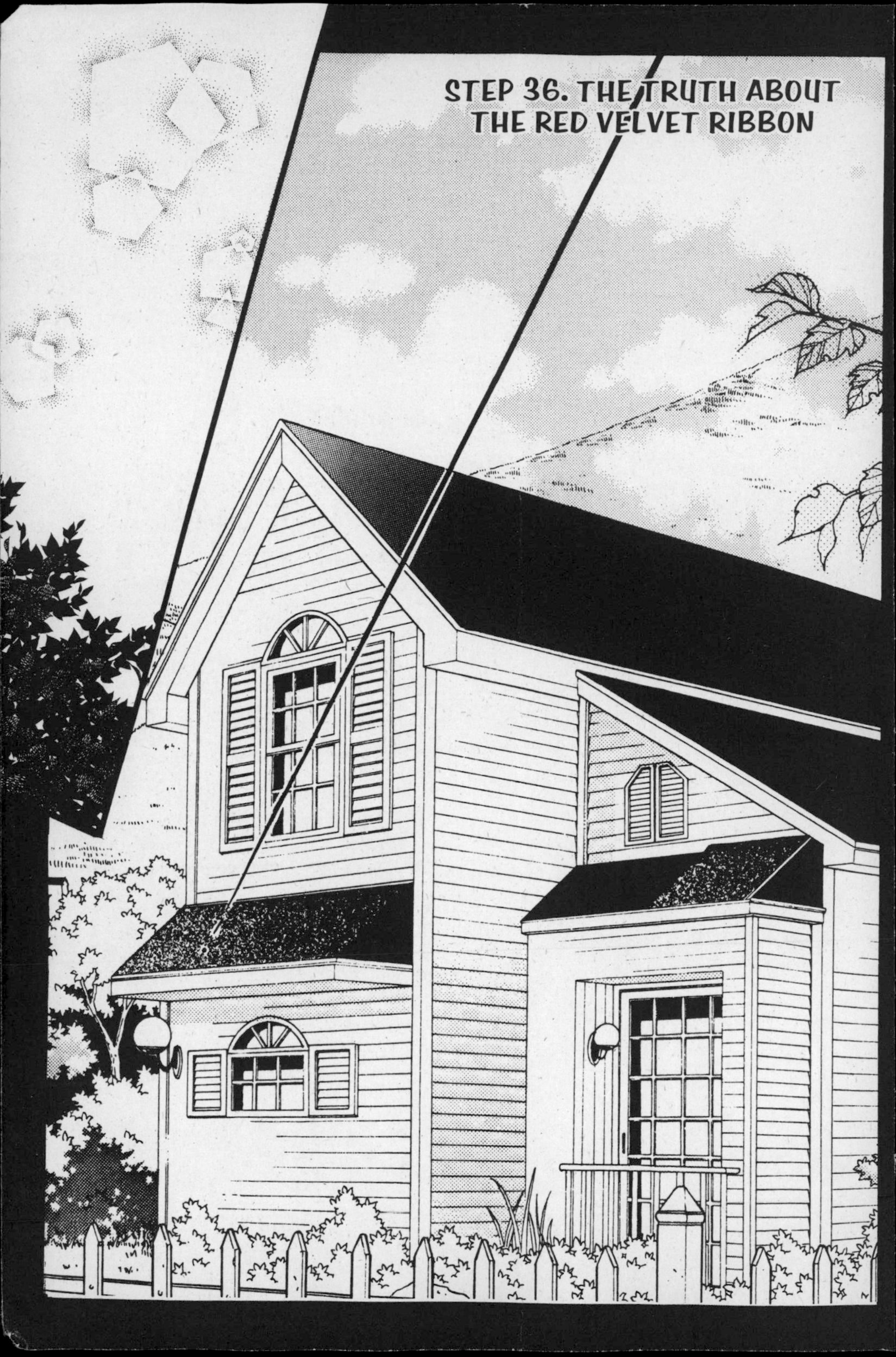
STEP 36. THE TRUTH ABOUT
THE RED VELVET RIBBON

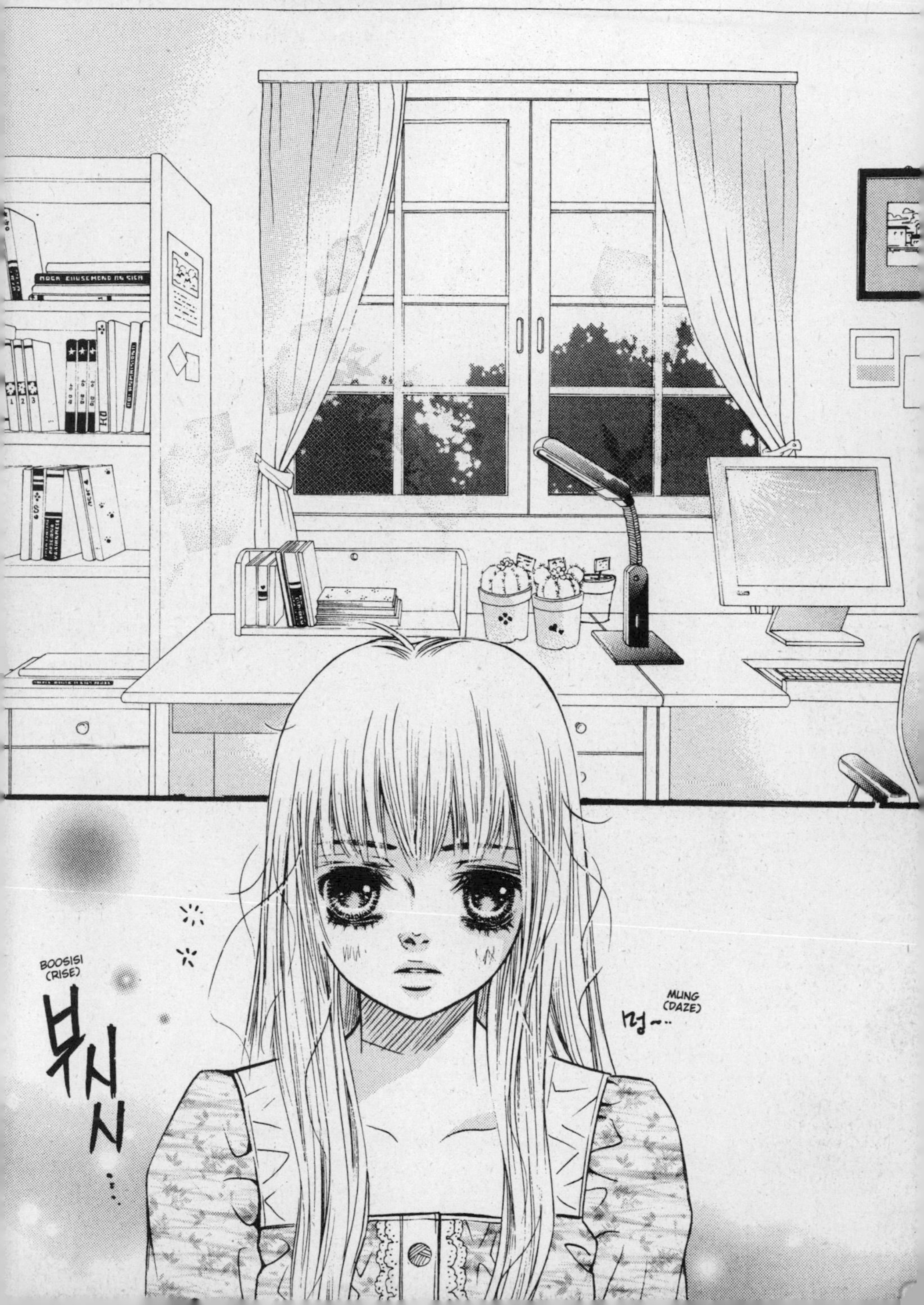
BOOSISI (RISE)
부시시…
MUNG (DAZE)
멍~..

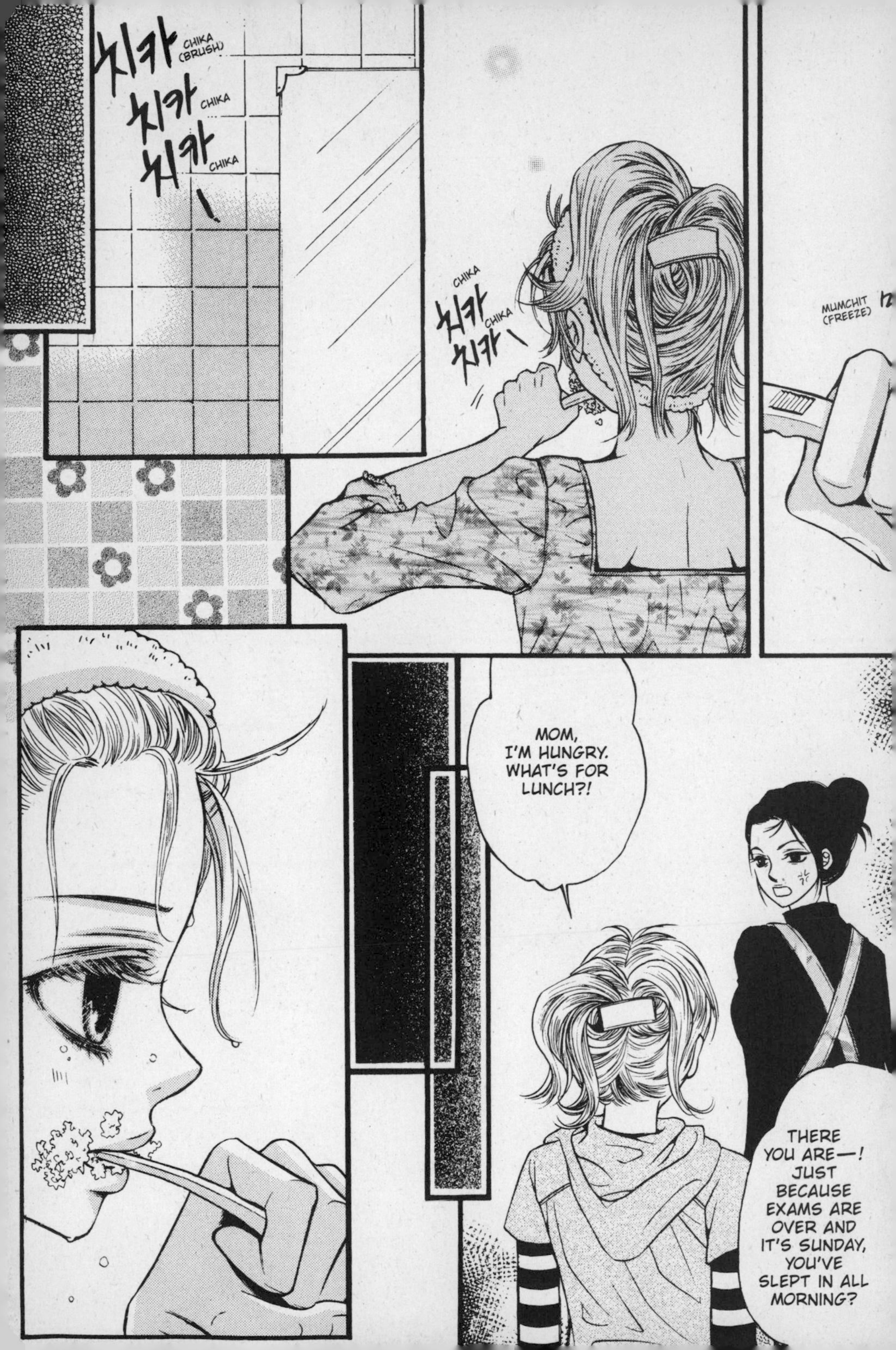

치카 CHIKA (BRUSH)
치카 CHIKA
치카 CHIKA
치카 CHIKA
치카 CHIKA
멈칫 MUMCHIT (FREEZE)
MOM, I'M HUNGRY. WHAT'S FOR LUNCH?!
THERE YOU ARE—! JUST BECAUSE EXAMS ARE OVER AND IT'S SUNDAY, YOU'VE SLEPT IN ALL MORNING?

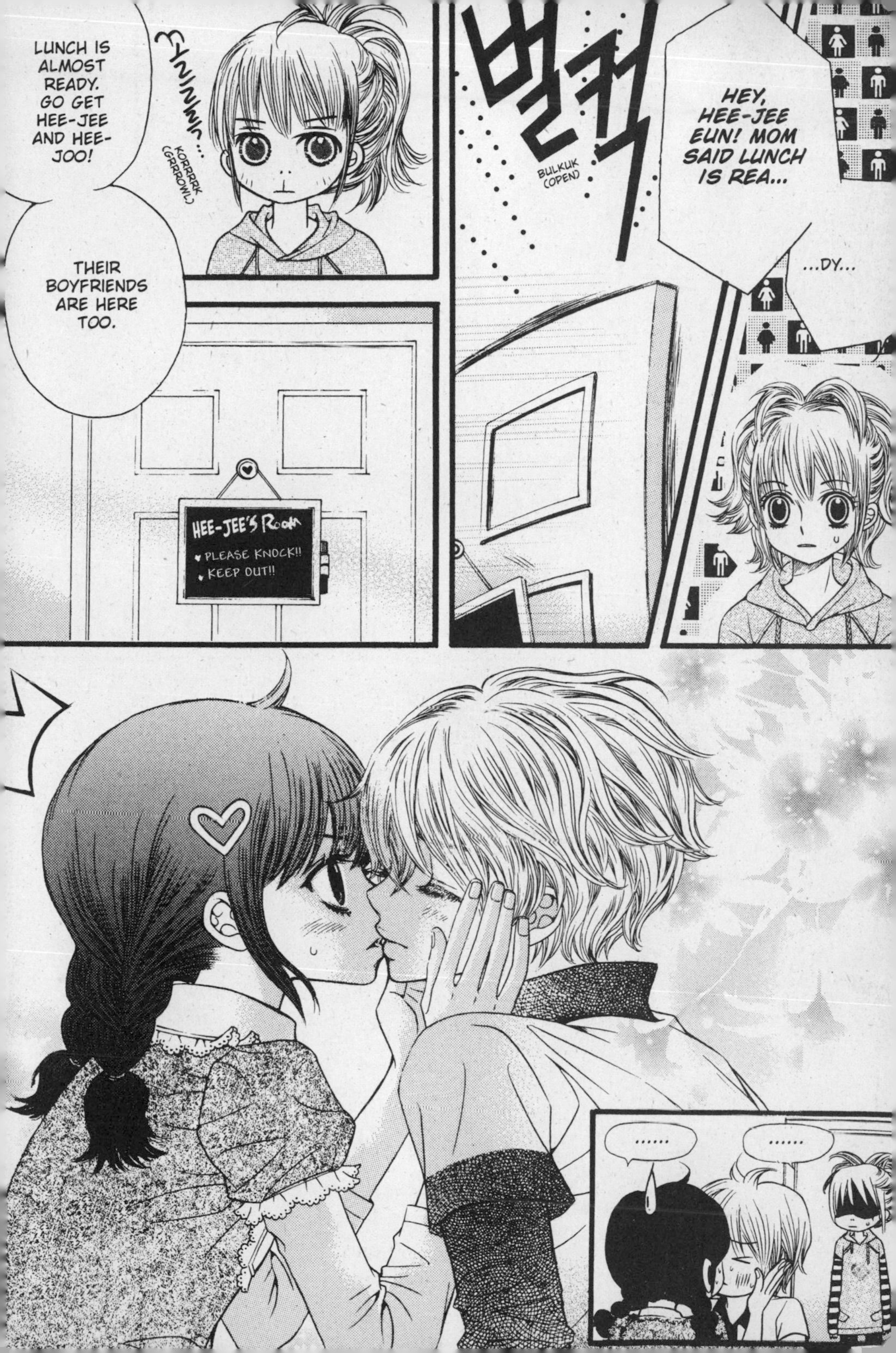

LUNCH IS ALMOST READY. GO GET HEE-JEE AND HEE-JOO!
KORRRRK (GRRROWL)
THEIR BOYFRIENDS ARE HERE TOO.
HEE-JEE'S Room
♥ PLEASE KNOCK!!
♥ KEEP OUT!!
벌컥
BULKUK (OPEN)
HEY, HEE-JEE EUN! MOM SAID LUNCH IS REA...
...DY...
......
......

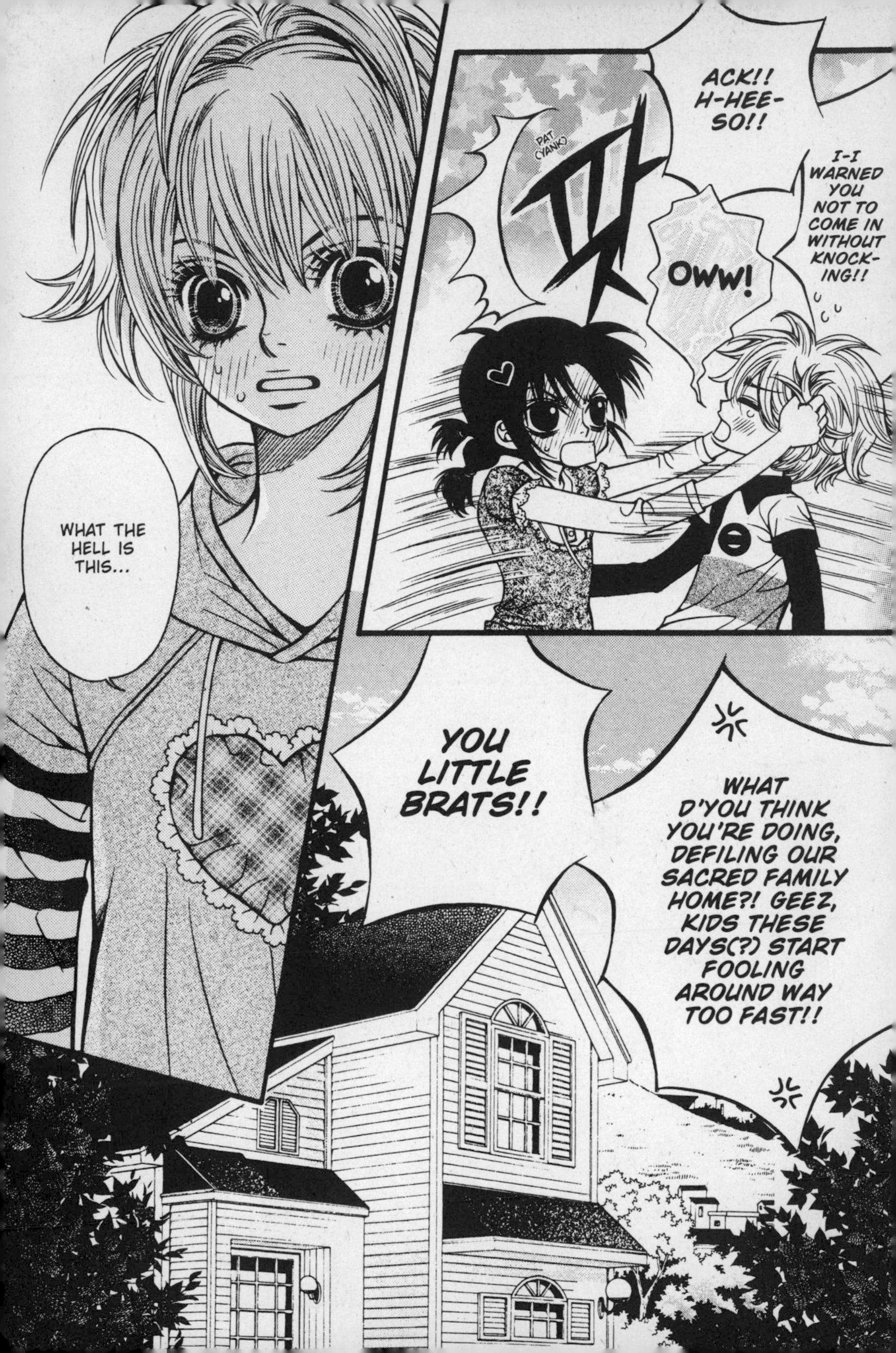
WHAT THE HELL IS THIS...
ACK!! H-HEE-SO!!
PAT (YANK)
I-I WARNED YOU NOT TO COME IN WITHOUT KNOCKING!!
OWW!
YOU LITTLE BRATS!!
WHAT D'YOU THINK YOU'RE DOING, DEFILING OUR SACRED FAMILY HOME?! GEEZ, KIDS THESE DAYS(?) START FOOLING AROUND WAY TOO FAST!!

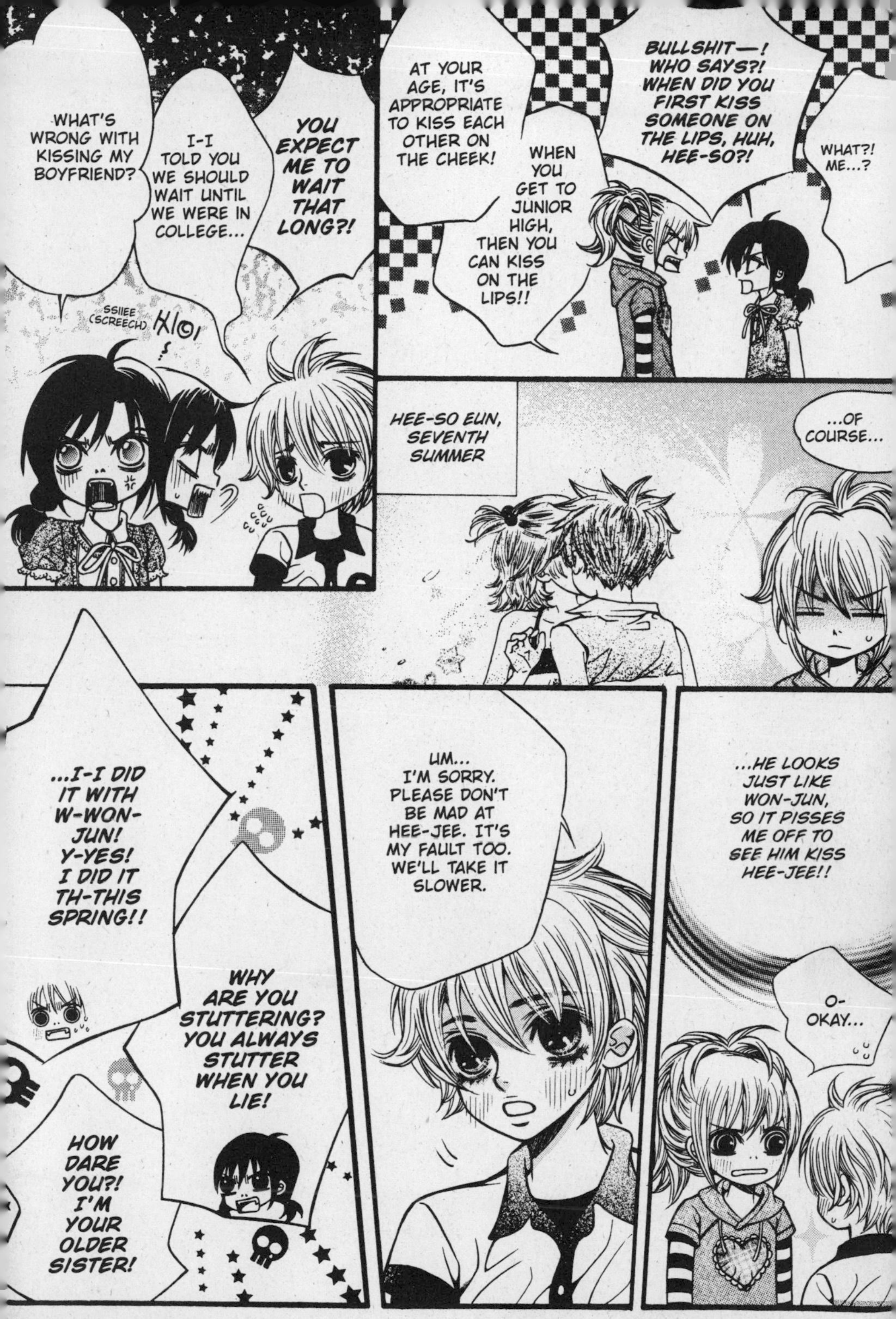
WHAT'S WRONG WITH KISSING MY BOYFRIEND?
I-I TOLD YOU WE SHOULD WAIT UNTIL WE WERE IN COLLEGE...
YOU EXPECT ME TO WAIT THAT LONG?!
SSIIEE (SCREECH)
AT YOUR AGE, IT'S APPROPRIATE TO KISS EACH OTHER ON THE CHEEK!
WHEN YOU GET TO JUNIOR HIGH, THEN YOU CAN KISS ON THE LIPS!!
BULLSHIT—! WHO SAYS?! WHEN DID YOU FIRST KISS SOMEONE ON THE LIPS, HUH, HEE-SO?!
WHAT?! ME...?
HEE-SO EUN, SEVENTH SUMMER
...OF COURSE...
...I-I DID IT WITH W-WON-JUN! Y-YES! I DID IT TH-THIS SPRING!!
WHY ARE YOU STUTTERING? YOU ALWAYS STUTTER WHEN YOU LIE!
HOW DARE YOU?! I'M YOUR OLDER SISTER!
UM... I'M SORRY. PLEASE DON'T BE MAD AT HEE-JEE. IT'S MY FAULT TOO. WE'LL TAKE IT SLOWER.
...HE LOOKS JUST LIKE WON-JUN, SO IT PISSES ME OFF TO SEE HIM KISS HEE-JEE!!
O-OKAY...

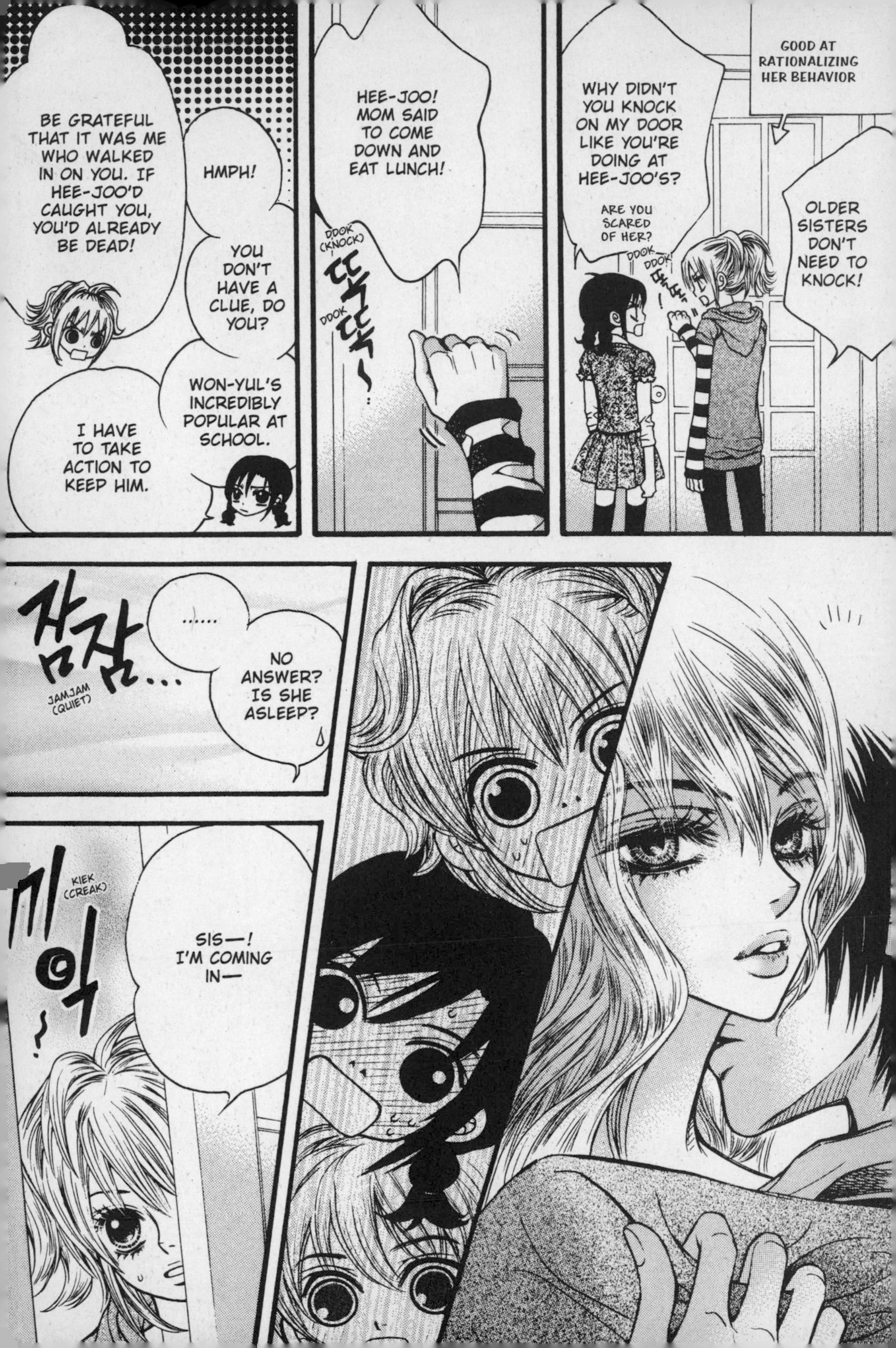
BE GRATEFUL THAT IT WAS ME WHO WALKED IN ON YOU. IF HEE-JOO'D CAUGHT YOU, YOU'D ALREADY BE DEAD!
HMPH!
YOU DON'T HAVE A CLUE, DO YOU?
WON-YUL'S INCREDIBLY POPULAR AT SCHOOL.
I HAVE TO TAKE ACTION TO KEEP HIM.
HEE-JOO! MOM SAID TO COME DOWN AND EAT LUNCH!
똑 똑~
DDOK (KNOCK)
DDOK
WHY DIDN'T YOU KNOCK ON MY DOOR LIKE YOU'RE DOING AT HEE-JOO'S?
ARE YOU SCARED OF HER?
GOOD AT RATIONALIZING HER BEHAVIOR
똑 똑
DDOK DDOK
OLDER SISTERS DON'T NEED TO KNOCK!
잠잠...
JAMJAM (QUIET)
......
NO ANSWER? IS SHE ASLEEP?
끼익~
KIEK (CREAK)
SIS—! I'M COMING IN—

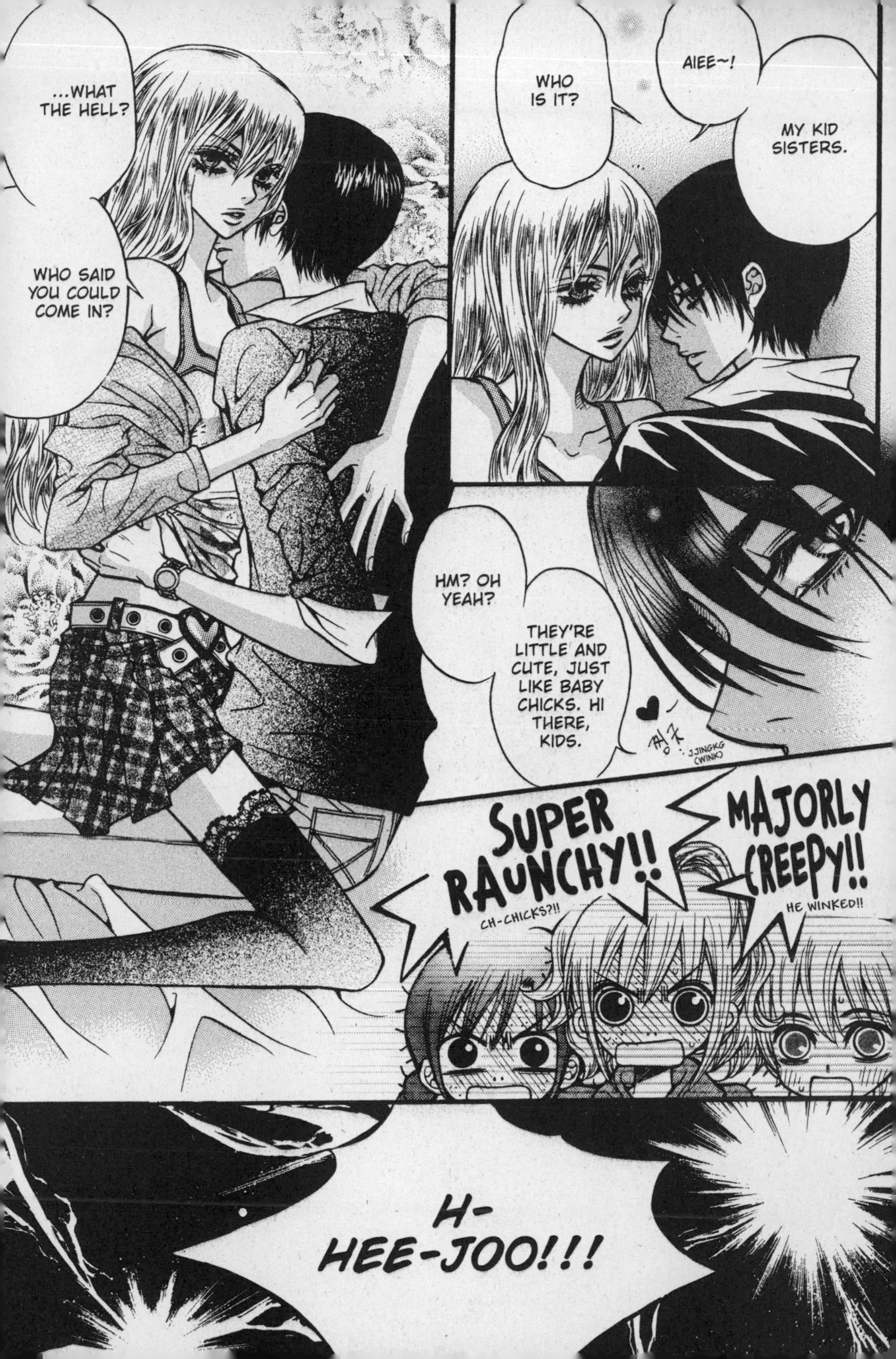
...WHAT THE HELL?
WHO SAID YOU COULD COME IN?
WHO IS IT?
AIEE~!
MY KID SISTERS.
HM? OH YEAH?
THEY'RE LITTLE AND CUTE, JUST LIKE BABY CHICKS. HI THERE, KIDS.
JJINGKG (WINK)
SUPER RAUNCHY!!
CH-CHICKS?!!
MAJORLY CREEPY!!
HE WINKED!!
H-HEE-JOO!!!

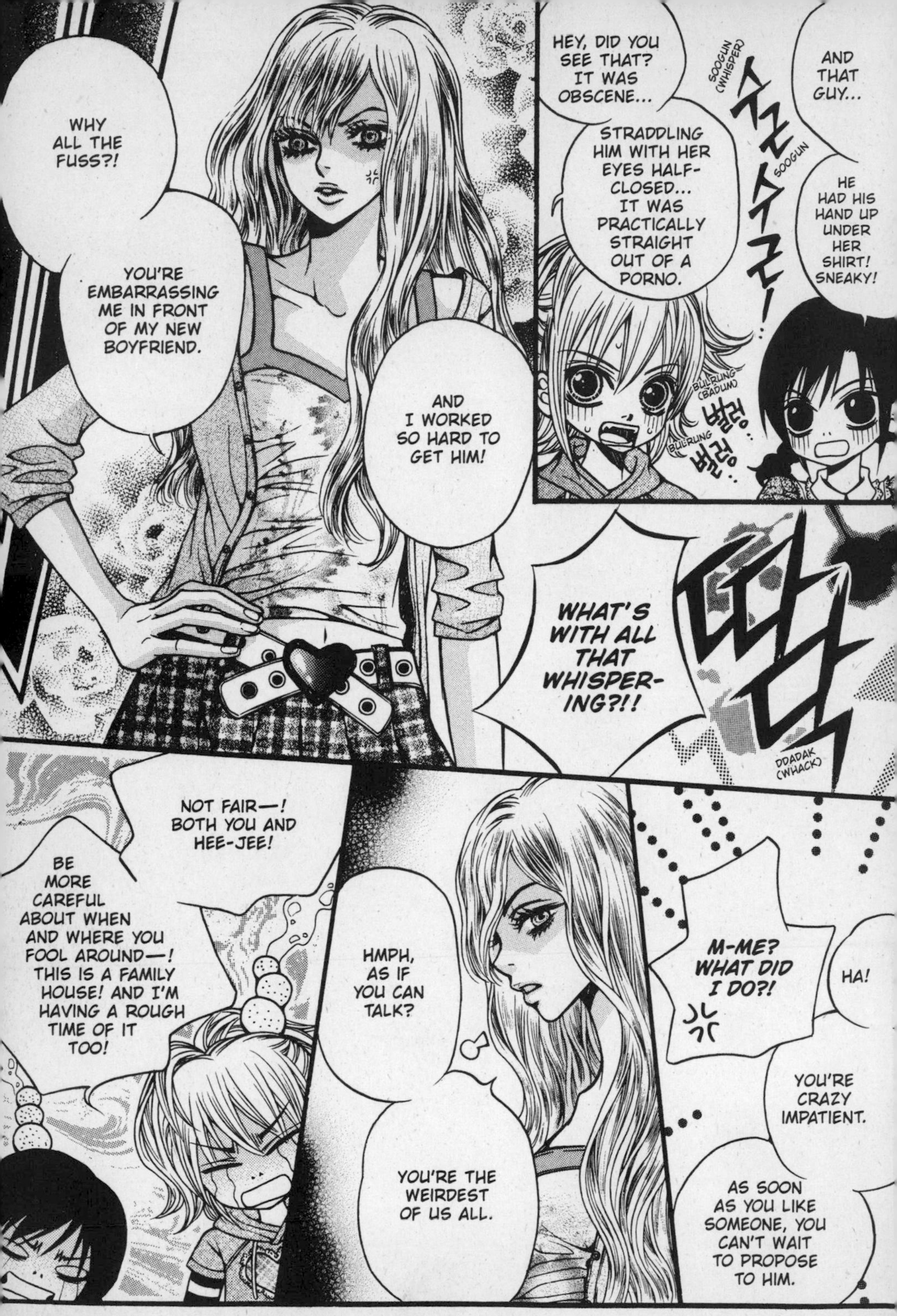
WHY ALL THE FUSS?!
YOU'RE EMBARRASSING ME IN FRONT OF MY NEW BOYFRIEND.
AND I WORKED SO HARD TO GET HIM!
HEY, DID YOU SEE THAT? IT WAS OBSCENE...
STRADDLING HIM WITH HER EYES HALF-CLOSED... IT WAS PRACTICALLY STRAIGHT OUT OF A PORNO.
SOOGUN (WHISPER)
SOOGUN
AND THAT GUY...
HE HAD HIS HAND UP UNDER HER SHIRT! SNEAKY!
BULRUNG (BADUM)
벌렁...
BULRUNG
벌렁...
WHAT'S WITH ALL THAT WHISPER-ING?!!
DDADAK (WHACK)
NOT FAIR—! BOTH YOU AND HEE-JEE!
BE MORE CAREFUL ABOUT WHEN AND WHERE YOU FOOL AROUND—! THIS IS A FAMILY HOUSE! AND I'M HAVING A ROUGH TIME OF IT TOO!
HMPH, AS IF YOU CAN TALK?
YOU'RE THE WEIRDEST OF US ALL.
M-ME? WHAT DID I DO?!
HA!
YOU'RE CRAZY IMPATIENT.
AS SOON AS YOU LIKE SOMEONE, YOU CAN'T WAIT TO PROPOSE TO HIM.

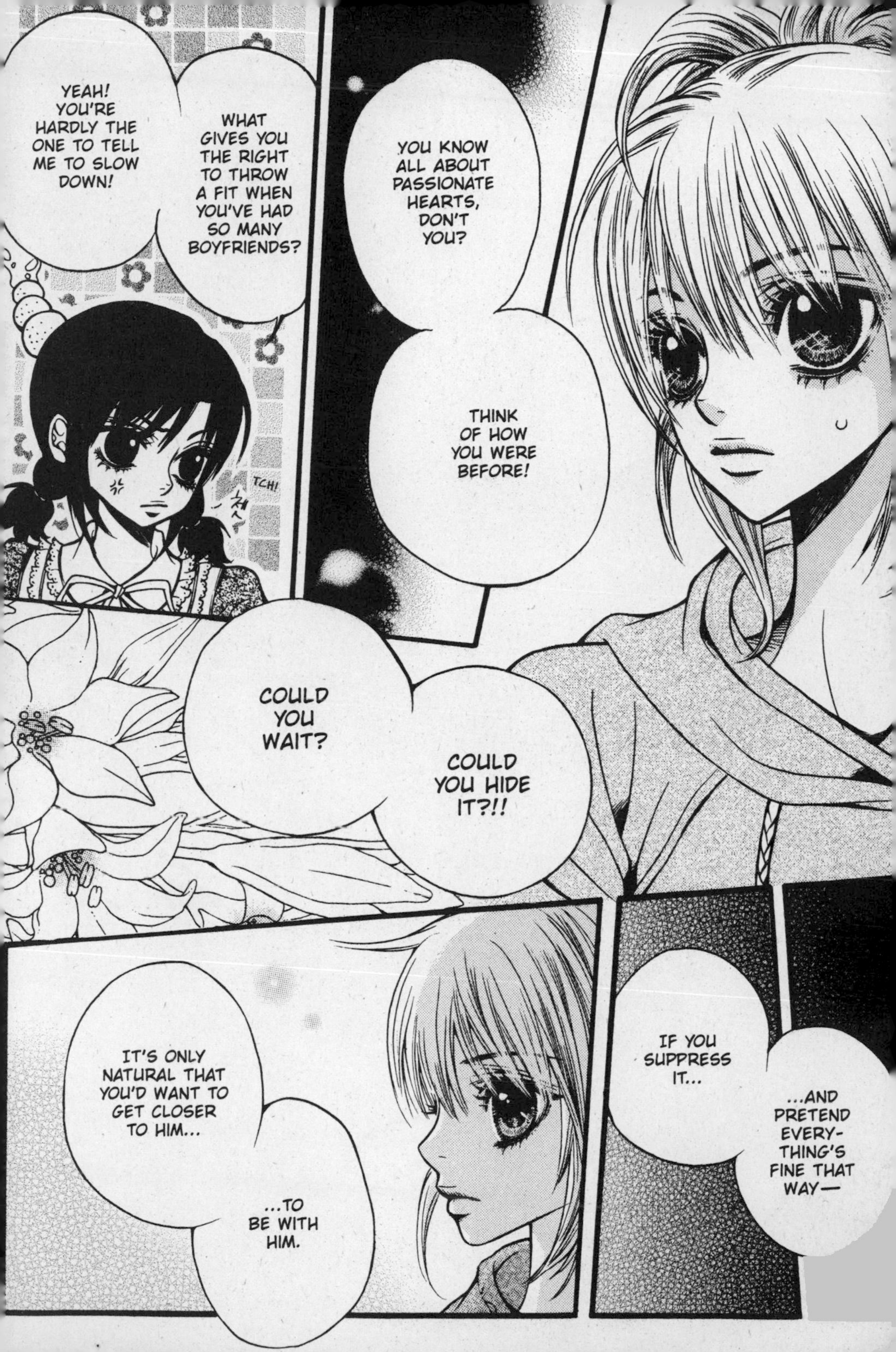
YEAH! YOU'RE HARDLY THE ONE TO TELL ME TO SLOW DOWN!
WHAT GIVES YOU THE RIGHT TO THROW A FIT WHEN YOU'VE HAD SO MANY BOYFRIENDS?
TCHI!
YOU KNOW ALL ABOUT PASSIONATE HEARTS, DON'T YOU?
THINK OF HOW YOU WERE BEFORE!
COULD YOU WAIT?
COULD YOU HIDE IT?!!
IT'S ONLY NATURAL THAT YOU'D WANT TO GET CLOSER TO HIM...
...TO BE WITH HIM.
IF YOU SUPPRESS IT...
...AND PRETEND EVERY-THING'S FINE THAT WAY—

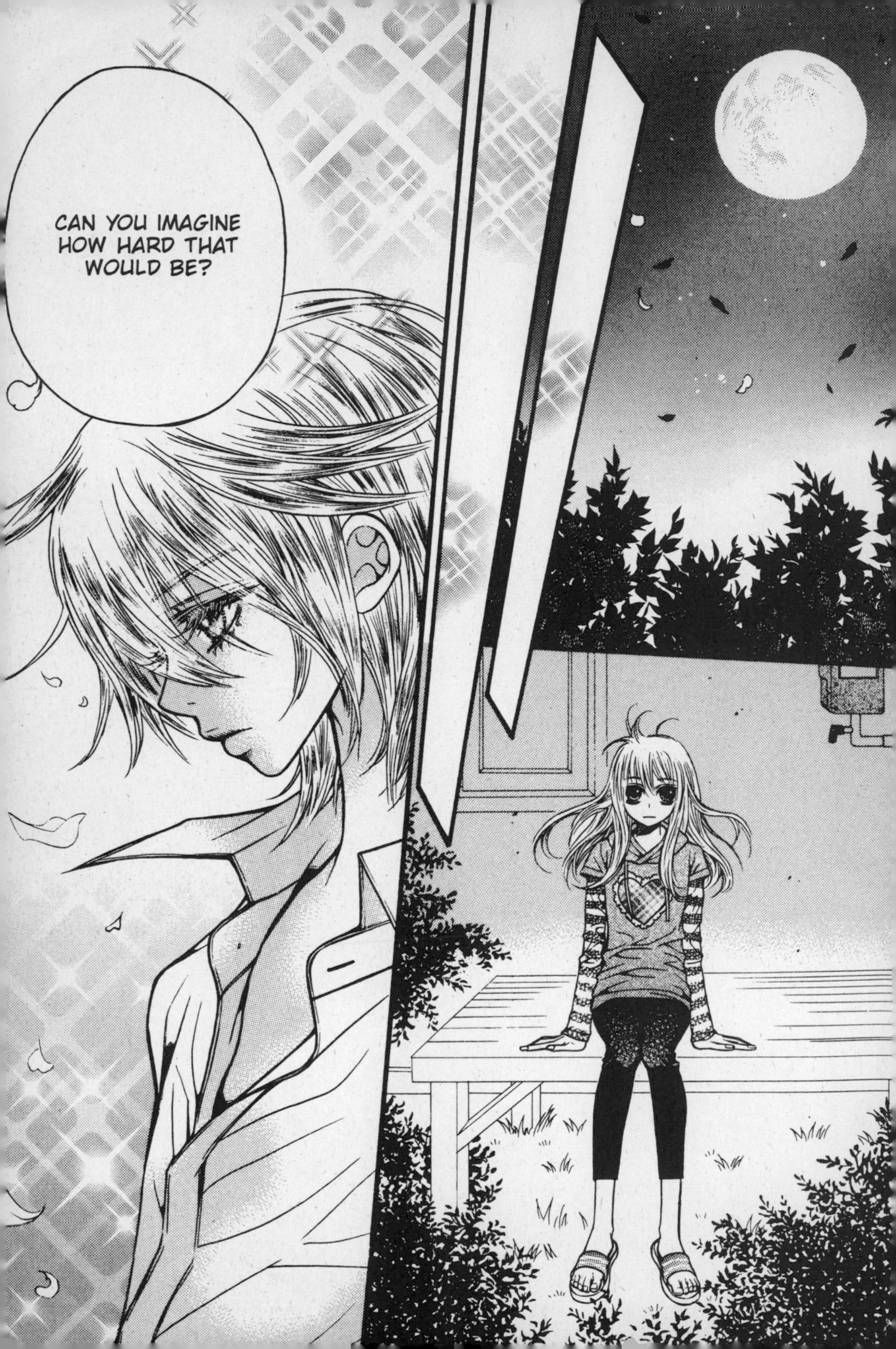
CAN YOU IMAGINE HOW HARD THAT WOULD BE?

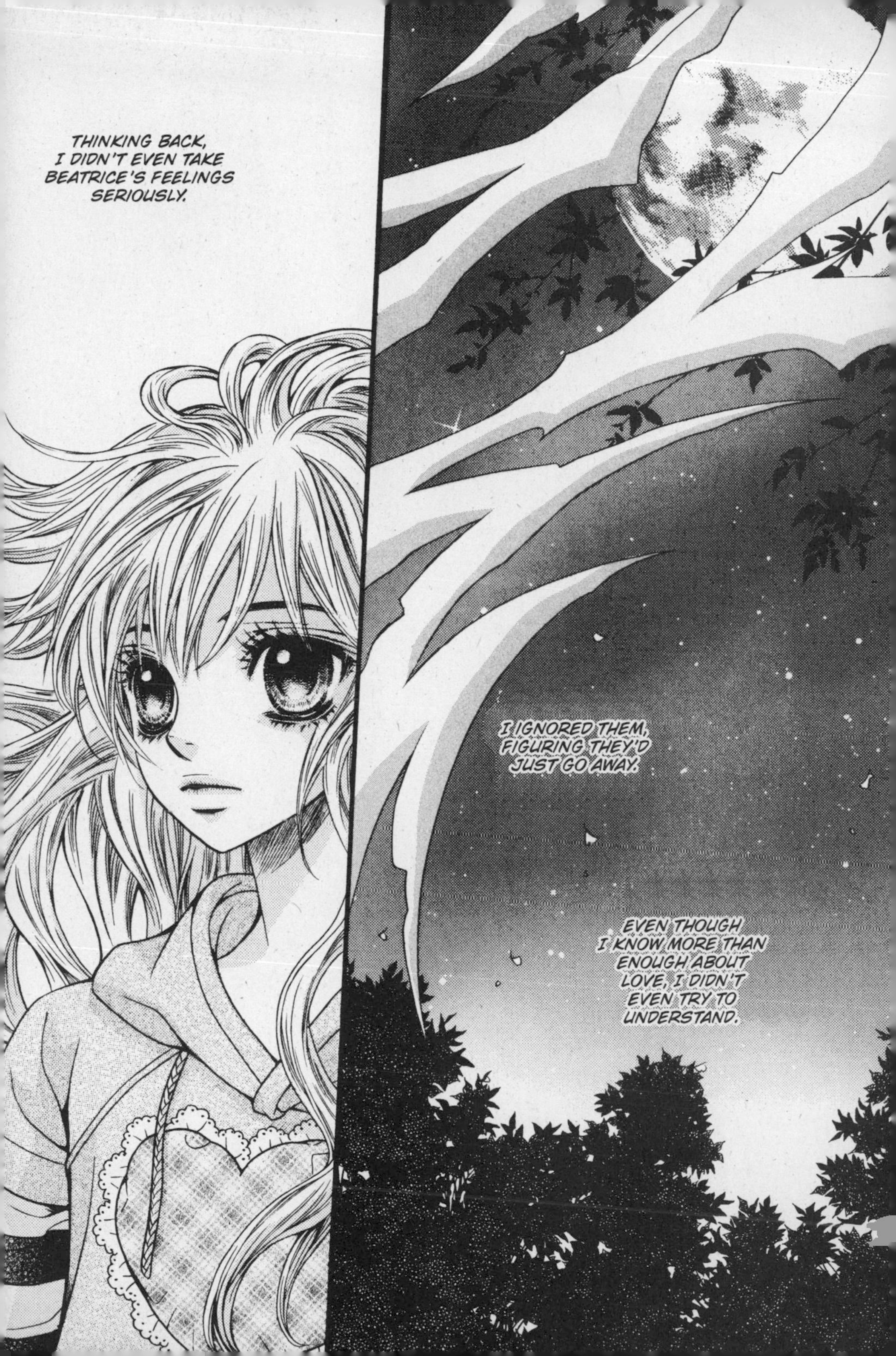
I IGNORED THEM, FIGURING THEY'D JUST GO AWAY.
EVEN THOUGH I KNOW MORE THAN ENOUGH ABOUT LOVE, I DIDN'T EVEN TRY TO UNDERSTAND.
THINKING BACK, I DIDN'T EVEN TAKE BEATRICE'S FEELINGS SERIOUSLY.

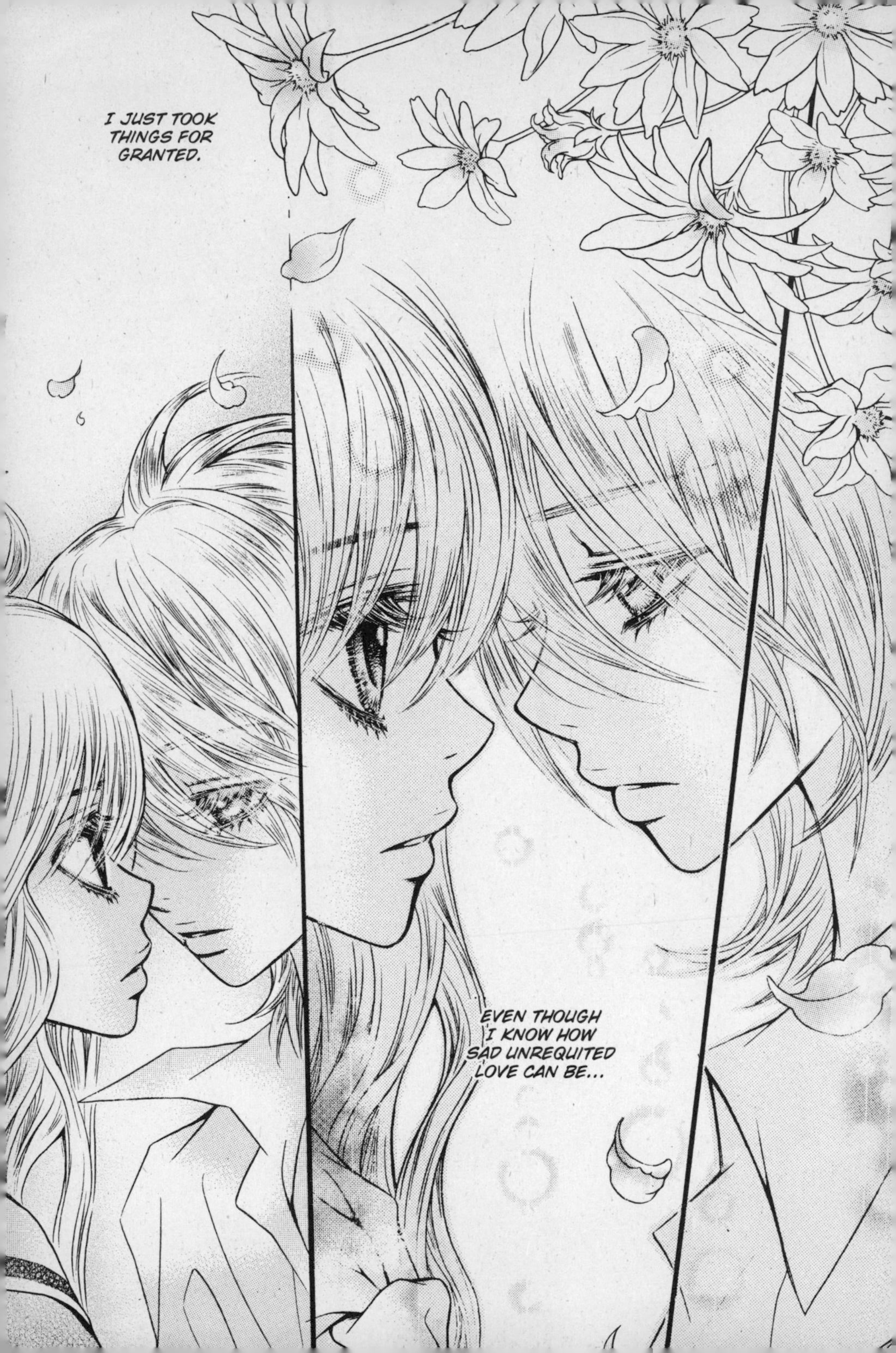
I JUST TOOK THINGS FOR GRANTED.
EVEN THOUGH I KNOW HOW SAD UNREQUITED LOVE CAN BE...

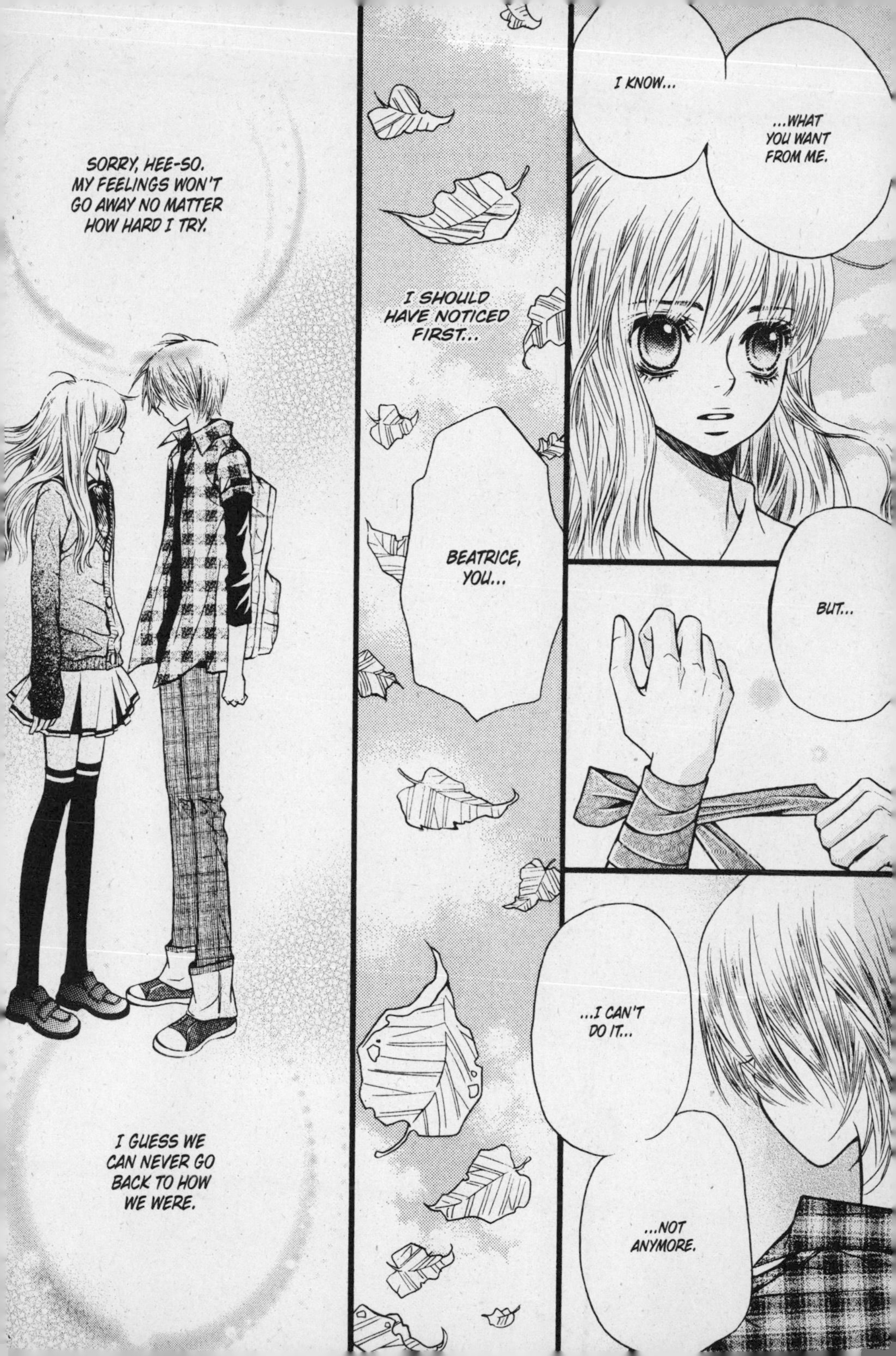
SORRY, HEE-SO. MY FEELINGS WON'T GO AWAY NO MATTER HOW HARD I TRY.
I GUESS WE CAN NEVER GO BACK TO HOW WE WERE.
I SHOULD HAVE NOTICED FIRST...
BEATRICE, YOU...
I KNOW...
...WHAT YOU WANT FROM ME.
BUT...
...I CAN'T DO IT...
...NOT ANYMORE.

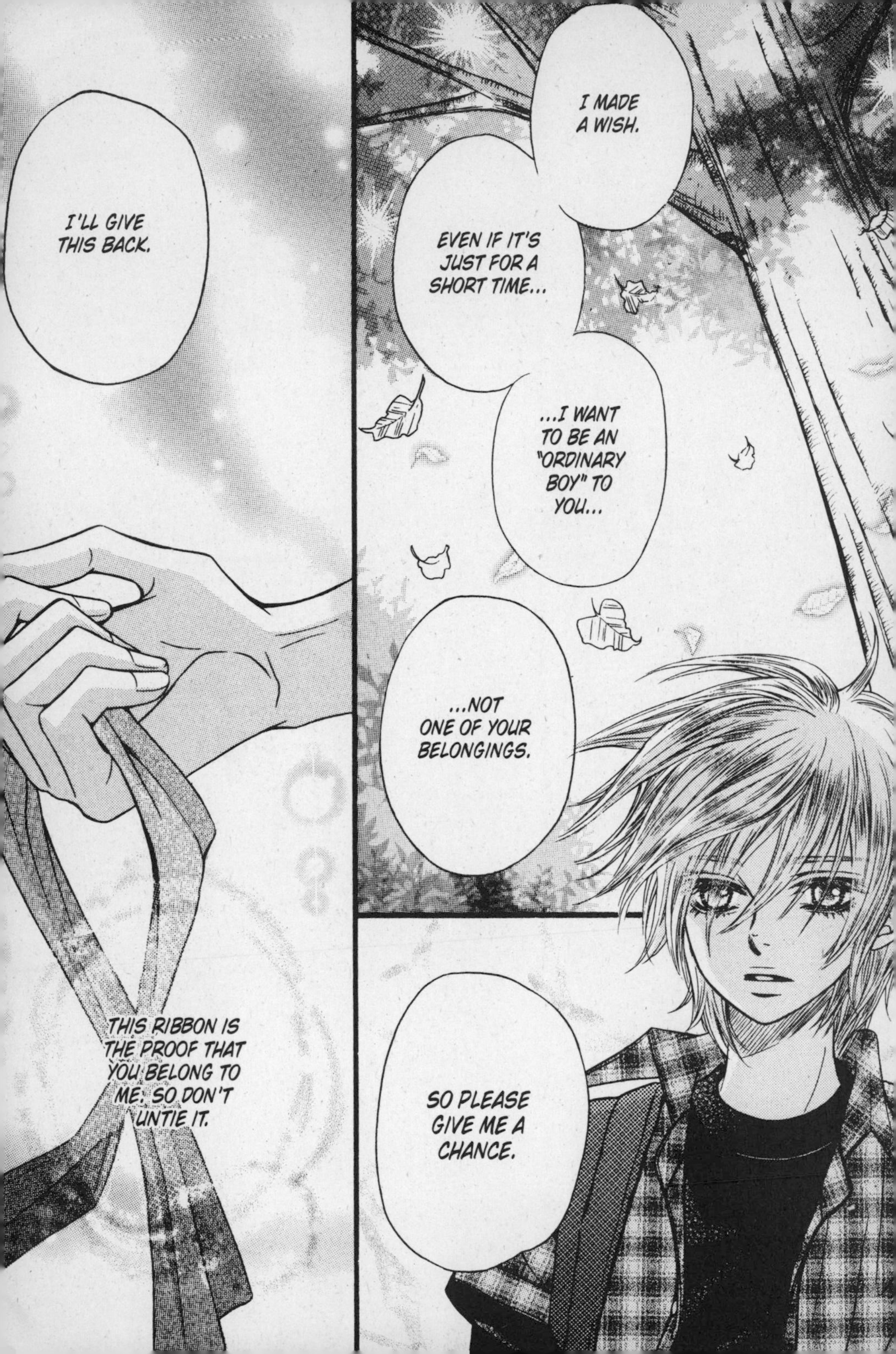
I MADE A WISH.
EVEN IF IT'S JUST FOR A SHORT TIME...
...I WANT TO BE AN "ORDINARY BOY" TO YOU...
...NOT ONE OF YOUR BELONGINGS.
SO PLEASE GIVE ME A CHANCE.
I'LL GIVE THIS BACK.
THIS RIBBON IS THE PROOF THAT YOU BELONG TO ME. SO DON'T UNTIE IT.

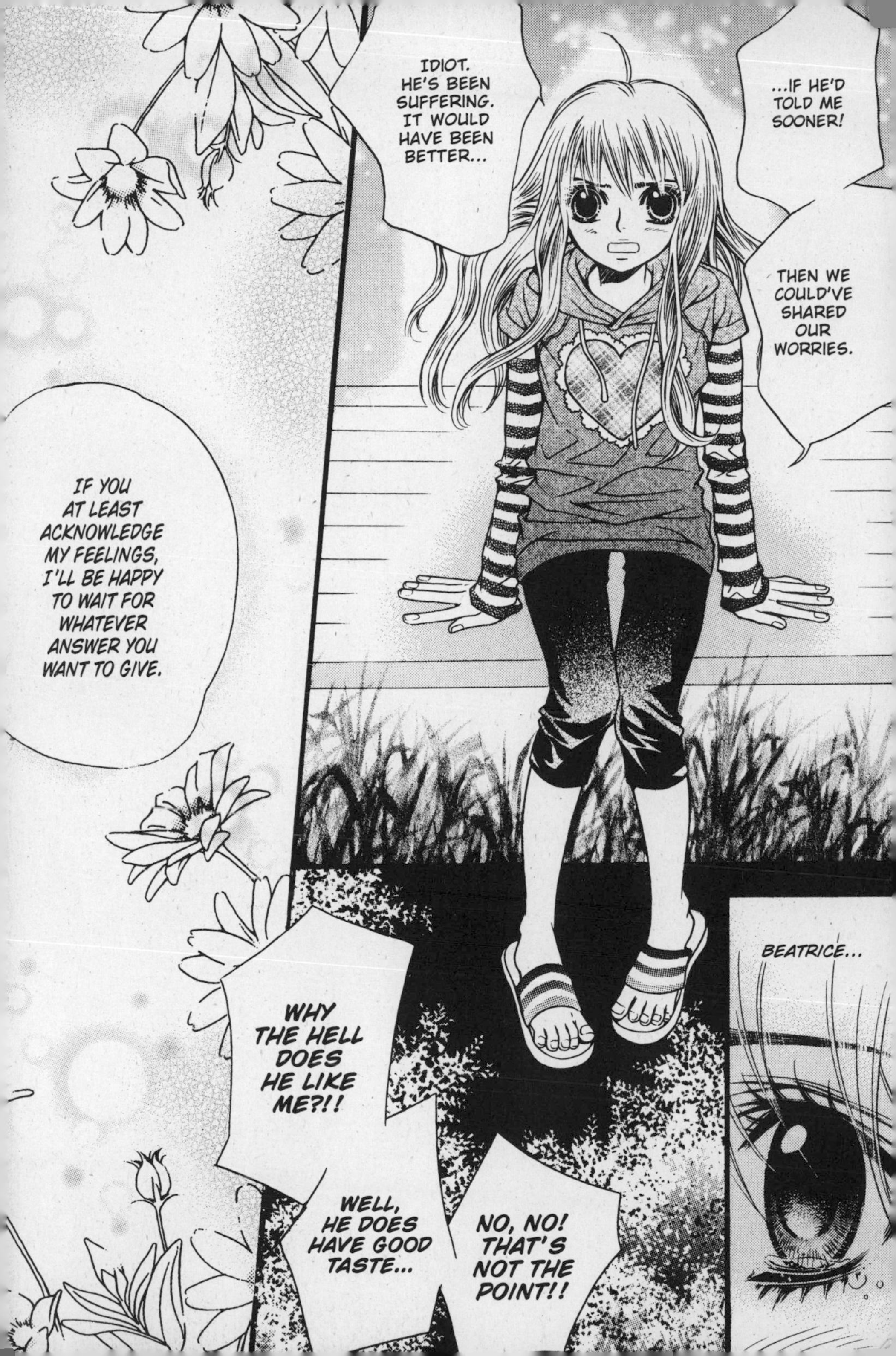
IDIOT. HE'S BEEN SUFFERING. IT WOULD HAVE BEEN BETTER...
...IF HE'D TOLD ME SOONER!
THEN WE COULD'VE SHARED OUR WORRIES.
IF YOU AT LEAST ACKNOWLEDGE MY FEELINGS, I'LL BE HAPPY TO WAIT FOR WHATEVER ANSWER YOU WANT TO GIVE.
BEATRICE...
WHY THE HELL DOES HE LIKE ME?!!
WELL, HE DOES HAVE GOOD TASTE...
NO, NO! THAT'S NOT THE POINT!!

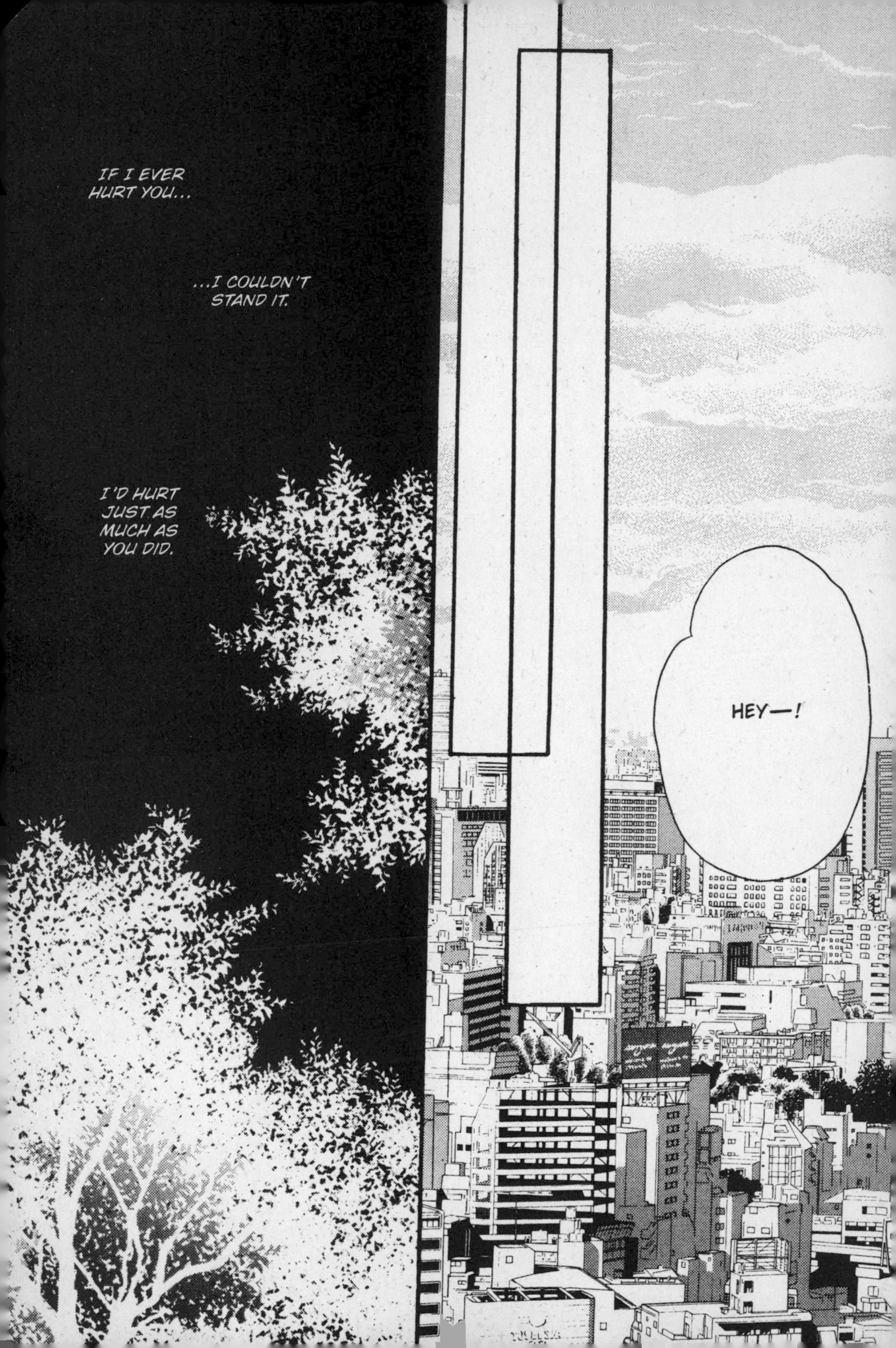
HEY—!
IF I EVER HURT YOU...
...I COULDN'T STAND IT.
I'D HURT JUST AS MUCH AS YOU DID.

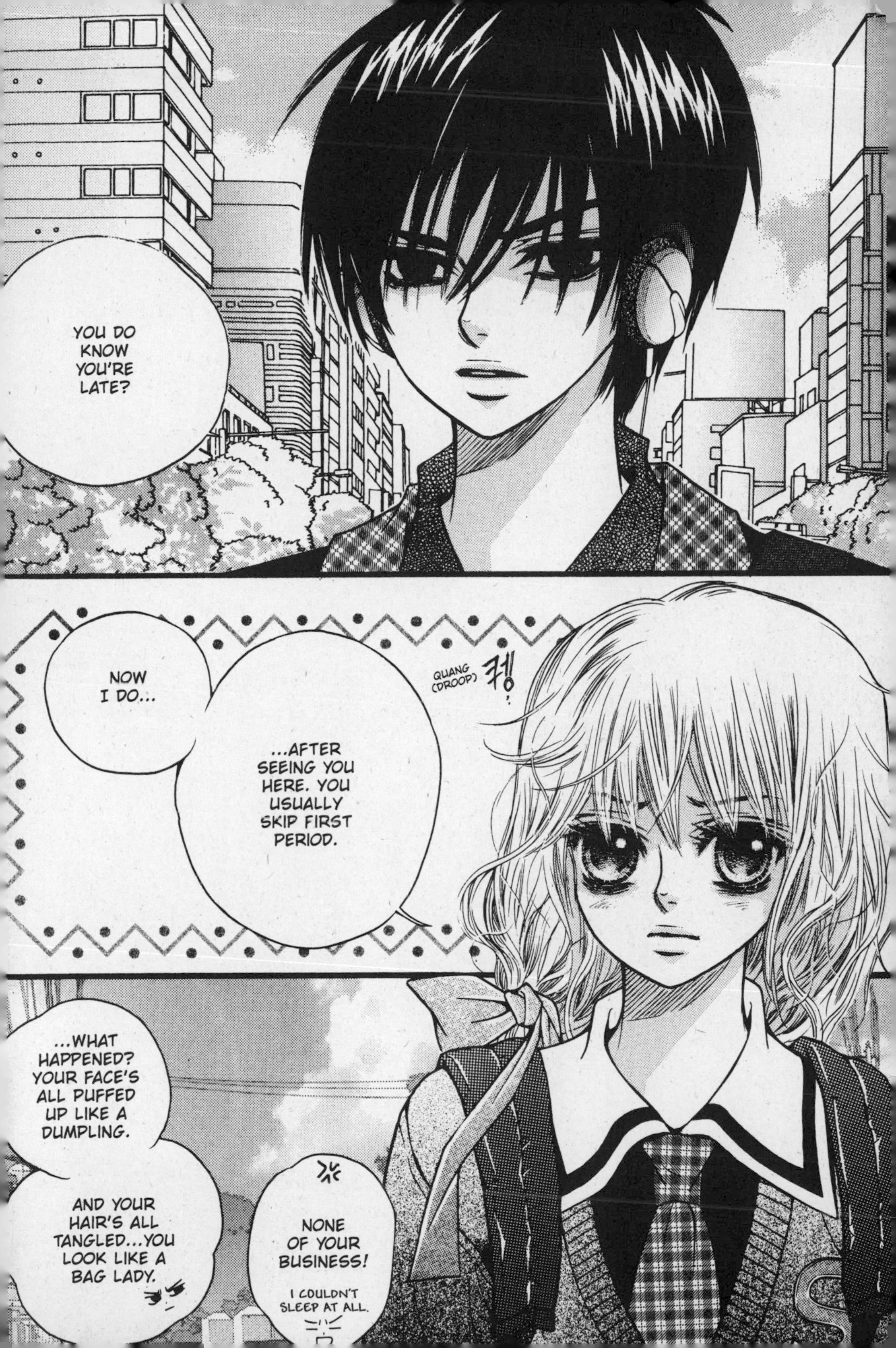
YOU DO KNOW YOU'RE LATE?
NOW I DO...
...AFTER SEEING YOU HERE. YOU USUALLY SKIP FIRST PERIOD.
QUANG (DROOP)
...WHAT HAPPENED? YOUR FACE'S ALL PUFFED UP LIKE A DUMPLING.
AND YOUR HAIR'S ALL TANGLED...YOU LOOK LIKE A BAG LADY.
NONE OF YOUR BUSINESS!
I COULDN'T SLEEP AT ALL.

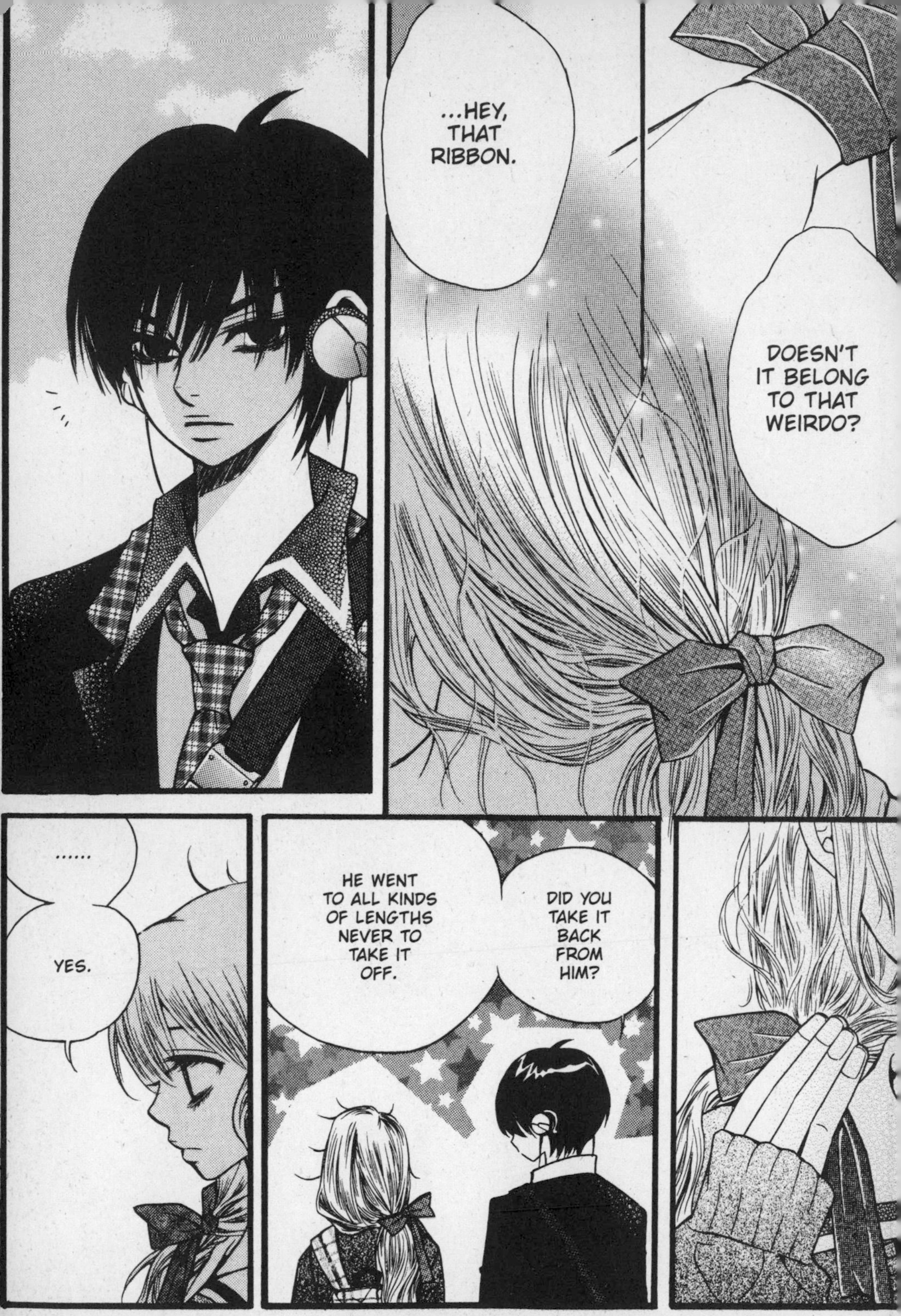
...HEY, THAT RIBBON.
DOESN'T IT BELONG TO THAT WEIRDO?
DID YOU TAKE IT BACK FROM HIM?
HE WENT TO ALL KINDS OF LENGTHS NEVER TO TAKE IT OFF.
......
YES.

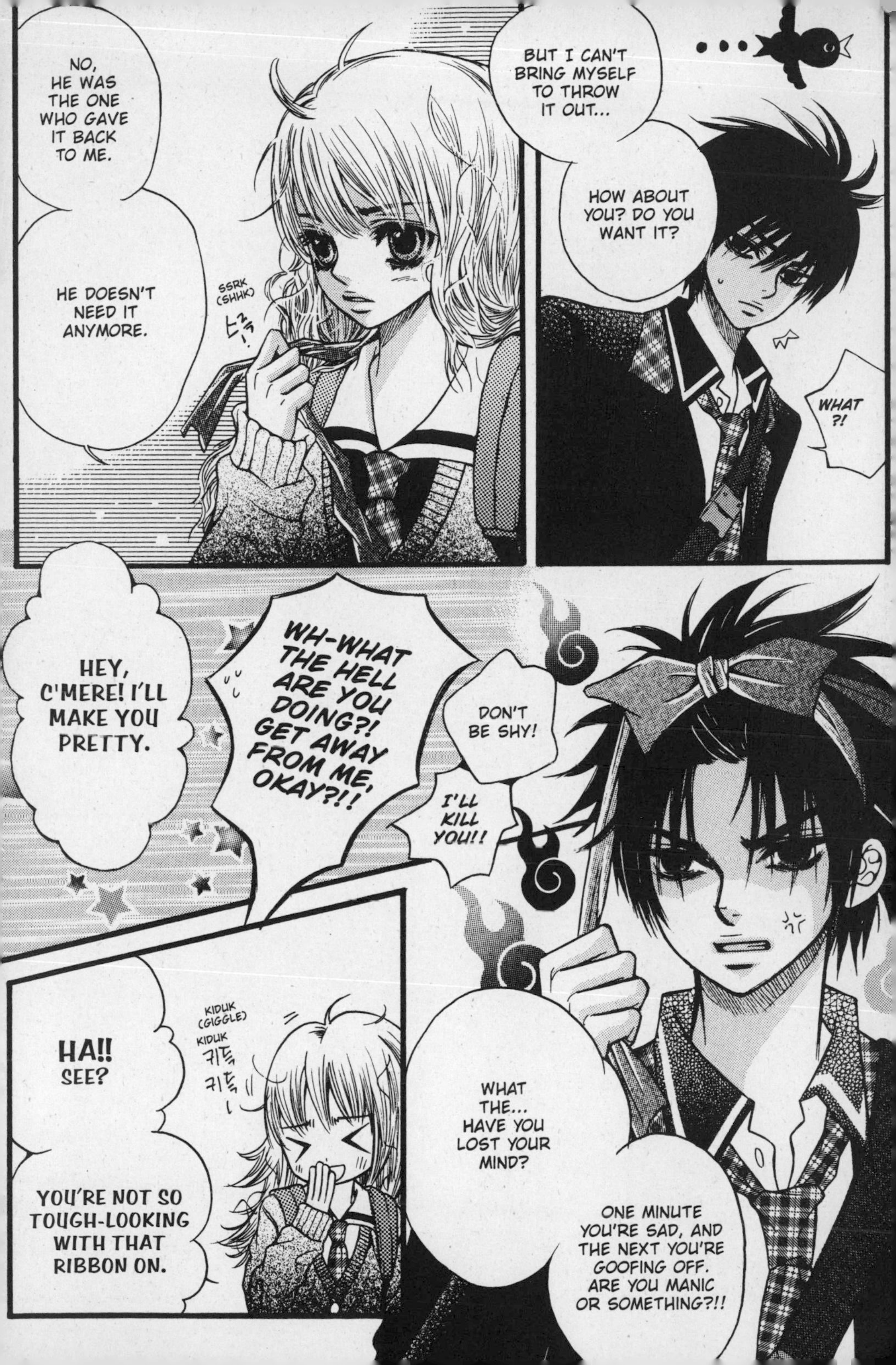

NO, HE WAS THE ONE WHO GAVE IT BACK TO ME.
HE DOESN'T NEED IT ANYMORE.
SSRK (SHHK)
BUT I CAN'T BRING MYSELF TO THROW IT OUT...
...
HOW ABOUT YOU? DO YOU WANT IT?
WHAT?!
HEY, C'MERE! I'LL MAKE YOU PRETTY.
WH-WHAT THE HELL ARE YOU DOING?! GET AWAY FROM ME, OKAY?!!
DON'T BE SHY!
I'LL KILL YOU!!
HA!! SEE?
KIDUK (GIGGLE) KIDUK
키득 키득
YOU'RE NOT SO TOUGH-LOOKING WITH THAT RIBBON ON.
WHAT THE... HAVE YOU LOST YOUR MIND?
ONE MINUTE YOU'RE SAD, AND THE NEXT YOU'RE GOOFING OFF. ARE YOU MANIC OR SOMETHING?!!

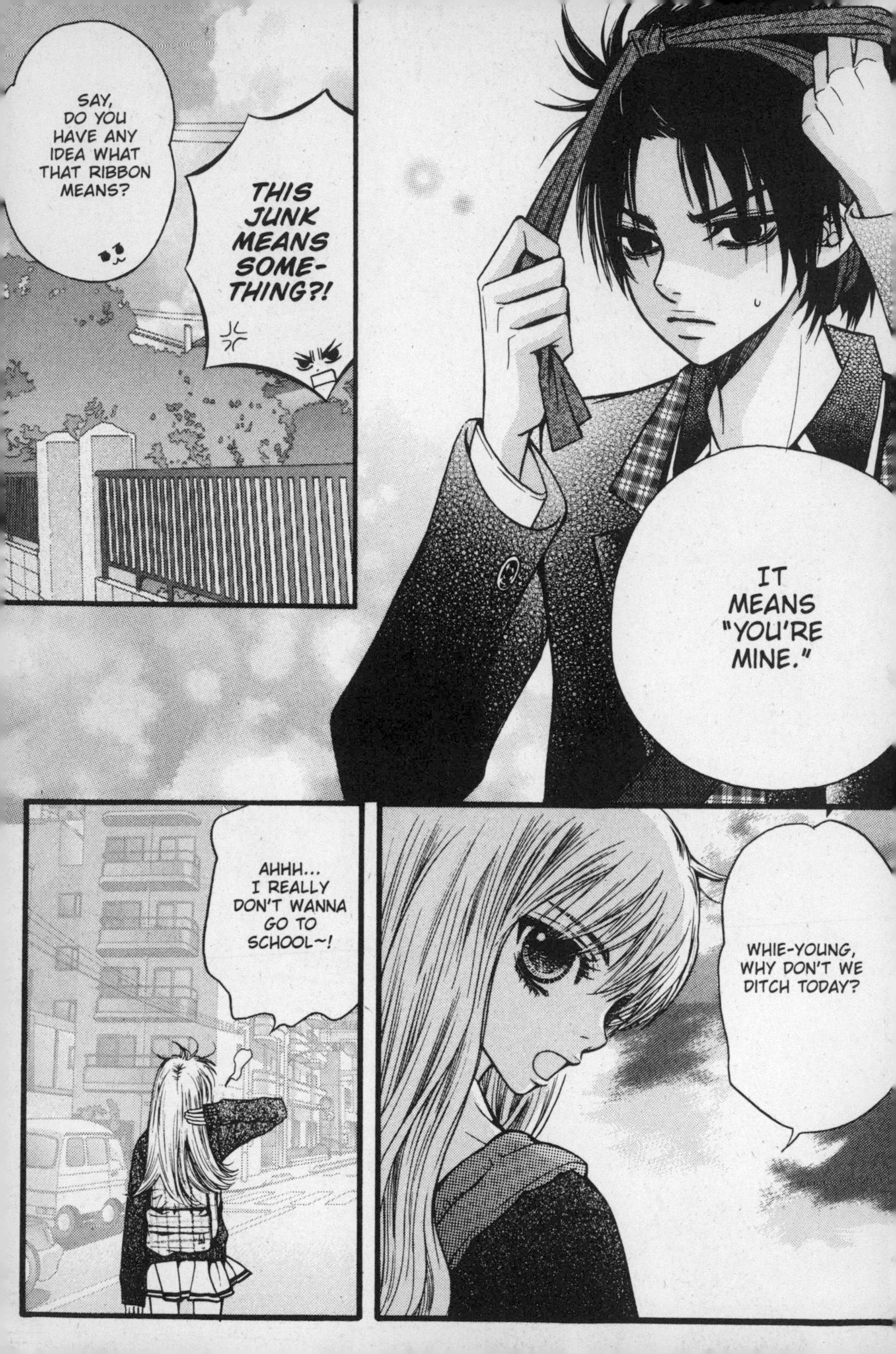
SAY, DO YOU HAVE ANY IDEA WHAT THAT RIBBON MEANS?
THIS JUNK MEANS SOME-THING?!
IT MEANS "YOU'RE MINE."
AHHH... I REALLY DON'T WANNA GO TO SCHOOL~!
WHIE-YOUNG, WHY DON'T WE DITCH TODAY?

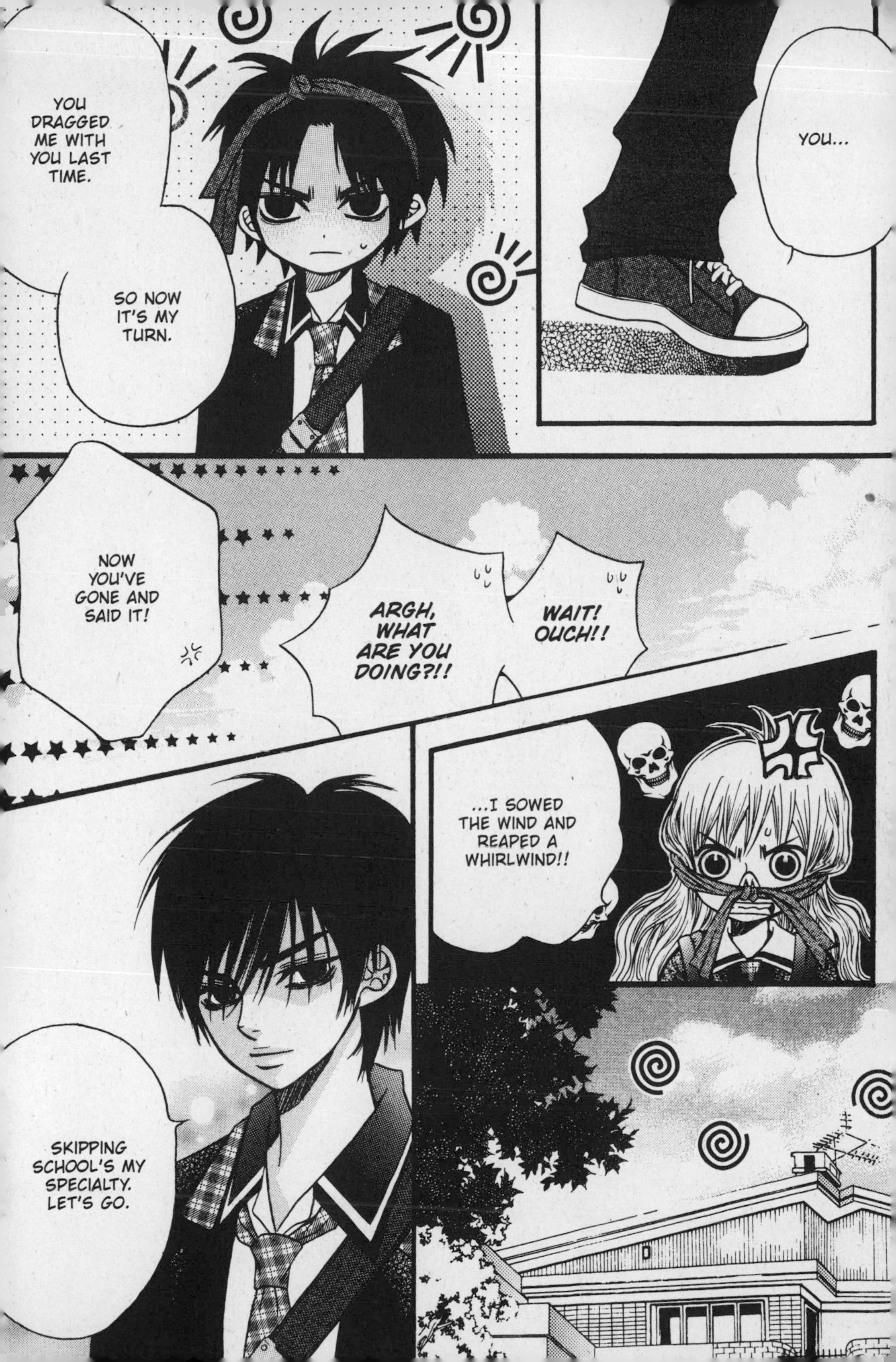
YOU...
YOU DRAGGED ME WITH YOU LAST TIME.
SO NOW IT'S MY TURN.
WAIT! OUCH!!
ARGH, WHAT ARE YOU DOING?!!
NOW YOU'VE GONE AND SAID IT!
...I SOWED THE WIND AND REAPED A WHIRLWIND!!
SKIPPING SCHOOL'S MY SPECIALTY. LET'S GO.

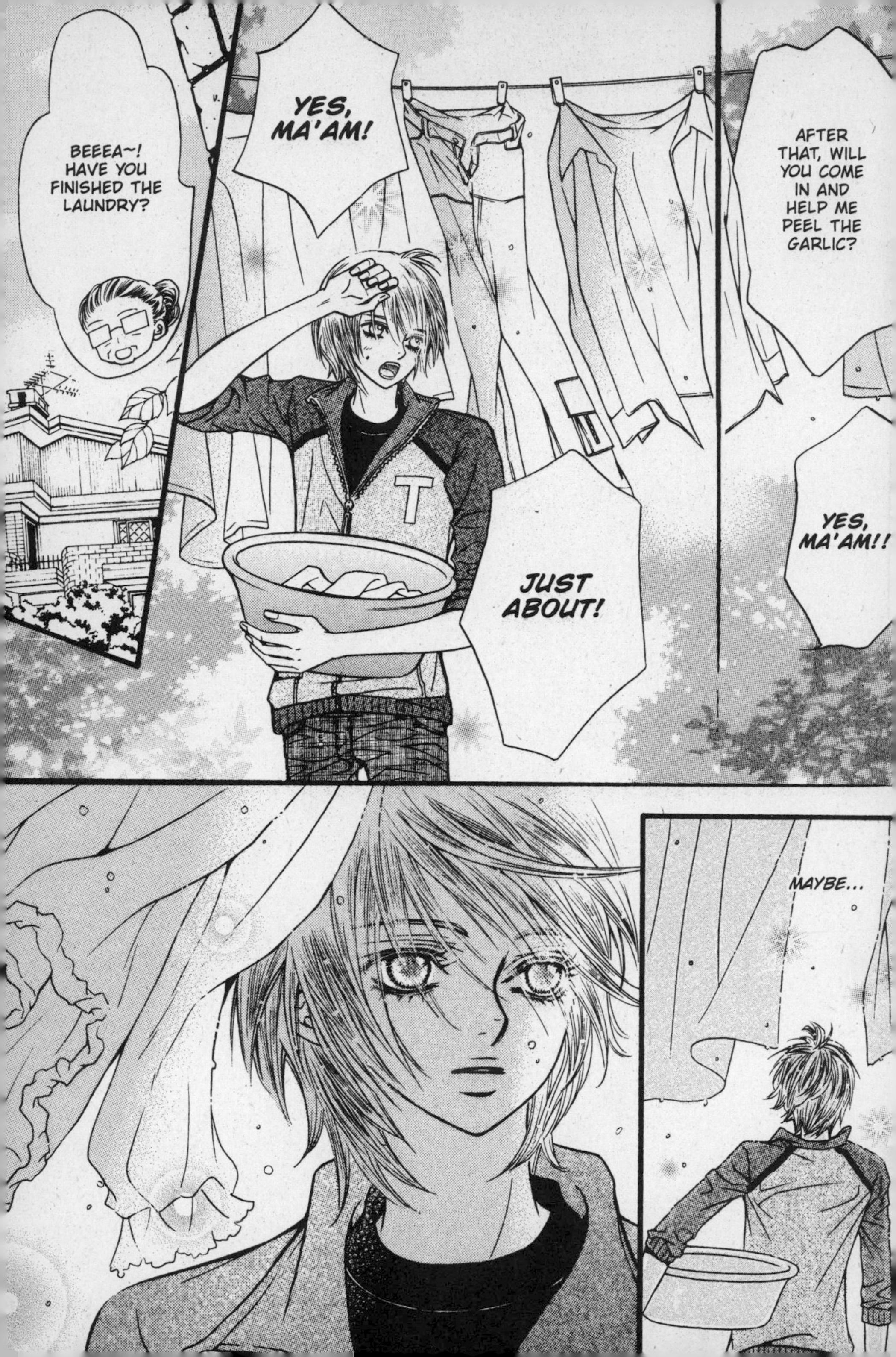
BEEEA~! HAVE YOU FINISHED THE LAUNDRY?
YES, MA'AM!
JUST ABOUT!
AFTER THAT, WILL YOU COME IN AND HELP ME PEEL THE GARLIC?
YES, MA'AM!!
MAYBE...

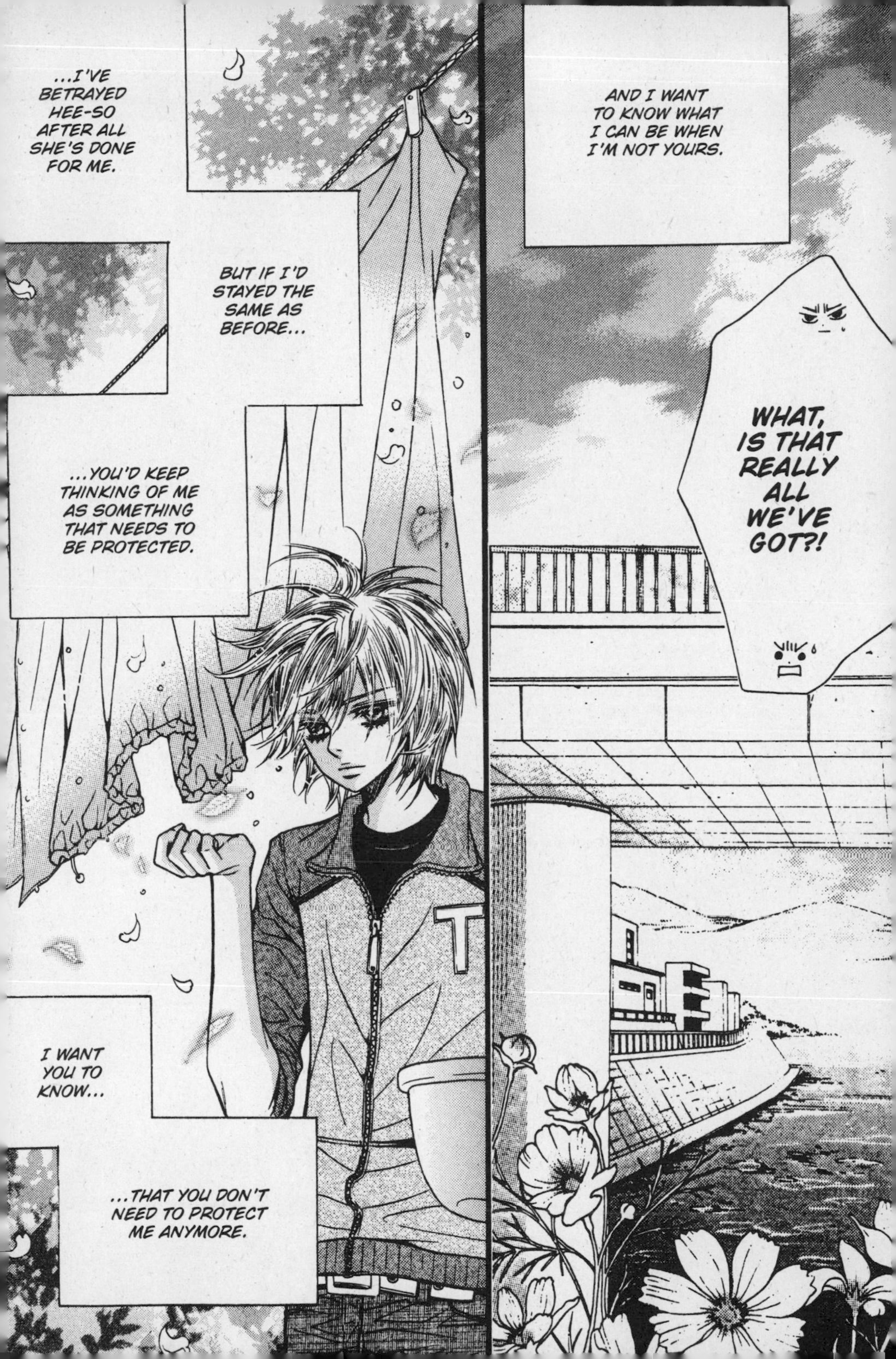
...I'VE BETRAYED HEE-SO AFTER ALL SHE'S DONE FOR ME.
BUT IF I'D STAYED THE SAME AS BEFORE...
...YOU'D KEEP THINKING OF ME AS SOMETHING THAT NEEDS TO BE PROTECTED.
I WANT YOU TO KNOW...
...THAT YOU DON'T NEED TO PROTECT ME ANYMORE.
AND I WANT TO KNOW WHAT I CAN BE WHEN I'M NOT YOURS.
WHAT, IS THAT REALLY ALL WE'VE GOT?!

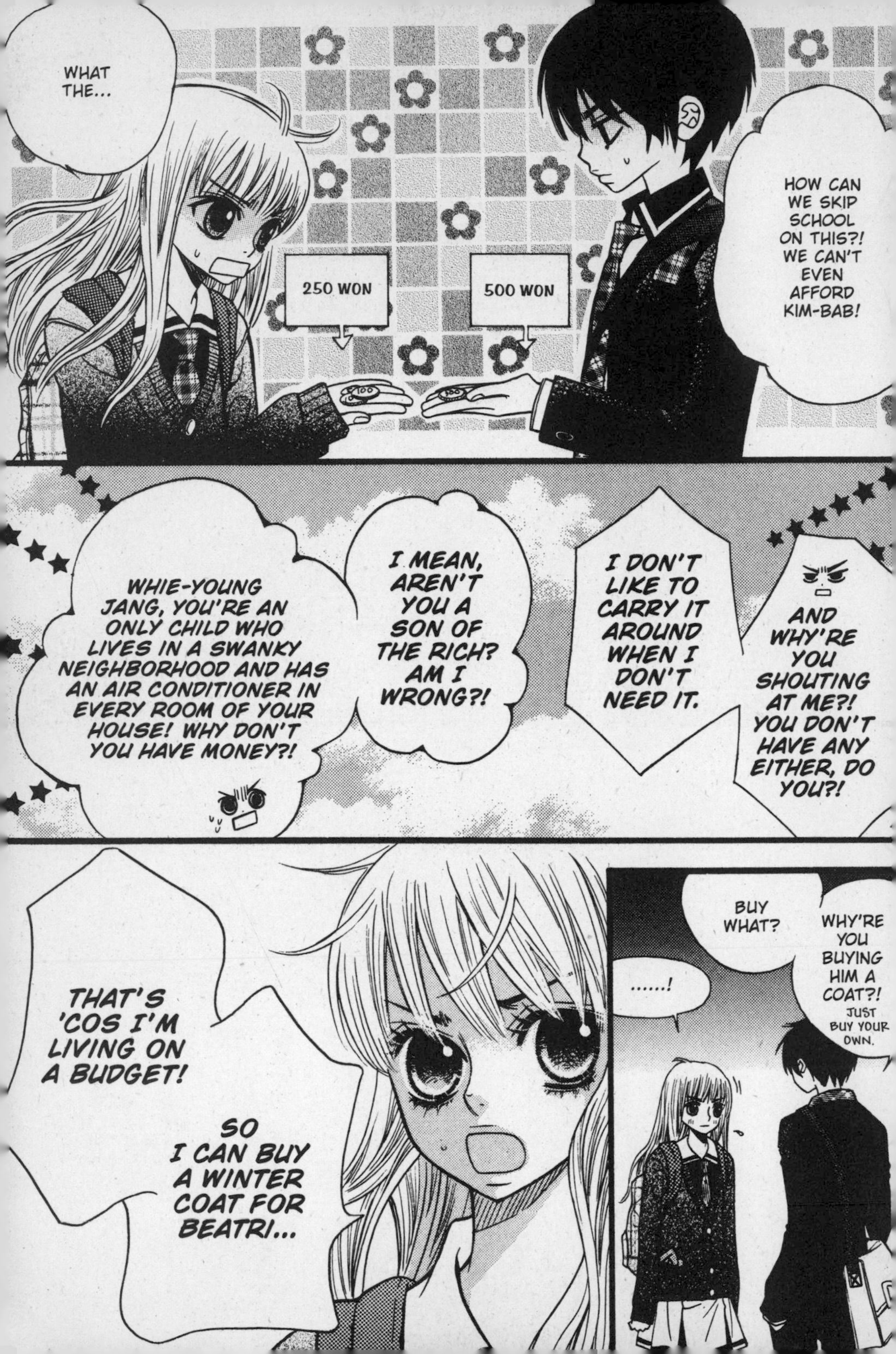
WHAT THE...
250 WON
500 WON
HOW CAN WE SKIP SCHOOL ON THIS?! WE CAN'T EVEN AFFORD KIM-BAB!
WHIE-YOUNG JANG, YOU'RE AN ONLY CHILD WHO LIVES IN A SWANKY NEIGHBORHOOD AND HAS AN AIR CONDITIONER IN EVERY ROOM OF YOUR HOUSE! WHY DON'T YOU HAVE MONEY?!
I MEAN, AREN'T YOU A SON OF THE RICH? AM I WRONG?!
I DON'T LIKE TO CARRY IT AROUND WHEN I DON'T NEED IT.
AND WHY'RE YOU SHOUTING AT ME?! YOU DON'T HAVE ANY EITHER, DO YOU?!
THAT'S 'COS I'M LIVING ON A BUDGET!
SO I CAN BUY A WINTER COAT FOR BEATRI...
BUY WHAT?
WHY'RE YOU BUYING HIM A COAT?! JUST BUY YOUR OWN.
......!

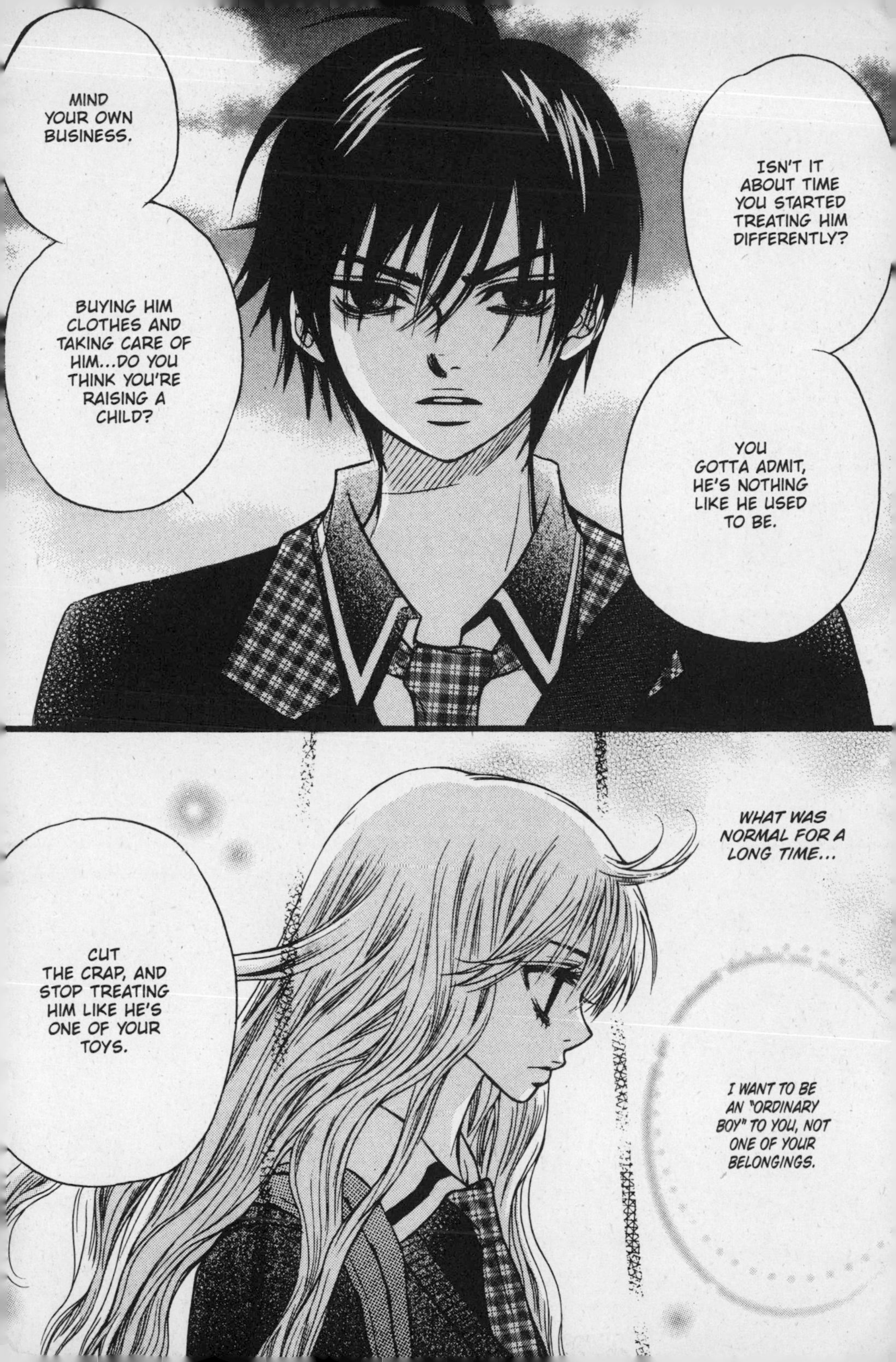
ISN'T IT ABOUT TIME YOU STARTED TREATING HIM DIFFERENTLY?
YOU GOTTA ADMIT, HE'S NOTHING LIKE HE USED TO BE.
MIND YOUR OWN BUSINESS.
BUYING HIM CLOTHES AND TAKING CARE OF HIM...DO YOU THINK YOU'RE RAISING A CHILD?
WHAT WAS NORMAL FOR A LONG TIME...
I WANT TO BE AN "ORDINARY BOY" TO YOU, NOT ONE OF YOUR BELONGINGS.
CUT THE CRAP, AND STOP TREATING HIM LIKE HE'S ONE OF YOUR TOYS.

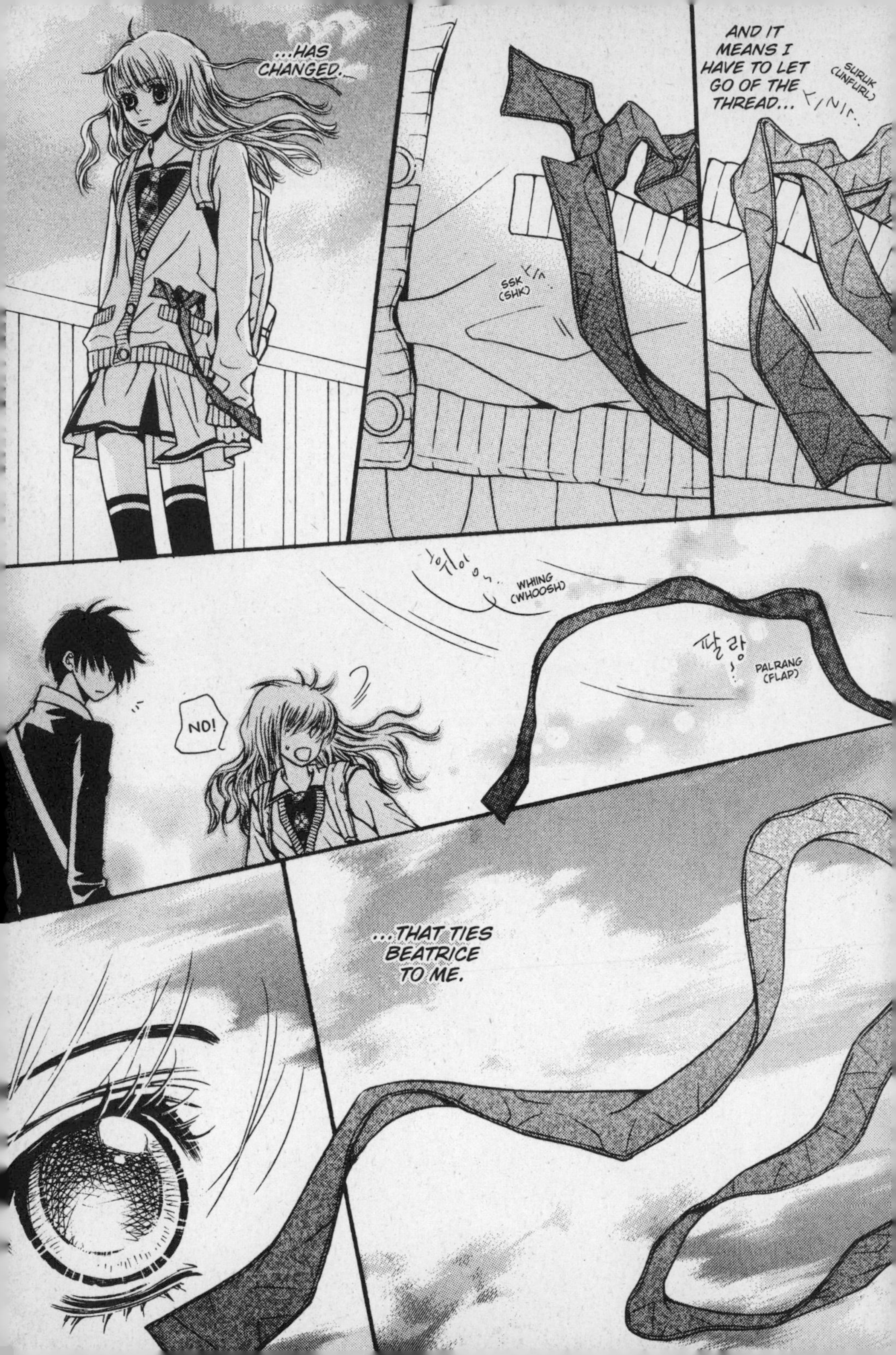
...HAS CHANGED.
SSK (SHK)
AND IT MEANS I HAVE TO LET GO OF THE THREAD...
SURUK (UNFURL)
WHIING (WHOOSH)
NO!
팔랑
PALRANG (FLAP)
...THAT TIES BEATRICE TO ME.

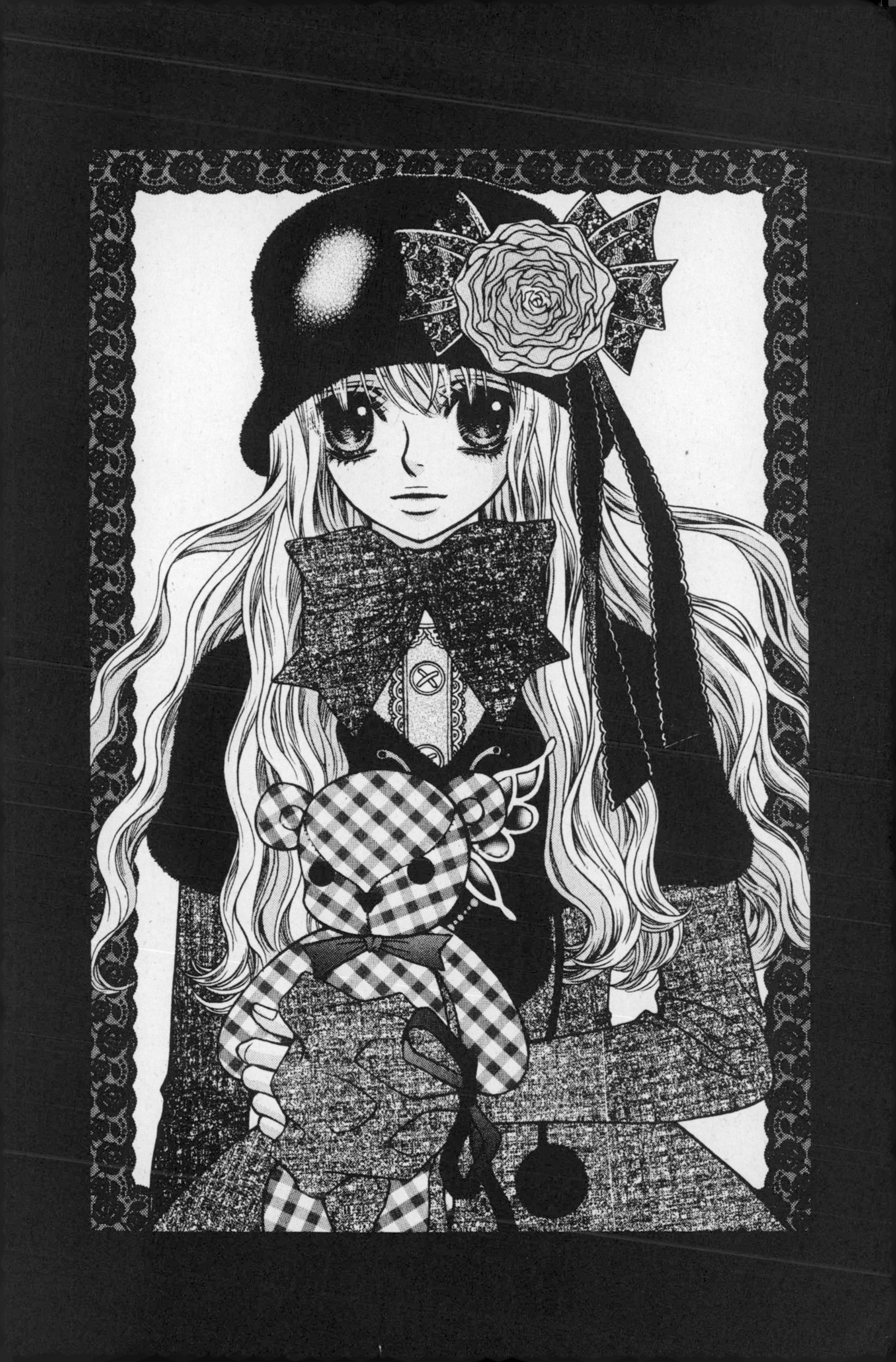

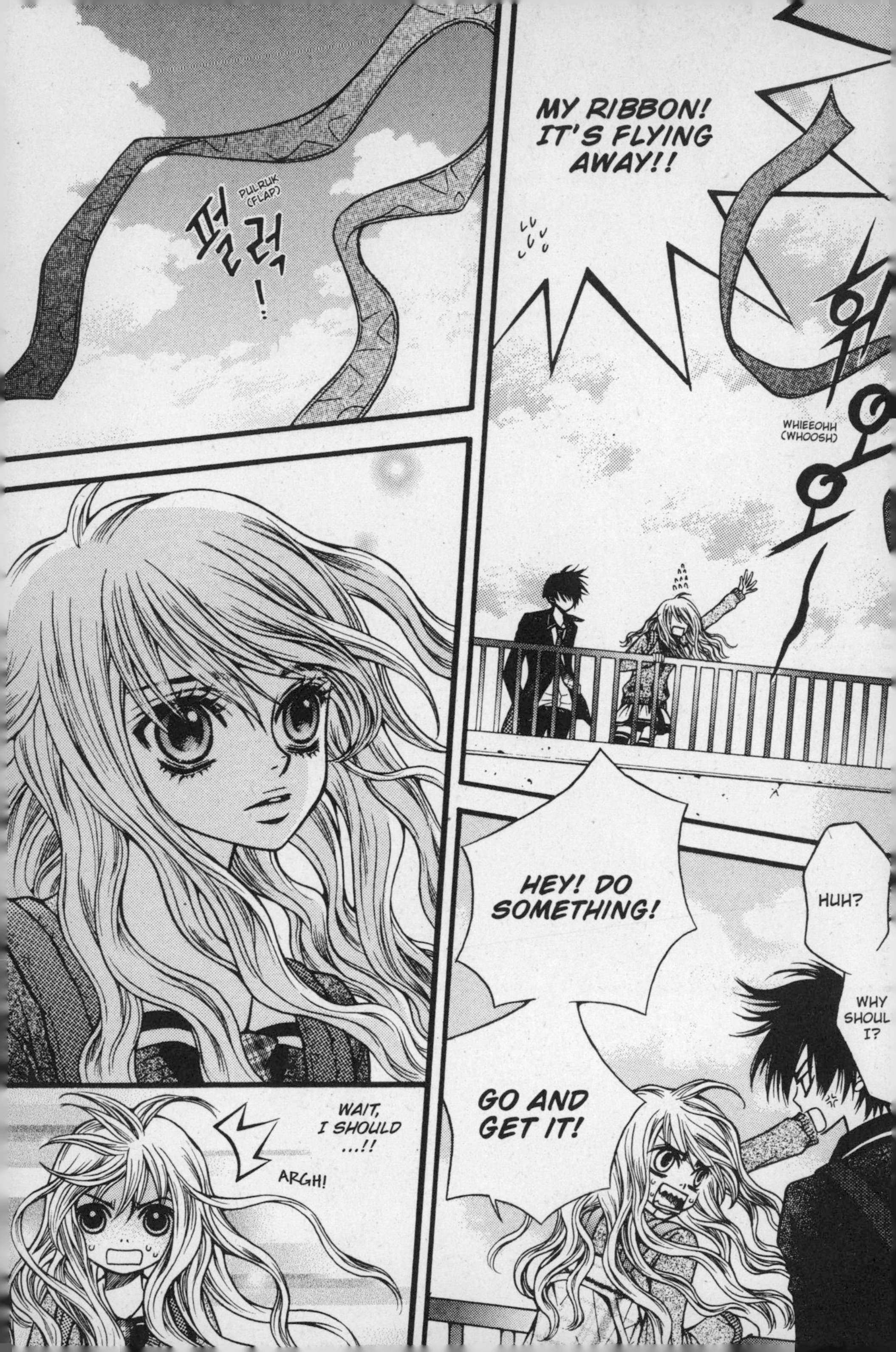
펄럭!!
PULRUK (FLAP)
MY RIBBON! IT'S FLYING AWAY!!
WHIEEOHH (WHOOSH)
WAIT, I SHOULD ...!!
ARGH!
HEY! DO SOMETHING!
HUH?
WHY SHOUL I?
GO AND GET IT!

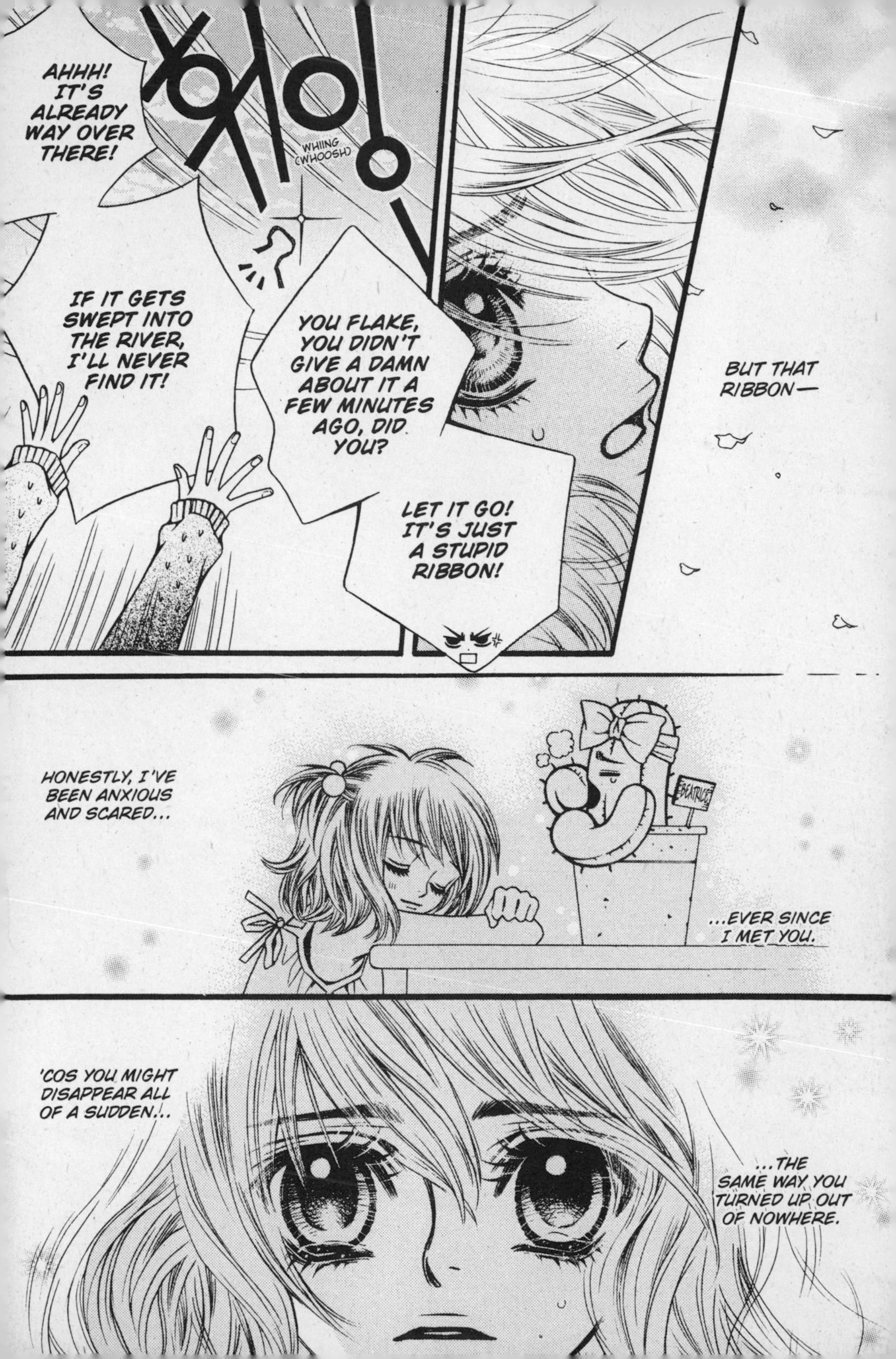

AHHH! IT'S ALREADY WAY OVER THERE!
WHIING (WHOOSH)
IF IT GETS SWEPT INTO THE RIVER, I'LL NEVER FIND IT!
YOU FLAKE, YOU DIDN'T GIVE A DAMN ABOUT IT A FEW MINUTES AGO, DID YOU?
LET IT GO! IT'S JUST A STUPID RIBBON!
BUT THAT RIBBON—
HONESTLY, I'VE BEEN ANXIOUS AND SCARED...
BEATRICE
...EVER SINCE I MET YOU.
'COS YOU MIGHT DISAPPEAR ALL OF A SUDDEN...
...THE SAME WAY YOU TURNED UP OUT OF NOWHERE.

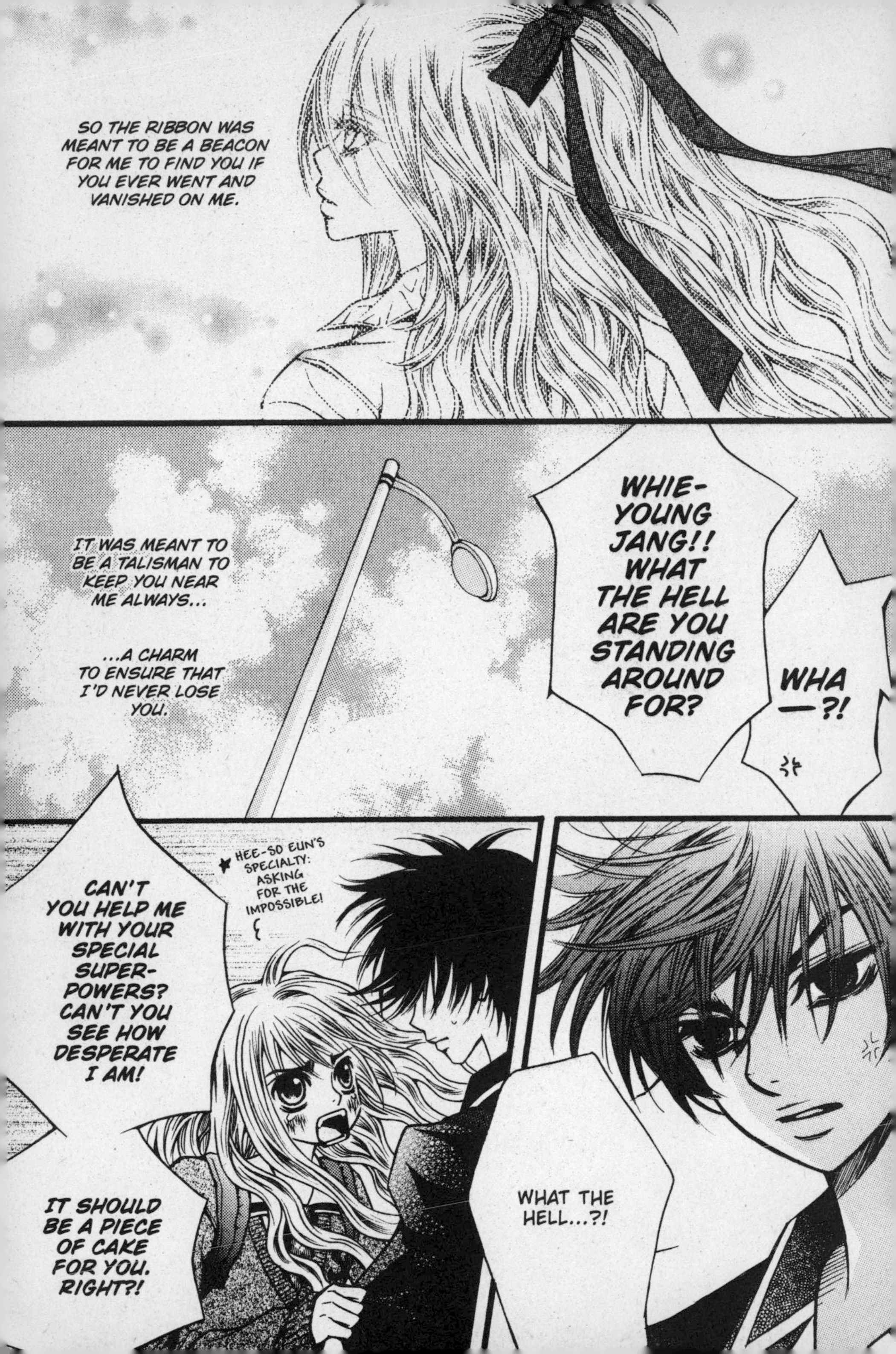

SO THE RIBBON WAS MEANT TO BE A BEACON FOR ME TO FIND YOU IF YOU EVER WENT AND VANISHED ON ME.
IT WAS MEANT TO BE A TALISMAN TO KEEP YOU NEAR ME ALWAYS...
...A CHARM TO ENSURE THAT I'D NEVER LOSE YOU.
WHIE-YOUNG JANG!! WHAT THE HELL ARE YOU STANDING AROUND FOR?
WHA—?!
CAN'T YOU HELP ME WITH YOUR SPECIAL SUPER-POWERS? CAN'T YOU SEE HOW DESPERATE I AM!
HEE-SO EUN'S SPECIALTY: ASKING FOR THE IMPOSSIBLE!
IT SHOULD BE A PIECE OF CAKE FOR YOU. RIGHT?!
WHAT THE HELL...?!

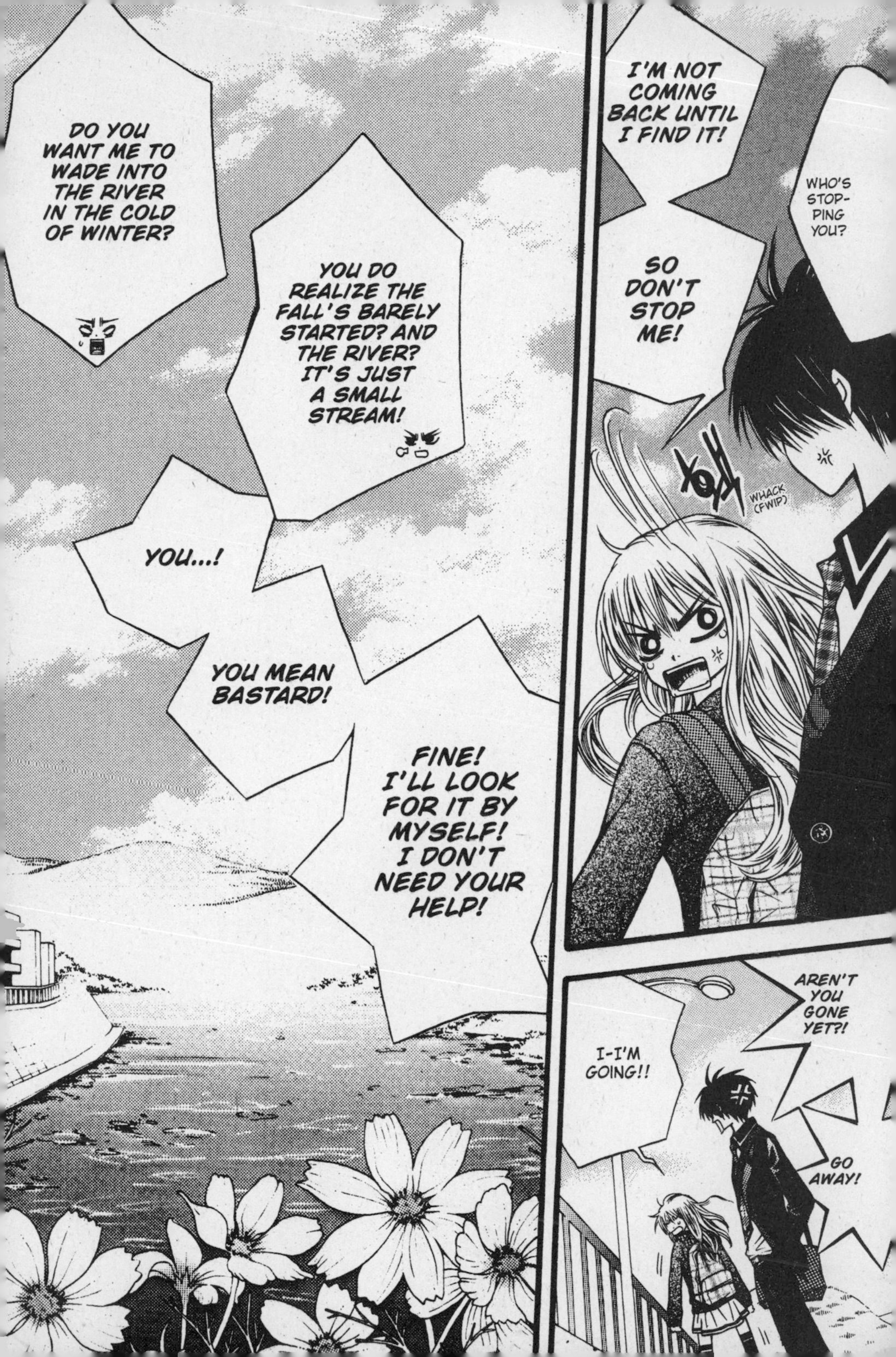

DO YOU WANT ME TO WADE INTO THE RIVER IN THE COLD OF WINTER?
YOU DO REALIZE THE FALL'S BARELY STARTED? AND THE RIVER? IT'S JUST A SMALL STREAM!
YOU...!
YOU MEAN BASTARD!
FINE! I'LL LOOK FOR IT BY MYSELF! I DON'T NEED YOUR HELP!
I'M NOT COMING BACK UNTIL I FIND IT!
SO DON'T STOP ME!
WHO'S STOP-PING YOU?
WHACK (FWIP)
AREN'T YOU GONE YET?!
I-I'M GOING!!
GO AWAY!

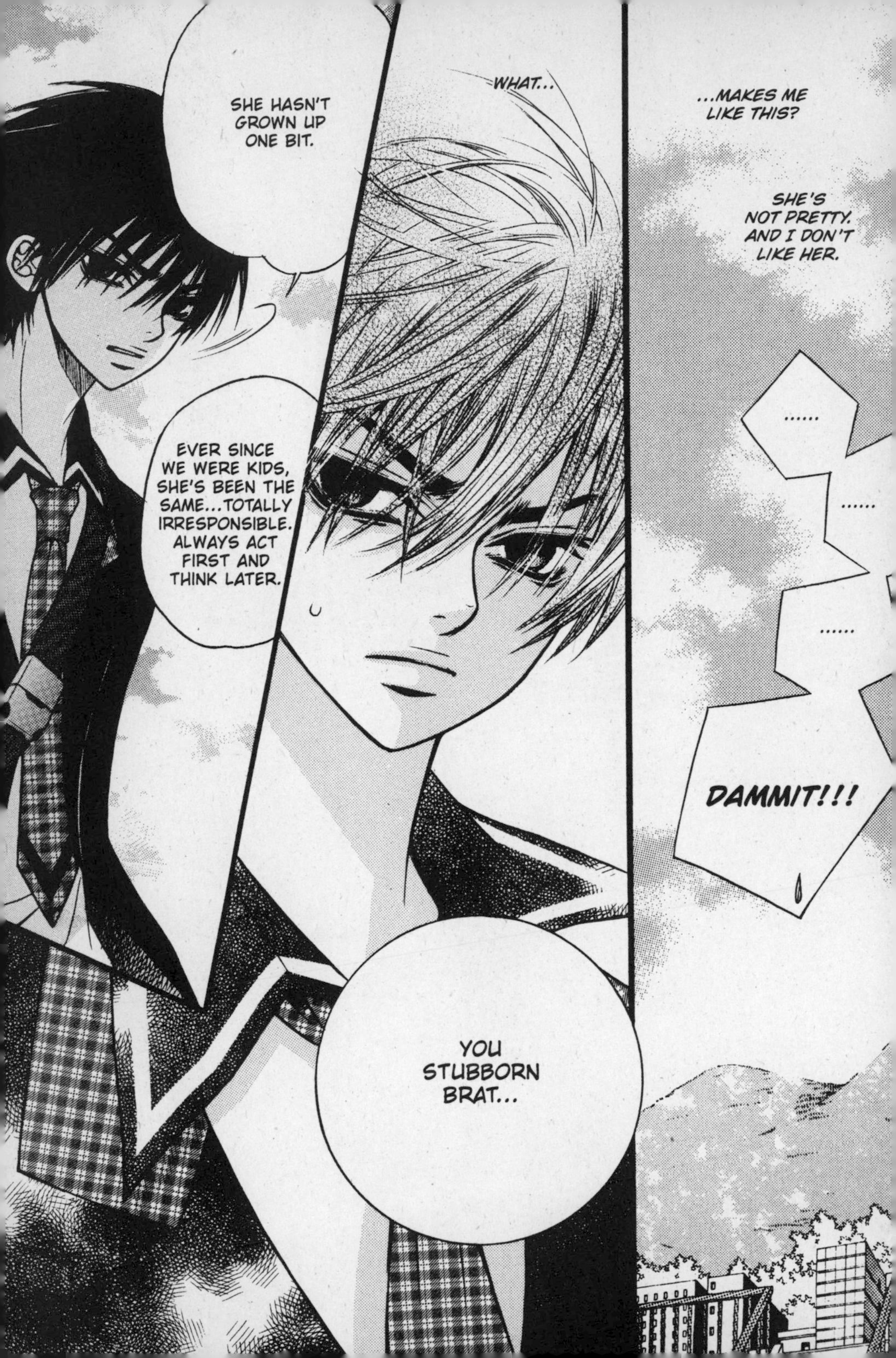
SHE HASN'T GROWN UP ONE BIT.
EVER SINCE WE WERE KIDS, SHE'S BEEN THE SAME...TOTALLY IRRESPONSIBLE. ALWAYS ACT FIRST AND THINK LATER.
YOU STUBBORN BRAT...
WHAT...
...MAKES ME LIKE THIS?
SHE'S NOT PRETTY. AND I DON'T LIKE HER.
......
......
......
DAMMIT!!!

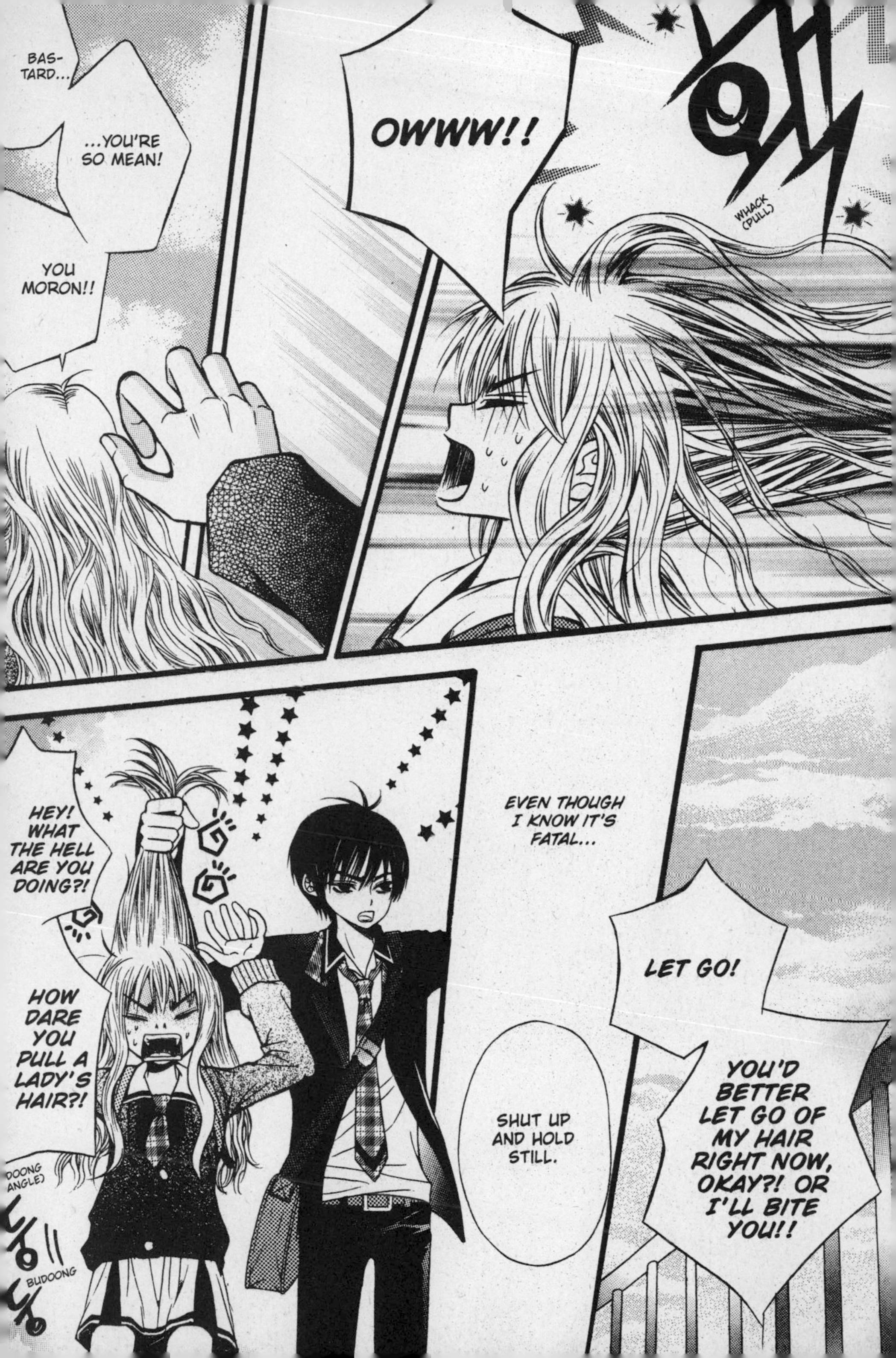
WHACK (PULL)
OWWW!!
BAS-TARD...
...YOU'RE SO MEAN!
YOU MORON!!
LET GO!
YOU'D BETTER LET GO OF MY HAIR RIGHT NOW, OKAY?! OR I'LL BITE YOU!!
EVEN THOUGH I KNOW IT'S FATAL...
SHUT UP AND HOLD STILL.
HEY! WHAT THE HELL ARE YOU DOING?!
HOW DARE YOU PULL A LADY'S HAIR?!
DOONG DANGLE)
BUDOONG

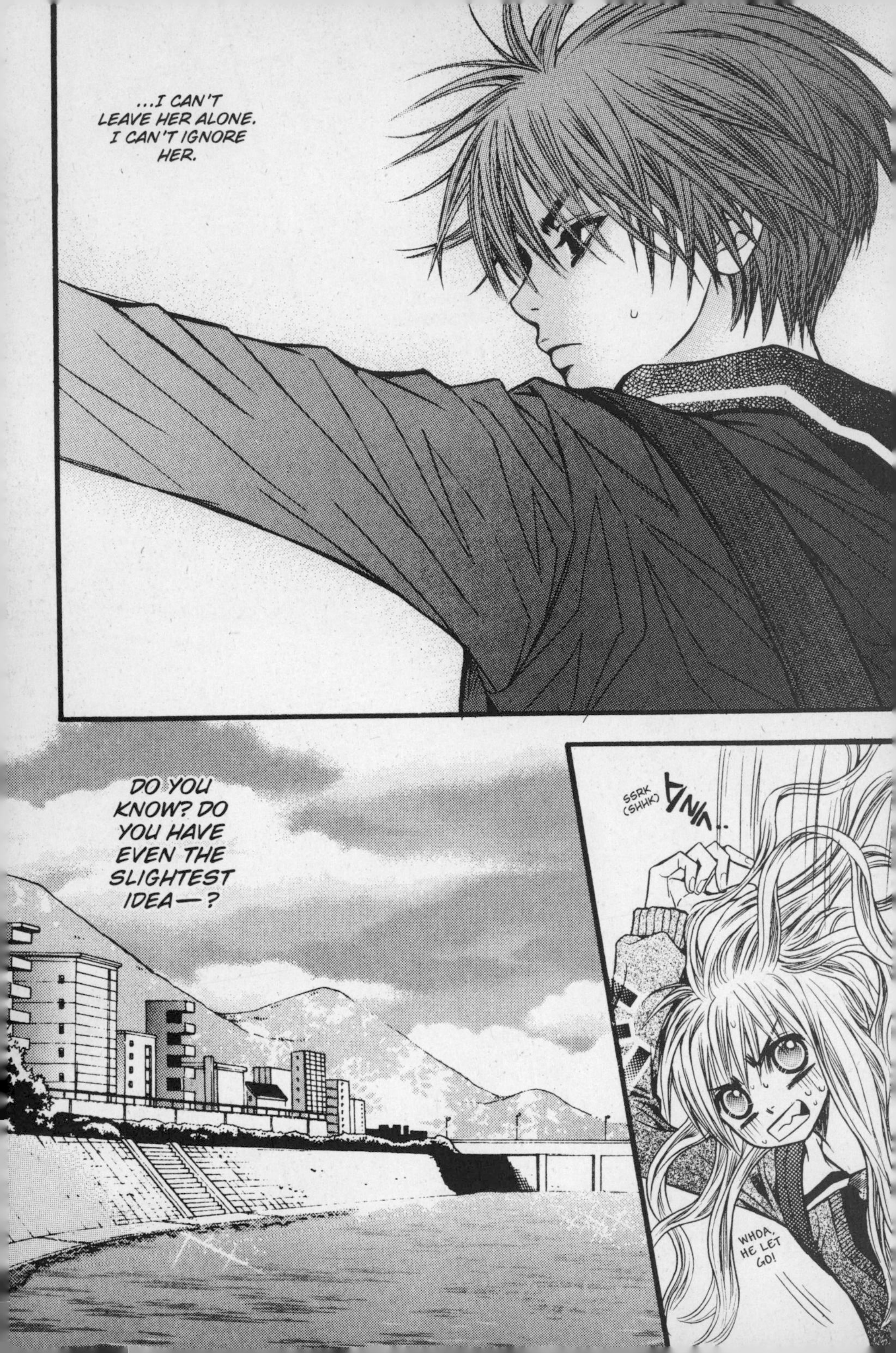
...I CAN'T LEAVE HER ALONE. I CAN'T IGNORE HER.
SSRK (SHHK)
WHOA, HE LET GO!
DO YOU KNOW? DO YOU HAVE EVEN THE SLIGHTEST IDEA—?

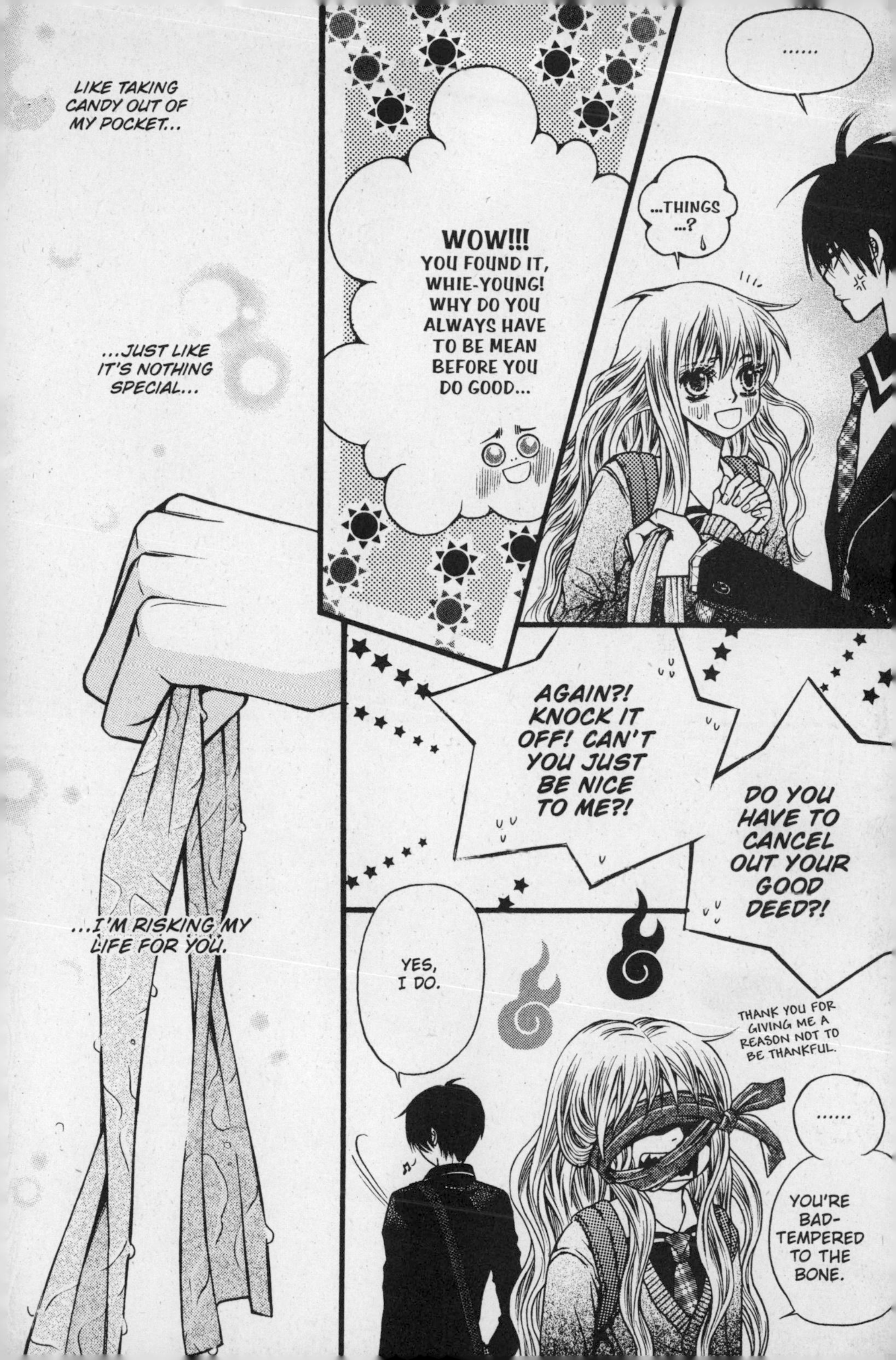
......
...THINGS ...?
WOW!!! YOU FOUND IT, WHIE-YOUNG! WHY DO YOU ALWAYS HAVE TO BE MEAN BEFORE YOU DO GOOD...
DO YOU HAVE TO CANCEL OUT YOUR GOOD DEED?!
AGAIN?! KNOCK IT OFF! CAN'T YOU JUST BE NICE TO ME?!
THANK YOU FOR GIVING ME A REASON NOT TO BE THANKFUL.
......
YOU'RE BAD-TEMPERED TO THE BONE.
YES, I DO.
LIKE TAKING CANDY OUT OF MY POCKET...
...JUST LIKE IT'S NOTHING SPECIAL...
...I'M RISKING MY LIFE FOR YOU.

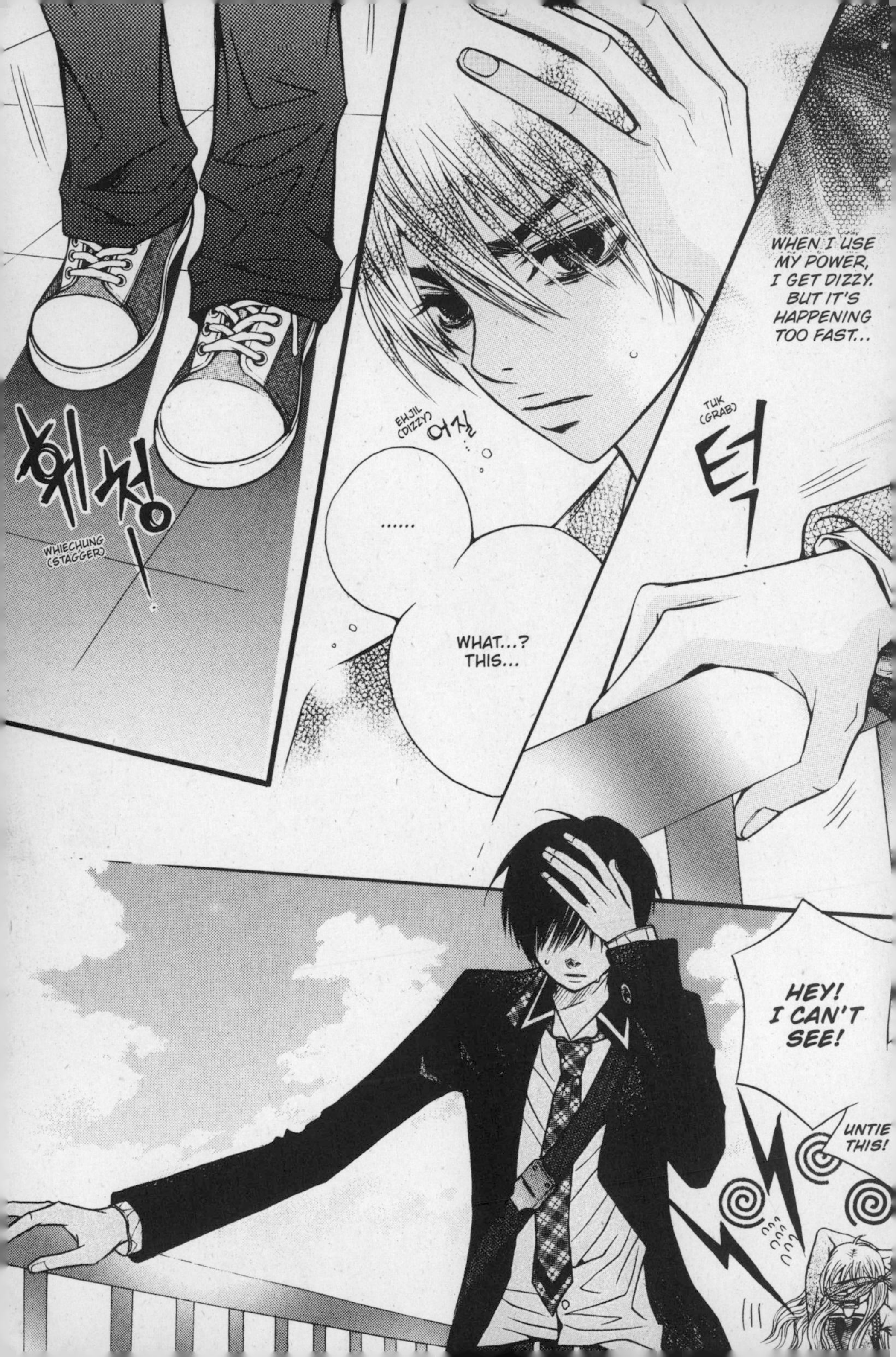

WHEN I USE MY POWER, I GET DIZZY. BUT IT'S HAPPENING TOO FAST...
TUK (GRAB)
턱
EHJIL (DIZZY)
어질
......
WHAT...? THIS...
휘청
WHIECHUNG (STAGGER)
HEY! I CAN'T SEE!
UNTIE THIS!

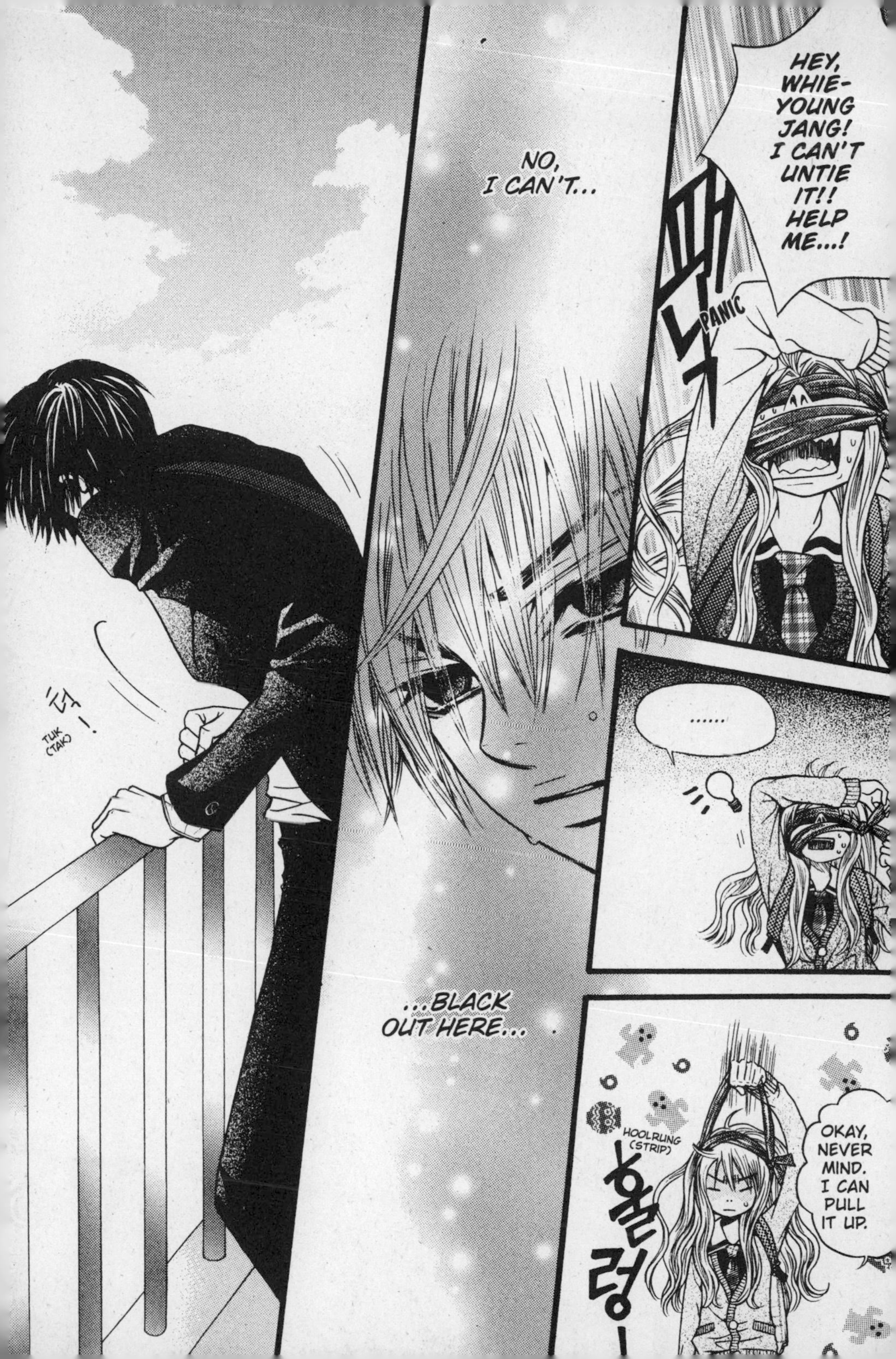
TUK (TAK)
!
NO, I CAN'T...
...BLACK OUT HERE...
HEY, WHIE-YOUNG JANG! I CAN'T UNTIE IT!! HELP ME...!
PANIC
......
HOOLRUNG (STRIP)
OKAY, NEVER MIND. I CAN PULL IT UP.

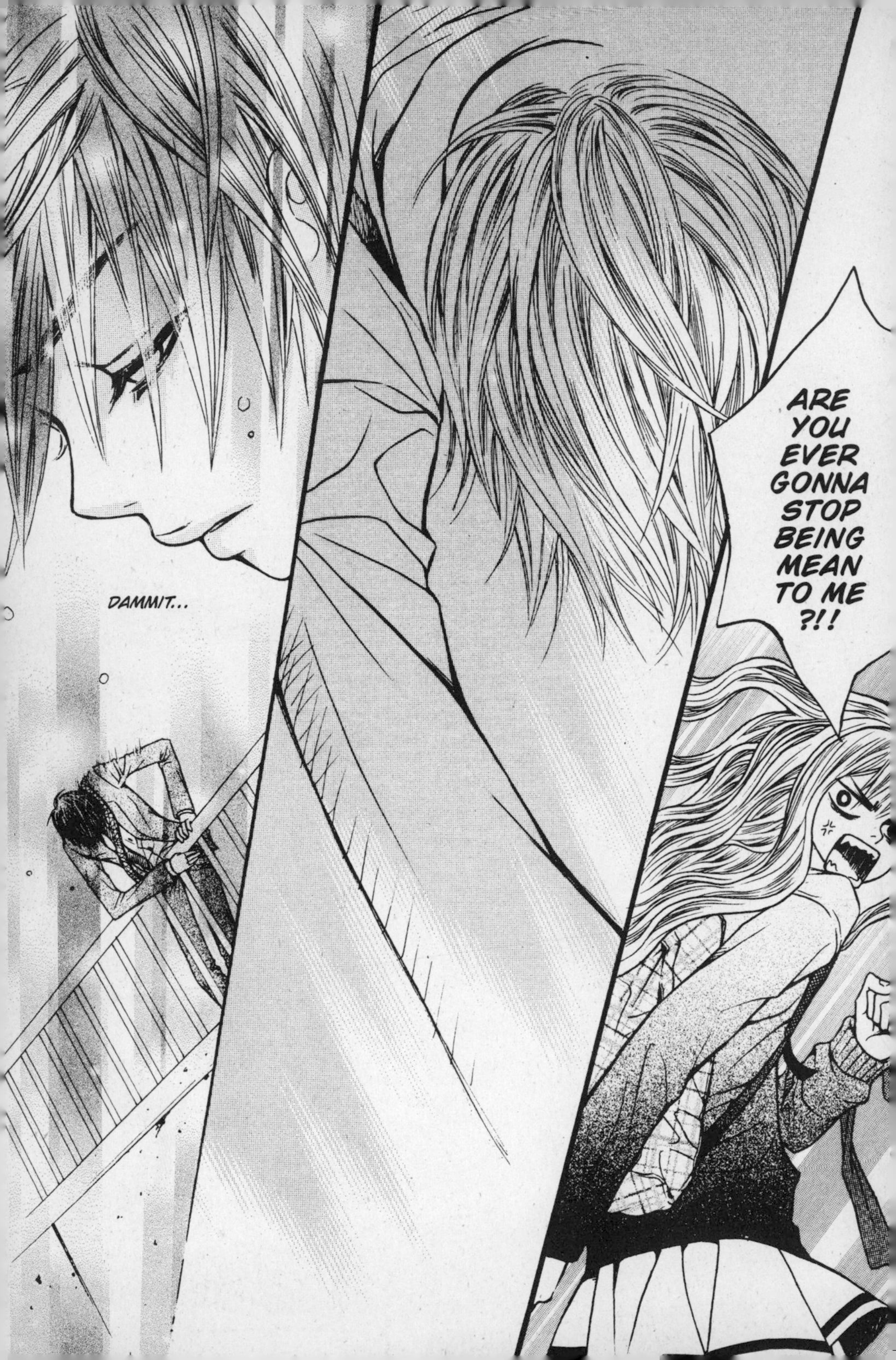
ARE YOU EVER GONNA STOP BEING MEAN TO ME ?!!
DAMMIT...

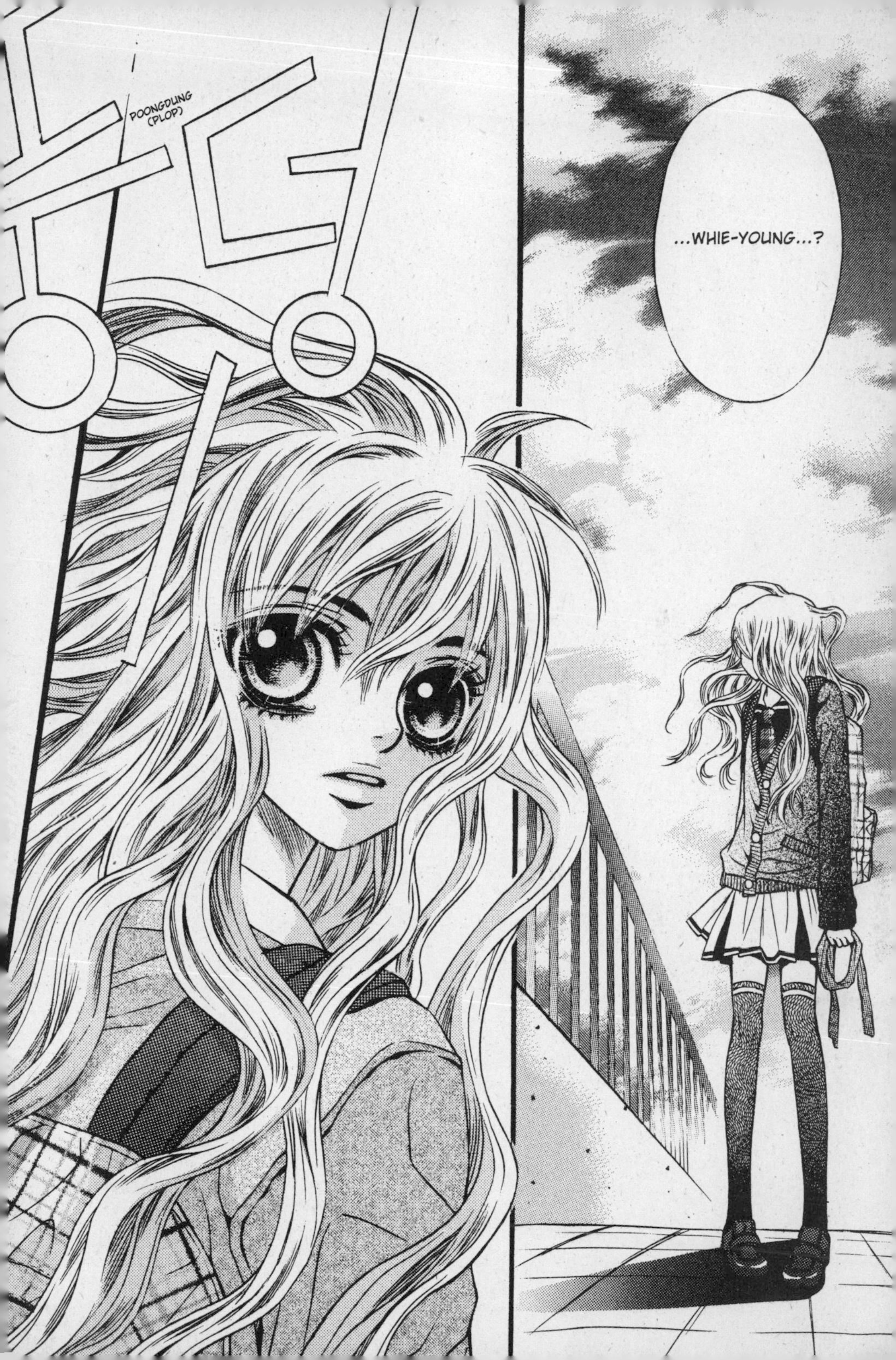
...WHIE-YOUNG...?
POONGDUNG
(PLOP)

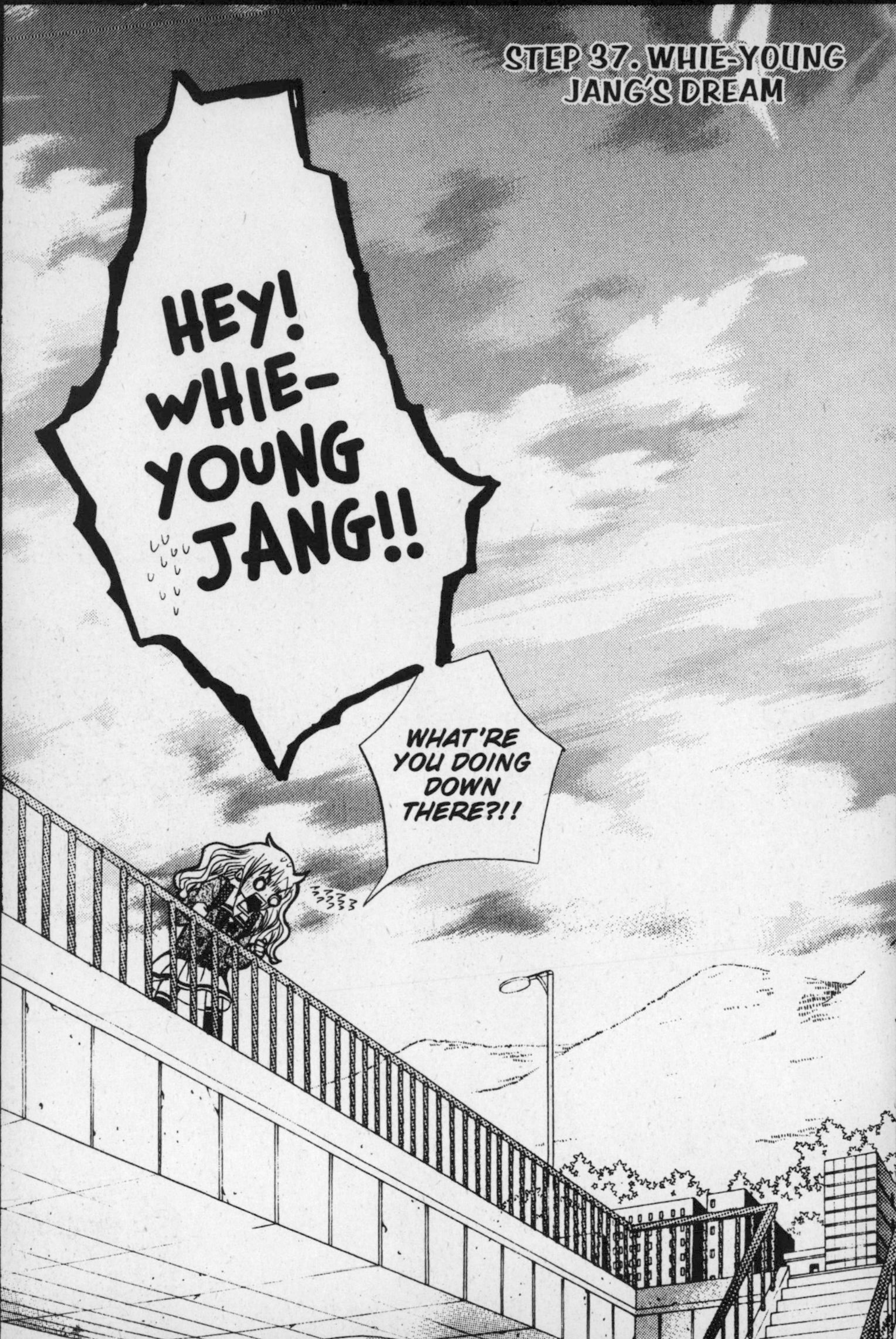
STEP 37. WHIE-YOUNG JANG'S DREAM
HEY! WHIE-YOUNG JANG!!
WHAT'RE YOU DOING DOWN THERE?!!

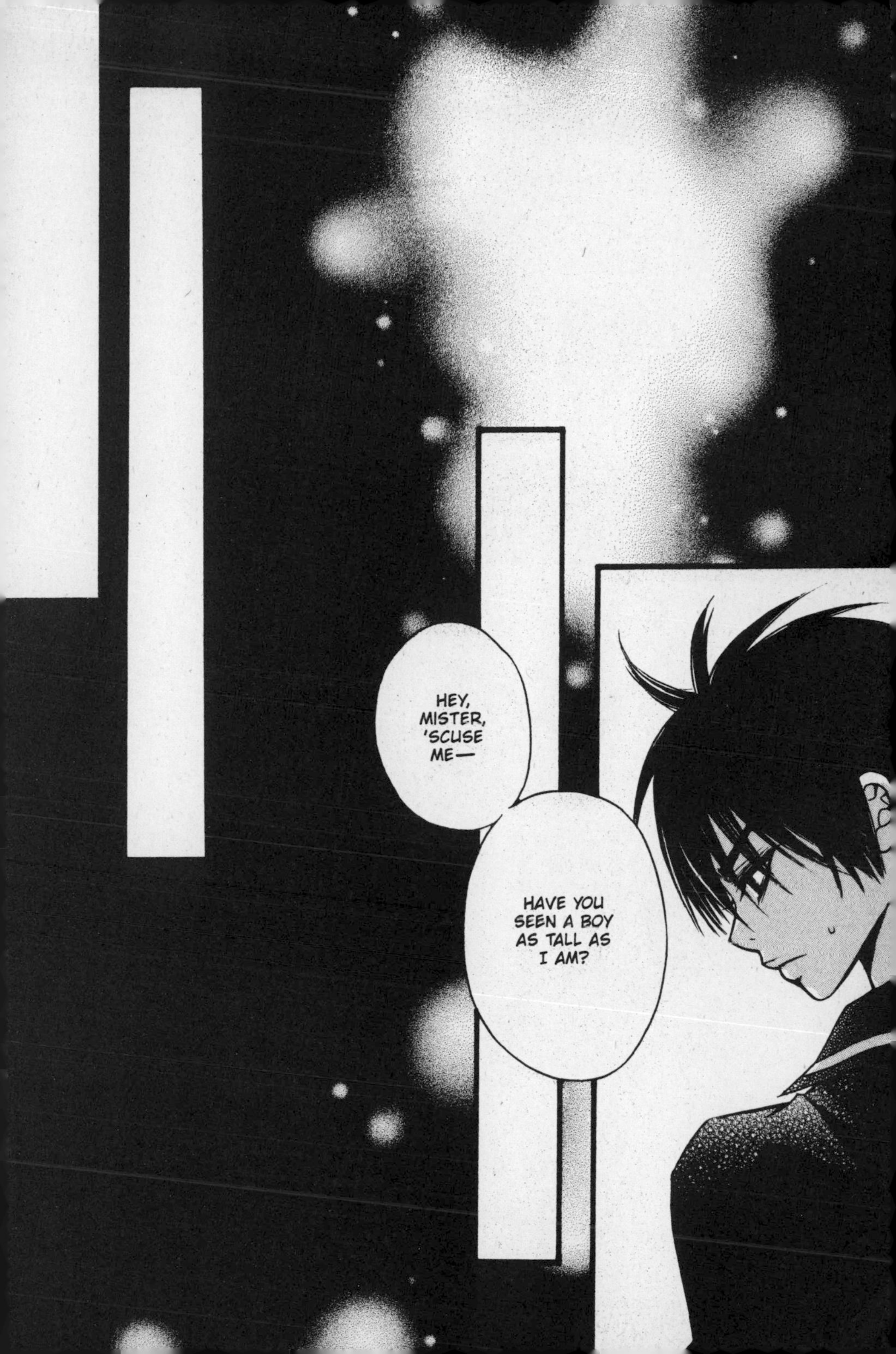
HEY, MISTER, 'SCUSE ME—
HAVE YOU SEEN A BOY AS TALL AS I AM?

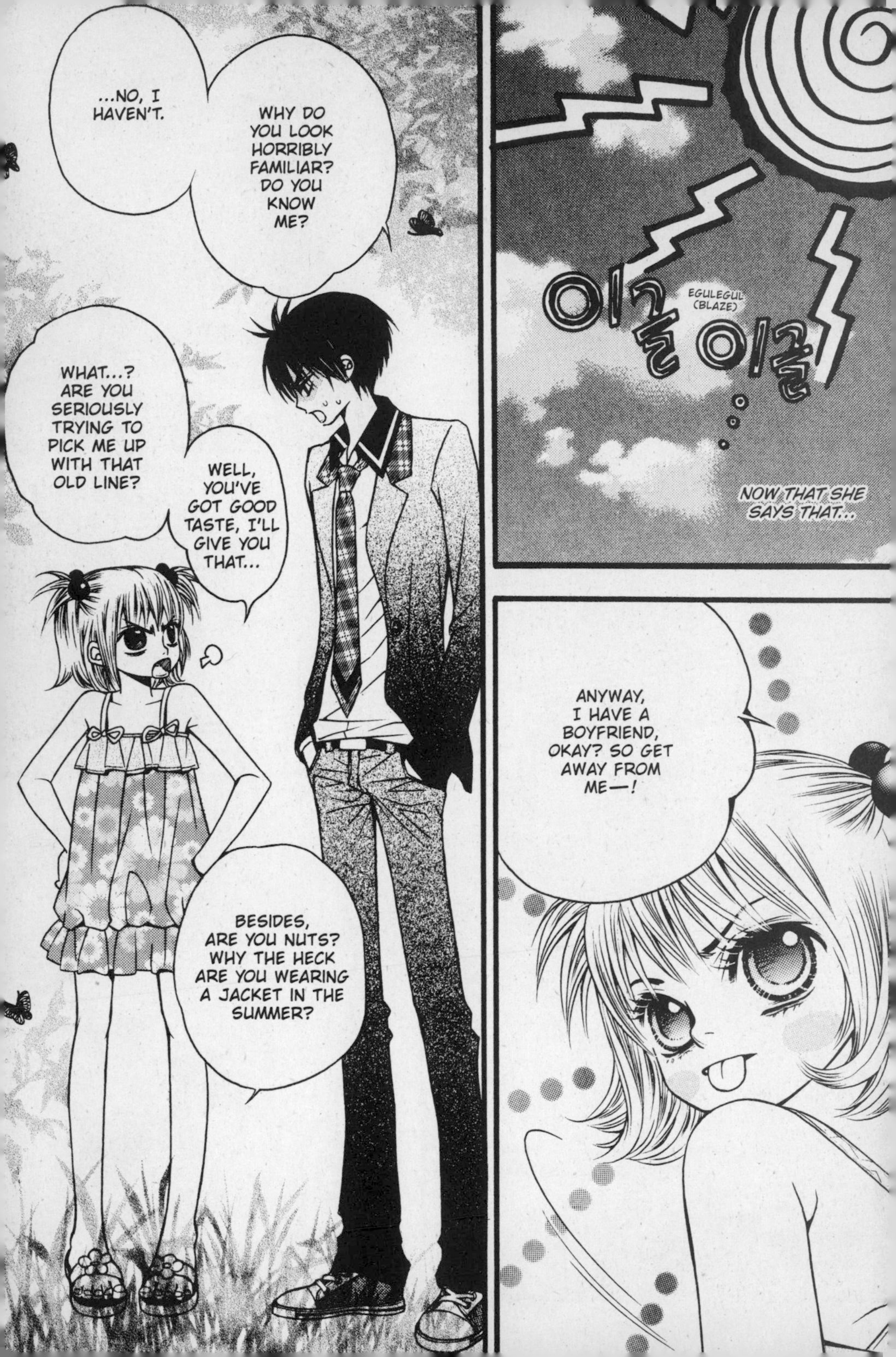
...NO, I HAVEN'T.
WHY DO YOU LOOK HORRIBLY FAMILIAR? DO YOU KNOW ME?
WHAT...? ARE YOU SERIOUSLY TRYING TO PICK ME UP WITH THAT OLD LINE?
WELL, YOU'VE GOT GOOD TASTE, I'LL GIVE YOU THAT...
BESIDES, ARE YOU NUTS? WHY THE HECK ARE YOU WEARING A JACKET IN THE SUMMER?
이글 이글
EGULEGUL (BLAZE)
NOW THAT SHE SAYS THAT...
ANYWAY, I HAVE A BOYFRIEND, OKAY? SO GET AWAY FROM ME—!

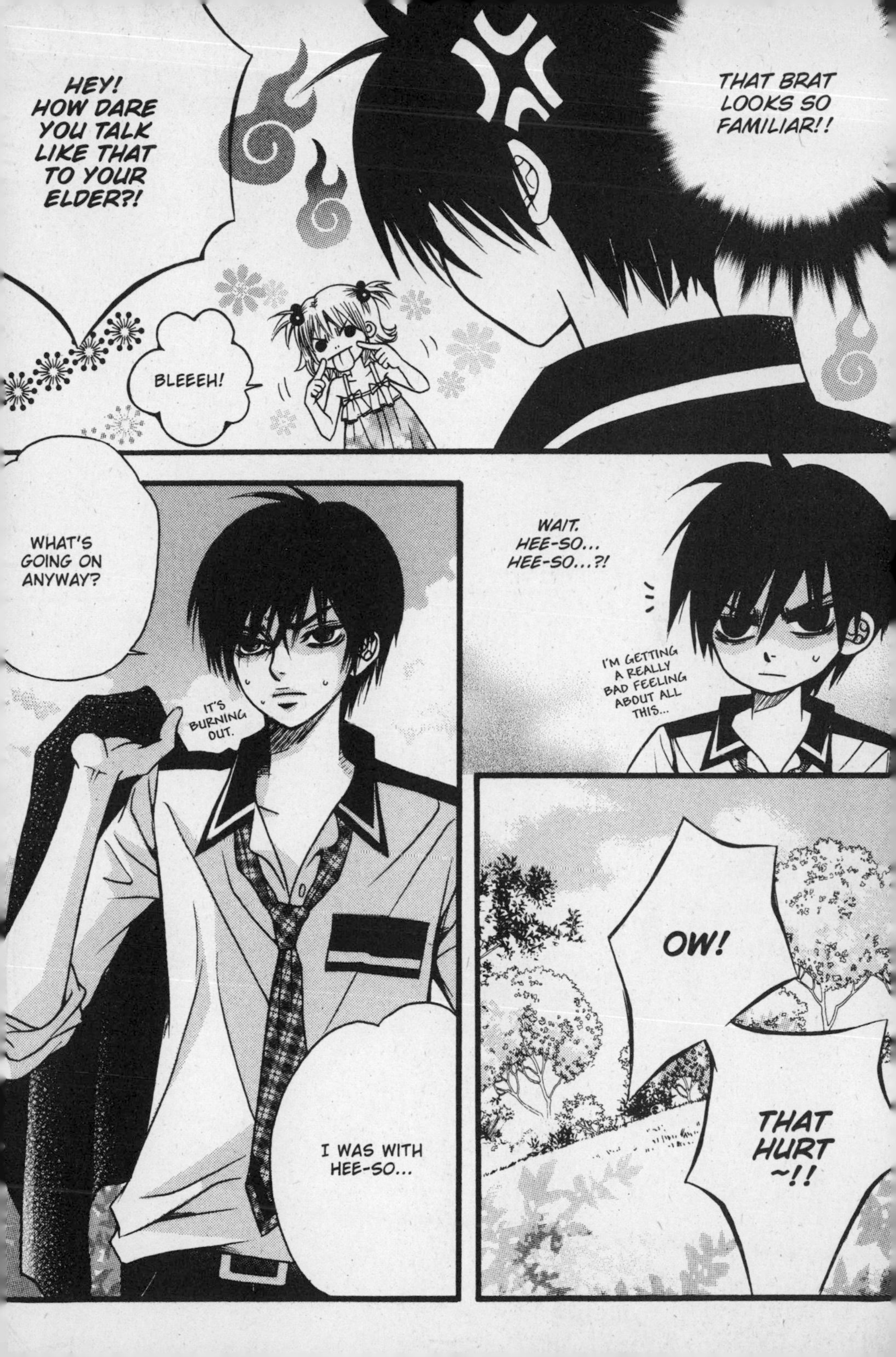
HEY! HOW DARE YOU TALK LIKE THAT TO YOUR ELDER?!
BLEEEH!
THAT BRAT LOOKS SO FAMILIAR!!
WHAT'S GOING ON ANYWAY?
IT'S BURNING OUT.
I WAS WITH HEE-SO...
WAIT. HEE-SO... HEE-SO...?!
I'M GETTING A REALLY BAD FEELING ABOUT ALL THIS...
OW!
THAT HURT ~!!

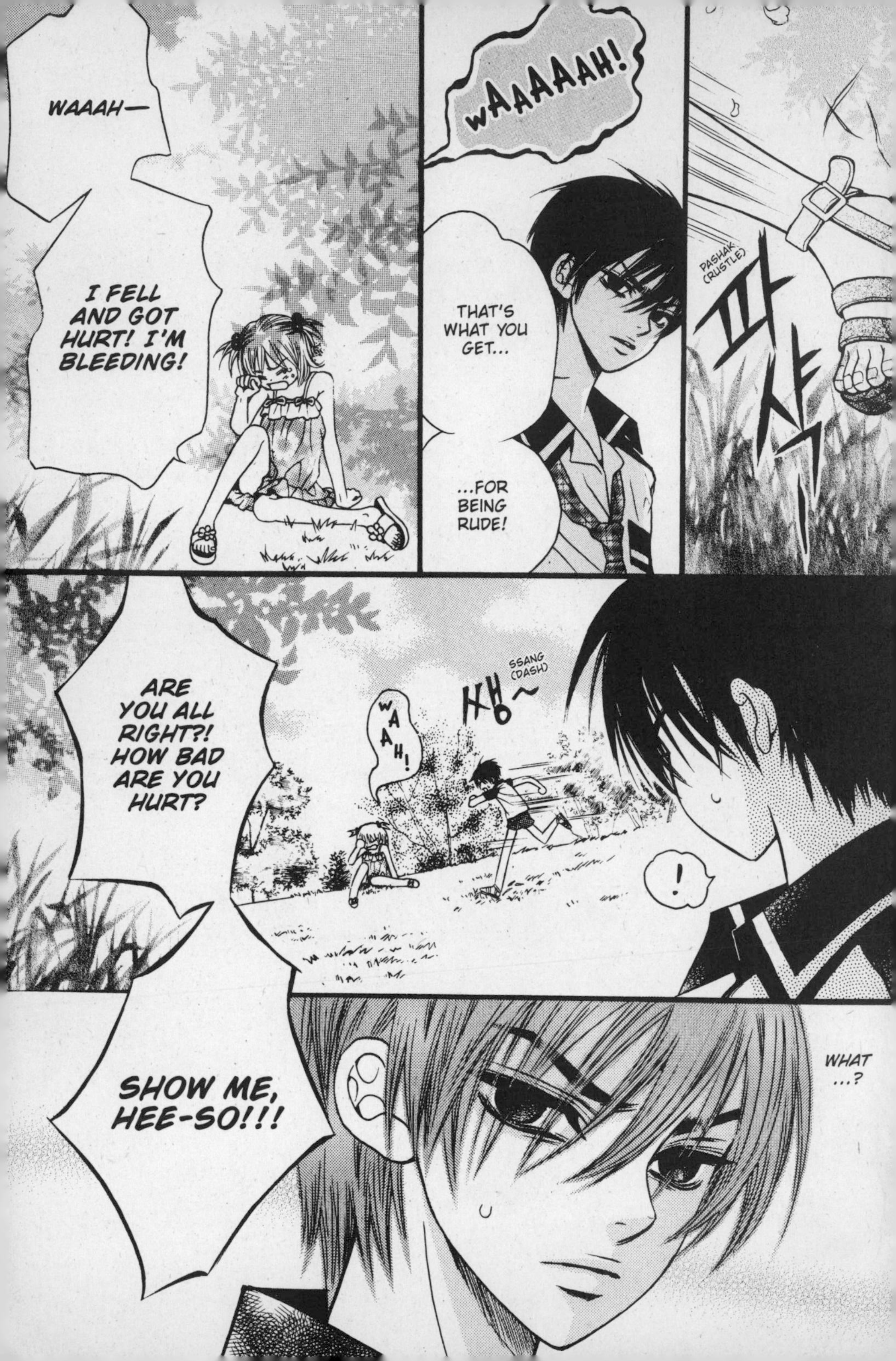
WAAAH—
I FELL AND GOT HURT! I'M BLEEDING!
wAAAAAH!
THAT'S WHAT YOU GET...
...FOR BEING RUDE!
PASHAK (RUSTLE)
ARE YOU ALL RIGHT?! HOW BAD ARE YOU HURT?
SSANG (DASH)
WAAH!
!
SHOW ME, HEE-SO!!!
WHAT ...?

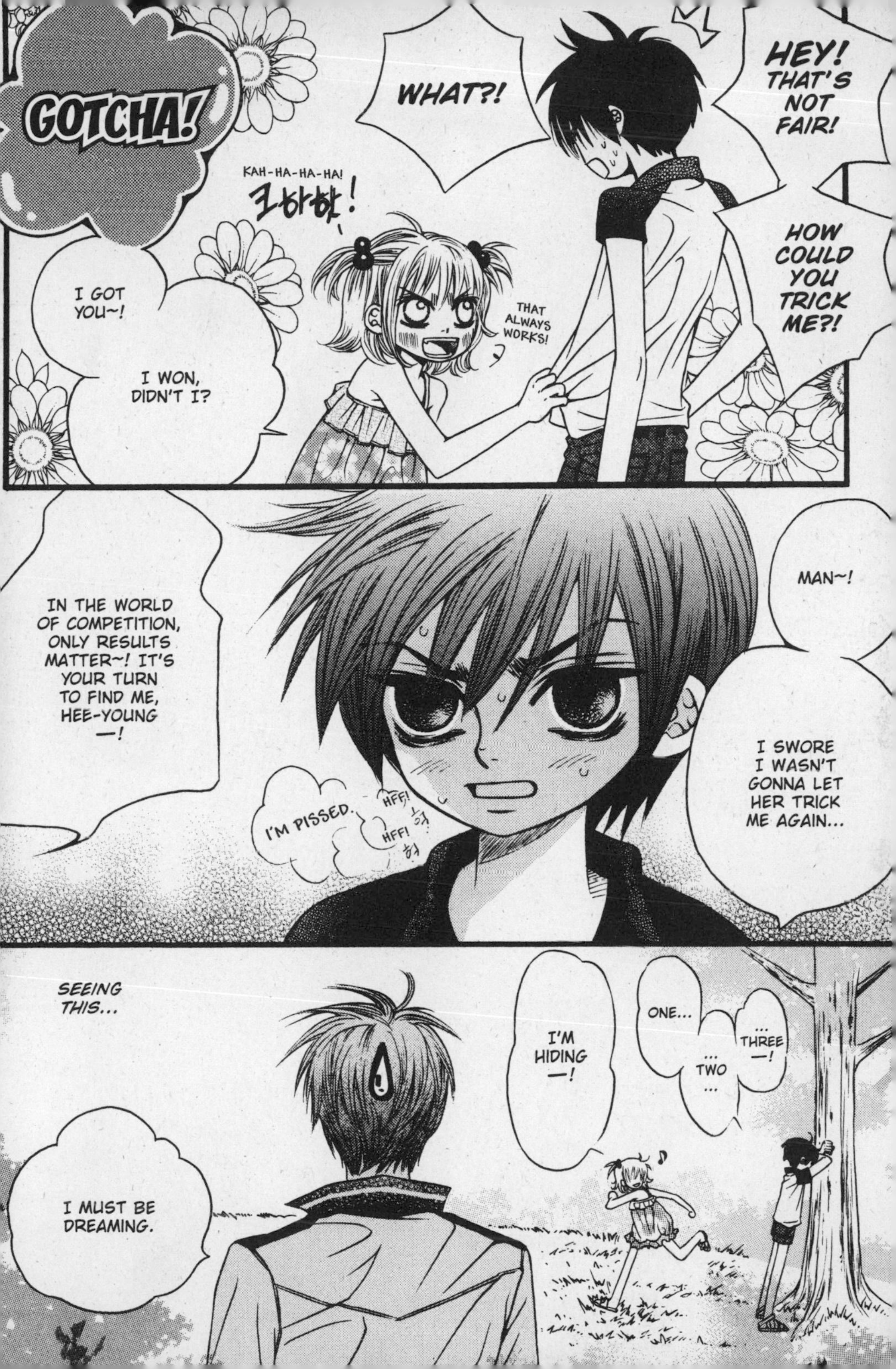
GOTCHA!
KAH-HA-HA-HA!
크하핫!
WHAT?!
HEY! THAT'S NOT FAIR!
HOW COULD YOU TRICK ME?!
I GOT YOU~!
I WON, DIDN'T I?
THAT ALWAYS WORKS!
IN THE WORLD OF COMPETITION, ONLY RESULTS MATTER~! IT'S YOUR TURN TO FIND ME, HEE-YOUNG—!
MAN~!
I SWORE I WASN'T GONNA LET HER TRICK ME AGAIN...
I'M PISSED.
HFF!
HFF!
SEEING THIS...
I MUST BE DREAMING.
I'M HIDING—!
ONE...
...TWO...
...THREE—!

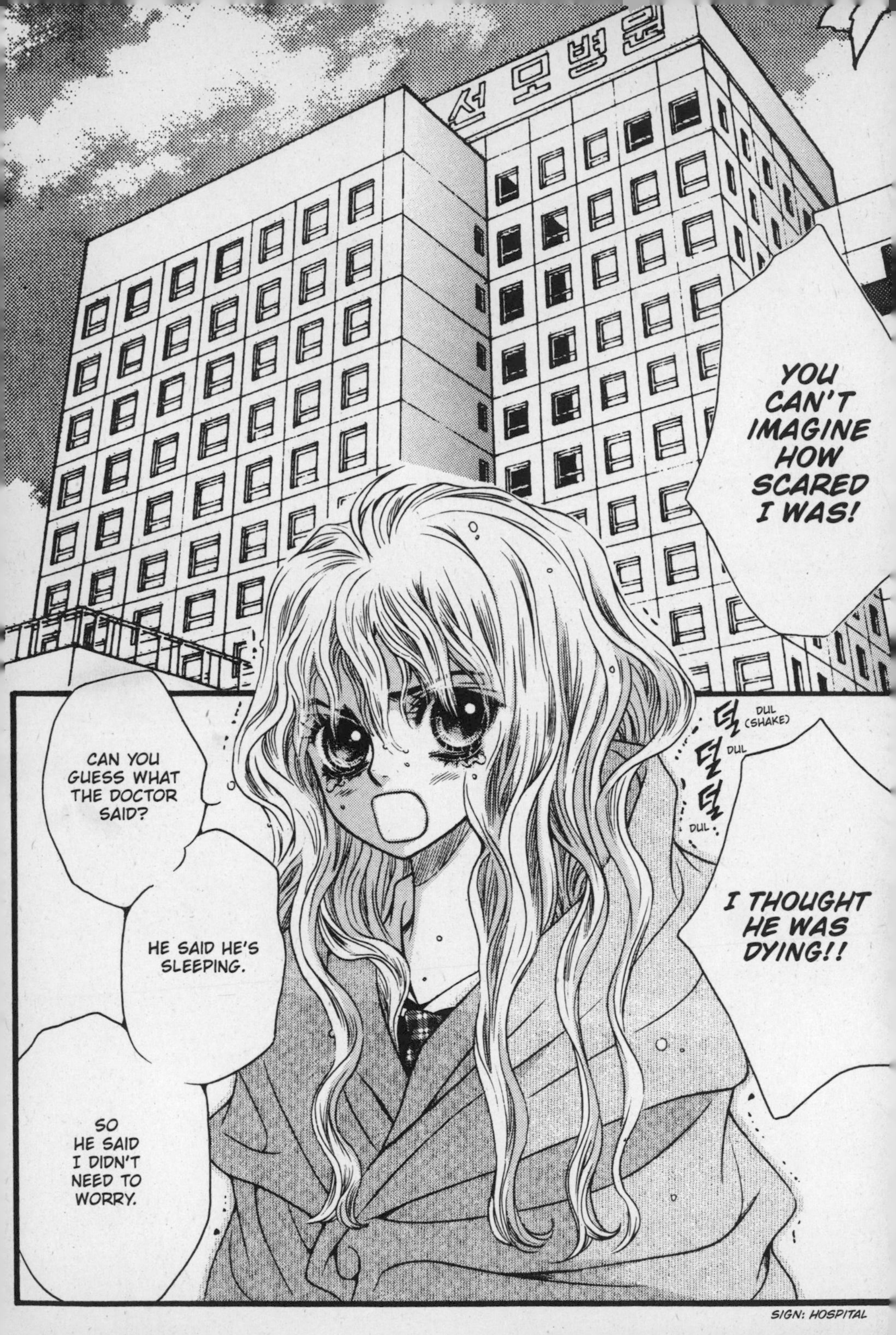
서모병원
YOU CAN'T IMAGINE HOW SCARED I WAS!
CAN YOU GUESS WHAT THE DOCTOR SAID?
HE SAID HE'S SLEEPING.
SO HE SAID I DIDN'T NEED TO WORRY.
덜 DUL (SHAKE)
덜 DUL
덜 DUL
I THOUGHT HE WAS DYING!!

SIGN: HOSPITAL

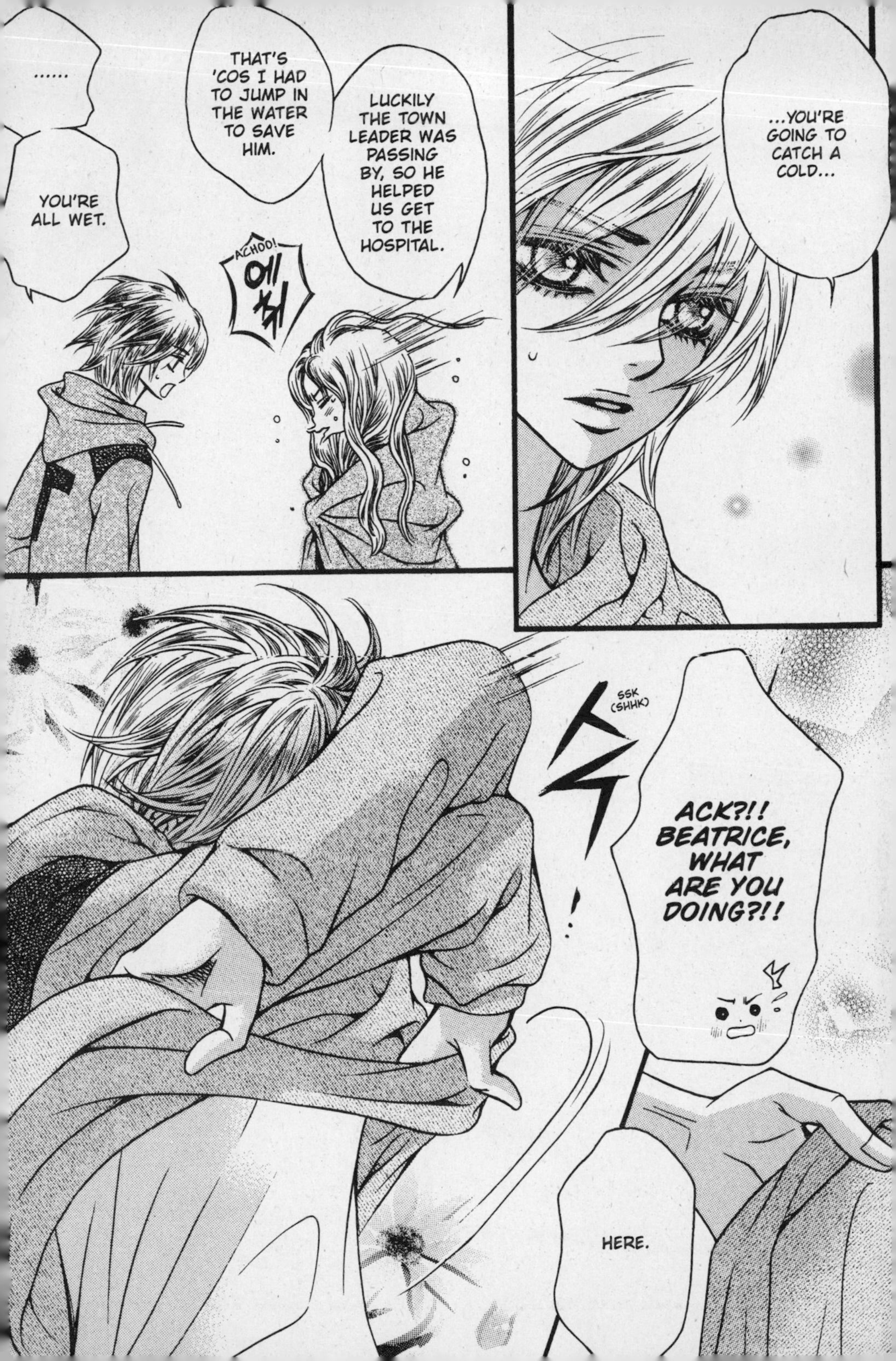
......
YOU'RE ALL WET.
THAT'S 'COS I HAD TO JUMP IN THE WATER TO SAVE HIM.
LUCKILY THE TOWN LEADER WAS PASSING BY, SO HE HELPED US GET TO THE HOSPITAL.
ACHOO!
에취
...YOU'RE GOING TO CATCH A COLD...
SSK (SHHK)
ACK?!! BEATRICE, WHAT ARE YOU DOING?!!
HERE.

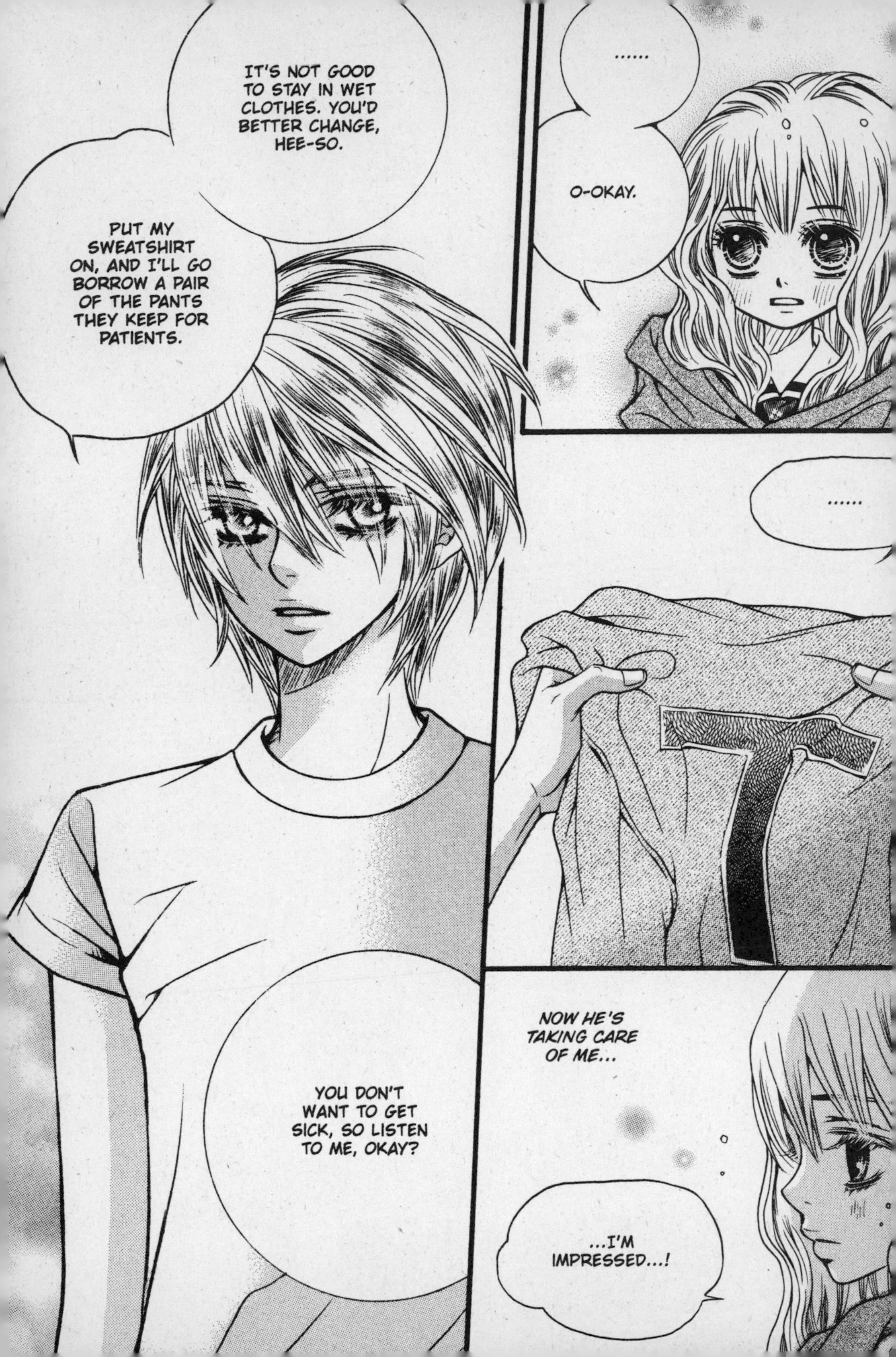

IT'S NOT GOOD TO STAY IN WET CLOTHES. YOU'D BETTER CHANGE, HEE-SO.
PUT MY SWEATSHIRT ON, AND I'LL GO BORROW A PAIR OF THE PANTS THEY KEEP FOR PATIENTS.
YOU DON'T WANT TO GET SICK, SO LISTEN TO ME, OKAY?
......
O-OKAY.
......
NOW HE'S TAKING CARE OF ME...
...I'M IMPRESSED...!

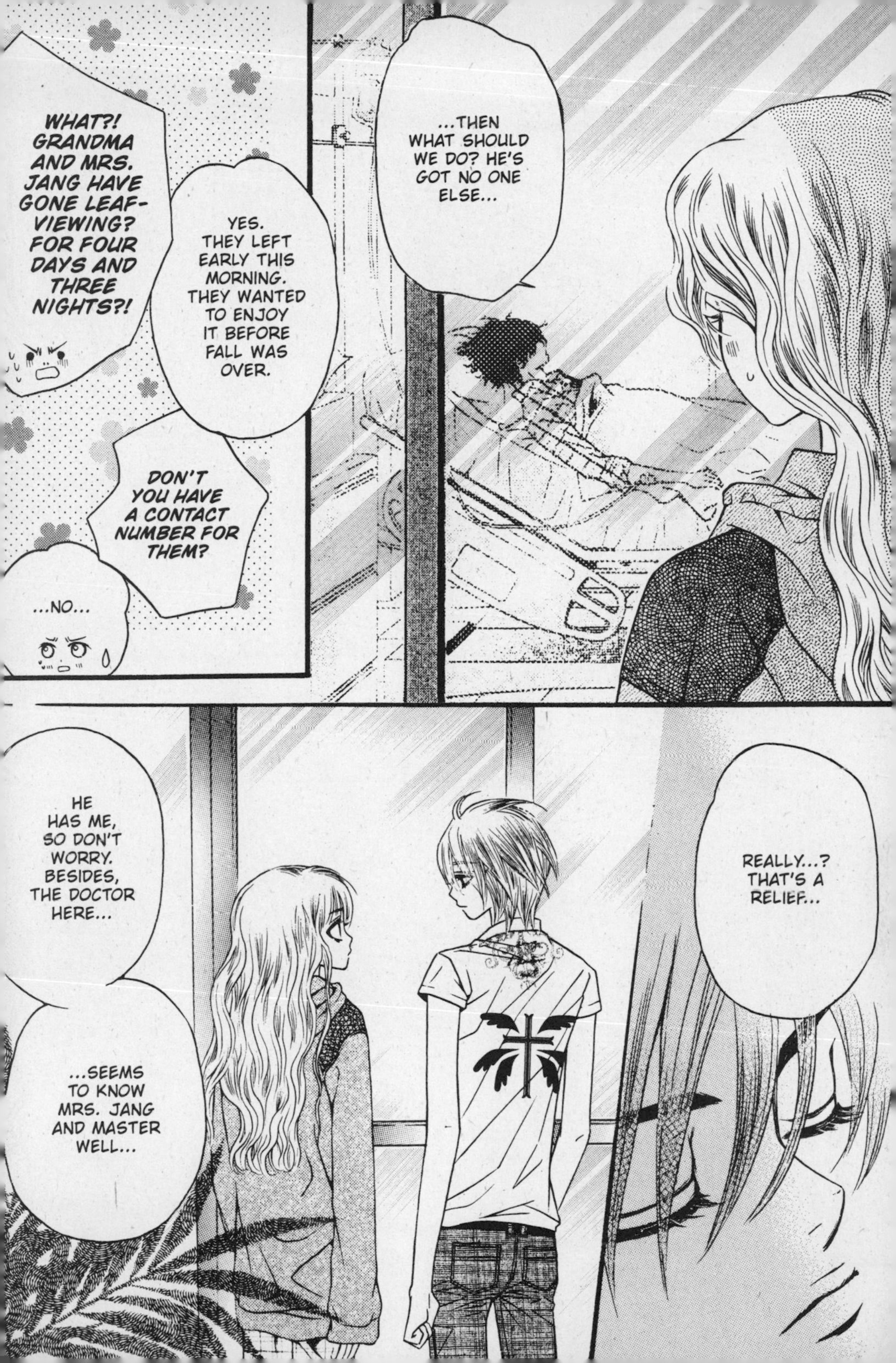
WHAT?! GRANDMA AND MRS. JANG HAVE GONE LEAF-VIEWING? FOR FOUR DAYS AND THREE NIGHTS?!
YES. THEY LEFT EARLY THIS MORNING. THEY WANTED TO ENJOY IT BEFORE FALL WAS OVER.
DON'T YOU HAVE A CONTACT NUMBER FOR THEM?
...NO...
...THEN WHAT SHOULD WE DO? HE'S GOT NO ONE ELSE...
REALLY...? THAT'S A RELIEF...
HE HAS ME, SO DON'T WORRY. BESIDES, THE DOCTOR HERE...
...SEEMS TO KNOW MRS. JANG AND MASTER WELL...

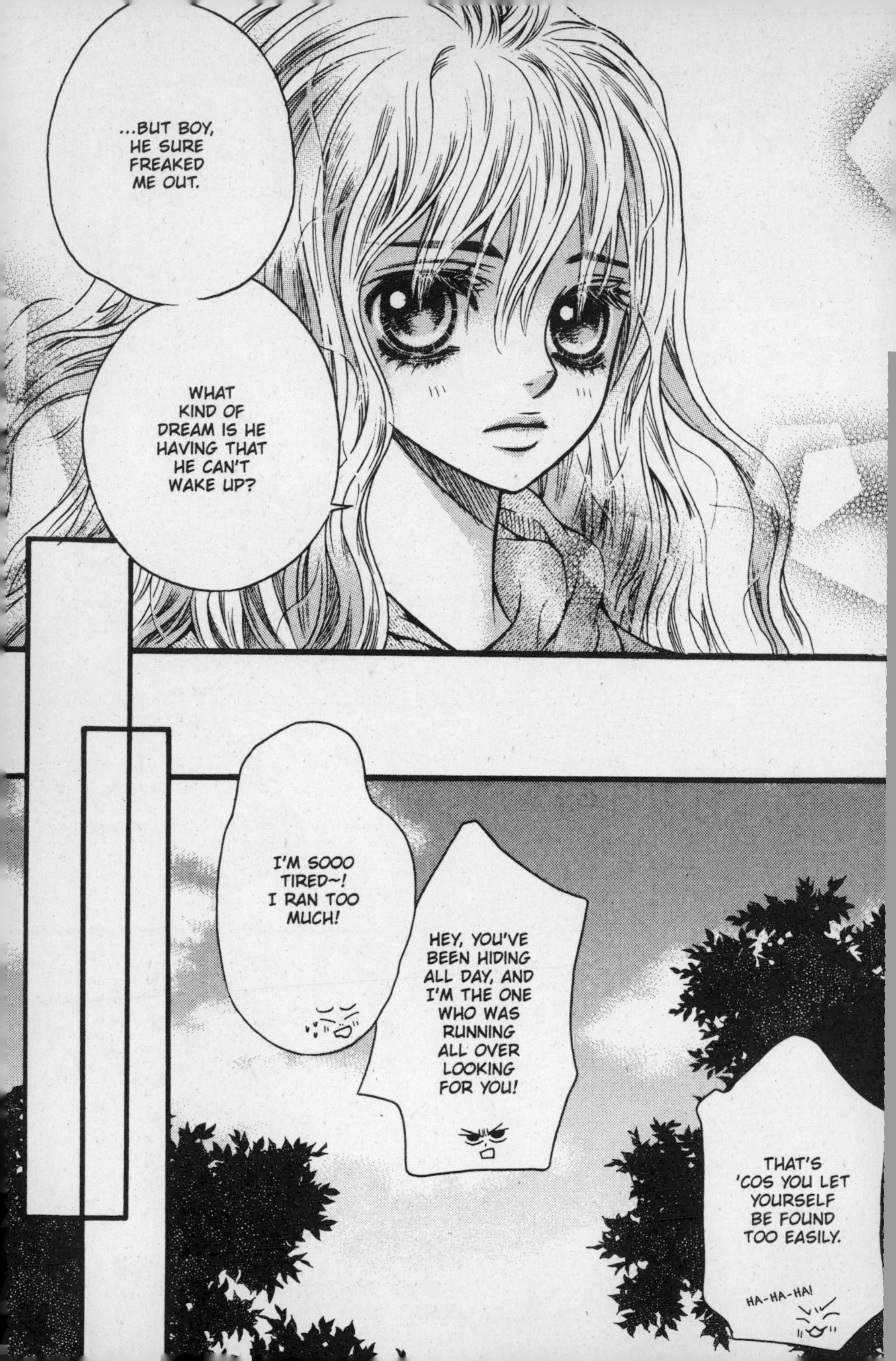
...BUT BOY, HE SURE FREAKED ME OUT.
WHAT KIND OF DREAM IS HE HAVING THAT HE CAN'T WAKE UP?
I'M SOOO TIRED~! I RAN TOO MUCH!
HEY, YOU'VE BEEN HIDING ALL DAY, AND I'M THE ONE WHO WAS RUNNING ALL OVER LOOKING FOR YOU!
THAT'S 'COS YOU LET YOURSELF BE FOUND TOO EASILY.
HA-HA-HA!

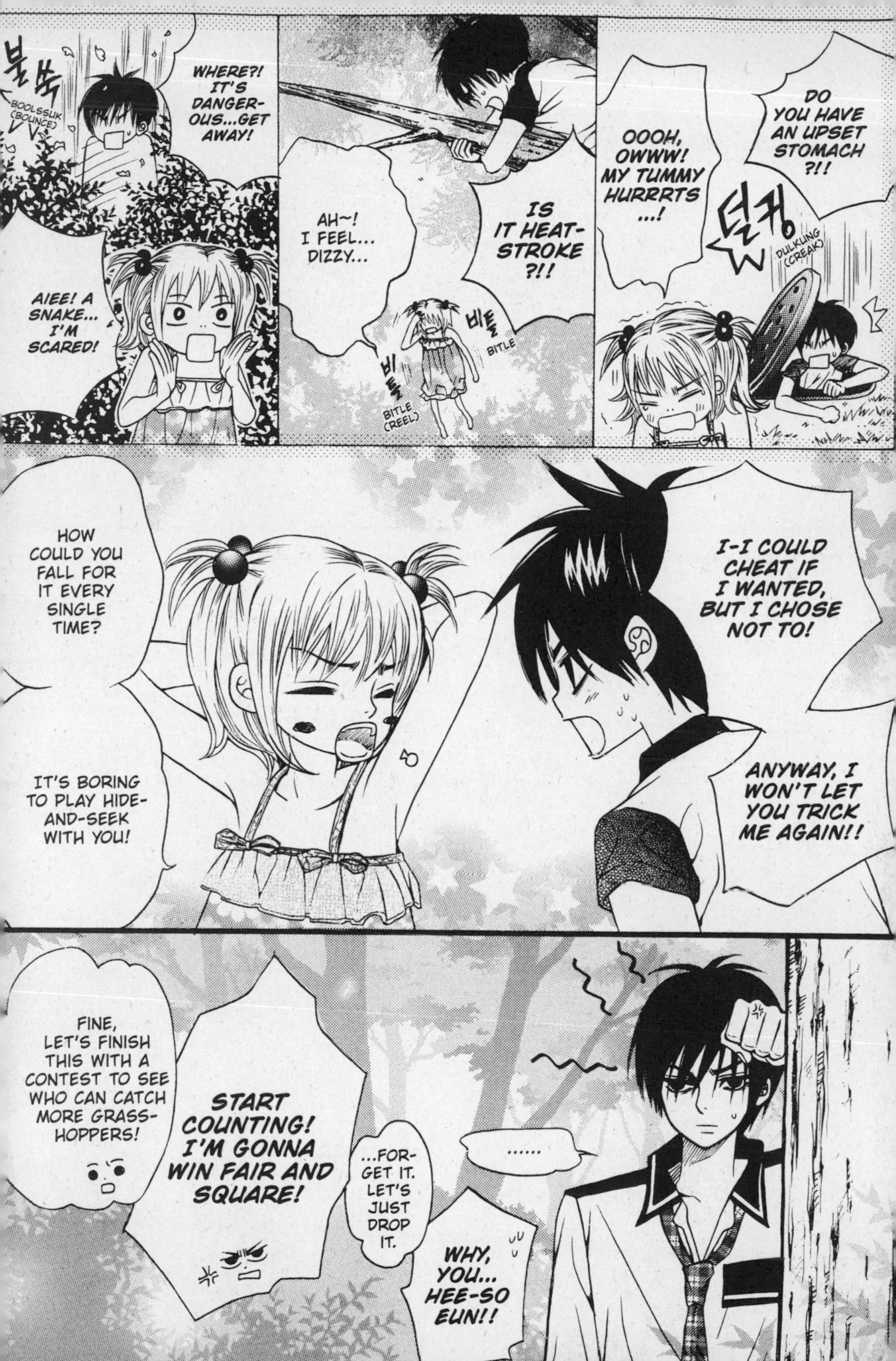

불쑥
BOOLSSUK (BOUNCE)
WHERE?! IT'S DANGER-OUS...GET AWAY!
AIEE! A SNAKE... I'M SCARED!
AH~! I FEEL... DIZZY...
IS IT HEAT-STROKE?!!
비틀
BITLE
비틀
BITLE (REEL)
OOOH, OWWW! MY TUMMY HURRRTS...!
DO YOU HAVE AN UPSET STOMACH?!!
덜컹
DULKUNG (CREAK)
HOW COULD YOU FALL FOR IT EVERY SINGLE TIME?
IT'S BORING TO PLAY HIDE-AND-SEEK WITH YOU!
I-I COULD CHEAT IF I WANTED, BUT I CHOSE NOT TO!
ANYWAY, I WON'T LET YOU TRICK ME AGAIN!!
FINE, LET'S FINISH THIS WITH A CONTEST TO SEE WHO CAN CATCH MORE GRASS-HOPPERS!
START COUNTING! I'M GONNA WIN FAIR AND SQUARE!
......
...FOR-GET IT. LET'S JUST DROP IT.
WHY, YOU... HEE-SO EUN!!

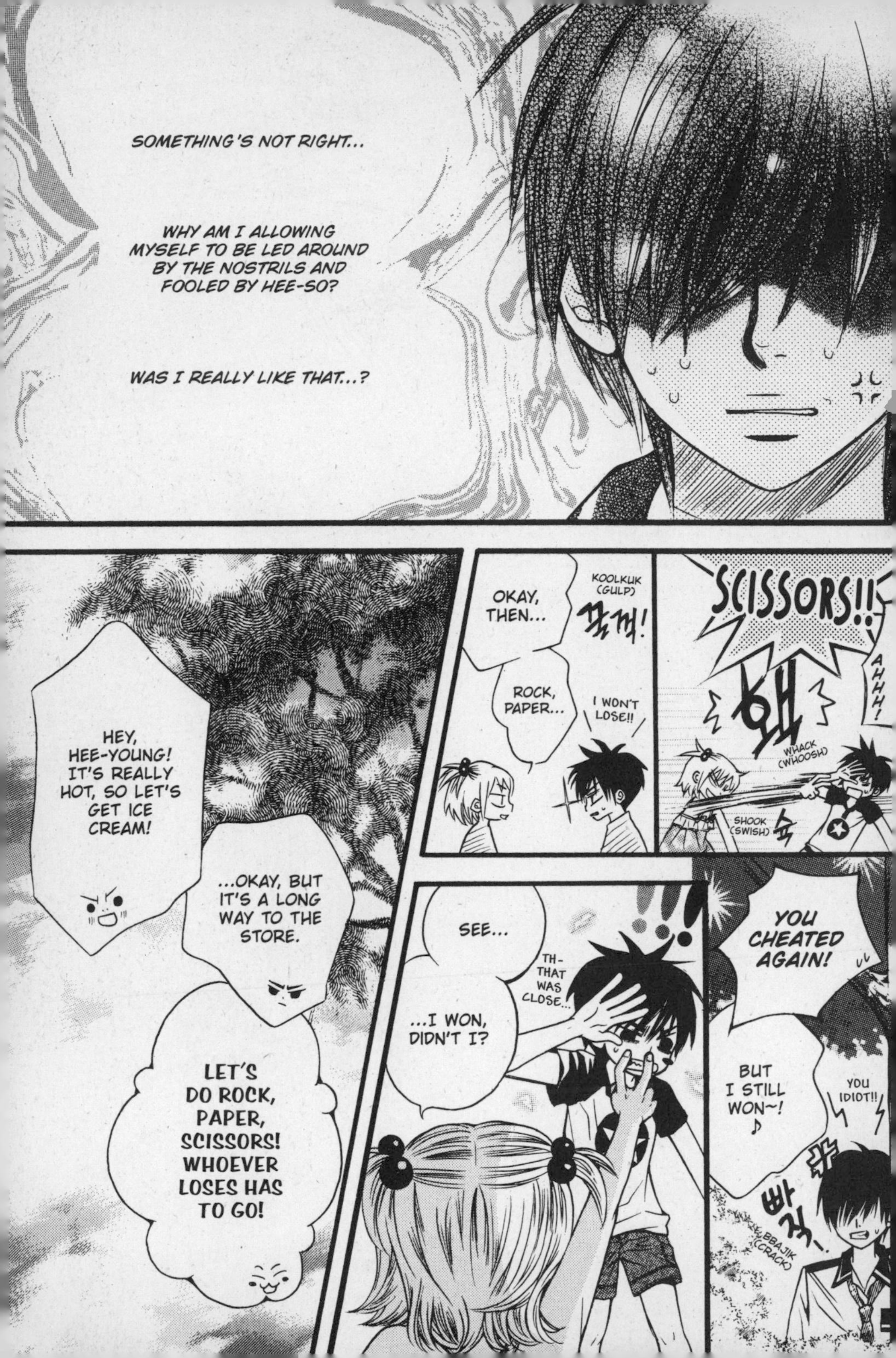

SOMETHING'S NOT RIGHT...
WHY AM I ALLOWING MYSELF TO BE LED AROUND BY THE NOSTRILS AND FOOLED BY HEE-SO?
WAS I REALLY LIKE THAT...?
HEY, HEE-YOUNG! IT'S REALLY HOT, SO LET'S GET ICE CREAM!
...OKAY, BUT IT'S A LONG WAY TO THE STORE.
LET'S DO ROCK, PAPER, SCISSORS! WHOEVER LOSES HAS TO GO!
OKAY, THEN...
KOOLKUK (GULP)
꿀꺽!
ROCK, PAPER...
I WON'T LOSE!!
SCISSORS!!
AHHH!
왝
WHACK (WHOOSH)
SHOOK (SWISH)
슉
SEE...
...I WON, DIDN'T I?
TH-THAT WAS CLOSE...
YOU CHEATED AGAIN!
BUT I STILL WON~! ♪
YOU IDIOT!!
빠직
BBAJIK (CRACK)

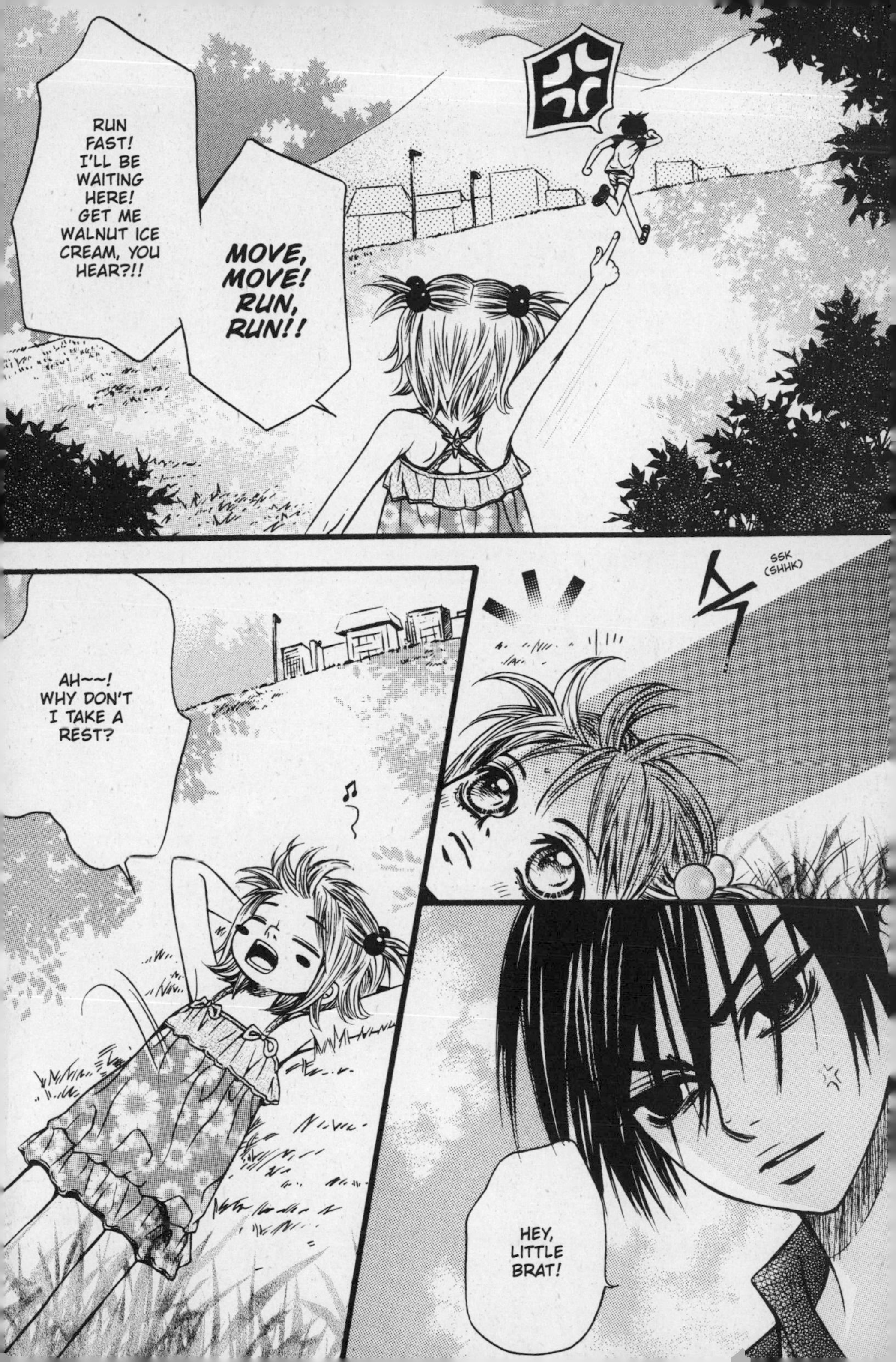
RUN FAST! I'LL BE WAITING HERE! GET ME WALNUT ICE CREAM, YOU HEAR?!!
MOVE, MOVE! RUN, RUN!!
SSK (SHHK)
AH~~! WHY DON'T I TAKE A REST?
HEY, LITTLE BRAT!

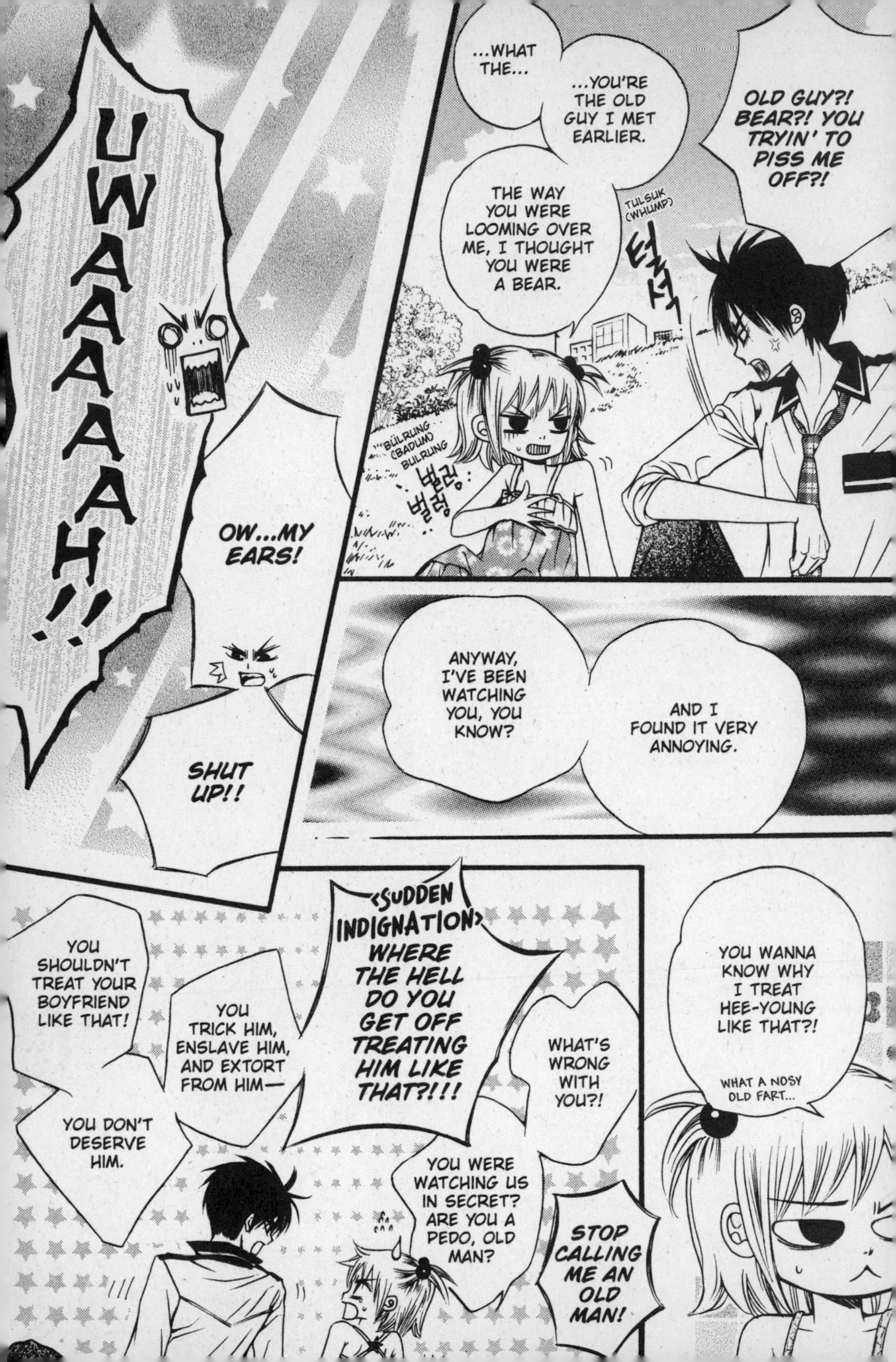
UWAAAAAH!!
OW...MY EARS!
SHUT UP!!
...WHAT THE...
...YOU'RE THE OLD GUY I MET EARLIER.
THE WAY YOU WERE LOOMING OVER ME, I THOUGHT YOU WERE A BEAR.
BÜLRUNG (BADUM) BULRUNG
벌렁 벌렁
TULSUK (WHUMP)
털석
OLD GUY?! BEAR?! YOU TRYIN' TO PISS ME OFF?!
ANYWAY, I'VE BEEN WATCHING YOU, YOU KNOW?
AND I FOUND IT VERY ANNOYING.
YOU SHOULDN'T TREAT YOUR BOYFRIEND LIKE THAT!
YOU TRICK HIM, ENSLAVE HIM, AND EXTORT FROM HIM—
YOU DON'T DESERVE HIM.
<SUDDEN INDIGNATION> WHERE THE HELL DO YOU GET OFF TREATING HIM LIKE THAT?!!!
WHAT'S WRONG WITH YOU?!
YOU WERE WATCHING US IN SECRET? ARE YOU A PEDO, OLD MAN?
STOP CALLING ME AN OLD MAN!
YOU WANNA KNOW WHY I TREAT HEE-YOUNG LIKE THAT?!
WHAT A NOSY OLD FART...

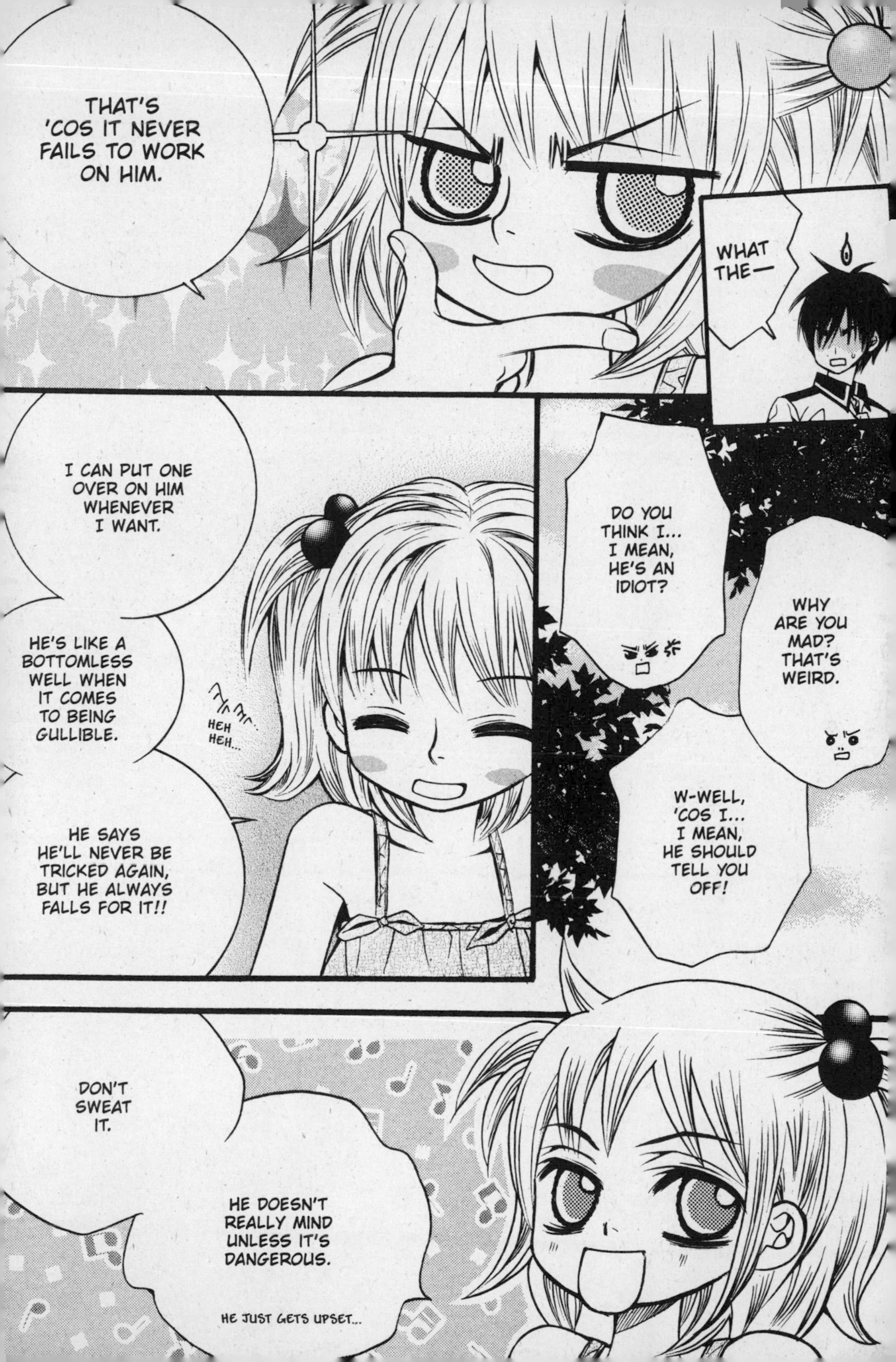
THAT'S 'COS IT NEVER FAILS TO WORK ON HIM.
WHAT THE—
DO YOU THINK I... I MEAN, HE'S AN IDIOT?
WHY ARE YOU MAD? THAT'S WEIRD.
W-WELL, 'COS I... I MEAN, HE SHOULD TELL YOU OFF!
I CAN PUT ONE OVER ON HIM WHENEVER I WANT.
HE'S LIKE A BOTTOMLESS WELL WHEN IT COMES TO BEING GULLIBLE.
HEH HEH...
HE SAYS HE'LL NEVER BE TRICKED AGAIN, BUT HE ALWAYS FALLS FOR IT!!
DON'T SWEAT IT.
HE DOESN'T REALLY MIND UNLESS IT'S DANGEROUS.
HE JUST GETS UPSET...

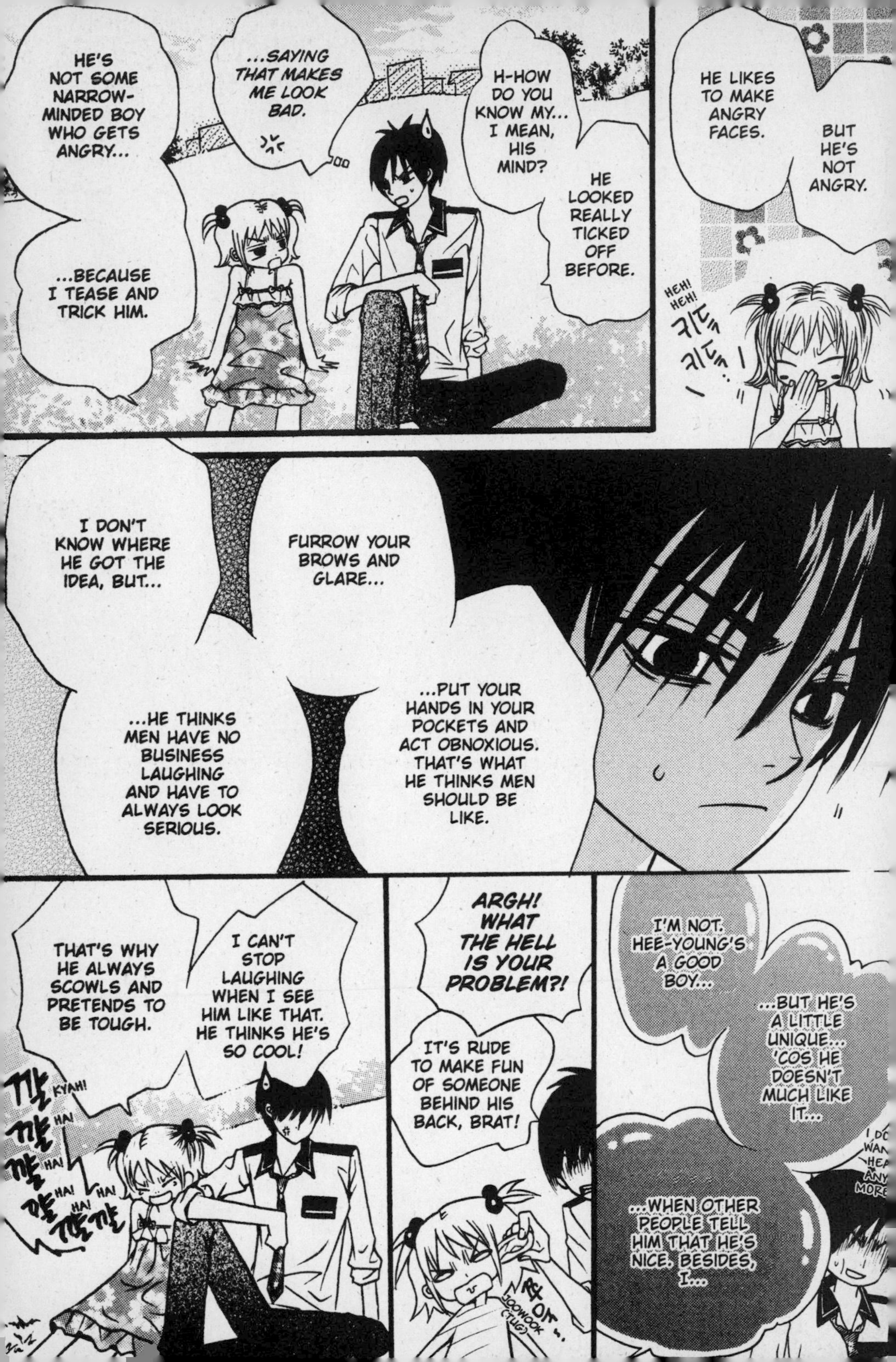
HE'S NOT SOME NARROW-MINDED BOY WHO GETS ANGRY...
...BECAUSE I TEASE AND TRICK HIM.
...SAYING THAT MAKES ME LOOK BAD.
H-HOW DO YOU KNOW MY... I MEAN, HIS MIND?
HE LOOKED REALLY TICKED OFF BEFORE.
HE LIKES TO MAKE ANGRY FACES.
BUT HE'S NOT ANGRY.
HEH! HEH!
I DON'T KNOW WHERE HE GOT THE IDEA, BUT...
...HE THINKS MEN HAVE NO BUSINESS LAUGHING AND HAVE TO ALWAYS LOOK SERIOUS.
FURROW YOUR BROWS AND GLARE...
...PUT YOUR HANDS IN YOUR POCKETS AND ACT OBNOXIOUS. THAT'S WHAT HE THINKS MEN SHOULD BE LIKE.
THAT'S WHY HE ALWAYS SCOWLS AND PRETENDS TO BE TOUGH.
I CAN'T STOP LAUGHING WHEN I SEE HIM LIKE THAT. HE THINKS HE'S SO COOL!
KYAH! HA! HA! HA! HA! HA!
ARGH! WHAT THE HELL IS YOUR PROBLEM?!
IT'S RUDE TO MAKE FUN OF SOMEONE BEHIND HIS BACK, BRAT!
JOOWOOK (TUG)
I'M NOT. HEE-YOUNG'S A GOOD BOY...
...BUT HE'S A LITTLE UNIQUE... 'COS HE DOESN'T MUCH LIKE IT...
...WHEN OTHER PEOPLE TELL HIM THAT HE'S NICE. BESIDES, I...

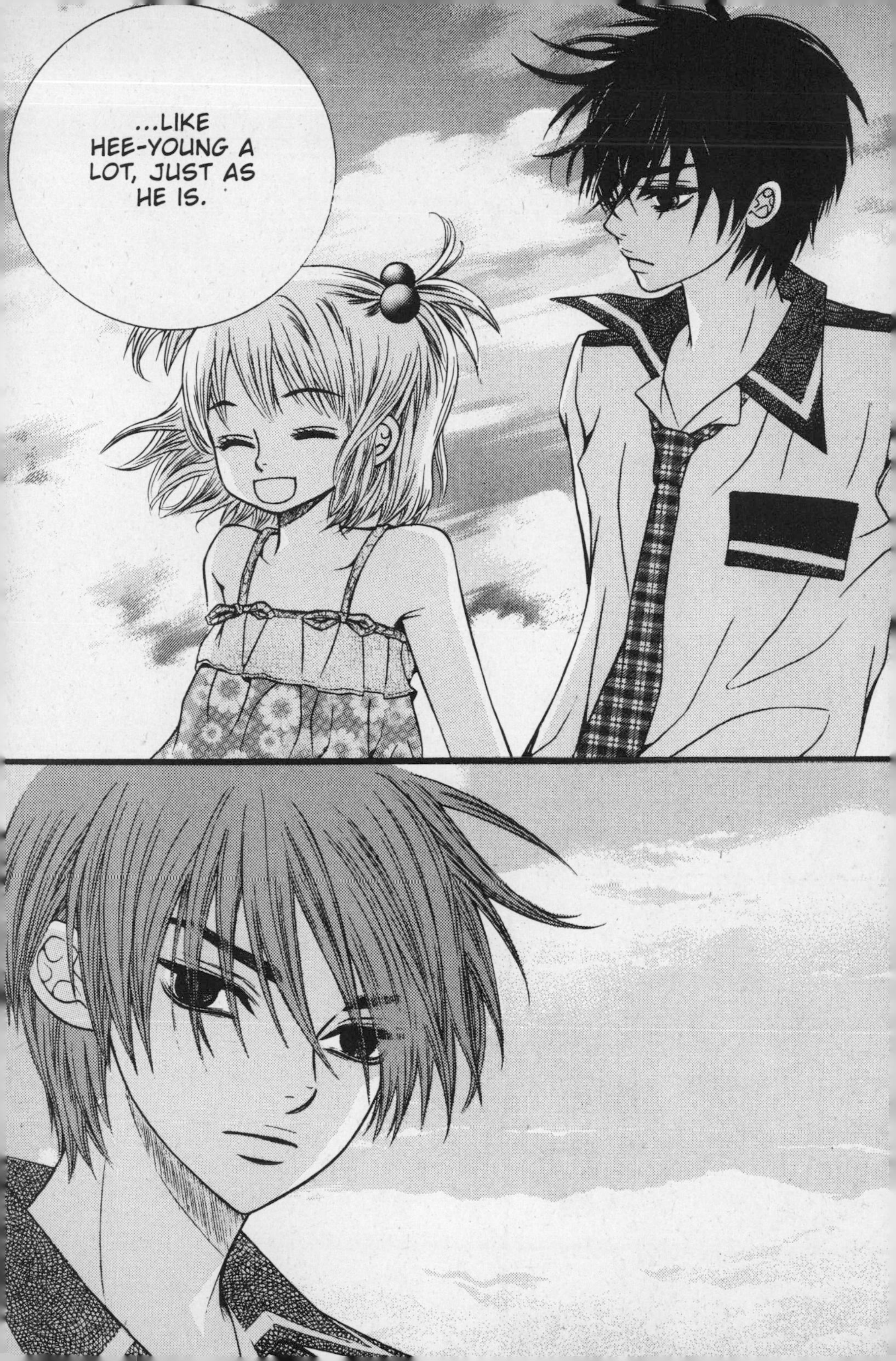
...LIKE HEE-YOUNG A LOT, JUST AS HE IS.

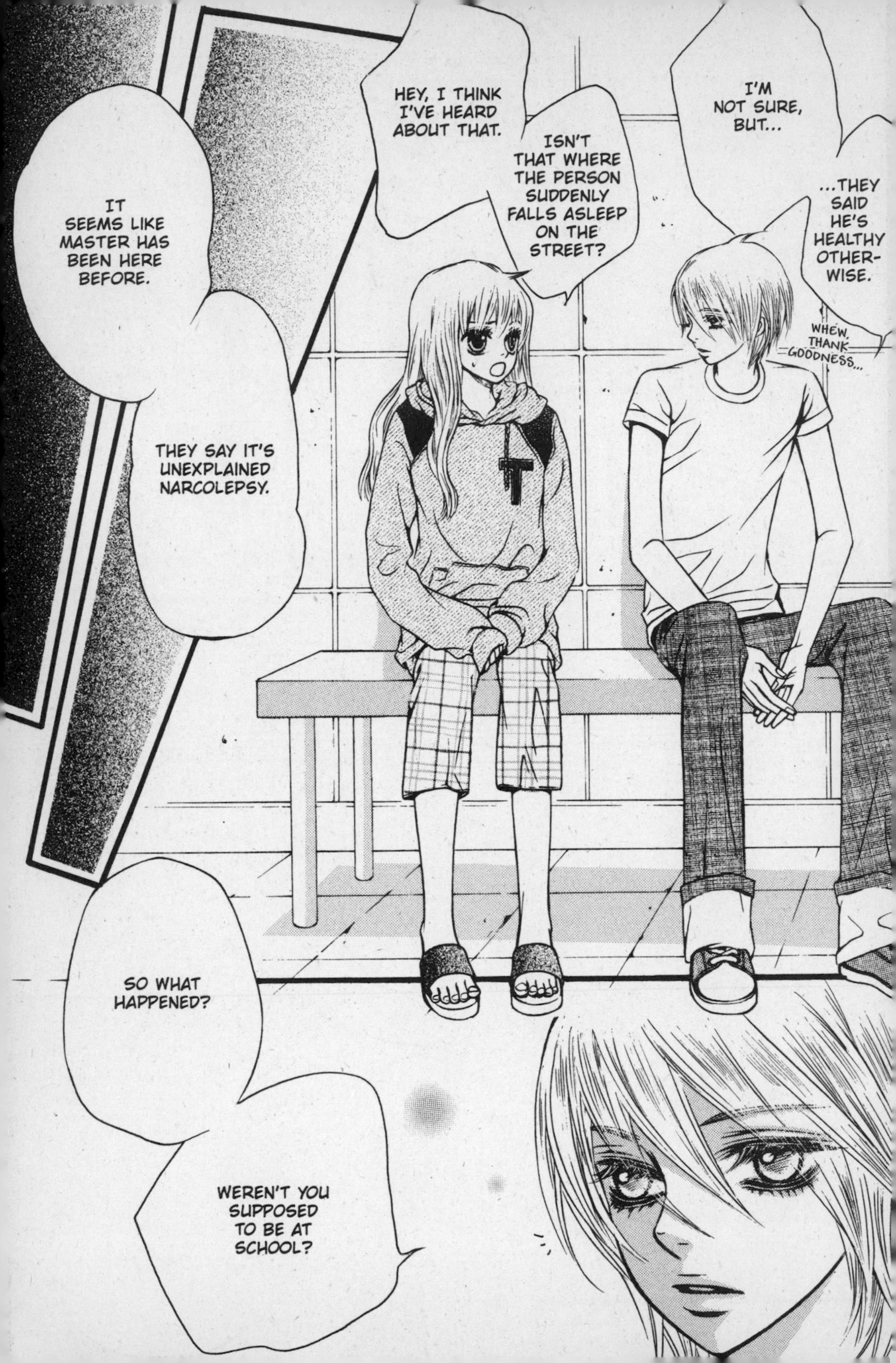
I'M NOT SURE, BUT...
...THEY SAID HE'S HEALTHY OTHER-WISE.
WHEW, THANK GOODNESS...
HEY, I THINK I'VE HEARD ABOUT THAT.
ISN'T THAT WHERE THE PERSON SUDDENLY FALLS ASLEEP ON THE STREET?
IT SEEMS LIKE MASTER HAS BEEN HERE BEFORE.
THEY SAY IT'S UNEXPLAINED NARCOLEPSY.
SO WHAT HAPPENED?
WEREN'T YOU SUPPOSED TO BE AT SCHOOL?

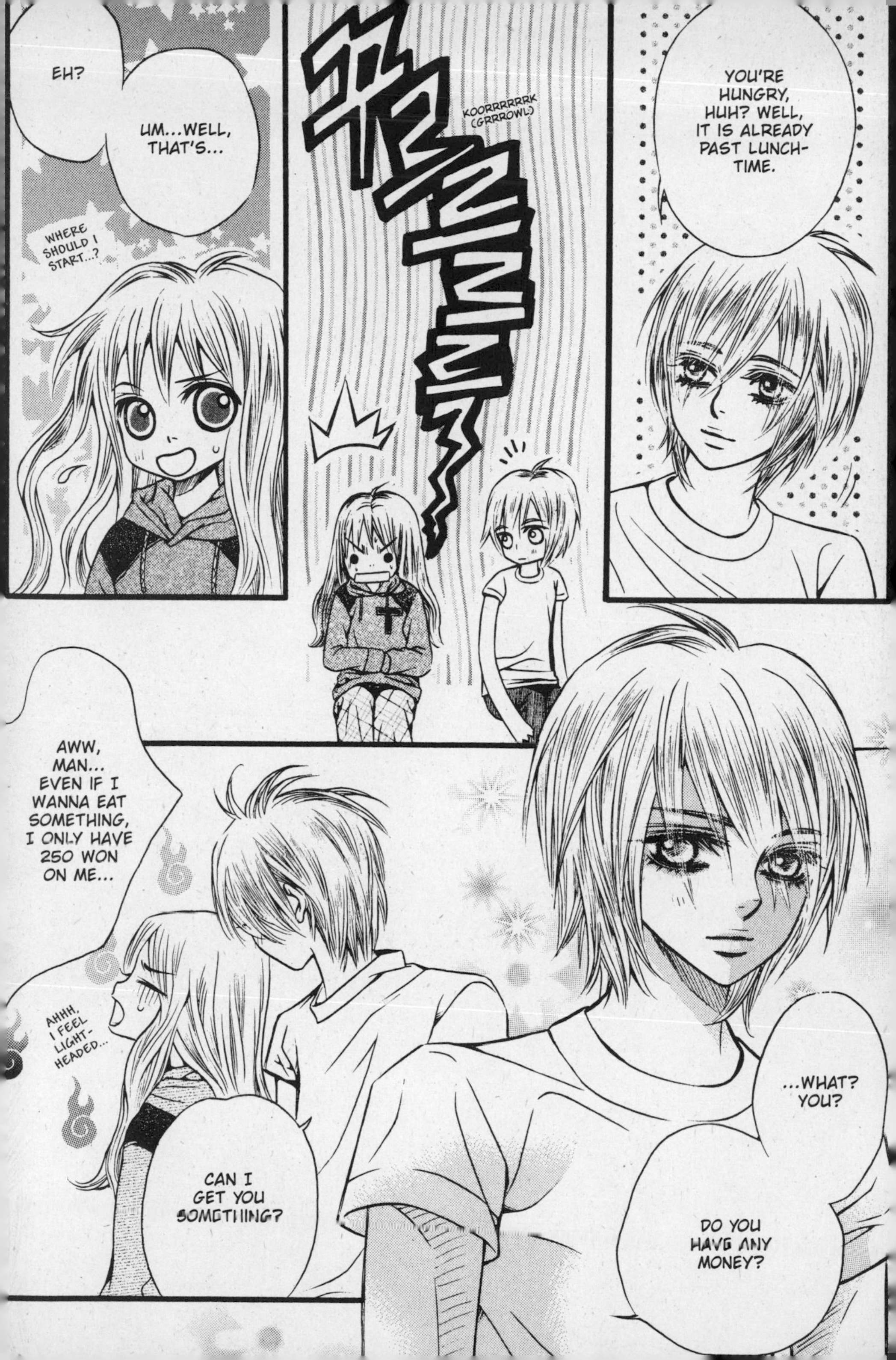
EH?
UM...WELL, THAT'S...
WHERE SHOULD I START...?
KOORRRRRRK (GRRROWL)
YOU'RE HUNGRY, HUH? WELL, IT IS ALREADY PAST LUNCH-TIME.
AWW, MAN... EVEN IF I WANNA EAT SOMETHING, I ONLY HAVE 250 WON ON ME...
AHHH, I FEEL LIGHT-HEADED...
CAN I GET YOU SOMETHING?
...WHAT? YOU?
DO YOU HAVE ANY MONEY?

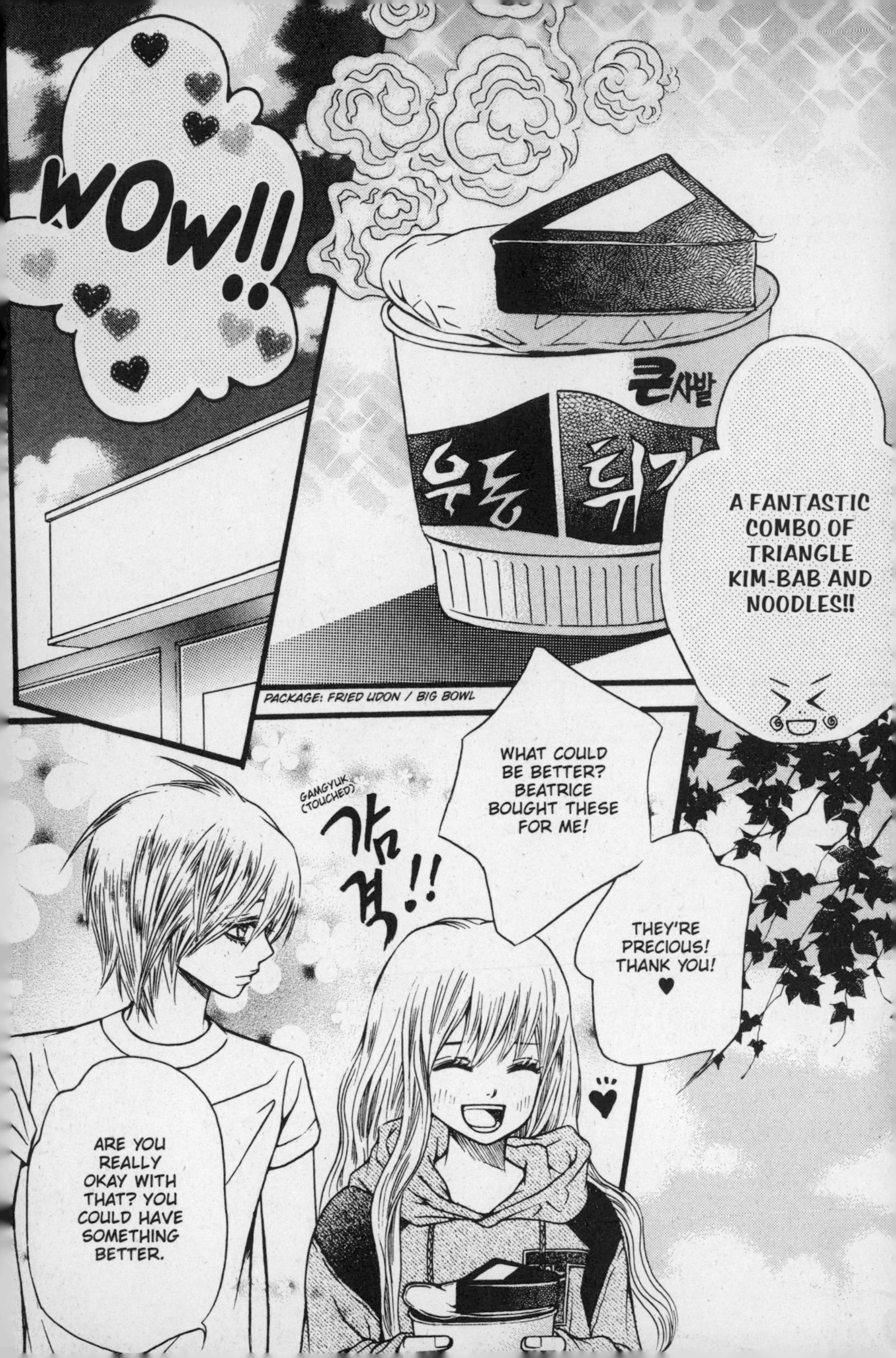
WOW!!
큰사발
A FANTASTIC COMBO OF TRIANGLE KIM-BAB AND NOODLES!!
PACKAGE: FRIED UDON / BIG BOWL
GAMGYUK (TOUCHED)
감격!!
WHAT COULD BE BETTER? BEATRICE BOUGHT THESE FOR ME!
THEY'RE PRECIOUS! THANK YOU! ♥
ARE YOU REALLY OKAY WITH THAT? YOU COULD HAVE SOMETHING BETTER.

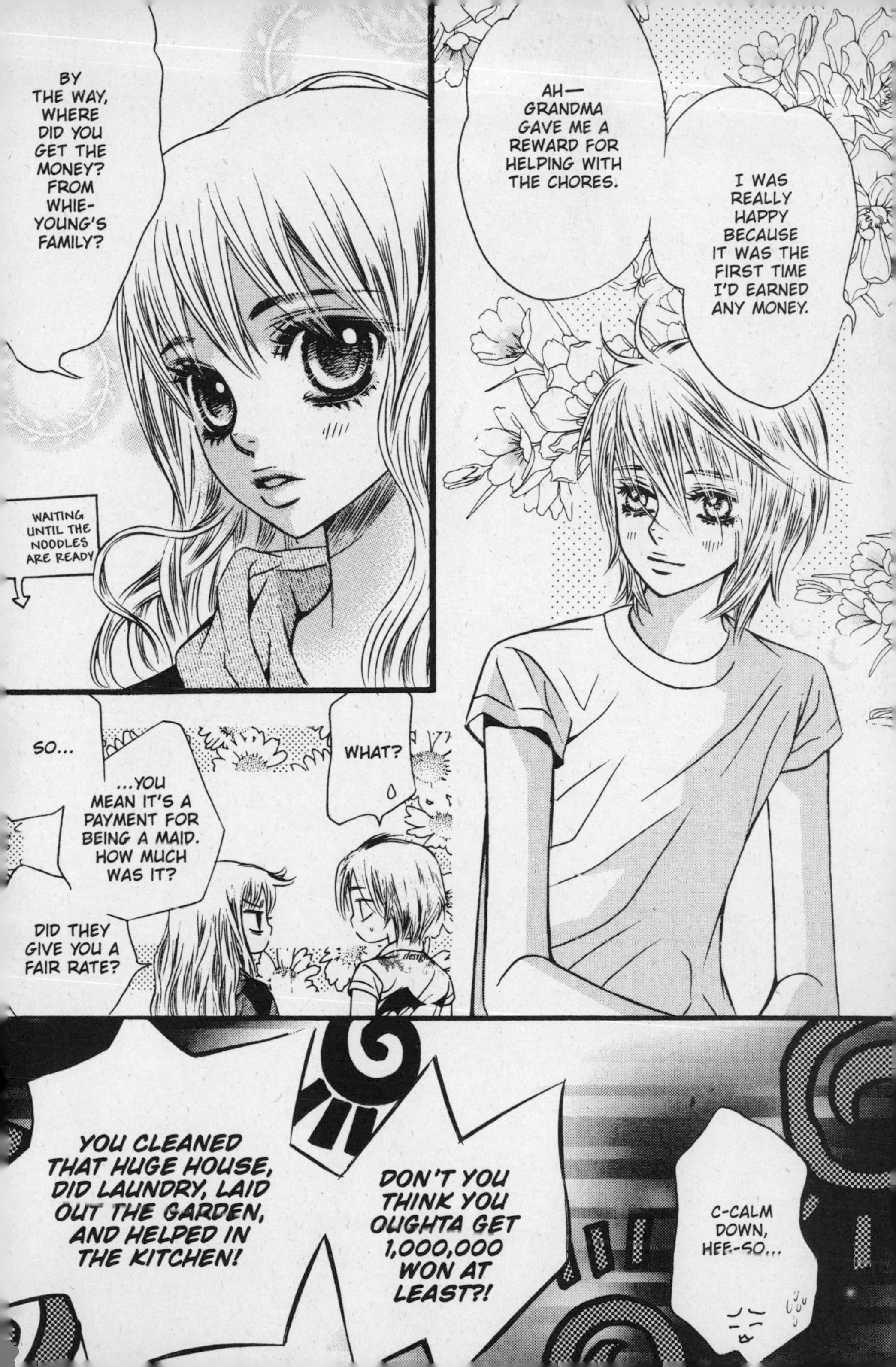
BY THE WAY, WHERE DID YOU GET THE MONEY? FROM WHIE-YOUNG'S FAMILY?
WAITING UNTIL THE NOODLES ARE READY
AH—GRANDMA GAVE ME A REWARD FOR HELPING WITH THE CHORES.
I WAS REALLY HAPPY BECAUSE IT WAS THE FIRST TIME I'D EARNED ANY MONEY.
SO...
...YOU MEAN IT'S A PAYMENT FOR BEING A MAID. HOW MUCH WAS IT?
WHAT?
DID THEY GIVE YOU A FAIR RATE?
YOU CLEANED THAT HUGE HOUSE, DID LAUNDRY, LAID OUT THE GARDEN, AND HELPED IN THE KITCHEN!
DON'T YOU THINK YOU OUGHTA GET 1,000,000 WON AT LEAST?!
C-CALM DOWN, HEE-SO...

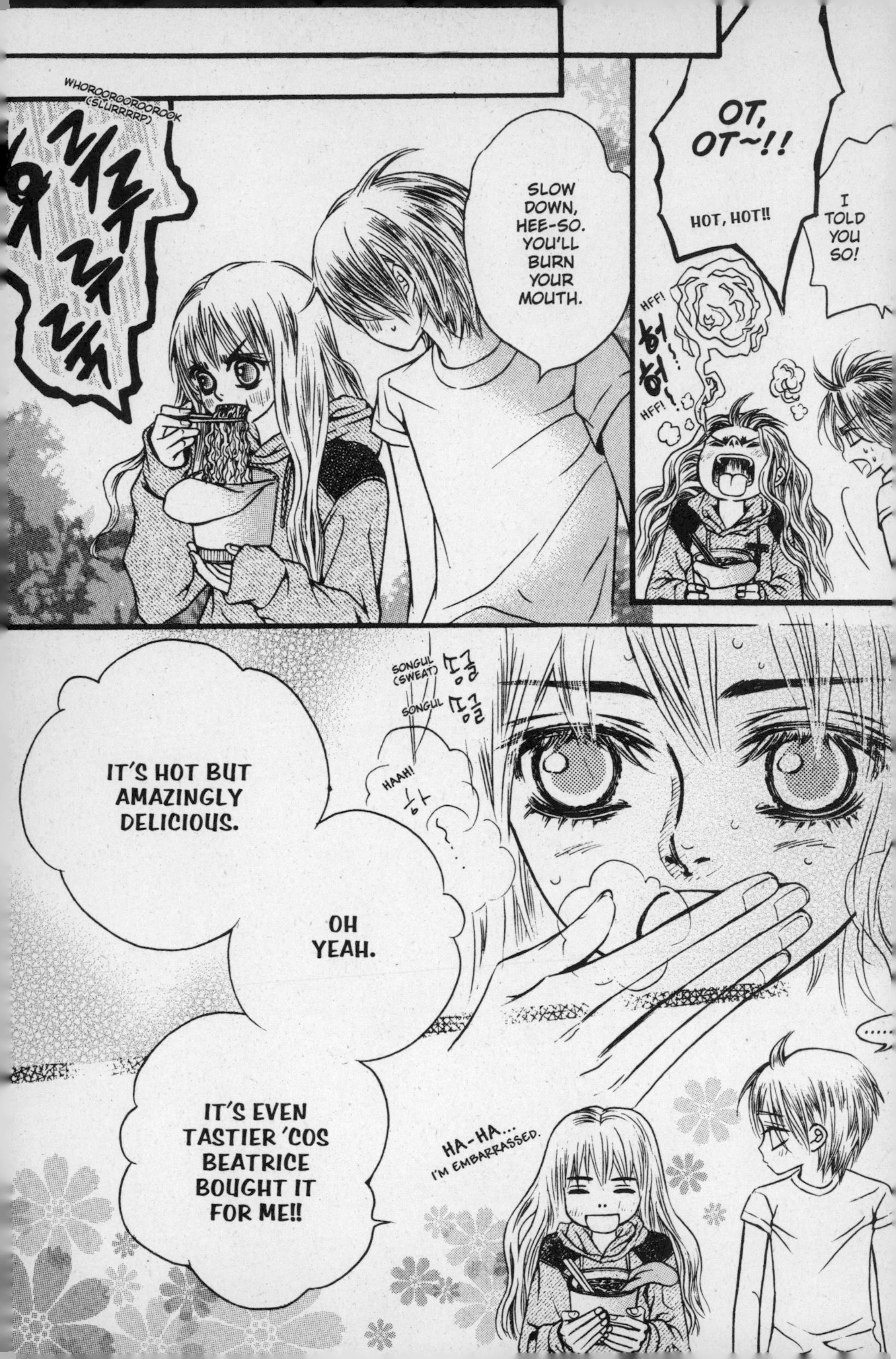
WHOROOROOROOROOK (SLURRRRP)
SLOW DOWN, HEE-SO. YOU'LL BURN YOUR MOUTH.
OT, OT~!!
HOT, HOT!!
HFF! HFF!
I TOLD YOU SO!
SONGUL (SWEAT) SONGUL
HAAH!
IT'S HOT BUT AMAZINGLY DELICIOUS.
OH YEAH.
IT'S EVEN TASTIER 'COS BEATRICE BOUGHT IT FOR ME!!
HA-HA... I'M EMBARRASSED.
.....

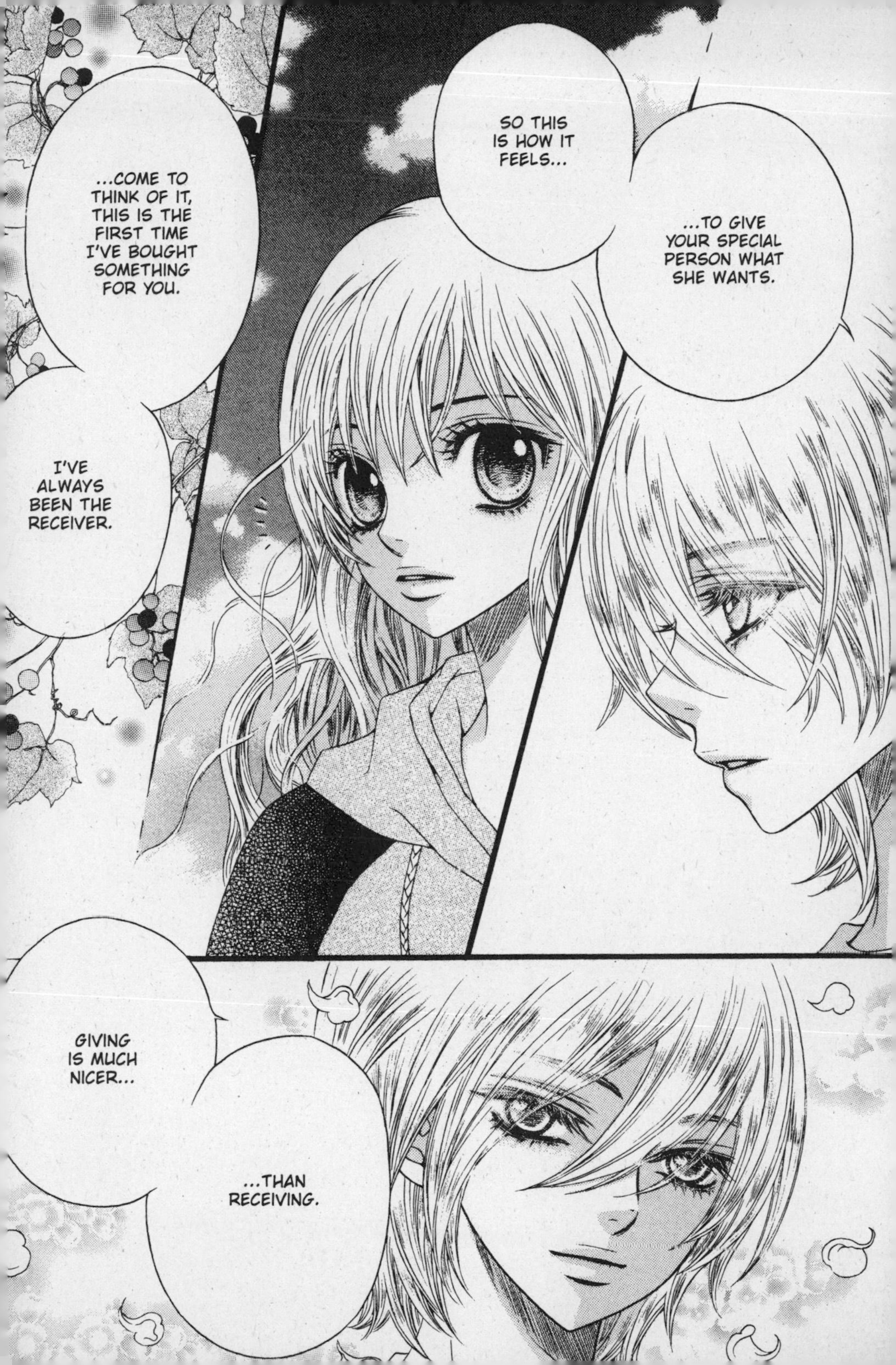
SO THIS IS HOW IT FEELS...
...TO GIVE YOUR SPECIAL PERSON WHAT SHE WANTS.
...COME TO THINK OF IT, THIS IS THE FIRST TIME I'VE BOUGHT SOMETHING FOR YOU.
I'VE ALWAYS BEEN THE RECEIVER.
GIVING IS MUCH NICER...
...THAN RECEIVING.

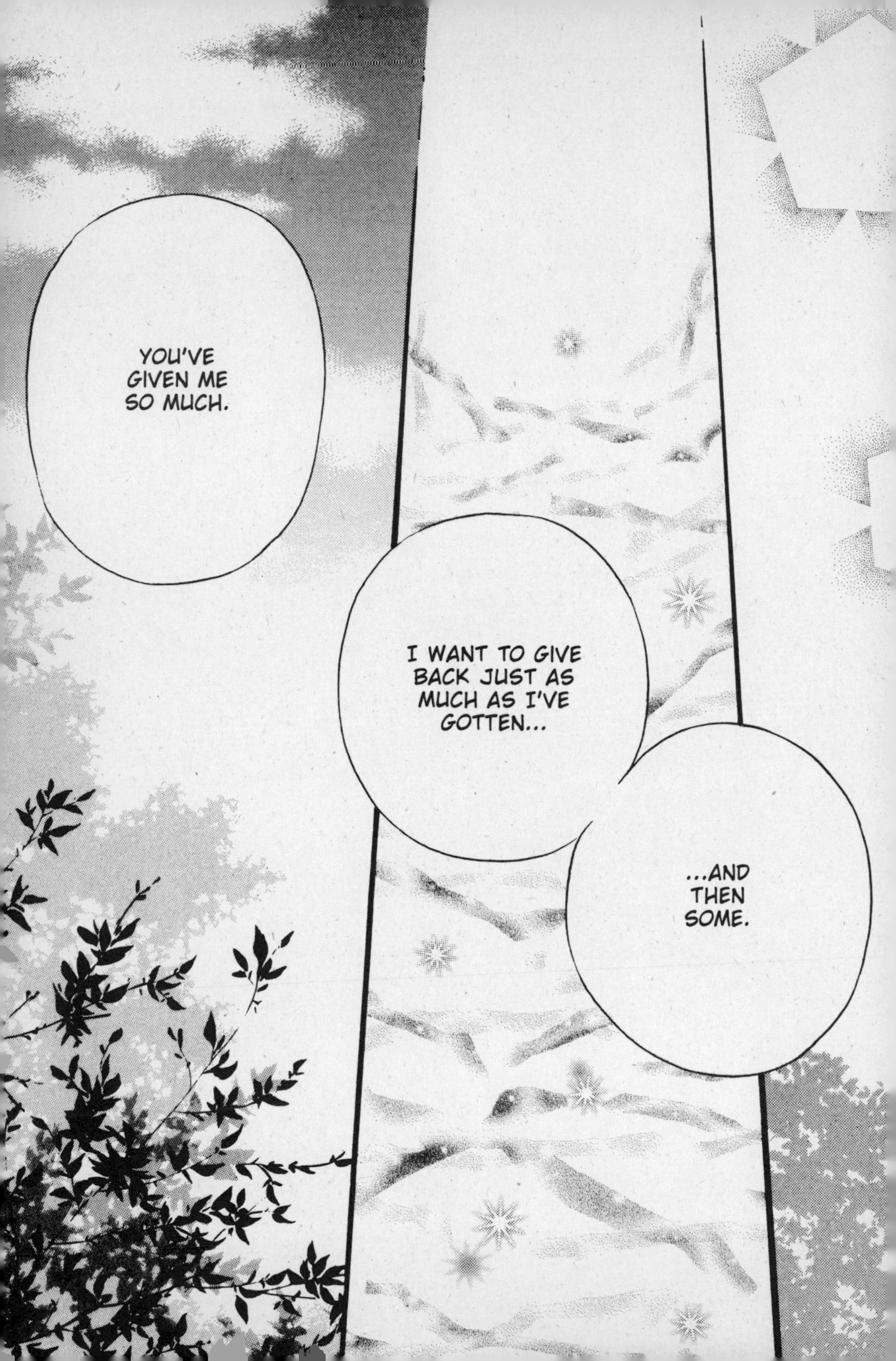
YOU'VE GIVEN ME SO MUCH.
I WANT TO GIVE BACK JUST AS MUCH AS I'VE GOTTEN...
...AND THEN SOME.

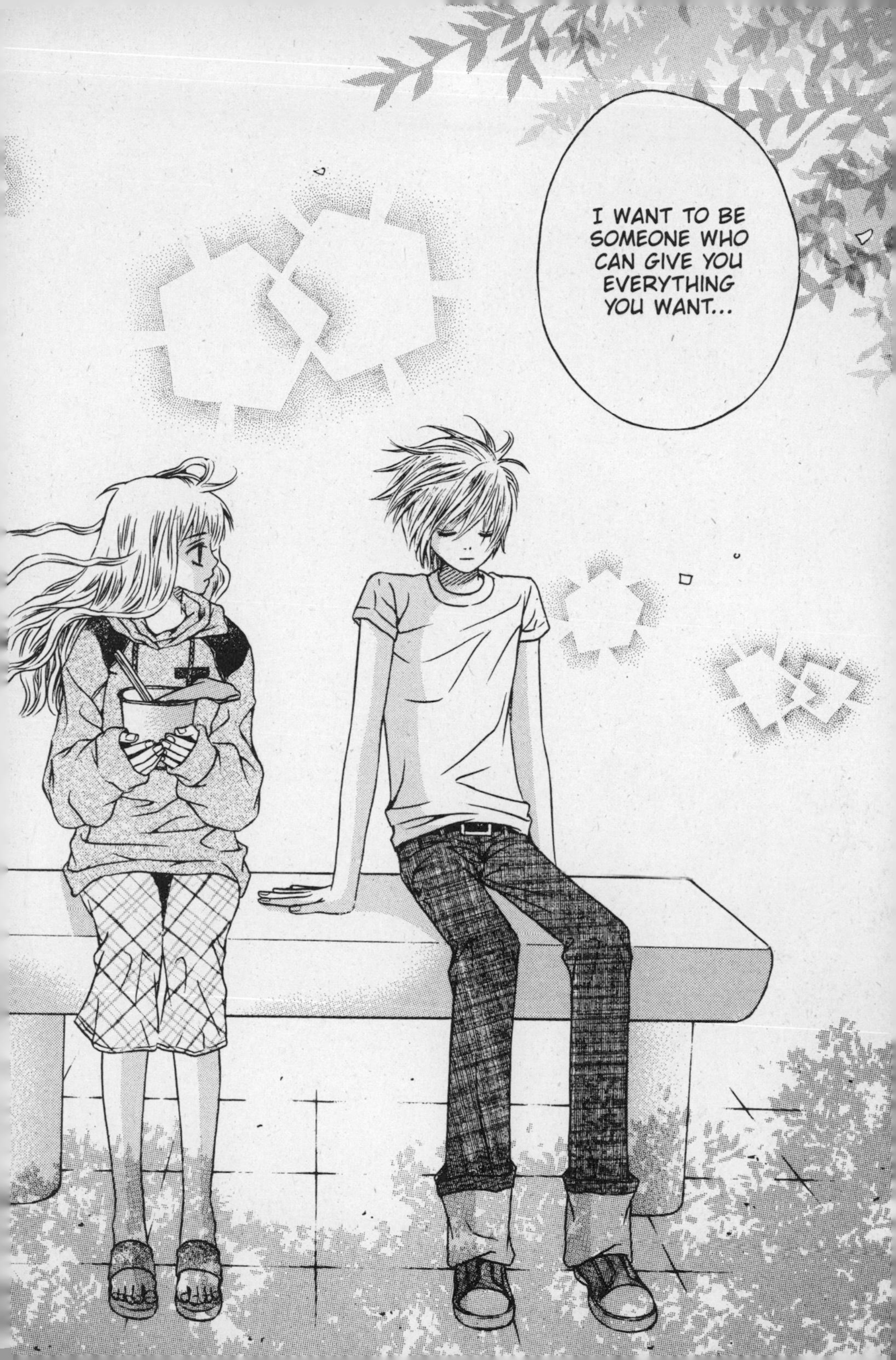
I WANT TO BE SOMEONE WHO CAN GIVE YOU EVERYTHING YOU WANT...

13th Boy

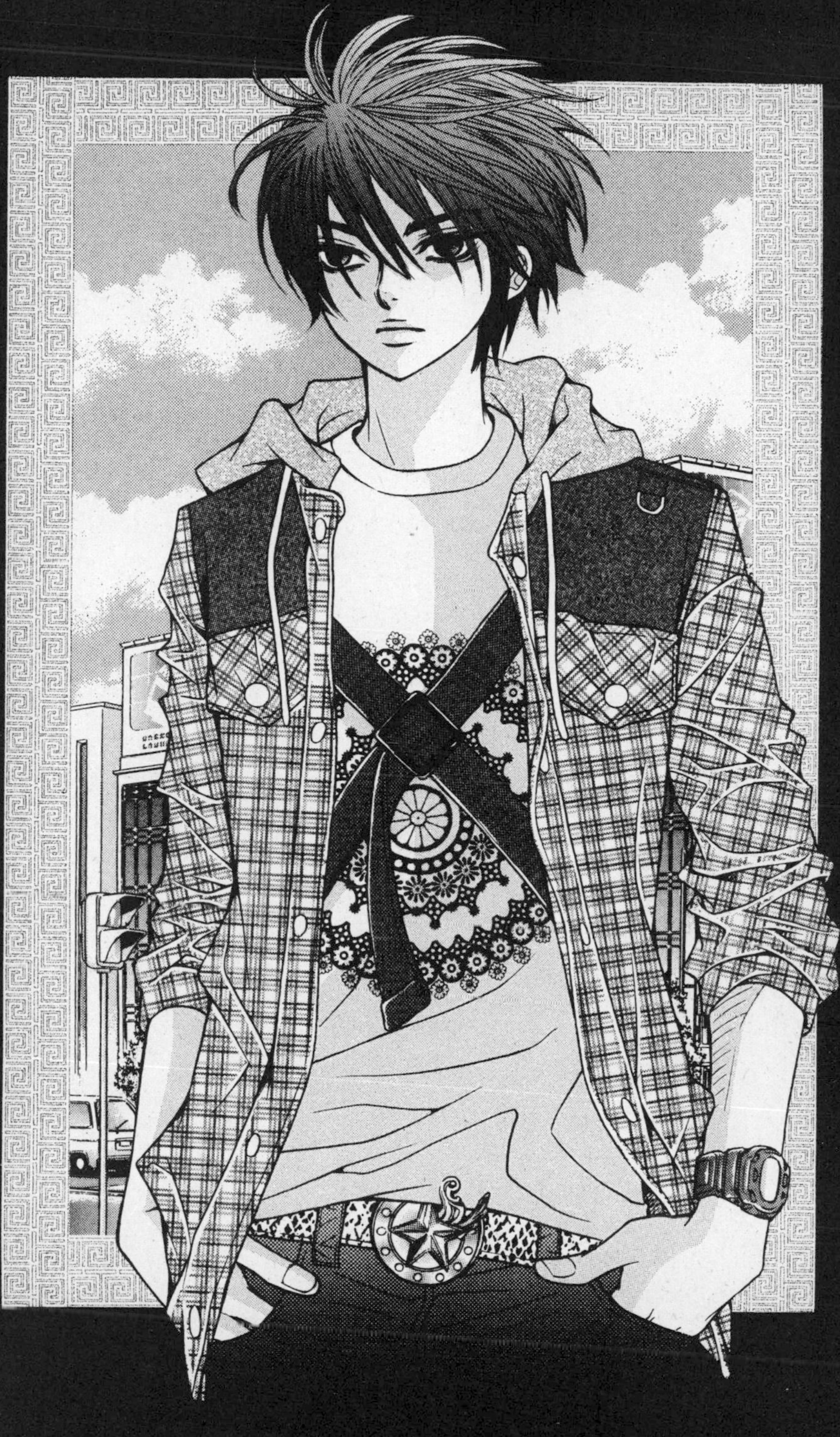

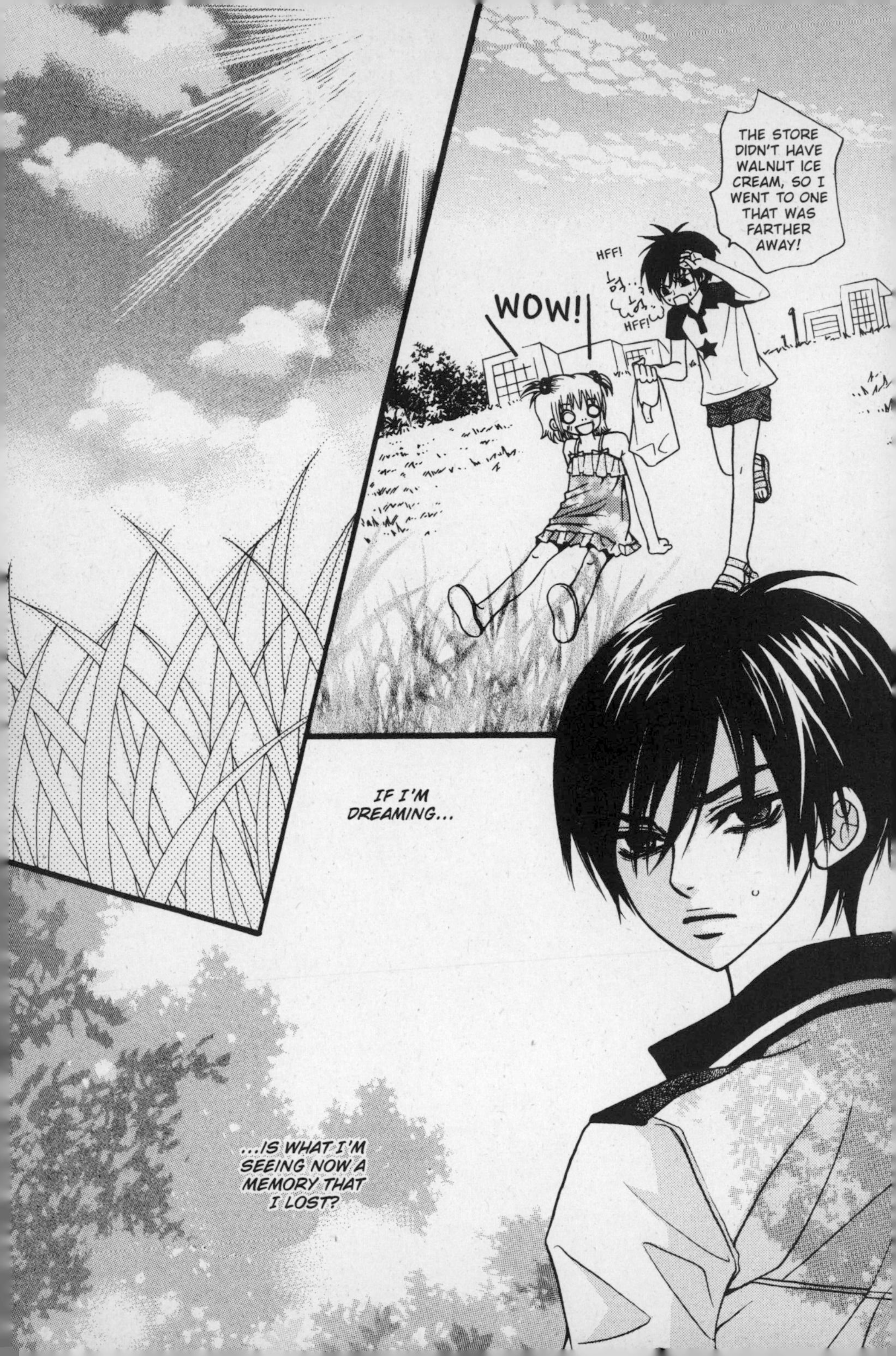
THE STORE DIDN'T HAVE WALNUT ICE CREAM, SO I WENT TO ONE THAT WAS FARTHER AWAY!
HFF!
HFF!
WOW!
IF I'M DREAMING...
...IS WHAT I'M SEEING NOW A MEMORY THAT I LOST?

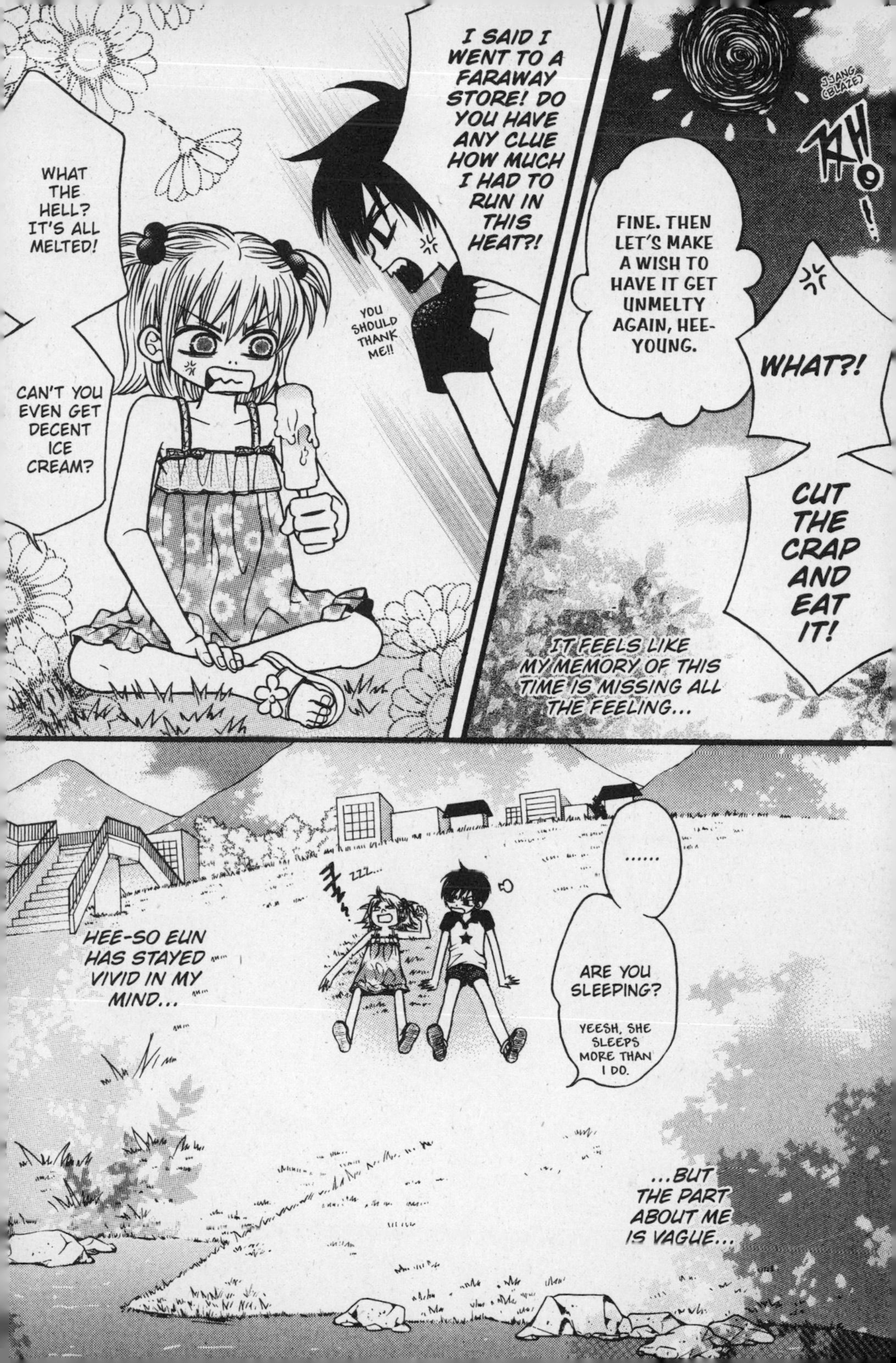
WHAT THE HELL? IT'S ALL MELTED!
CAN'T YOU EVEN GET DECENT ICE CREAM?
I SAID I WENT TO A FARAWAY STORE! DO YOU HAVE ANY CLUE HOW MUCH I HAD TO RUN IN THIS HEAT?!
YOU SHOULD THANK ME!!
FINE. THEN LET'S MAKE A WISH TO HAVE IT GET UNMELTY AGAIN, HEE-YOUNG.
JJANG (BLAZE)
WHAT?!
CUT THE CRAP AND EAT IT!
IT FEELS LIKE MY MEMORY OF THIS TIME IS MISSING ALL THE FEELING...
HEE-SO EUN HAS STAYED VIVID IN MY MIND...
ZZZ...
......
ARE YOU SLEEPING?
YEESH, SHE SLEEPS MORE THAN I DO.
...BUT THE PART ABOUT ME IS VAGUE...

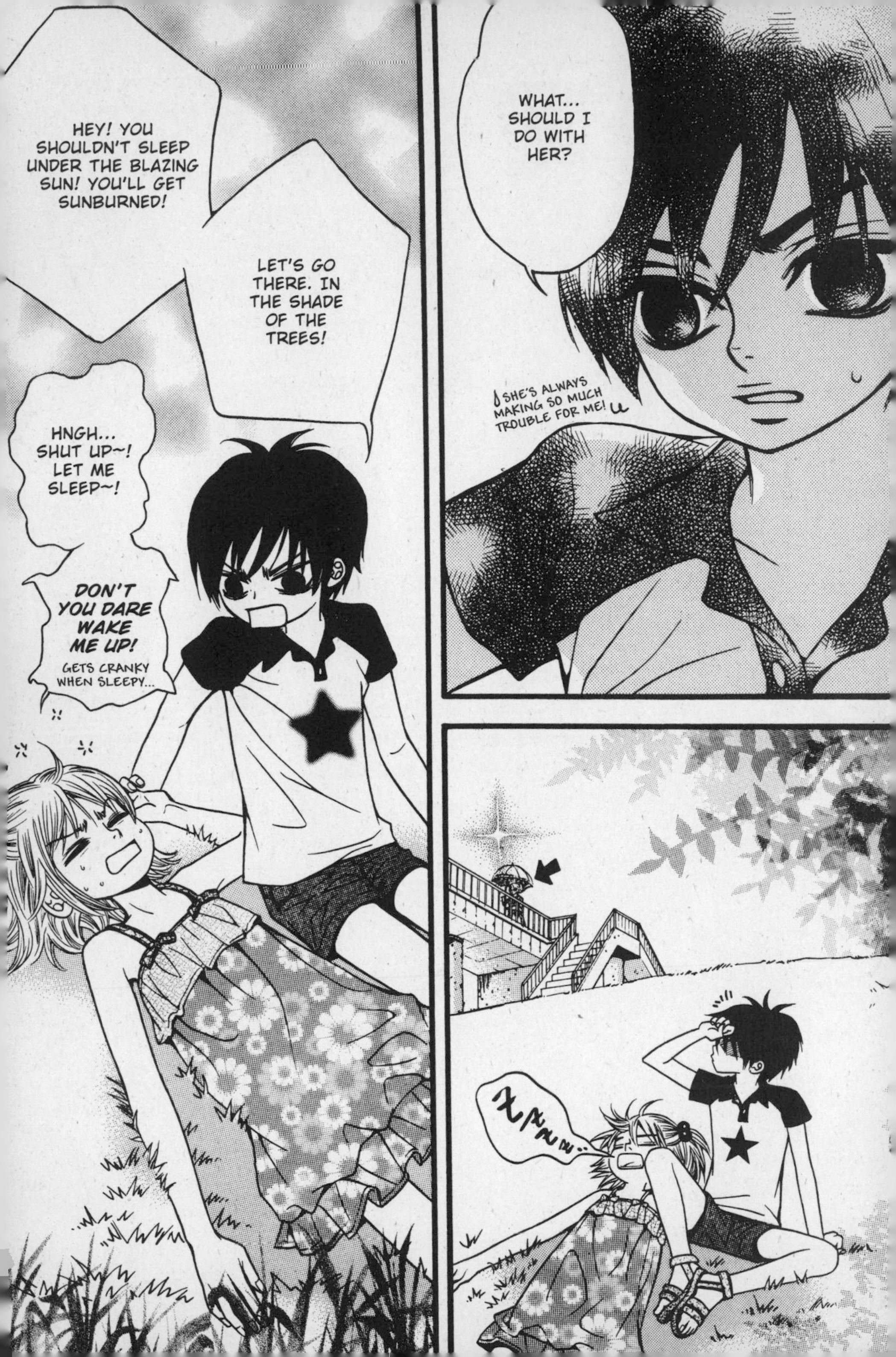
HEY! YOU SHOULDN'T SLEEP UNDER THE BLAZING SUN! YOU'LL GET SUNBURNED!
LET'S GO THERE. IN THE SHADE OF THE TREES!
HNGH... SHUT UP~! LET ME SLEEP~!
DON'T YOU DARE WAKE ME UP!
GETS CRANKY WHEN SLEEPY...
WHAT... SHOULD I DO WITH HER?
SHE'S ALWAYS MAKING SO MUCH TROUBLE FOR ME!

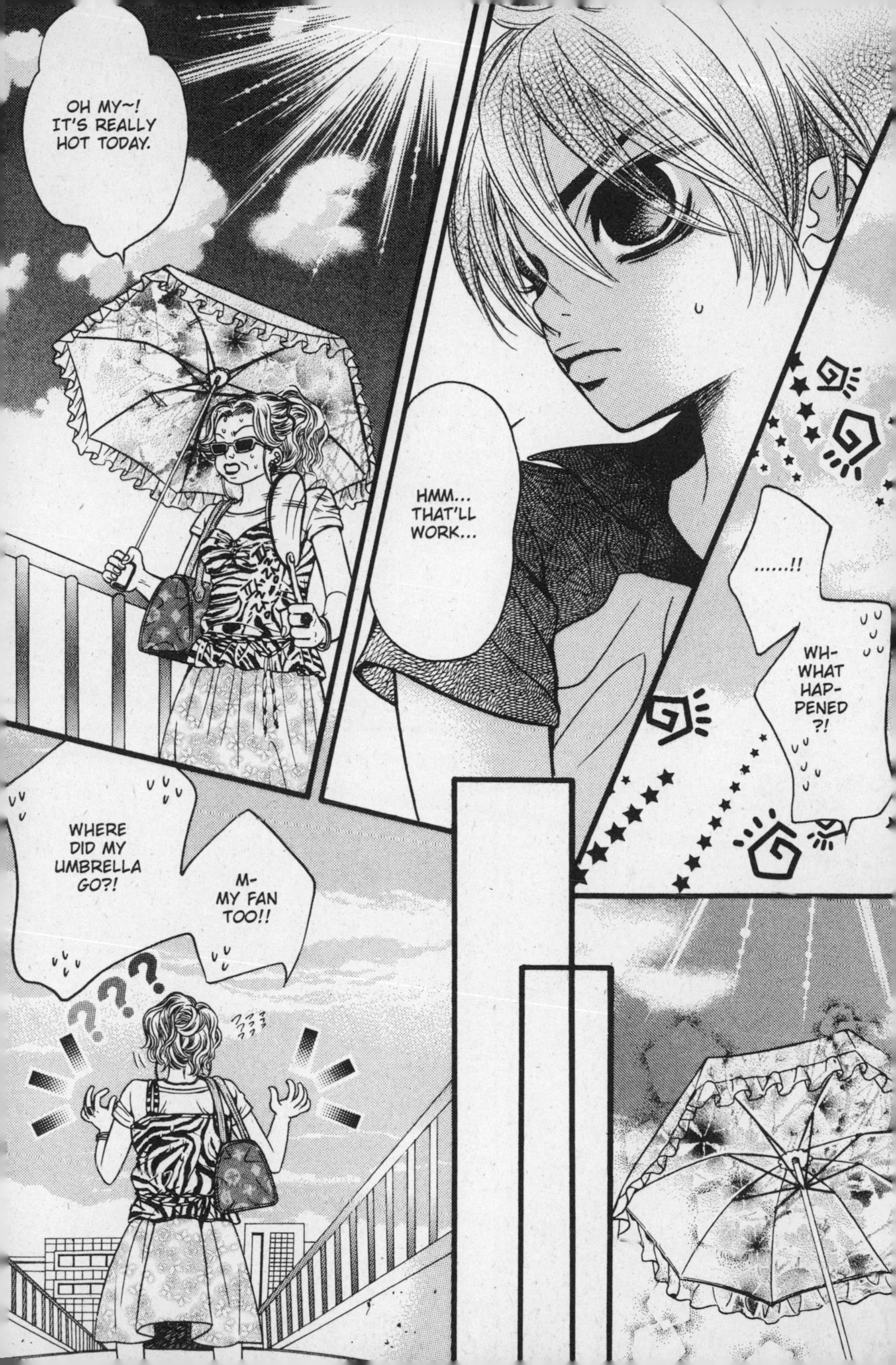
OH MY~! IT'S REALLY HOT TODAY.
HMM... THAT'LL WORK...
......!!
WH- WHAT HAP- PENED ?!
WHERE DID MY UMBRELLA GO?!
M- MY FAN TOO!!

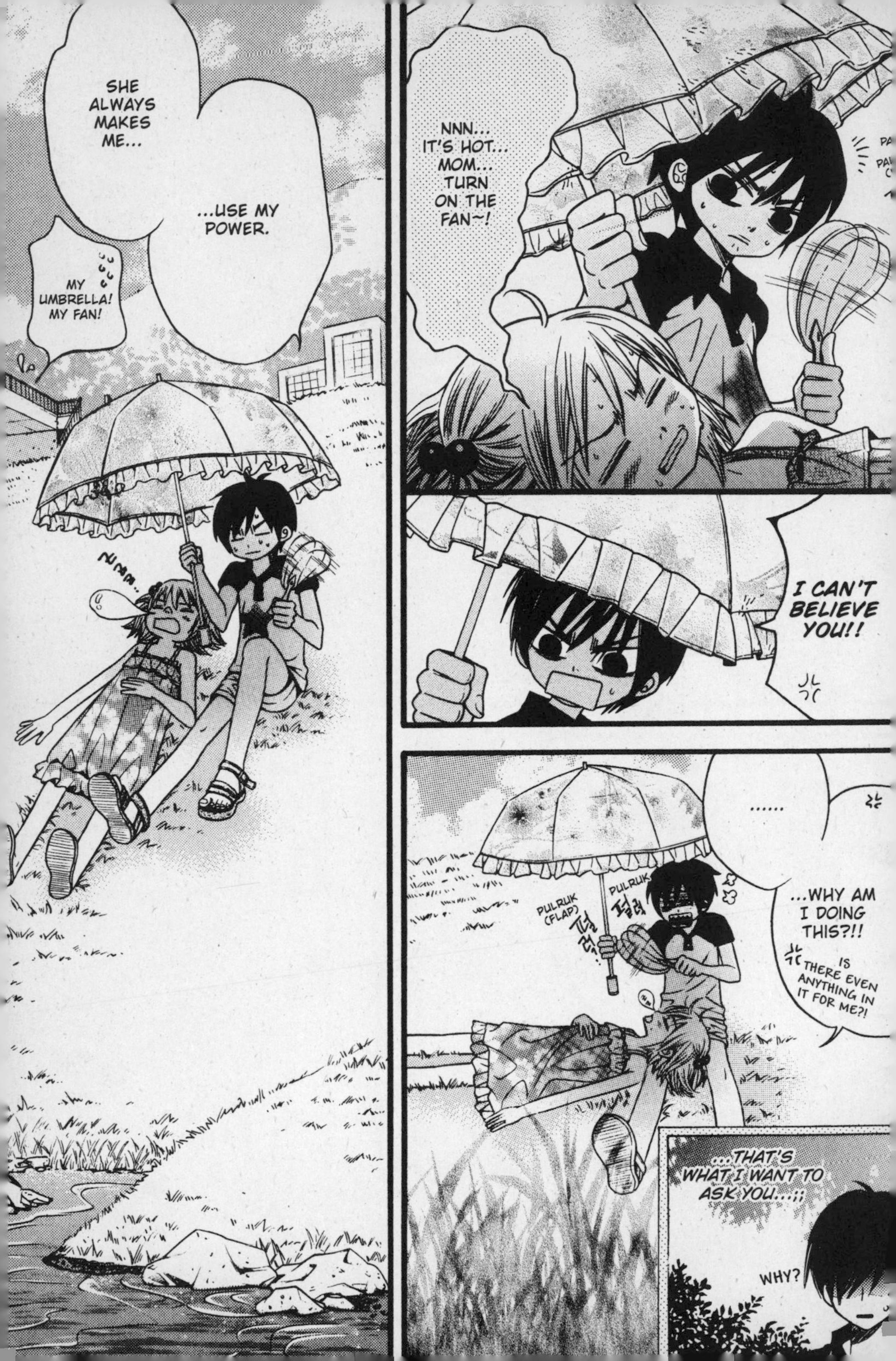
SHE ALWAYS MAKES ME...
...USE MY POWER.
MY UMBRELLA! MY FAN!
NNN... IT'S HOT... MOM... TURN ON THE FAN~!
I CAN'T BELIEVE YOU!!
......
...WHY AM I DOING THIS?!!
IS THERE EVEN ANYTHING IN IT FOR ME?!
PULRUK (FLAP)
PULRUK
...THAT'S WHAT I WANT TO ASK YOU...;;
WHY?

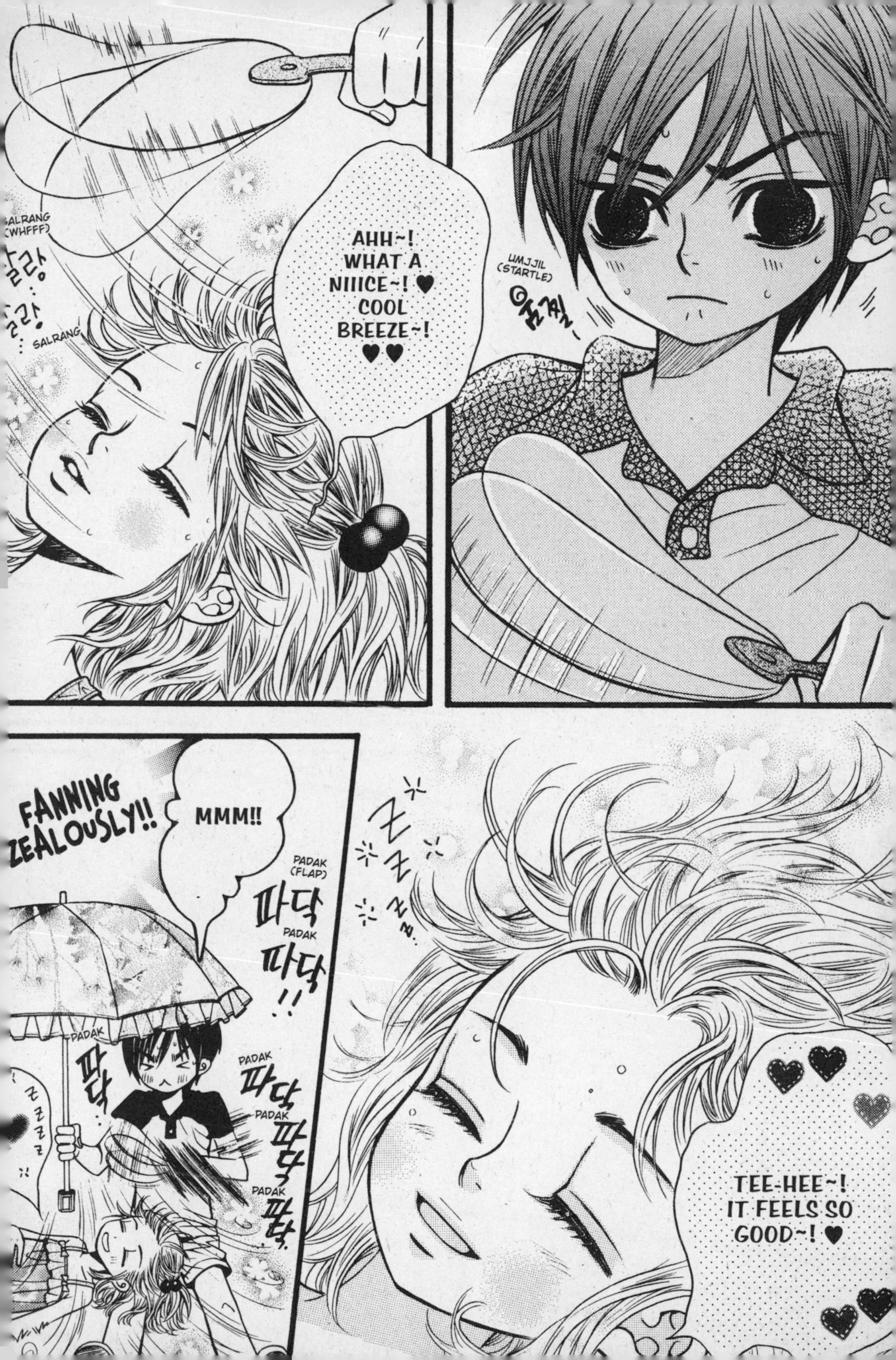
SALRANG (WHFFF)
살랑 살랑
SALRANG
AHH~! WHAT A NIIICE~! ♥ COOL BREEZE~! ♥♥
UMJJIL (STARTLE)
움찔
FANNING ZEALOUSLY!!
MMM!!
PADAK (FLAP)
파닥
PADAK
파닥!!
PADAK
파닥
PADAK
파닥
PADAK
파닥
PADAK
파닥
Z Z Z
TEE-HEE~! IT FEELS SO GOOD~! ♥

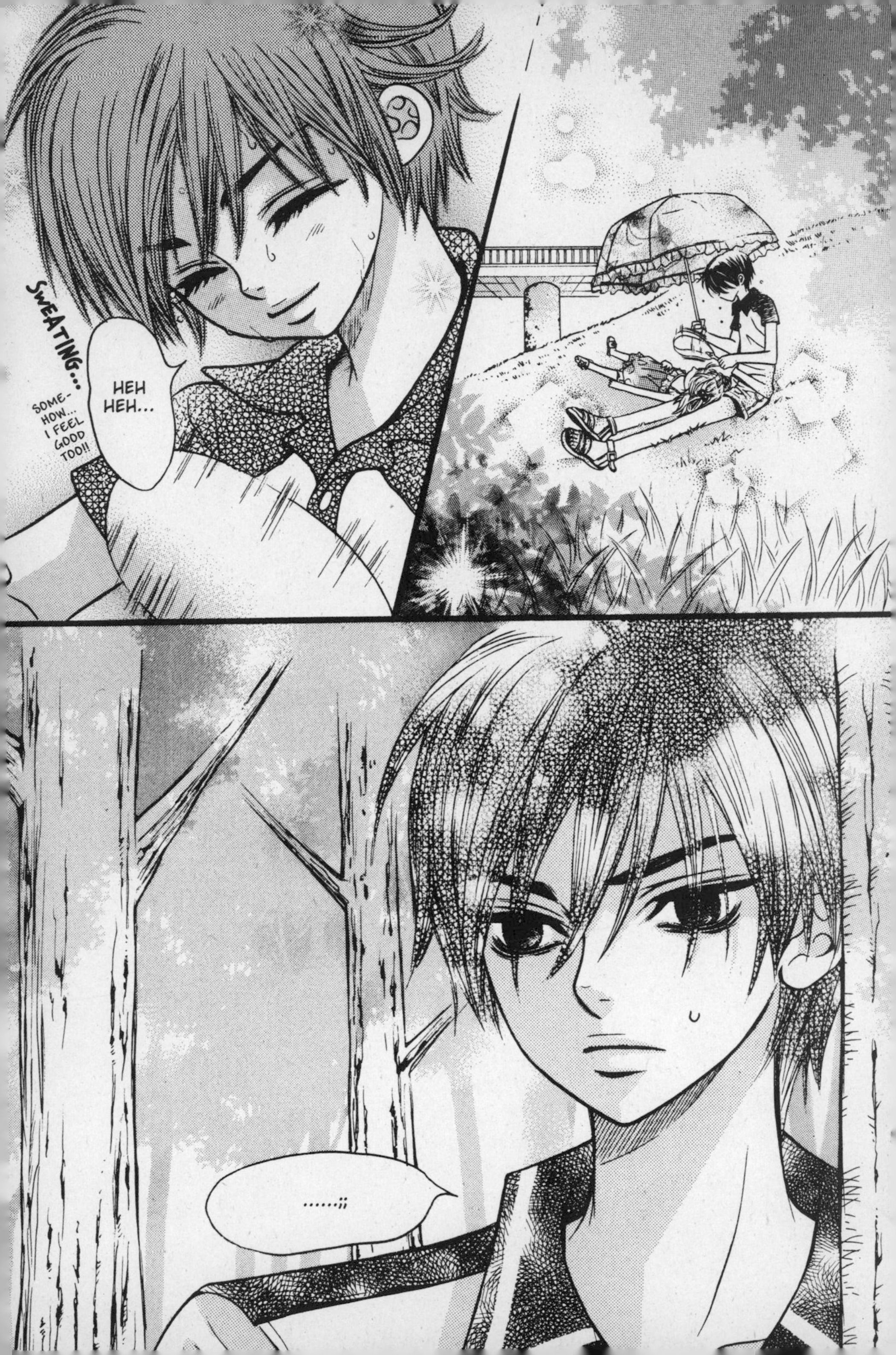
SWEATING...
HEH HEH...
SOME-HOW... I FEEL GOOD TOO!!
......;;

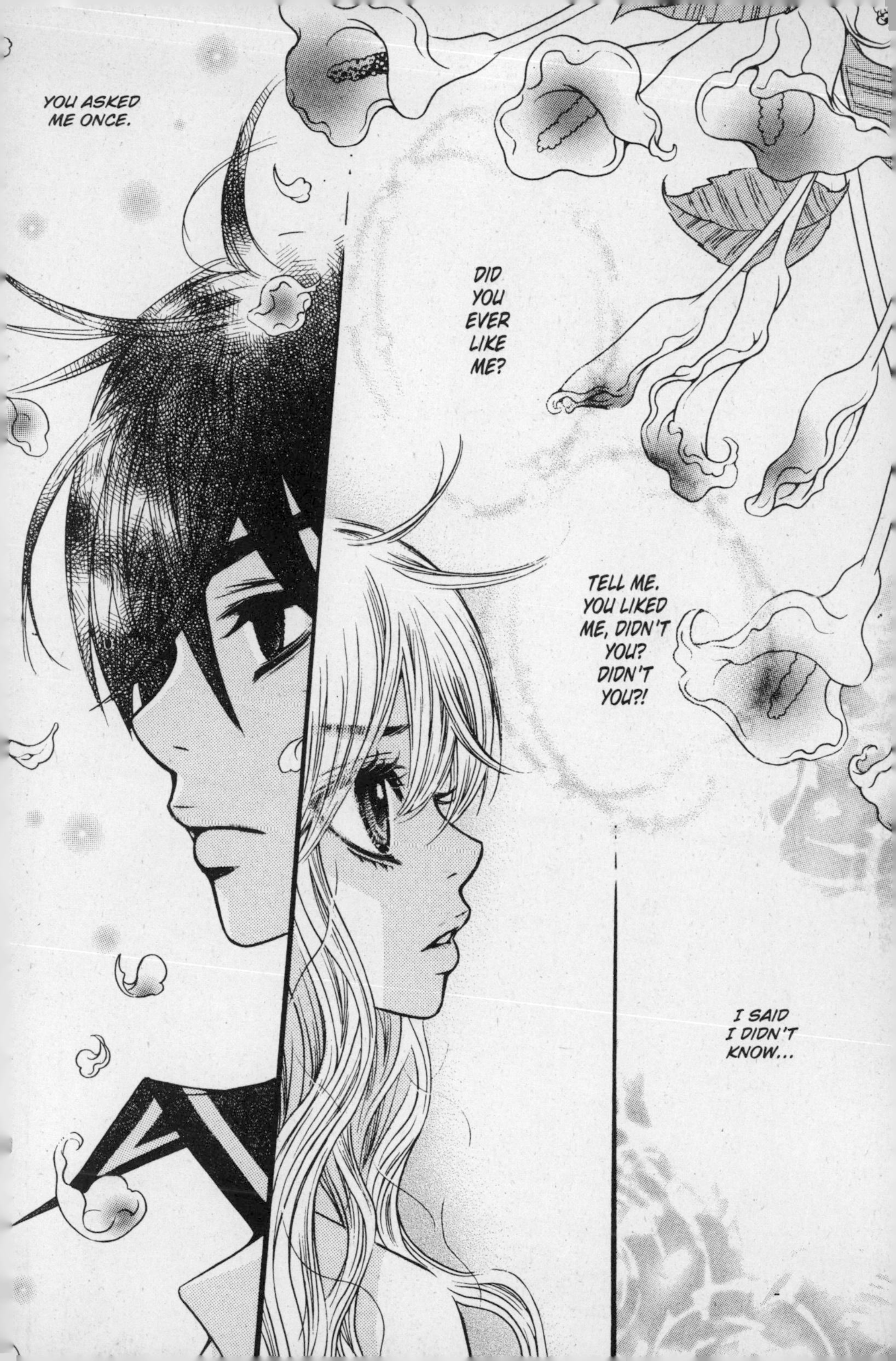
YOU ASKED ME ONCE.
DID YOU EVER LIKE ME?
TELL ME. YOU LIKED ME, DIDN'T YOU? DIDN'T YOU?!
I SAID I DIDN'T KNOW...

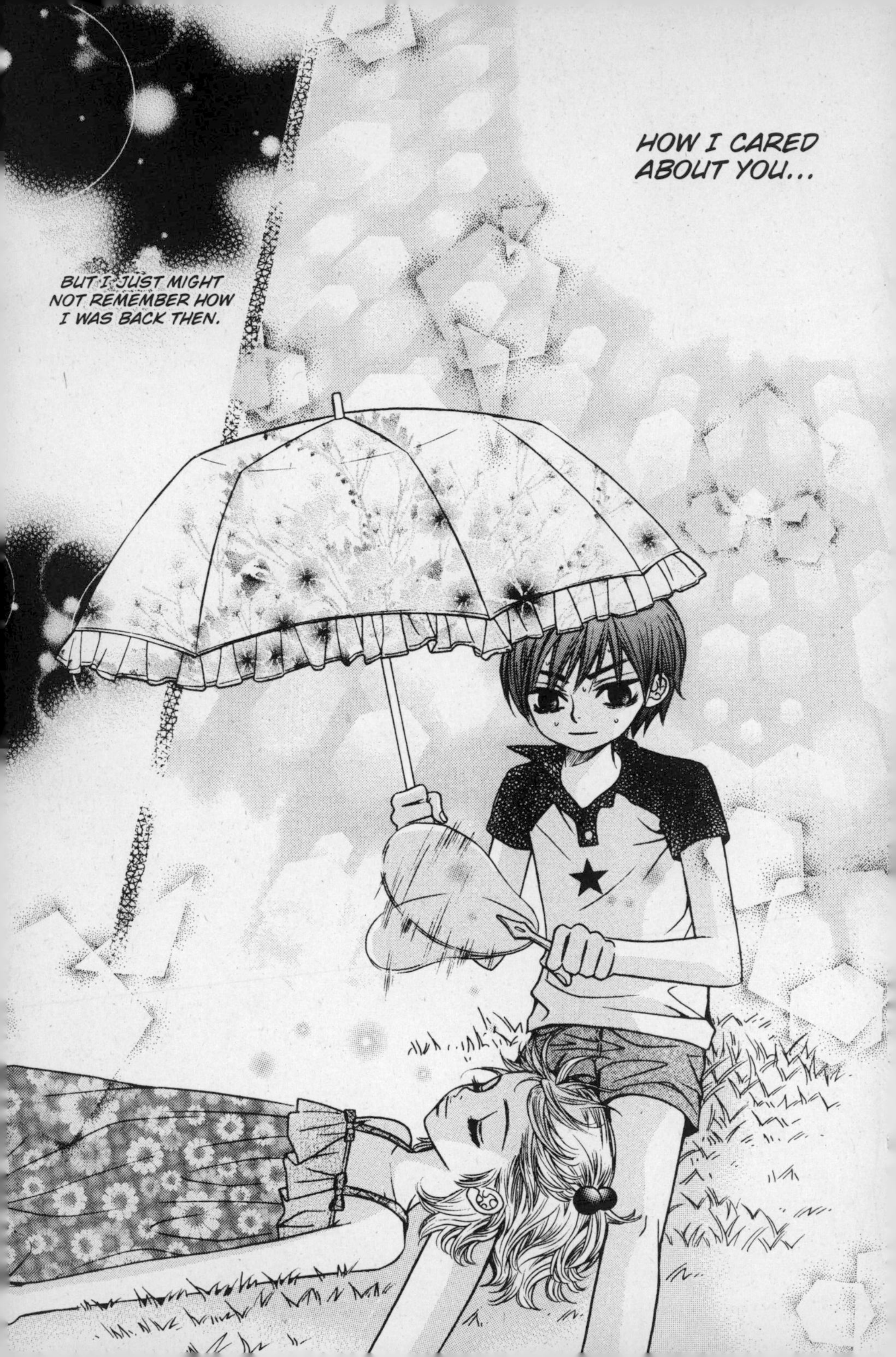
HOW I CARED ABOUT YOU...
BUT I JUST MIGHT NOT REMEMBER HOW I WAS BACK THEN.

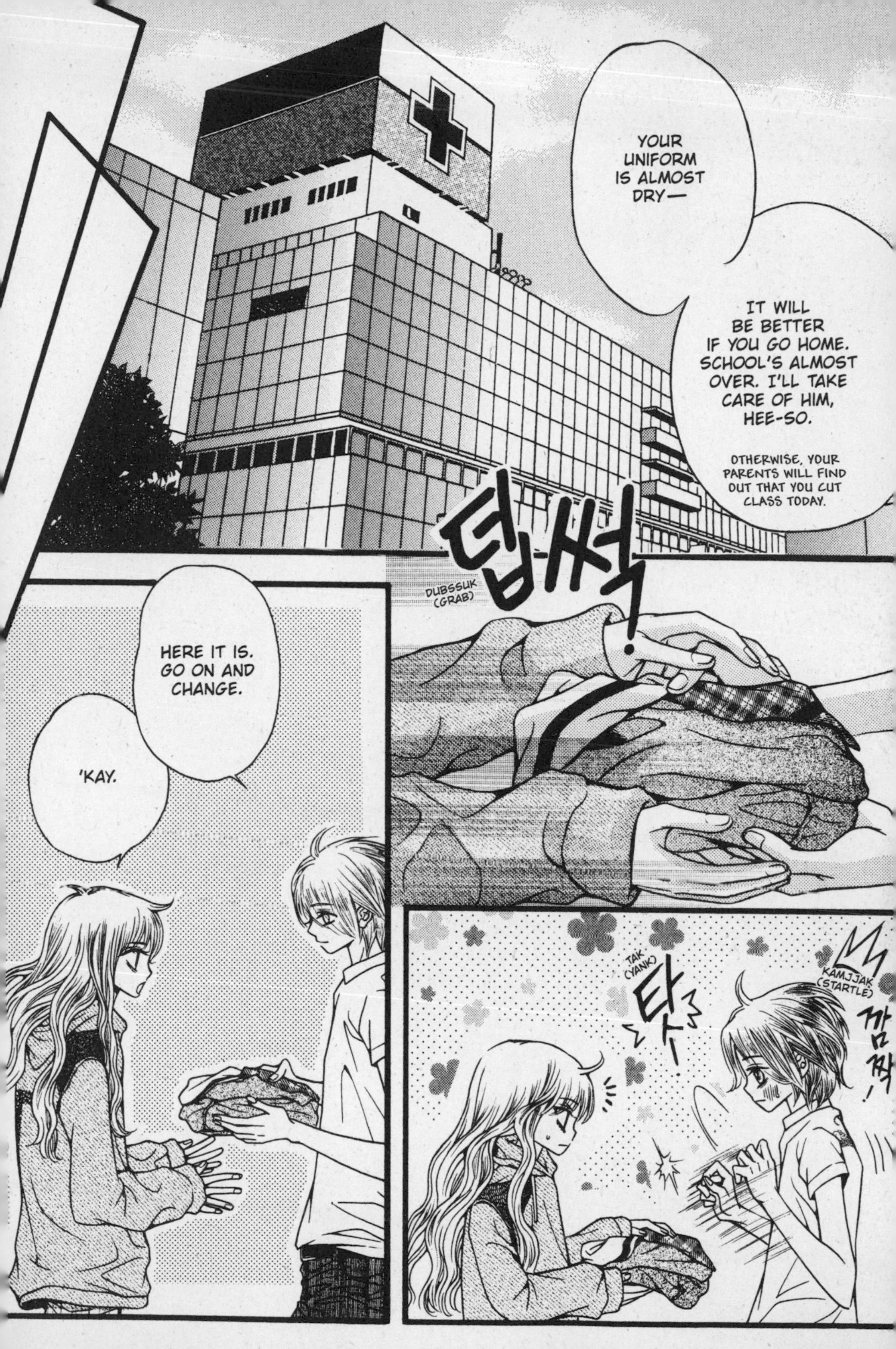
YOUR UNIFORM IS ALMOST DRY—
IT WILL BE BETTER IF YOU GO HOME. SCHOOL'S ALMOST OVER. I'LL TAKE CARE OF HIM, HEE-SO.
OTHERWISE, YOUR PARENTS WILL FIND OUT THAT YOU CUT CLASS TODAY.
HERE IT IS. GO ON AND CHANGE.
'KAY.
덥썩!
DUBSSUK (GRAB)
탁!
TAK (YANK)
깜짝!
KAMJJAK (STARTLE)

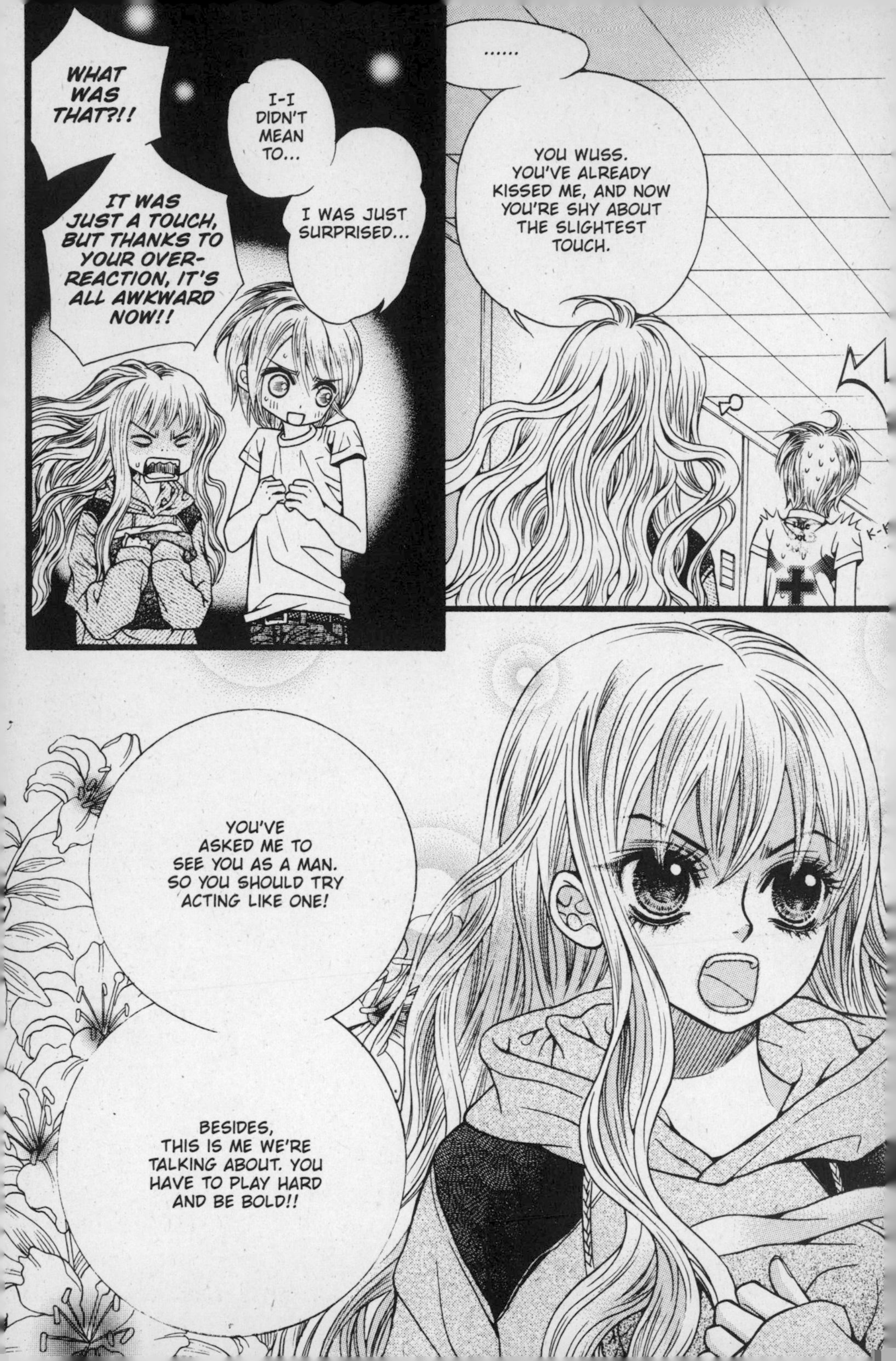
WHAT WAS THAT?!!
I-I DIDN'T MEAN TO...
I WAS JUST SURPRISED...
IT WAS JUST A TOUCH, BUT THANKS TO YOUR OVER-REACTION, IT'S ALL AWKWARD NOW!!
......
YOU WUSS. YOU'VE ALREADY KISSED ME, AND NOW YOU'RE SHY ABOUT THE SLIGHTEST TOUCH.
YOU'VE ASKED ME TO SEE YOU AS A MAN. SO YOU SHOULD TRY ACTING LIKE ONE!
BESIDES, THIS IS ME WE'RE TALKING ABOUT. YOU HAVE TO PLAY HARD AND BE BOLD!!

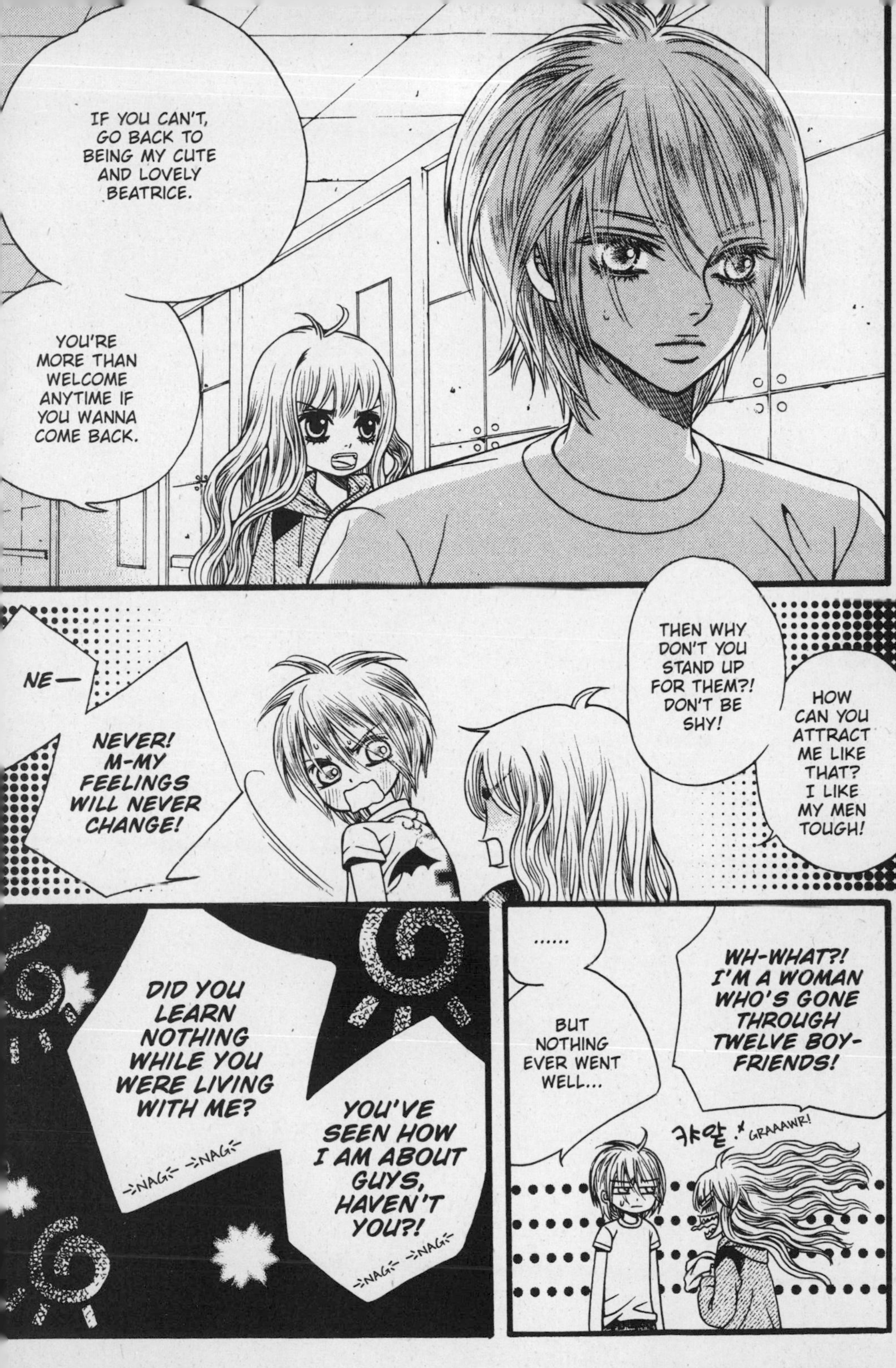
IF YOU CAN'T, GO BACK TO BEING MY CUTE AND LOVELY BEATRICE.
YOU'RE MORE THAN WELCOME ANYTIME IF YOU WANNA COME BACK.
NE—
NEVER! M-MY FEELINGS WILL NEVER CHANGE!
THEN WHY DON'T YOU STAND UP FOR THEM?! DON'T BE SHY!
HOW CAN YOU ATTRACT ME LIKE THAT? I LIKE MY MEN TOUGH!
DID YOU LEARN NOTHING WHILE YOU WERE LIVING WITH ME?
NAG NAG NAG
YOU'VE SEEN HOW I AM ABOUT GUYS, HAVEN'T YOU?!
NAG NAG
WH-WHAT?! I'M A WOMAN WHO'S GONE THROUGH TWELVE BOY-FRIENDS!
......
BUT NOTHING EVER WENT WELL...
캬알 GRAAAWR!

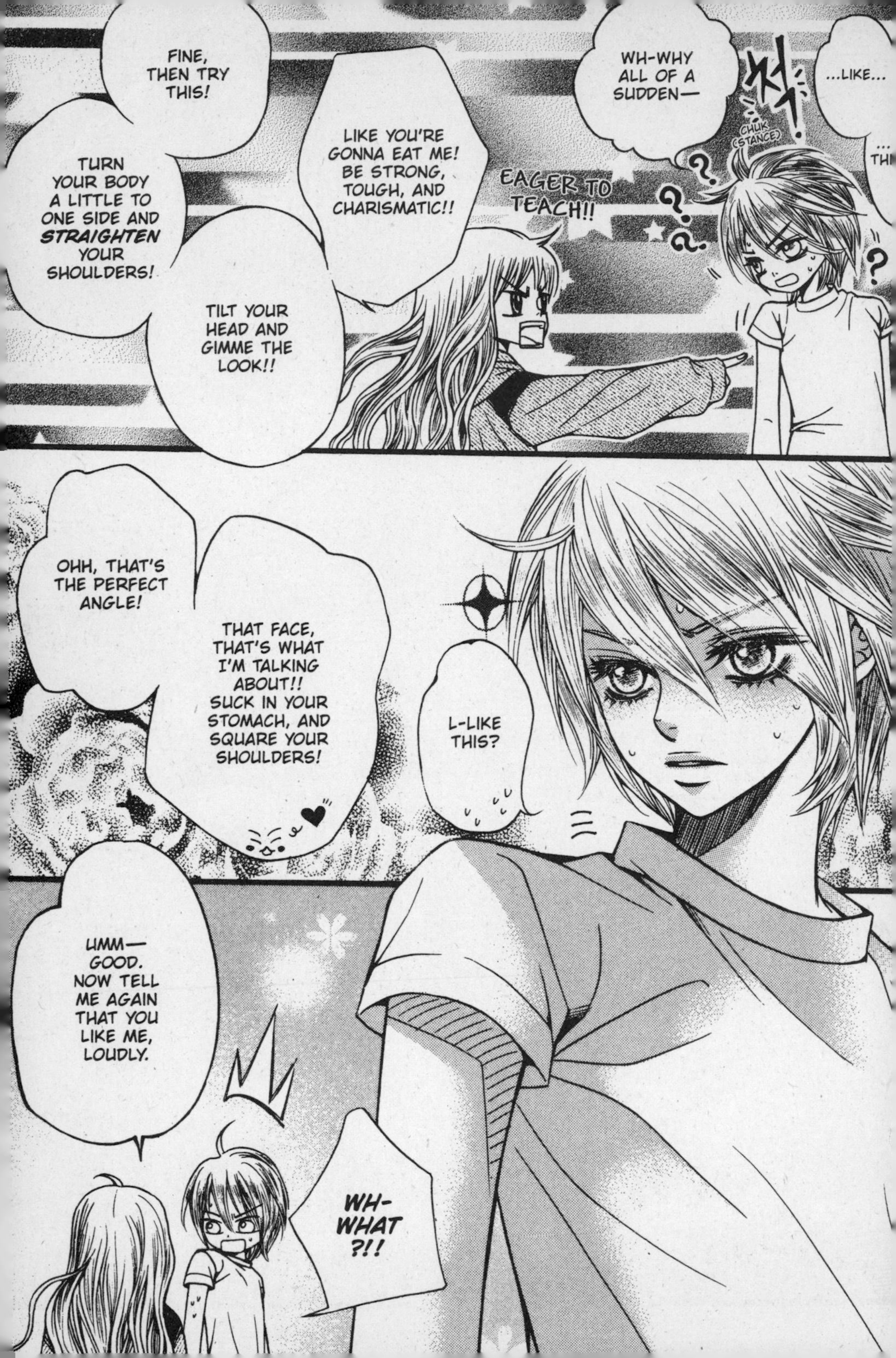
...LIKE...
WH-WHY ALL OF A SUDDEN—
CHUK (STANCE)
EAGER TO TEACH!!
LIKE YOU'RE GONNA EAT ME! BE STRONG, TOUGH, AND CHARISMATIC!!
FINE, THEN TRY THIS!
TURN YOUR BODY A LITTLE TO ONE SIDE AND STRAIGHTEN YOUR SHOULDERS!
TILT YOUR HEAD AND GIMME THE LOOK!!
L-LIKE THIS?
OHH, THAT'S THE PERFECT ANGLE!
THAT FACE, THAT'S WHAT I'M TALKING ABOUT!! SUCK IN YOUR STOMACH, AND SQUARE YOUR SHOULDERS!
UMM— GOOD. NOW TELL ME AGAIN THAT YOU LIKE ME, LOUDLY.
WH- WHAT ?!!

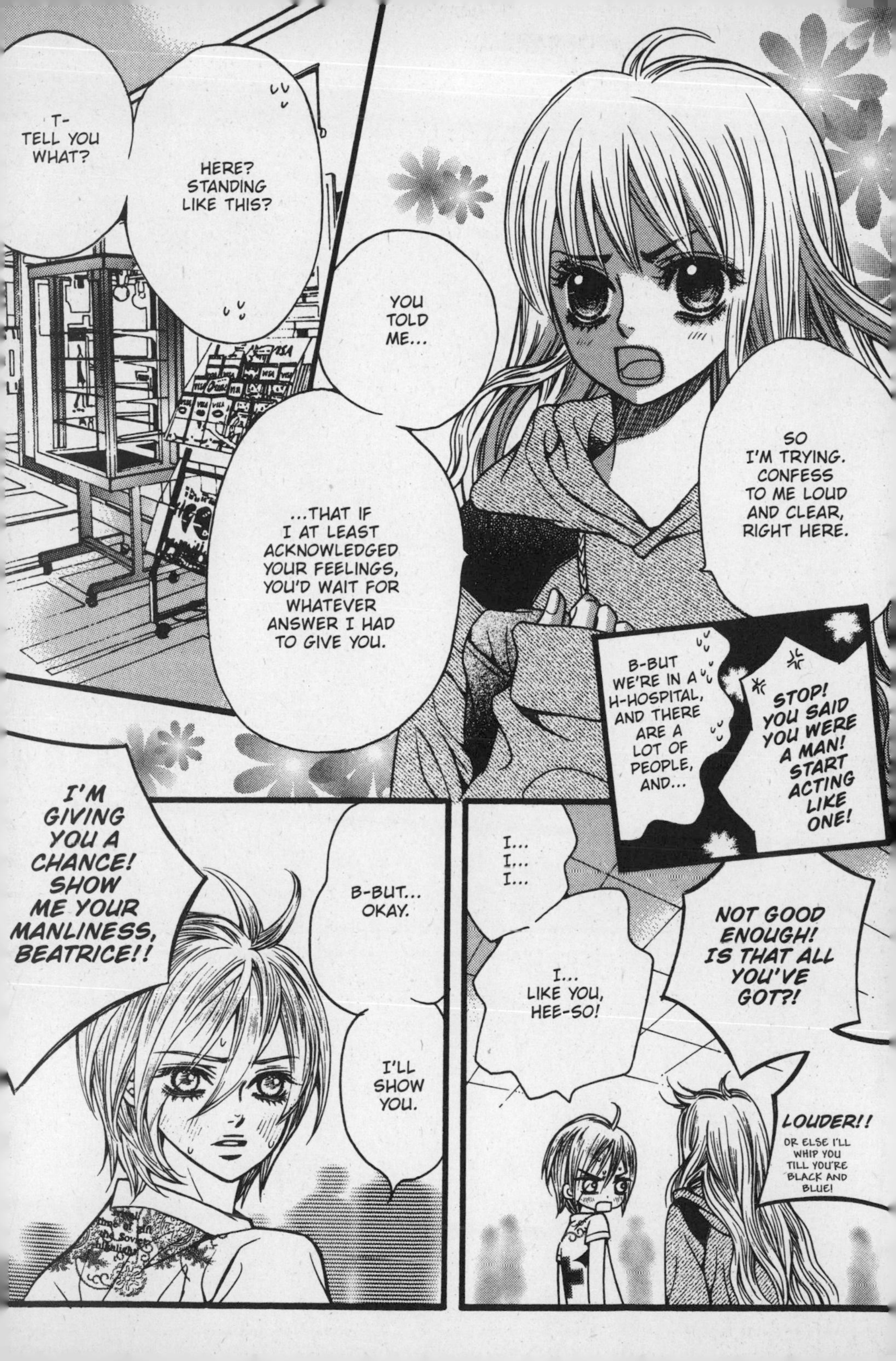
T- TELL YOU WHAT?
HERE? STANDING LIKE THIS?
YOU TOLD ME...
...THAT IF I AT LEAST ACKNOWLEDGED YOUR FEELINGS, YOU'D WAIT FOR WHATEVER ANSWER I HAD TO GIVE YOU.
SO I'M TRYING. CONFESS TO ME LOUD AND CLEAR, RIGHT HERE.
B-BUT WE'RE IN A H-HOSPITAL, AND THERE ARE A LOT OF PEOPLE, AND...
STOP! YOU SAID YOU WERE A MAN! START ACTING LIKE ONE!
I'M GIVING YOU A CHANCE! SHOW ME YOUR MANLINESS, BEATRICE!!
B-BUT... OKAY.
I'LL SHOW YOU.
I... I... I...
NOT GOOD ENOUGH! IS THAT ALL YOU'VE GOT?!
I... LIKE YOU, HEE-SO!
LOUDER!!
OR ELSE I'LL WHIP YOU TILL YOU'RE BLACK AND BLUE!

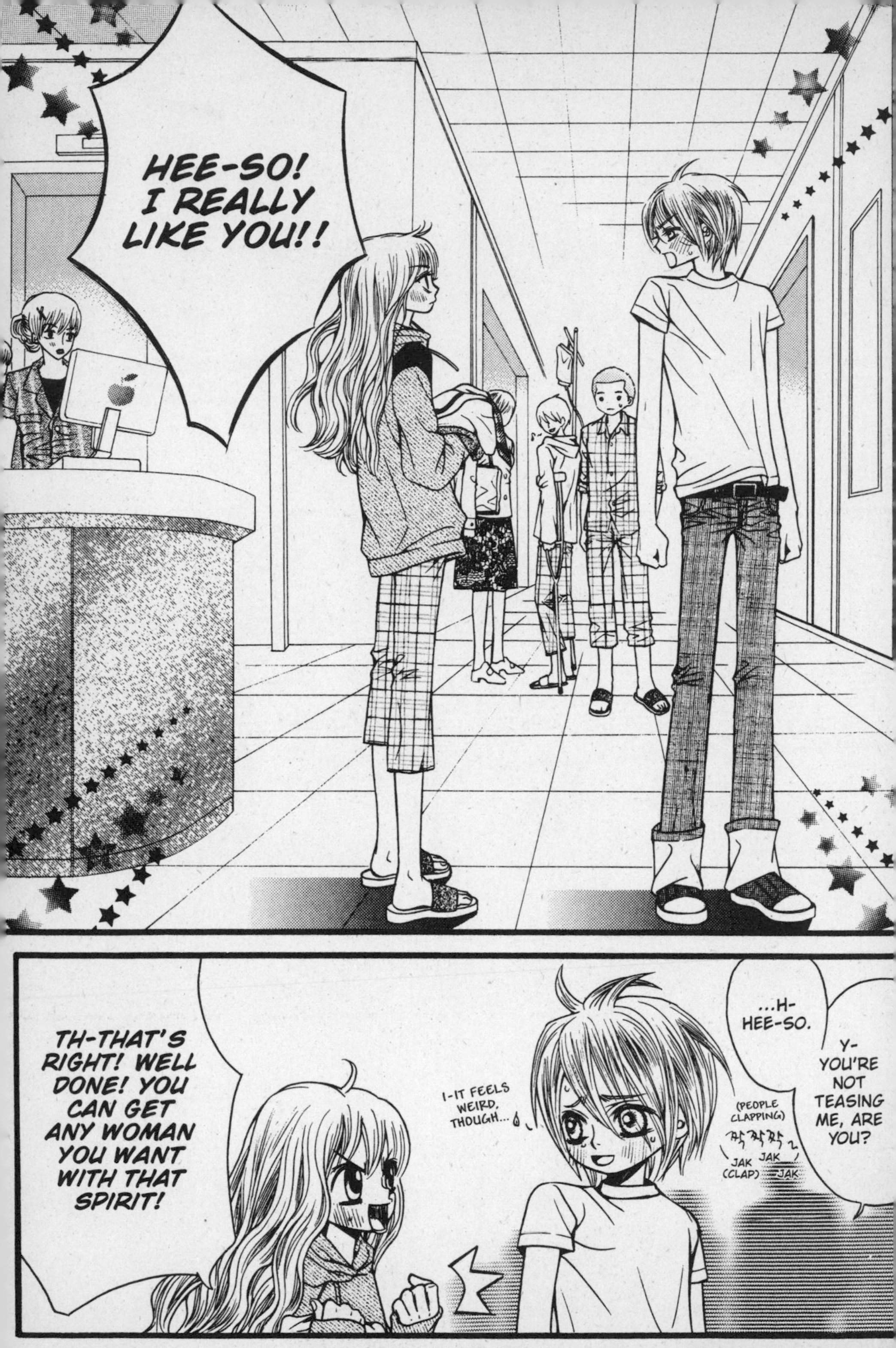
HEE-SO! I REALLY LIKE YOU!!
TH-THAT'S RIGHT! WELL DONE! YOU CAN GET ANY WOMAN YOU WANT WITH THAT SPIRIT!
I-IT FEELS WEIRD, THOUGH...
(PEOPLE CLAPPING)
짝짝짝
JAK JAK JAK (CLAP)
...H-HEE-SO.
Y-YOU'RE NOT TEASING ME, ARE YOU?

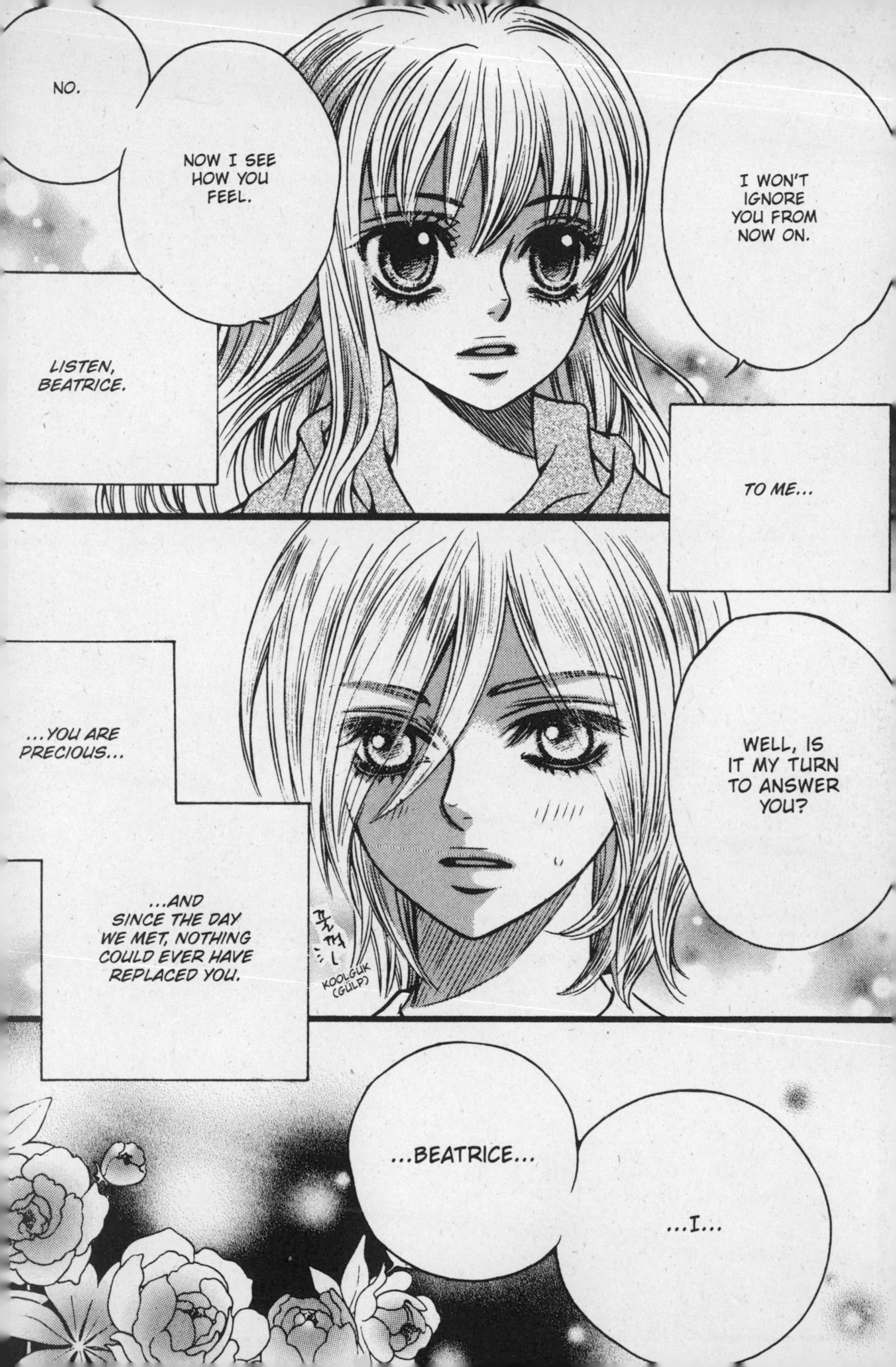

NO.
NOW I SEE HOW YOU FEEL.
I WON'T IGNORE YOU FROM NOW ON.
LISTEN, BEATRICE.
TO ME...
...YOU ARE PRECIOUS...
...AND SINCE THE DAY WE MET, NOTHING COULD EVER HAVE REPLACED YOU.
WELL, IS IT MY TURN TO ANSWER YOU?
꿀꺽
KOOLGUK (GULP)
...BEATRICE...
...I...

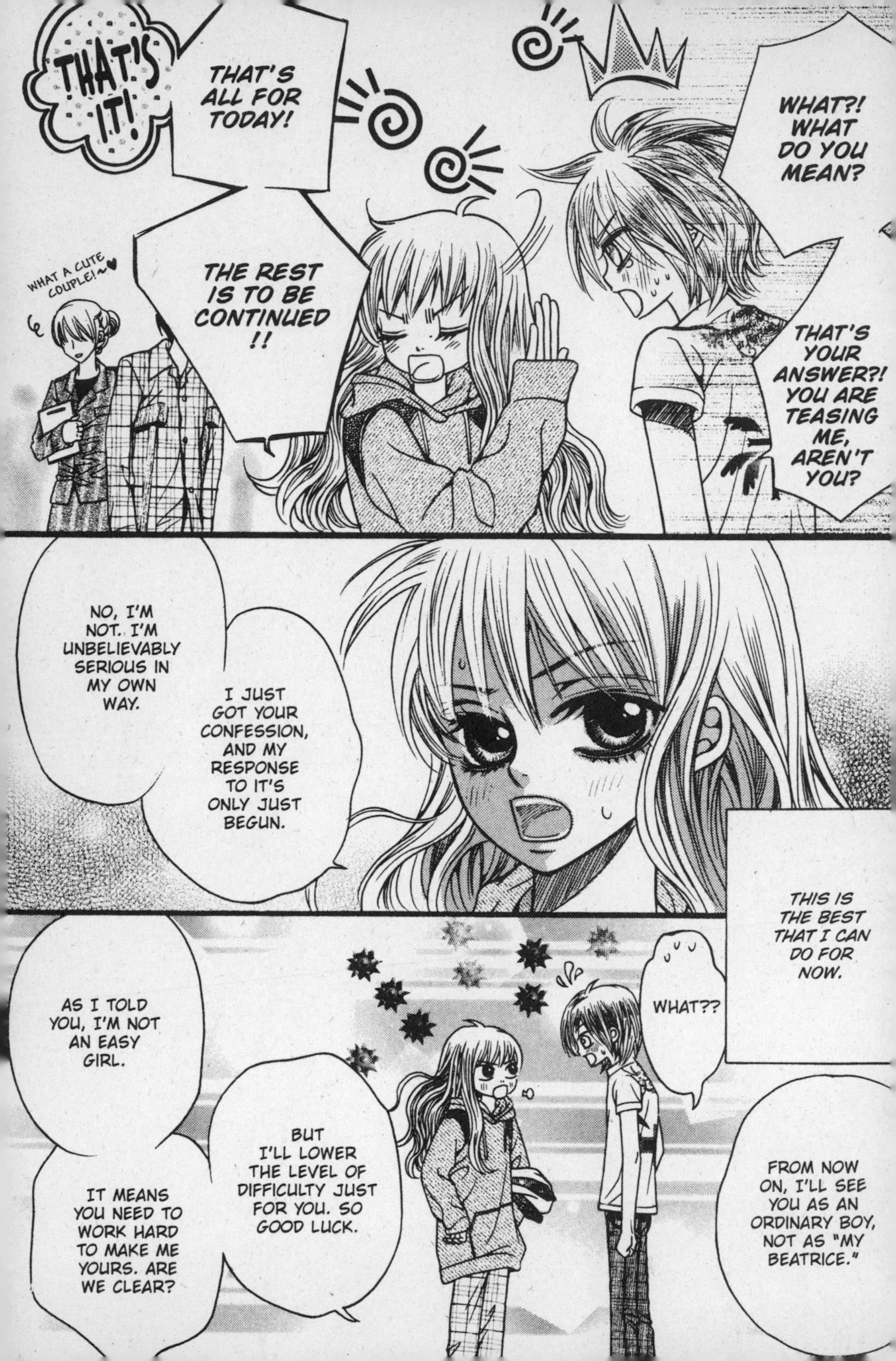
THAT'S IT!
THAT'S ALL FOR TODAY!
THE REST IS TO BE CONTINUED !!
WHAT A CUTE COUPLE!~♥
WHAT?! WHAT DO YOU MEAN?
THAT'S YOUR ANSWER?! YOU ARE TEASING ME, AREN'T YOU?
NO, I'M NOT. I'M UNBELIEVABLY SERIOUS IN MY OWN WAY.
I JUST GOT YOUR CONFESSION, AND MY RESPONSE TO IT'S ONLY JUST BEGUN.
THIS IS THE BEST THAT I CAN DO FOR NOW.
WHAT??
FROM NOW ON, I'LL SEE YOU AS AN ORDINARY BOY, NOT AS "MY BEATRICE."
AS I TOLD YOU, I'M NOT AN EASY GIRL.
BUT I'LL LOWER THE LEVEL OF DIFFICULTY JUST FOR YOU. SO GOOD LUCK.
IT MEANS YOU NEED TO WORK HARD TO MAKE ME YOURS. ARE WE CLEAR?

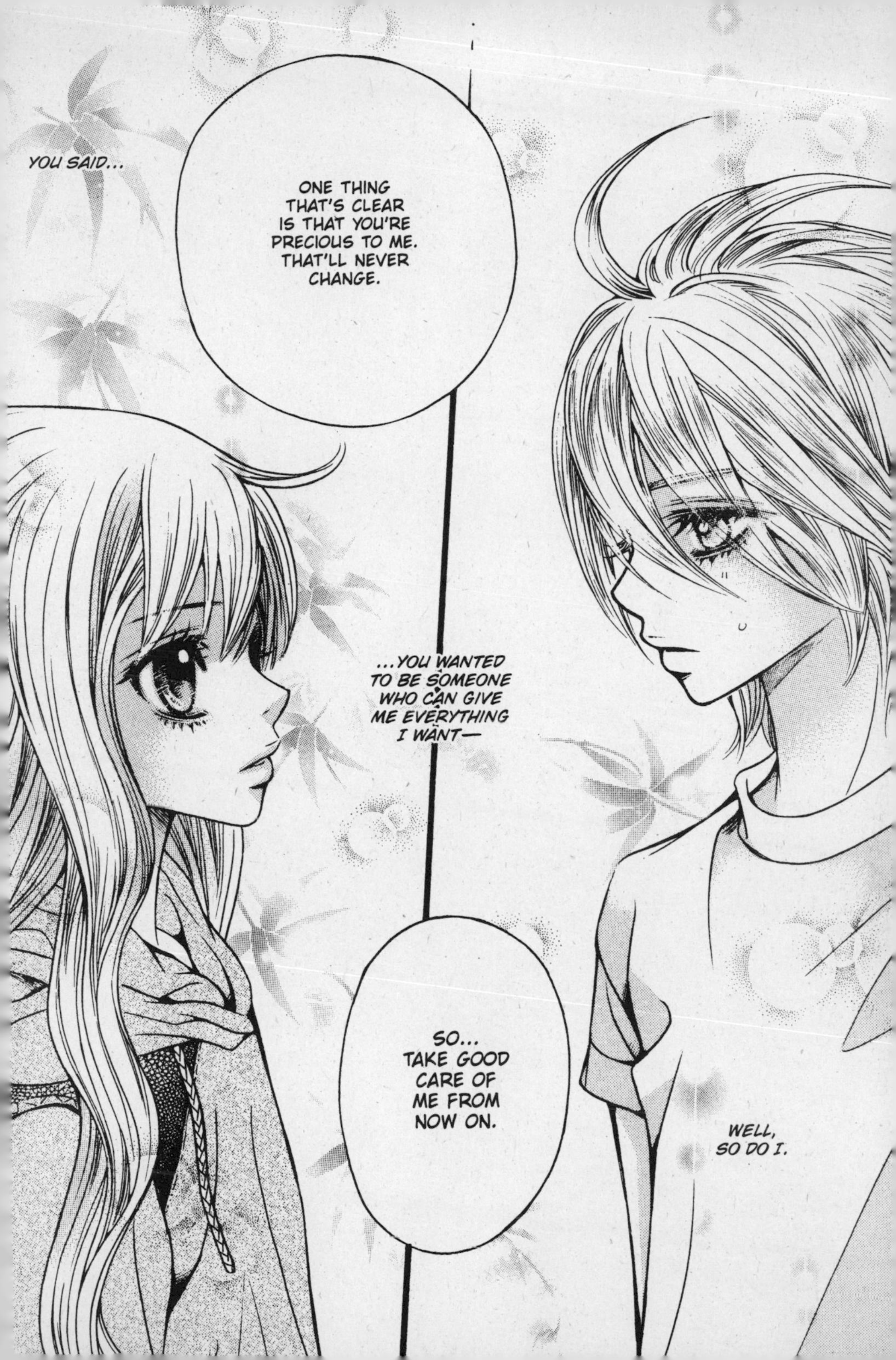
ONE THING THAT'S CLEAR IS THAT YOU'RE PRECIOUS TO ME. THAT'LL NEVER CHANGE.
YOU SAID...
...YOU WANTED TO BE SOMEONE WHO CAN GIVE ME EVERYTHING I WANT—
WELL, SO DO I.
SO... TAKE GOOD CARE OF ME FROM NOW ON.

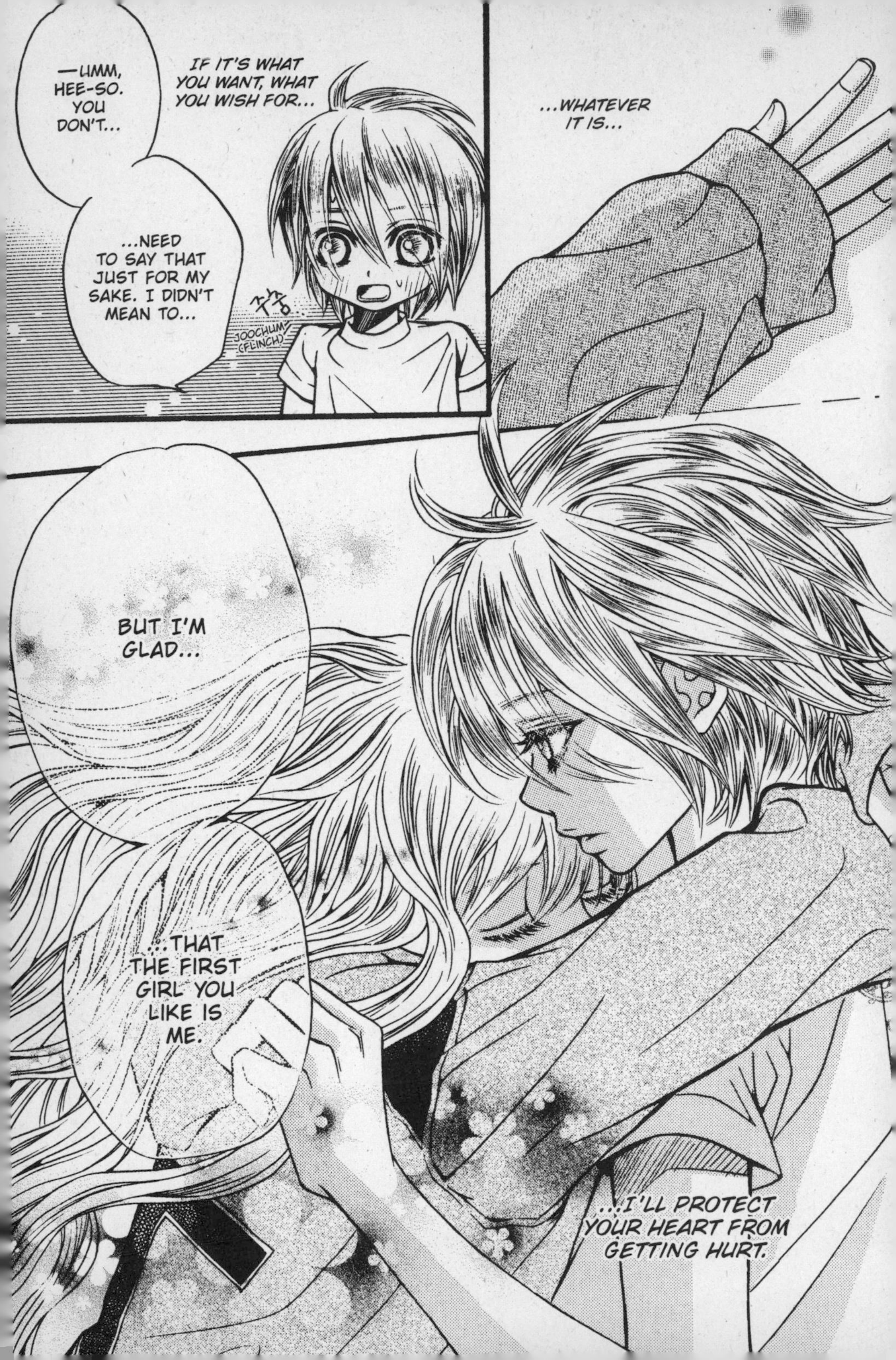

—UMM, HEE-SO. YOU DON'T...
...NEED TO SAY THAT JUST FOR MY SAKE. I DIDN'T MEAN TO...
IF IT'S WHAT YOU WANT, WHAT YOU WISH FOR...
주춤
JOOCHUM (FLINCH)
...WHATEVER IT IS...
BUT I'M GLAD...
...THAT THE FIRST GIRL YOU LIKE IS ME.
...I'LL PROTECT YOUR HEART FROM GETTING HURT.

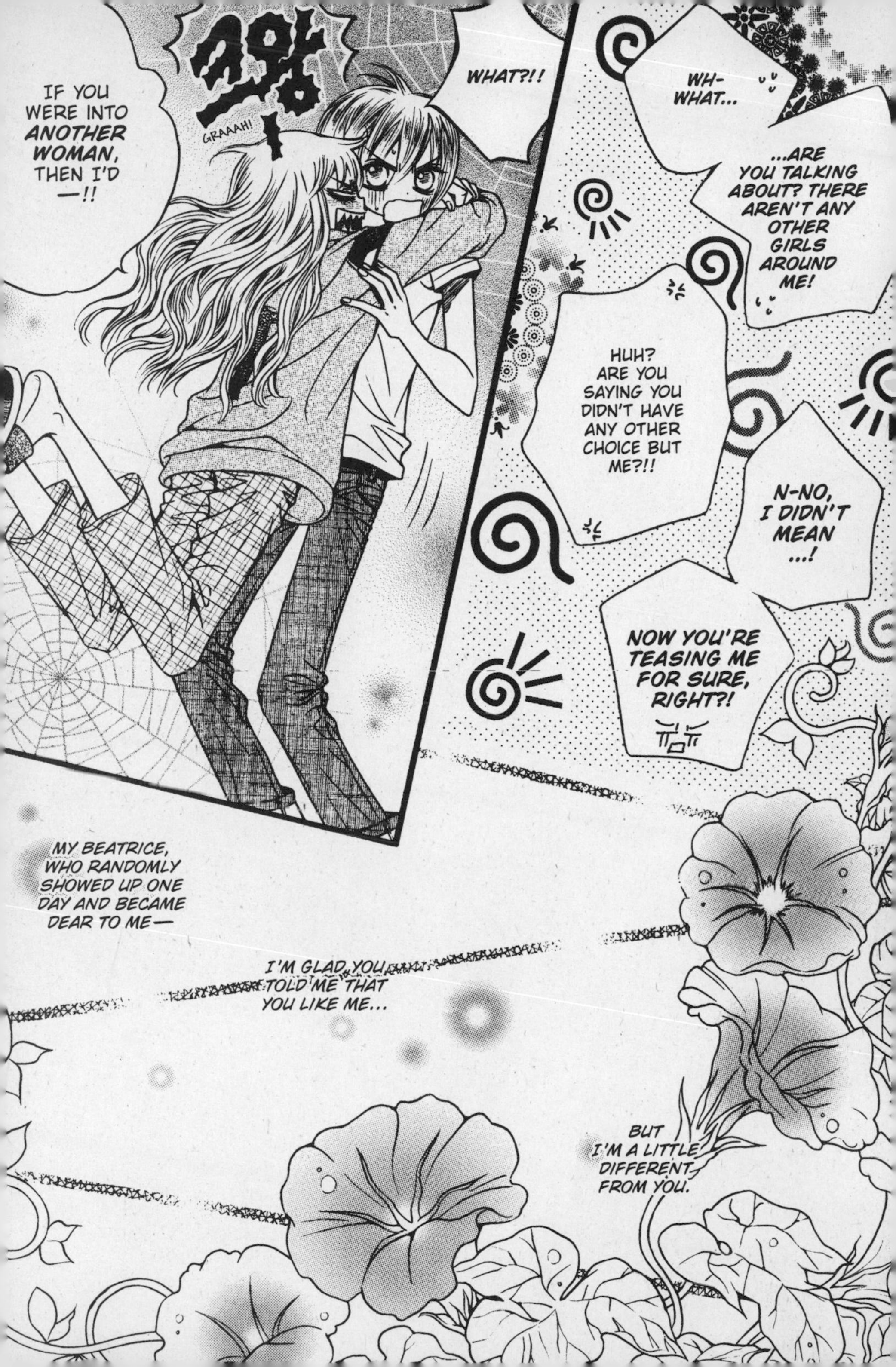
WH-WHAT...
...ARE YOU TALKING ABOUT? THERE AREN'T ANY OTHER GIRLS AROUND ME!
HUH? ARE YOU SAYING YOU DIDN'T HAVE ANY OTHER CHOICE BUT ME?!!
N-NO, I DIDN'T MEAN ...!
NOW YOU'RE TEASING ME FOR SURE, RIGHT?!
IF YOU WERE INTO **ANOTHER WOMAN**, THEN I'D —!!
GRAAAH!
WHAT?!!
MY BEATRICE, WHO RANDOMLY SHOWED UP ONE DAY AND BECAME DEAR TO ME—
I'M GLAD YOU TOLD ME THAT YOU LIKE ME...
BUT I'M A LITTLE DIFFERENT FROM YOU.

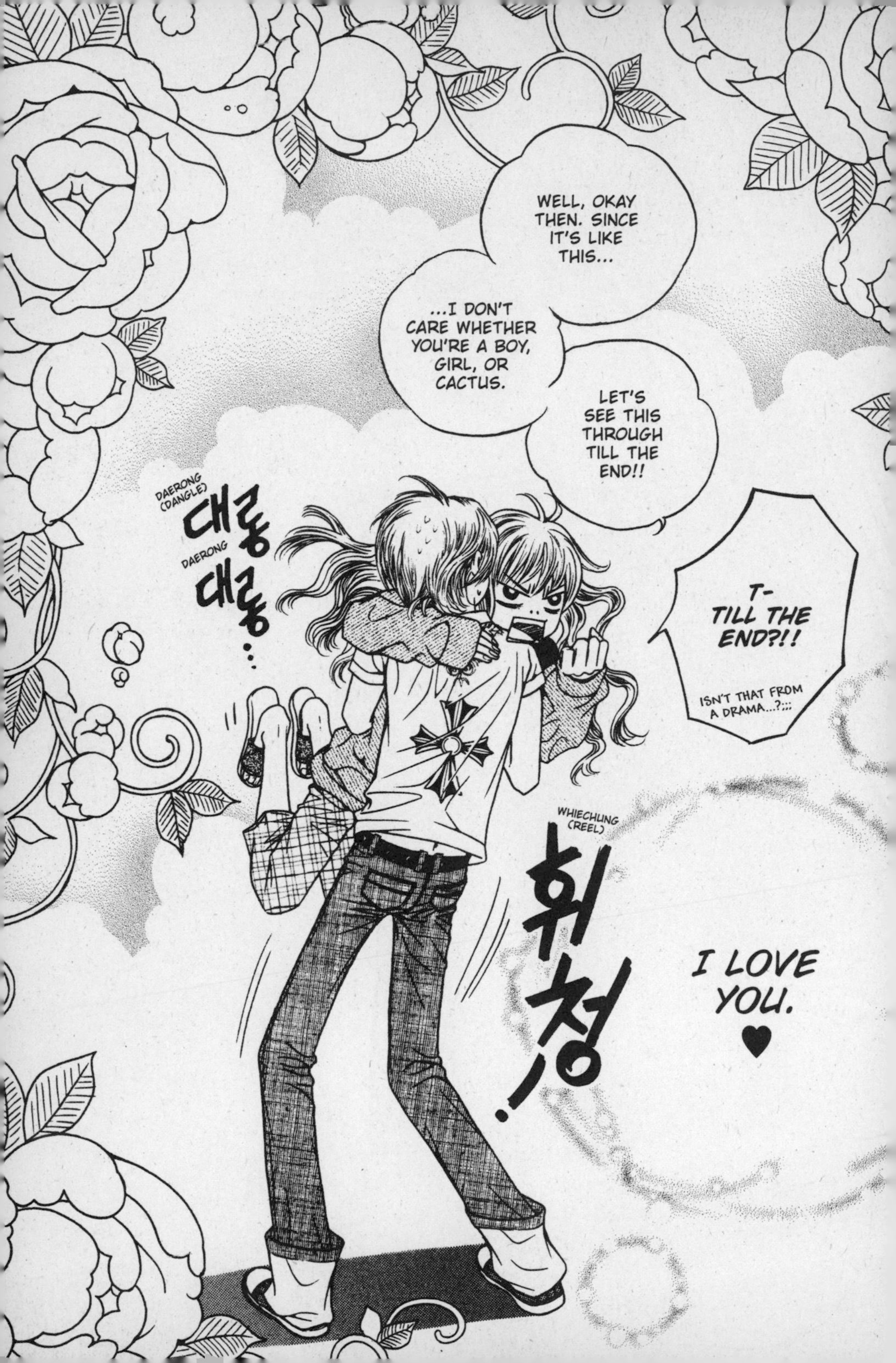

WELL, OKAY THEN. SINCE IT'S LIKE THIS...
...I DON'T CARE WHETHER YOU'RE A BOY, GIRL, OR CACTUS.
LET'S SEE THIS THROUGH TILL THE END!!
DAERONG (DANGLE)
대롱
DAERONG
대롱...
T- TILL THE END?!!
ISN'T THAT FROM A DRAMA...?;;;
WHIECHUNG (REEL)
휘청!
I LOVE YOU. ♥

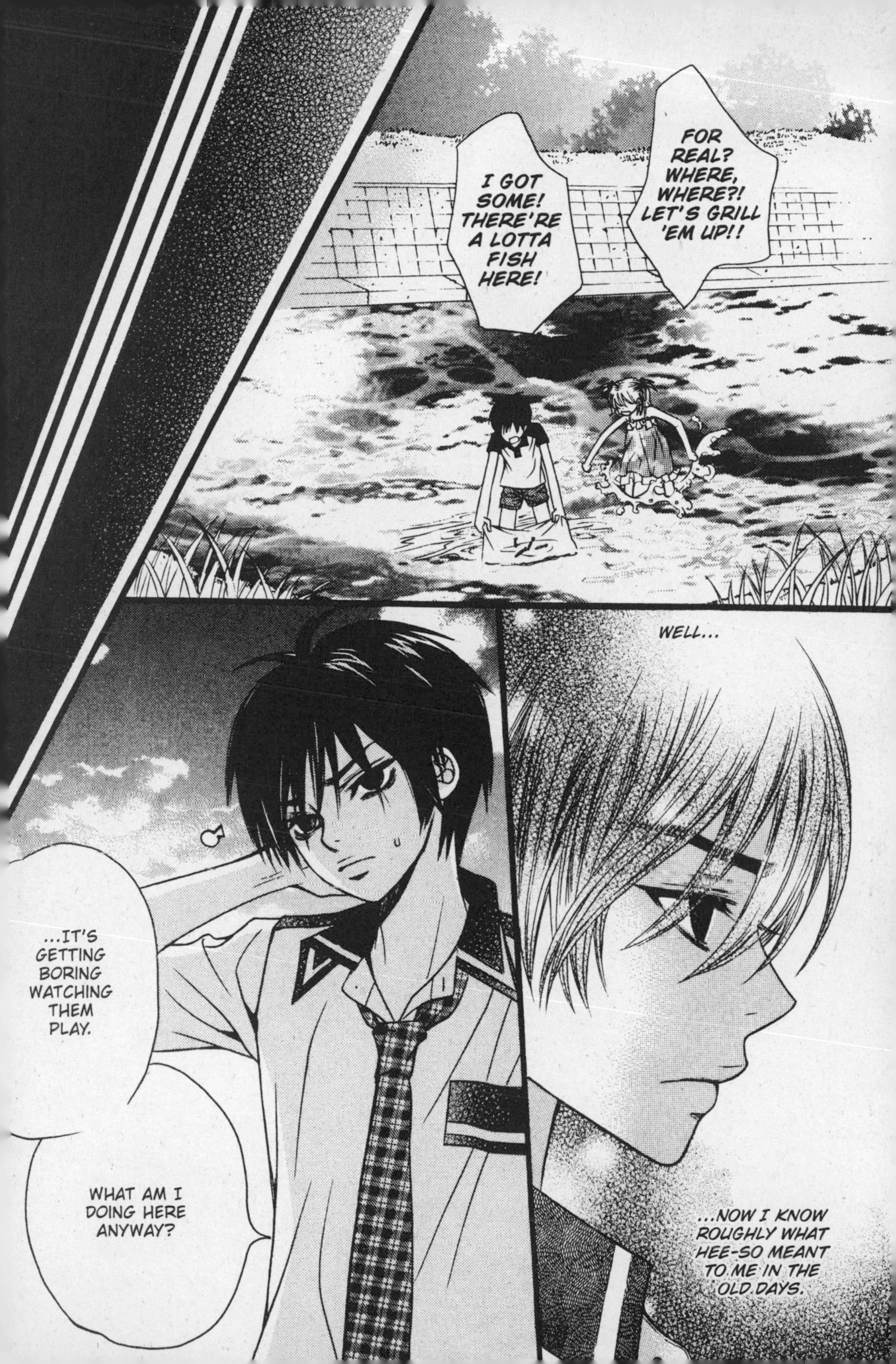
FOR REAL? WHERE, WHERE?! LET'S GRILL 'EM UP!!
I GOT SOME! THERE'RE A LOTTA FISH HERE!
WELL...
...IT'S GETTING BORING WATCHING THEM PLAY.
...NOW I KNOW ROUGHLY WHAT HEE-SO MEANT TO ME IN THE OLD DAYS.
WHAT AM I DOING HERE ANYWAY?

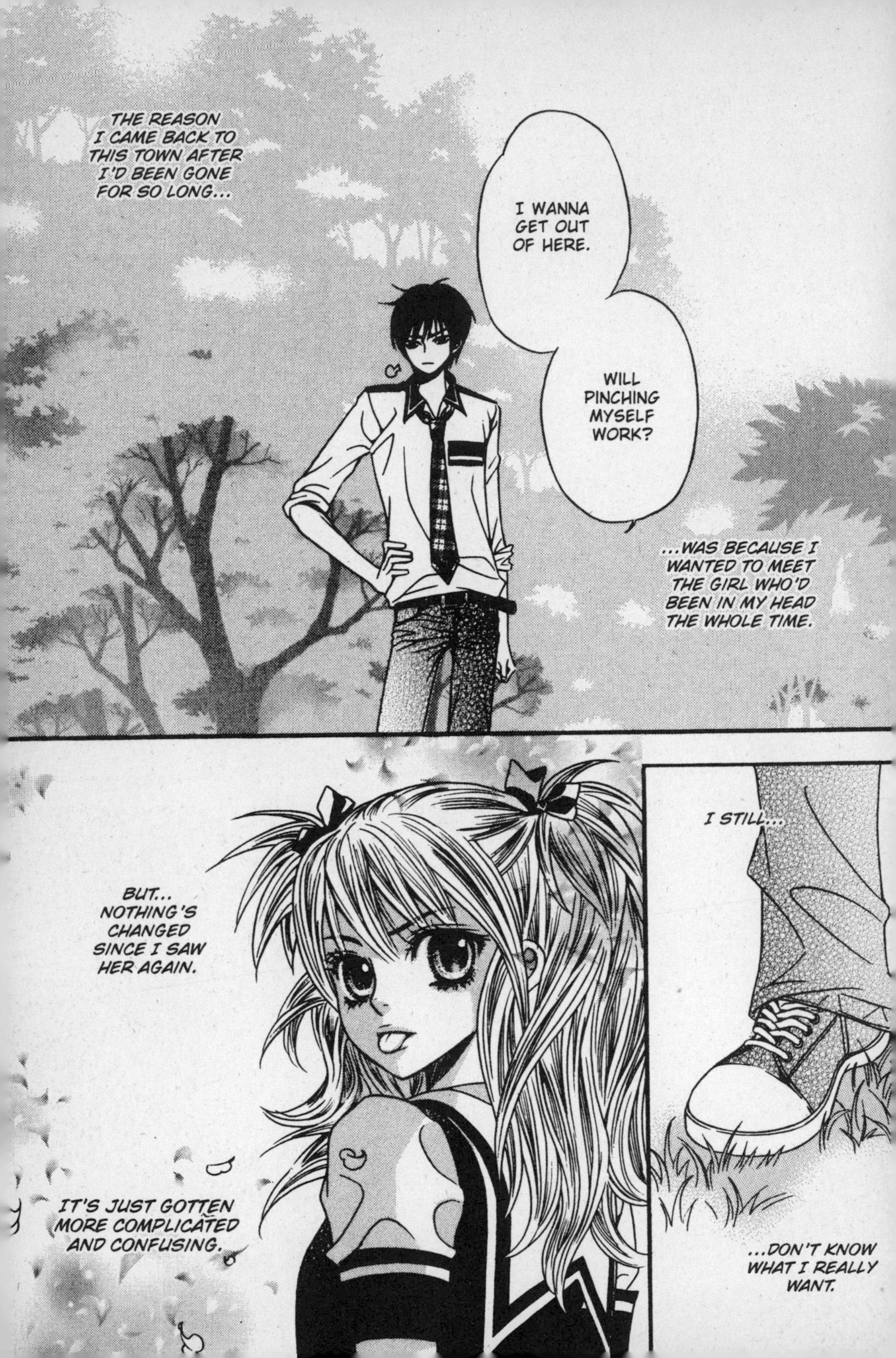
THE REASON I CAME BACK TO THIS TOWN AFTER I'D BEEN GONE FOR SO LONG...
I WANNA GET OUT OF HERE.
WILL PINCHING MYSELF WORK?
...WAS BECAUSE I WANTED TO MEET THE GIRL WHO'D BEEN IN MY HEAD THE WHOLE TIME.
BUT... NOTHING'S CHANGED SINCE I SAW HER AGAIN.
IT'S JUST GOTTEN MORE COMPLICATED AND CONFUSING.
I STILL...
...DON'T KNOW WHAT I REALLY WANT.

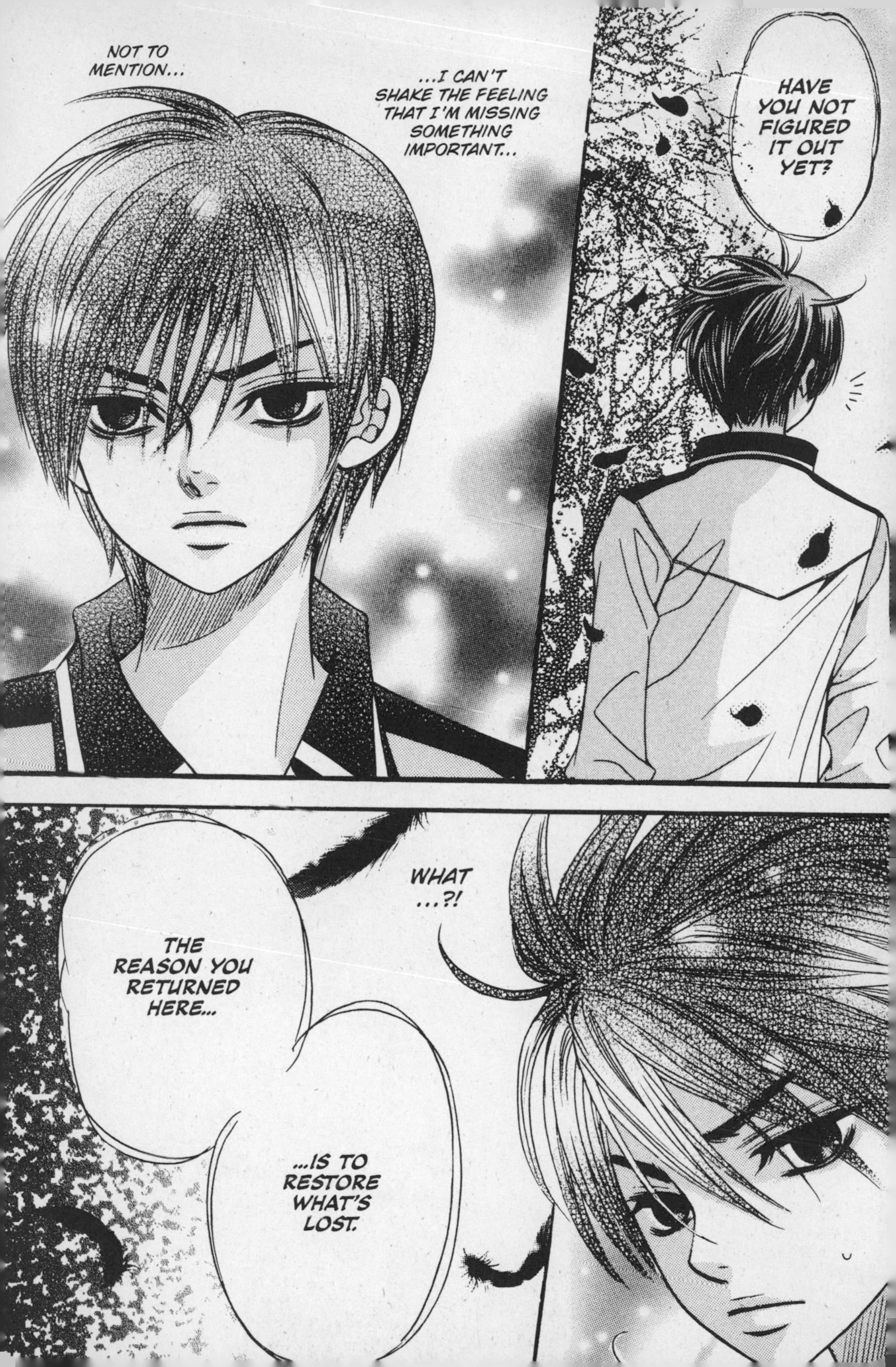
HAVE YOU NOT FIGURED IT OUT YET?
NOT TO MENTION...
...I CAN'T SHAKE THE FEELING THAT I'M MISSING SOMETHING IMPORTANT...
WHAT ...?!
THE REASON YOU RETURNED HERE...
...IS TO RESTORE WHAT'S LOST.

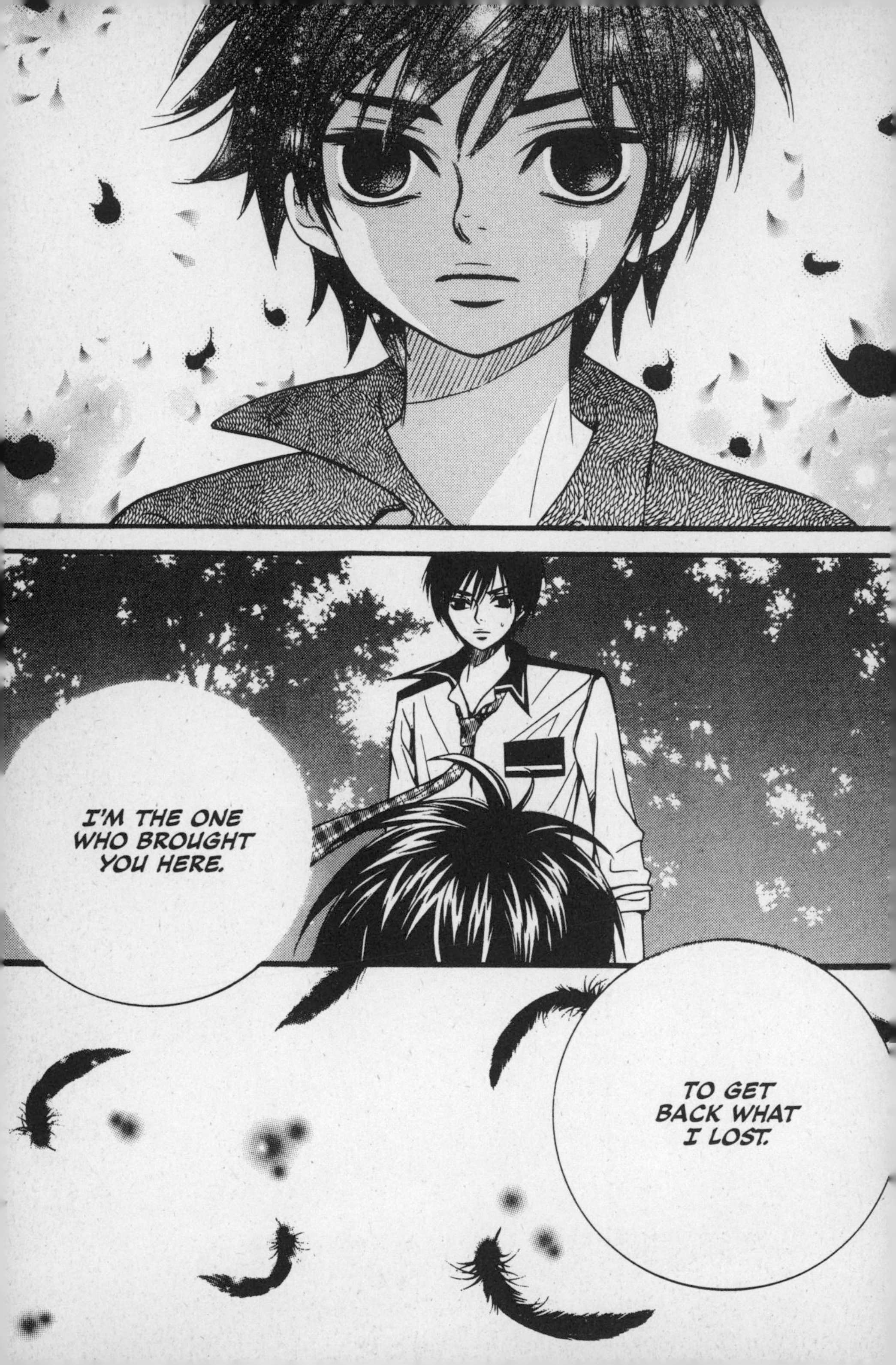
I'M THE ONE WHO BROUGHT YOU HERE.
TO GET BACK WHAT I LOST.

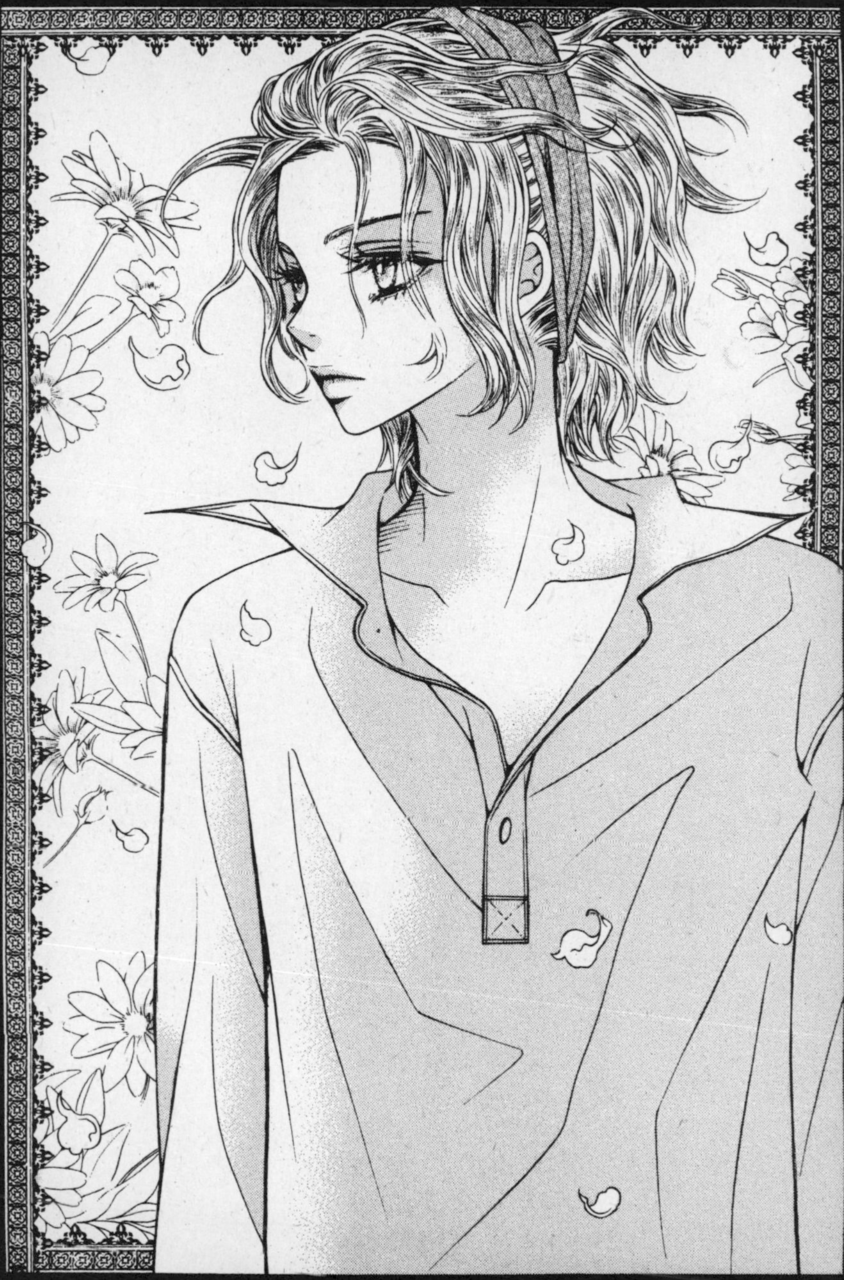

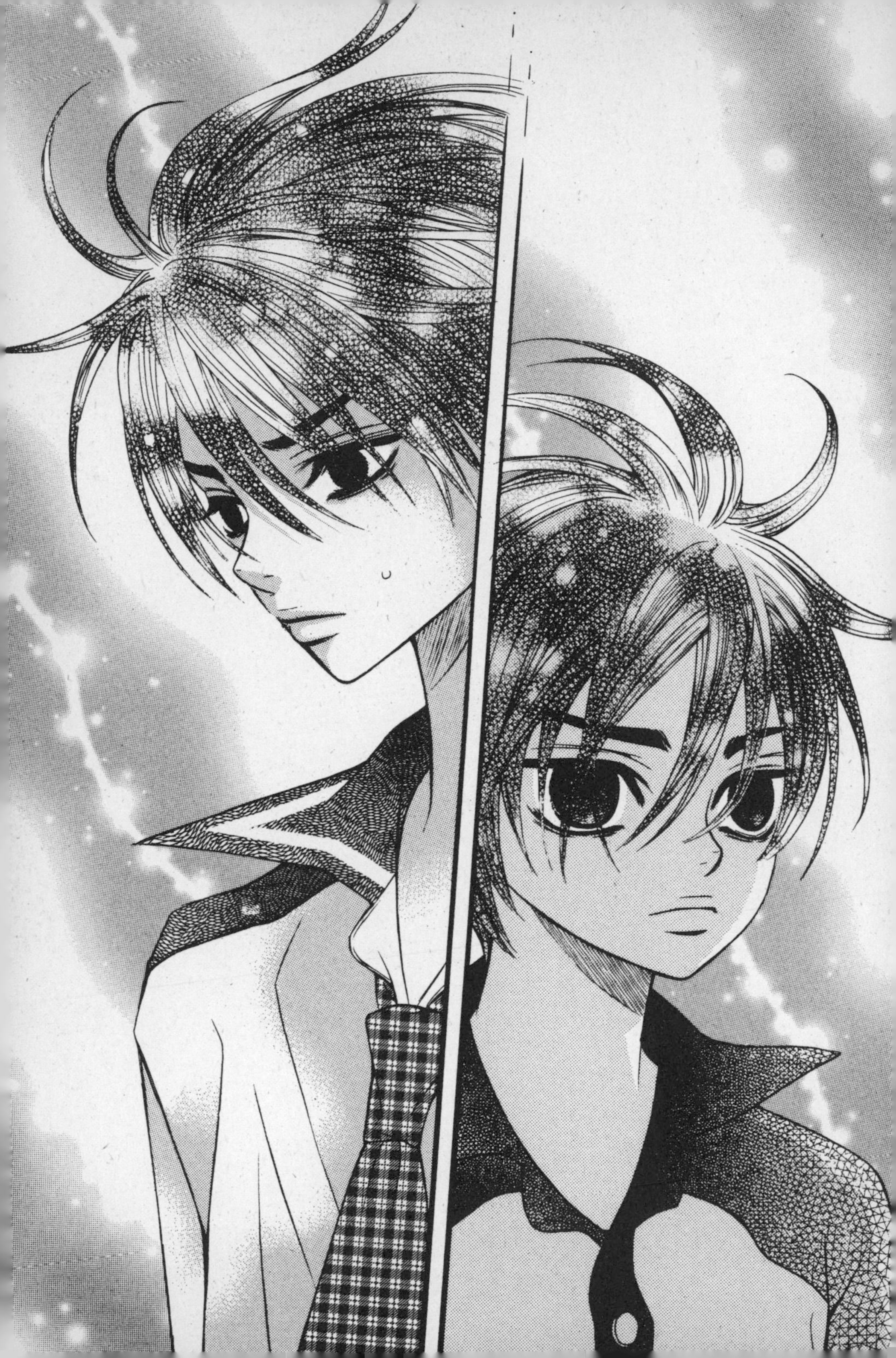

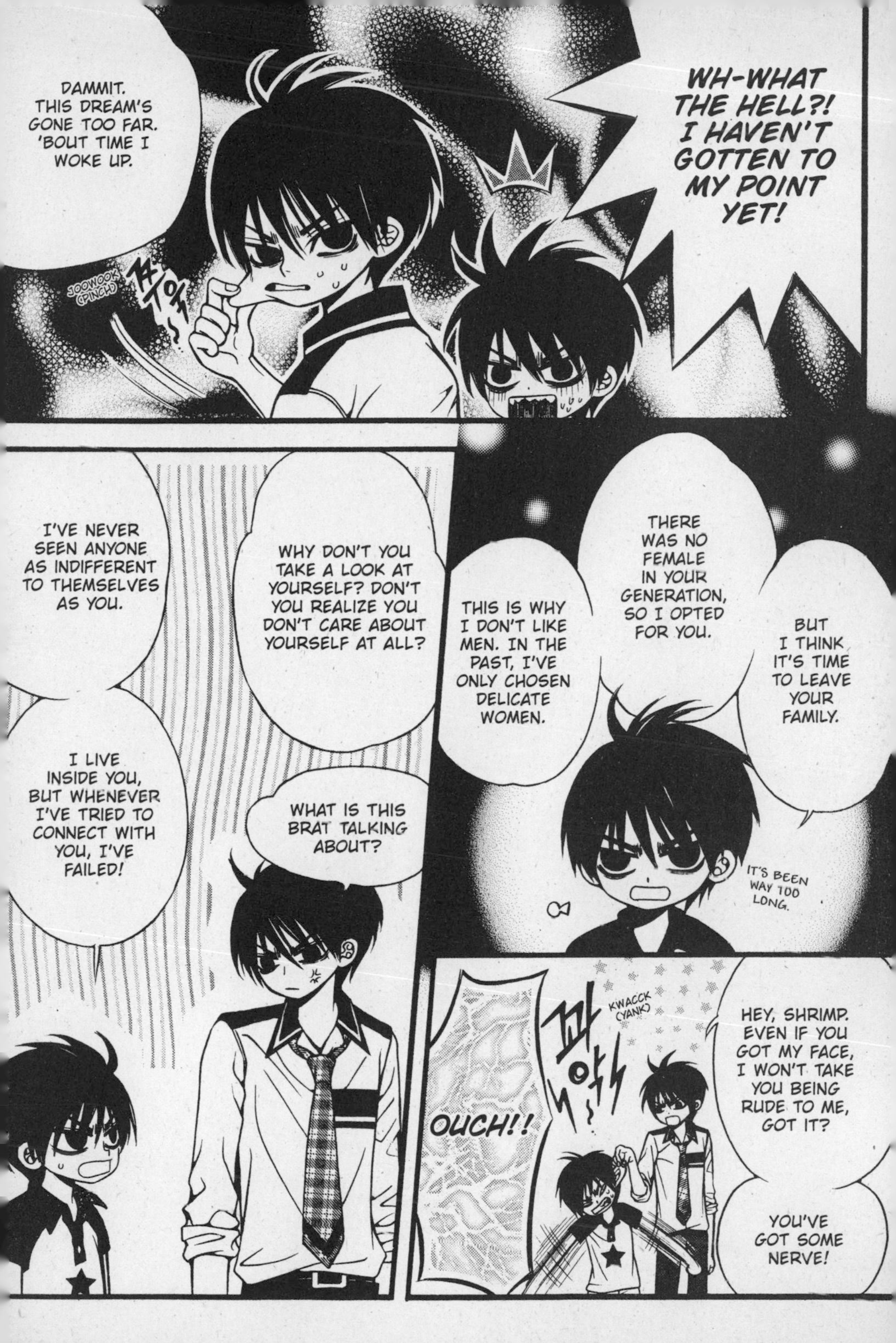
DAMMIT. THIS DREAM'S GONE TOO FAR. 'BOUT TIME I WOKE UP.
JOOWOOK (PINCH)
WH-WHAT THE HELL?! I HAVEN'T GOTTEN TO MY POINT YET!
I'VE NEVER SEEN ANYONE AS INDIFFERENT TO THEMSELVES AS YOU.
WHY DON'T YOU TAKE A LOOK AT YOURSELF? DON'T YOU REALIZE YOU DON'T CARE ABOUT YOURSELF AT ALL?
I LIVE INSIDE YOU, BUT WHENEVER I'VE TRIED TO CONNECT WITH YOU, I'VE FAILED!
WHAT IS THIS BRAT TALKING ABOUT?
THIS IS WHY I DON'T LIKE MEN. IN THE PAST, I'VE ONLY CHOSEN DELICATE WOMEN.
THERE WAS NO FEMALE IN YOUR GENERATION, SO I OPTED FOR YOU.
BUT I THINK IT'S TIME TO LEAVE YOUR FAMILY.
IT'S BEEN WAY TOO LONG.
KWACCK (YANK)
OUCH!!
HEY, SHRIMP. EVEN IF YOU GOT MY FACE, I WON'T TAKE YOU BEING RUDE TO ME, GOT IT?
YOU'VE GOT SOME NERVE!

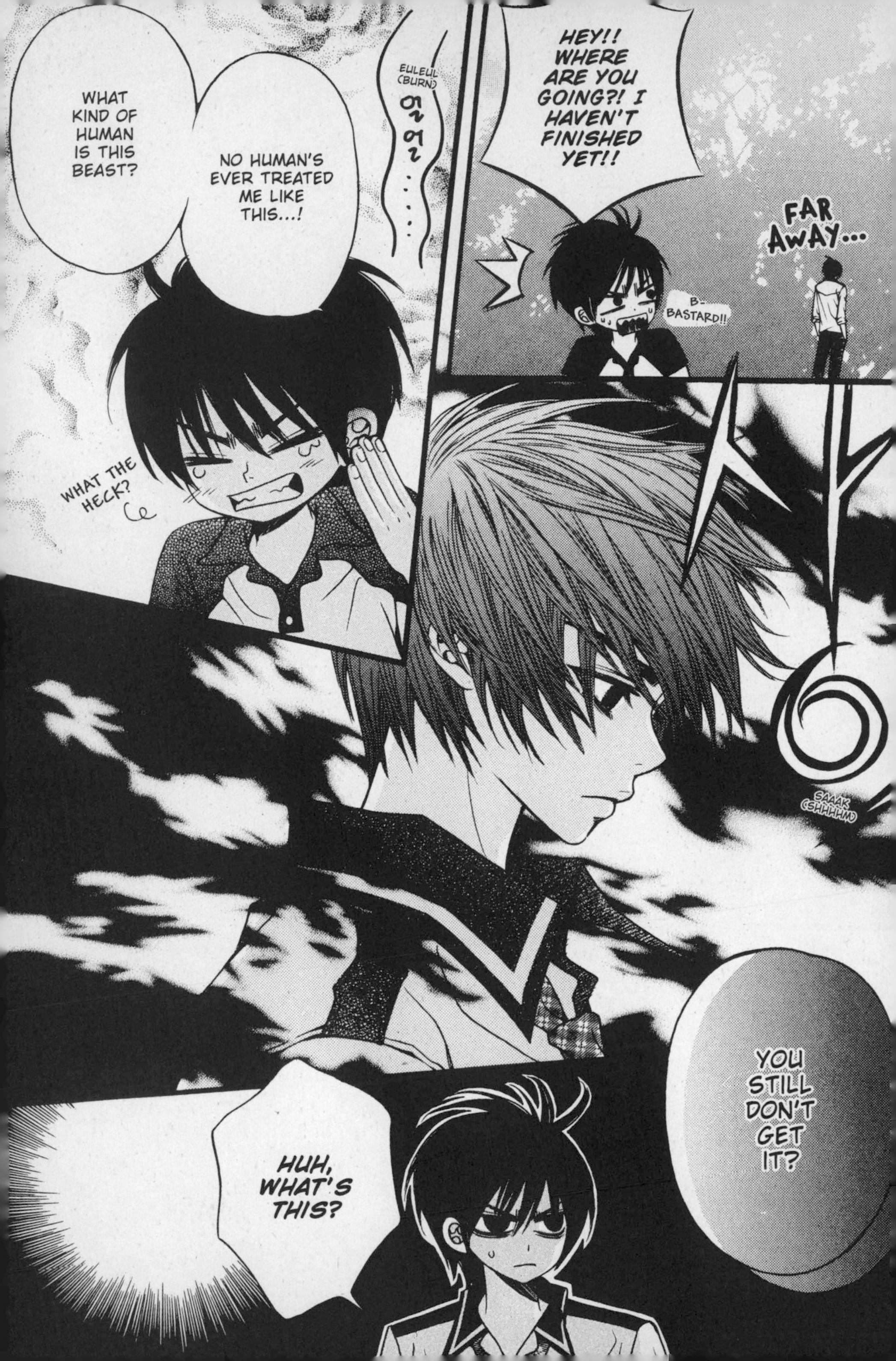

HEY!! WHERE ARE YOU GOING?! I HAVEN'T FINISHED YET!!
FAR AWAY...
B-BASTARD!!
EULEUL (BURN)
NO HUMAN'S EVER TREATED ME LIKE THIS...!
WHAT KIND OF HUMAN IS THIS BEAST?
WHAT THE HECK?
SAAAK (SHHHHM)
YOU STILL DON'T GET IT?
HUH, WHAT'S THIS?

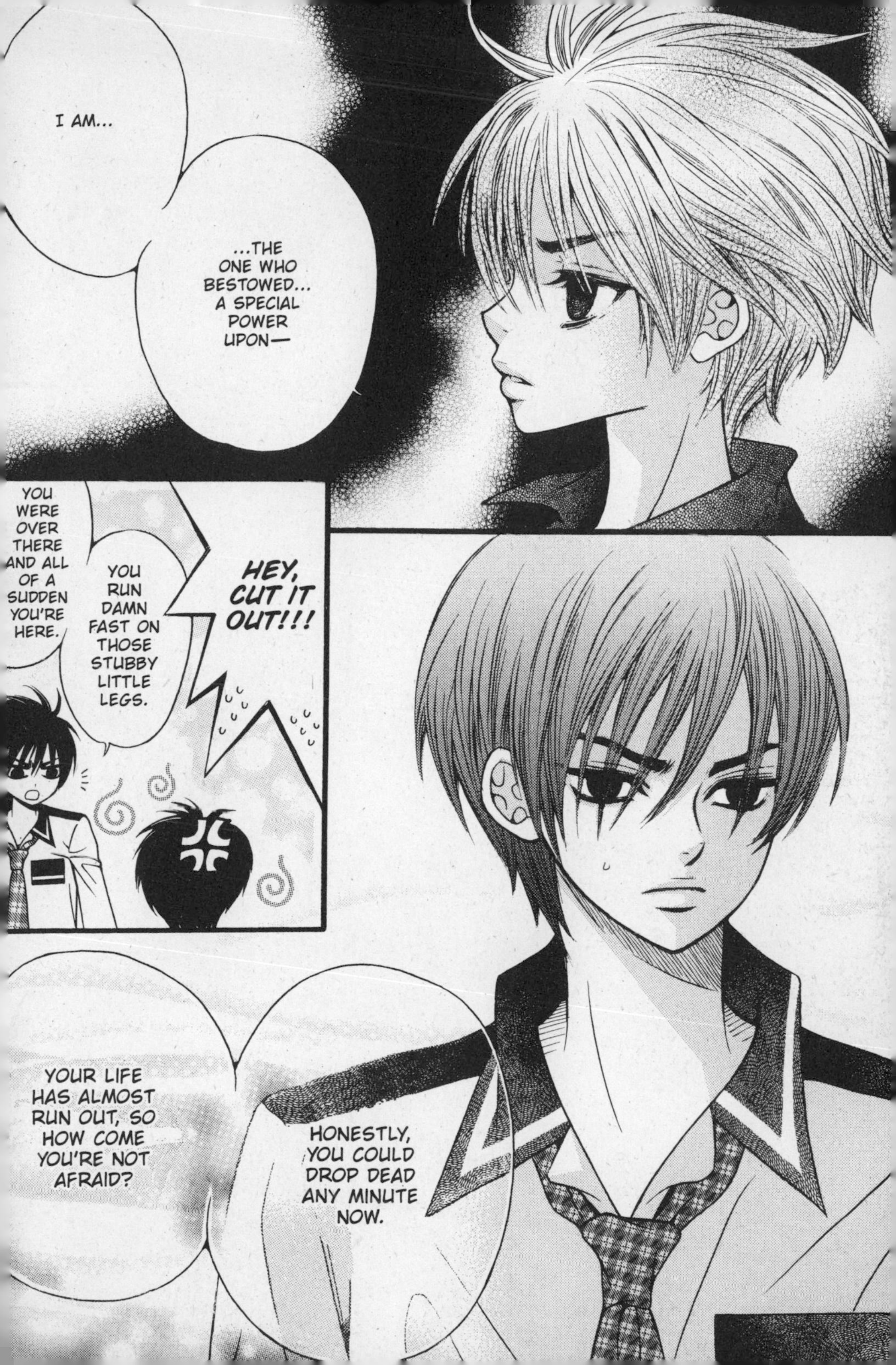
I AM...
...THE ONE WHO BESTOWED... A SPECIAL POWER UPON—
YOU WERE OVER THERE AND ALL OF A SUDDEN YOU'RE HERE.
YOU RUN DAMN FAST ON THOSE STUBBY LITTLE LEGS.
HEY, CUT IT OUT!!!
HONESTLY, YOU COULD DROP DEAD ANY MINUTE NOW.
YOUR LIFE HAS ALMOST RUN OUT, SO HOW COME YOU'RE NOT AFRAID?

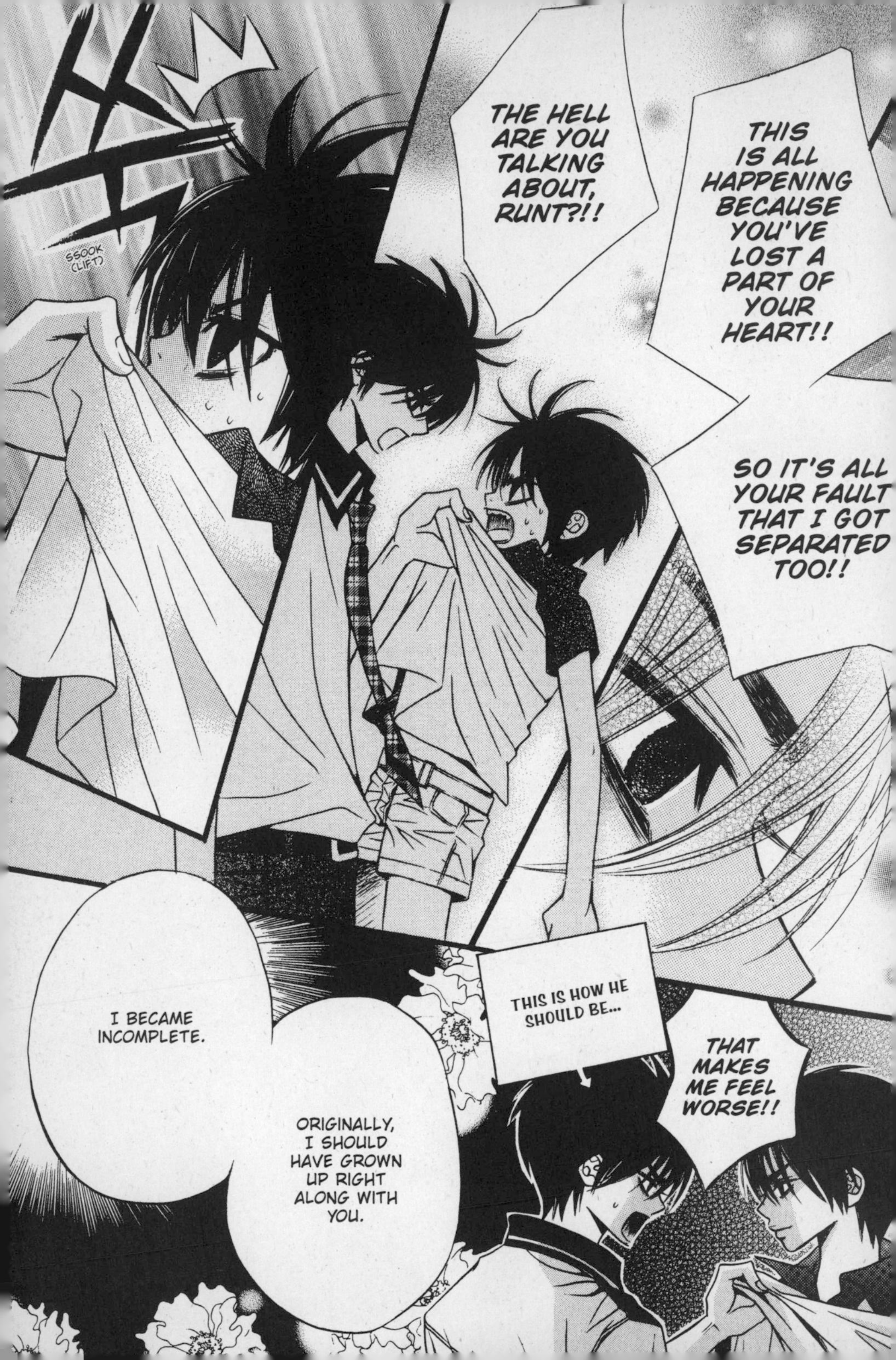
THE HELL ARE YOU TALKING ABOUT, RUNT?!!
THIS IS ALL HAPPENING BECAUSE YOU'VE LOST A PART OF YOUR HEART!!
SSOOK (LIFT)
SO IT'S ALL YOUR FAULT THAT I GOT SEPARATED TOO!!
THIS IS HOW HE SHOULD BE...
THAT MAKES ME FEEL WORSE!!
I BECAME INCOMPLETE.
ORIGINALLY, I SHOULD HAVE GROWN UP RIGHT ALONG WITH YOU.

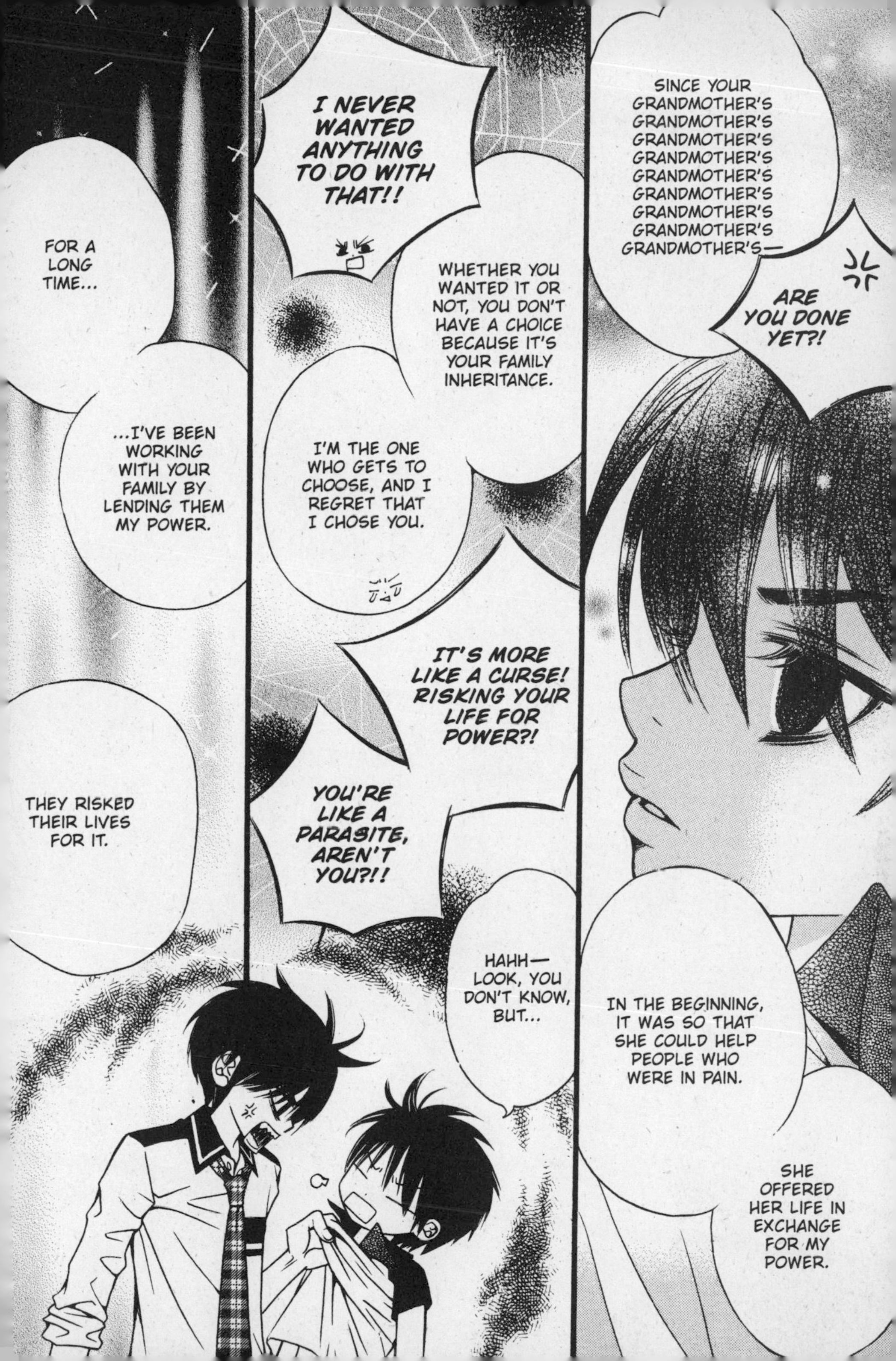
FOR A LONG TIME...
...I'VE BEEN WORKING WITH YOUR FAMILY BY LENDING THEM MY POWER.
THEY RISKED THEIR LIVES FOR IT.
I NEVER WANTED ANYTHING TO DO WITH THAT!!
WHETHER YOU WANTED IT OR NOT, YOU DON'T HAVE A CHOICE BECAUSE IT'S YOUR FAMILY INHERITANCE.
I'M THE ONE WHO GETS TO CHOOSE, AND I REGRET THAT I CHOSE YOU.
IT'S MORE LIKE A CURSE! RISKING YOUR LIFE FOR POWER?!
YOU'RE LIKE A PARASITE, AREN'T YOU?!!
HAHH— LOOK, YOU DON'T KNOW, BUT...
SINCE YOUR GRANDMOTHER'S GRANDMOTHER'S GRANDMOTHER'S GRANDMOTHER'S GRANDMOTHER'S GRANDMOTHER'S GRANDMOTHER'S GRANDMOTHER'S GRANDMOTHER'S—
ARE YOU DONE YET?!
IN THE BEGINNING, IT WAS SO THAT SHE COULD HELP PEOPLE WHO WERE IN PAIN.
SHE OFFERED HER LIFE IN EXCHANGE FOR MY POWER.

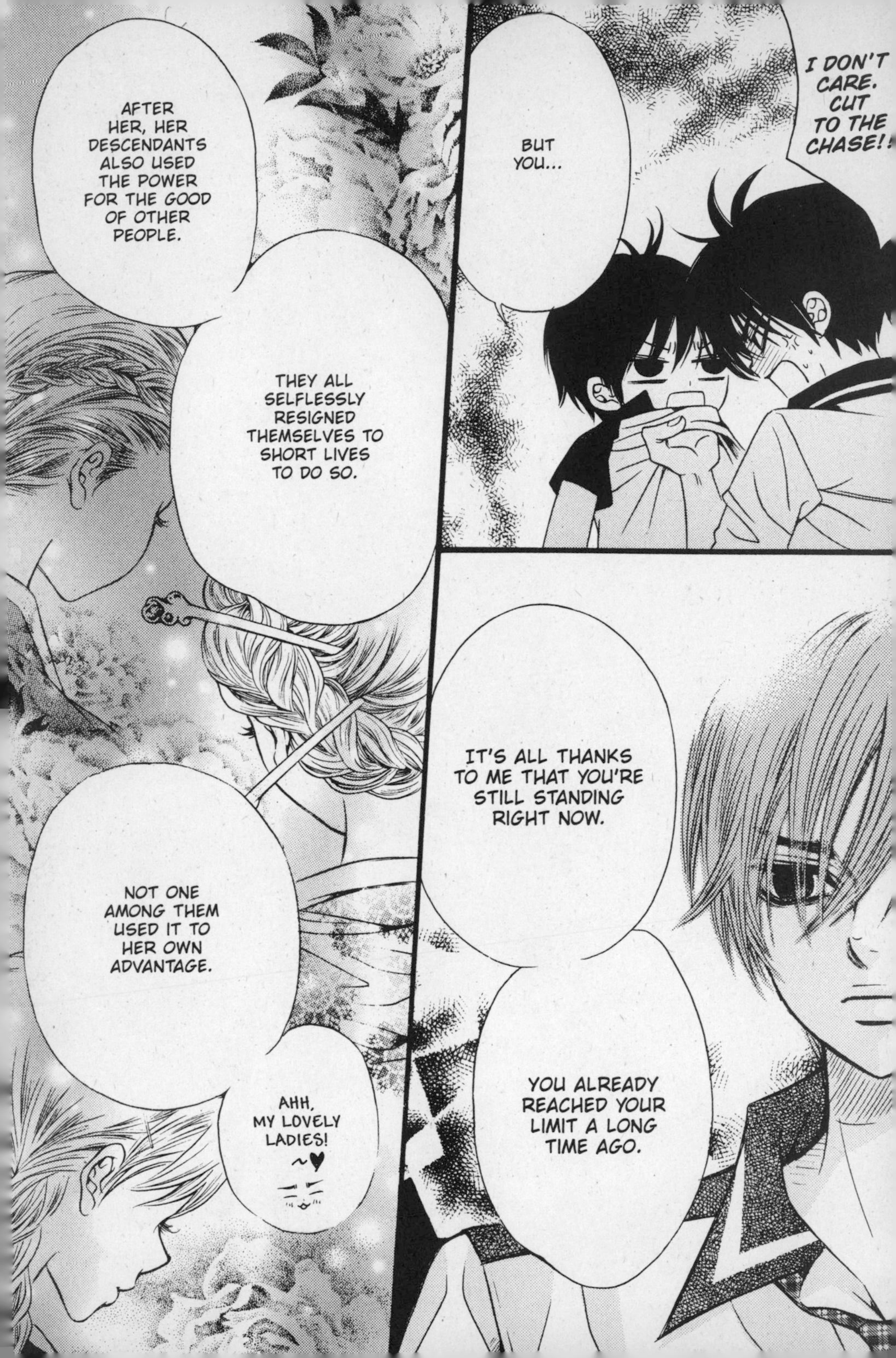
I DON'T CARE. CUT TO THE CHASE!!
BUT YOU...
IT'S ALL THANKS TO ME THAT YOU'RE STILL STANDING RIGHT NOW.
YOU ALREADY REACHED YOUR LIMIT A LONG TIME AGO.
AFTER HER, HER DESCENDANTS ALSO USED THE POWER FOR THE GOOD OF OTHER PEOPLE.
THEY ALL SELFLESSLY RESIGNED THEMSELVES TO SHORT LIVES TO DO SO.
NOT ONE AMONG THEM USED IT TO HER OWN ADVANTAGE.
AHH, MY LOVELY LADIES! ~♥

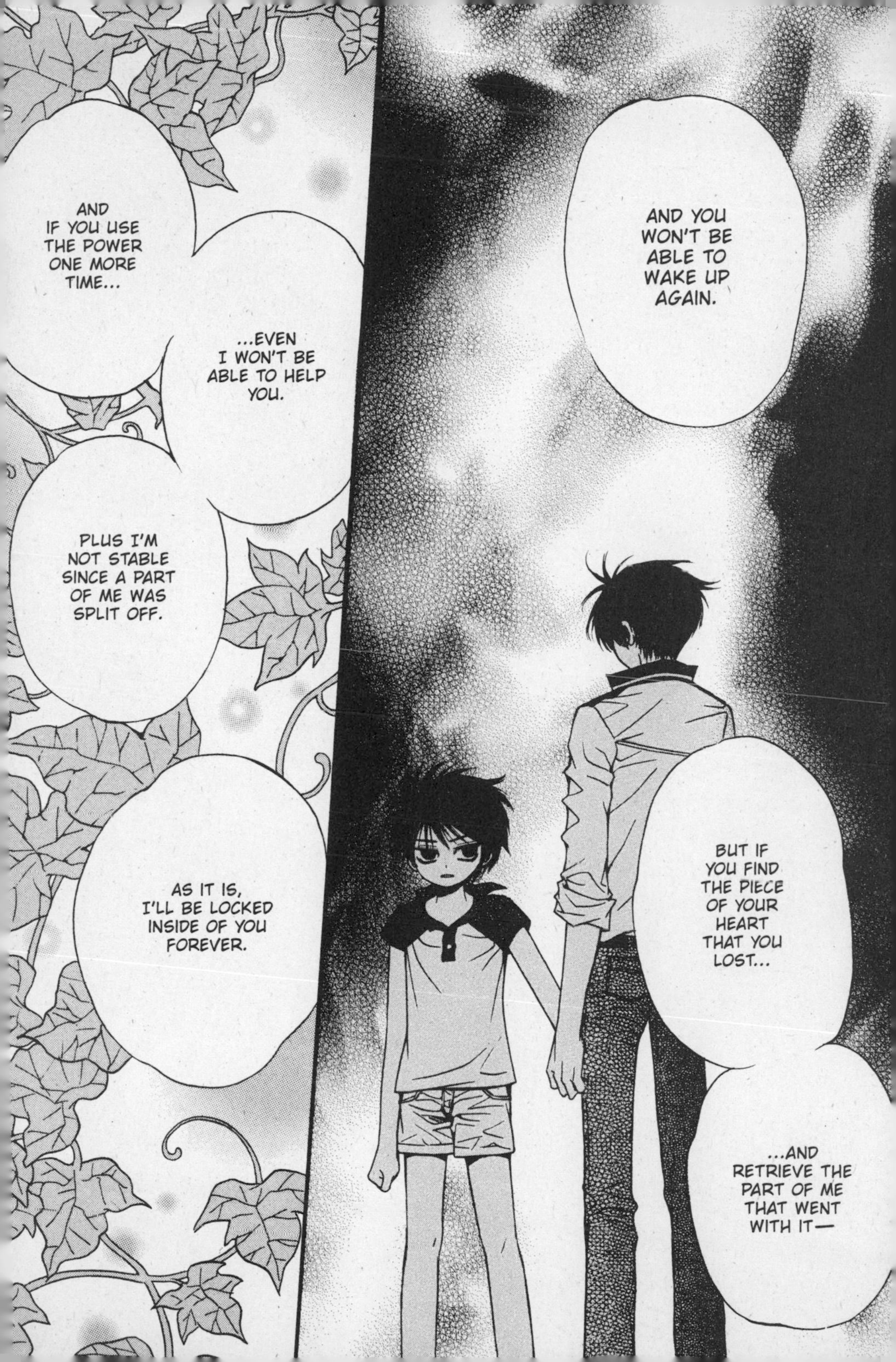
AND IF YOU USE THE POWER ONE MORE TIME...
...EVEN I WON'T BE ABLE TO HELP YOU.
PLUS I'M NOT STABLE SINCE A PART OF ME WAS SPLIT OFF.
AS IT IS, I'LL BE LOCKED INSIDE OF YOU FOREVER.
AND YOU WON'T BE ABLE TO WAKE UP AGAIN.
BUT IF YOU FIND THE PIECE OF YOUR HEART THAT YOU LOST...
...AND RETRIEVE THE PART OF ME THAT WENT WITH IT—

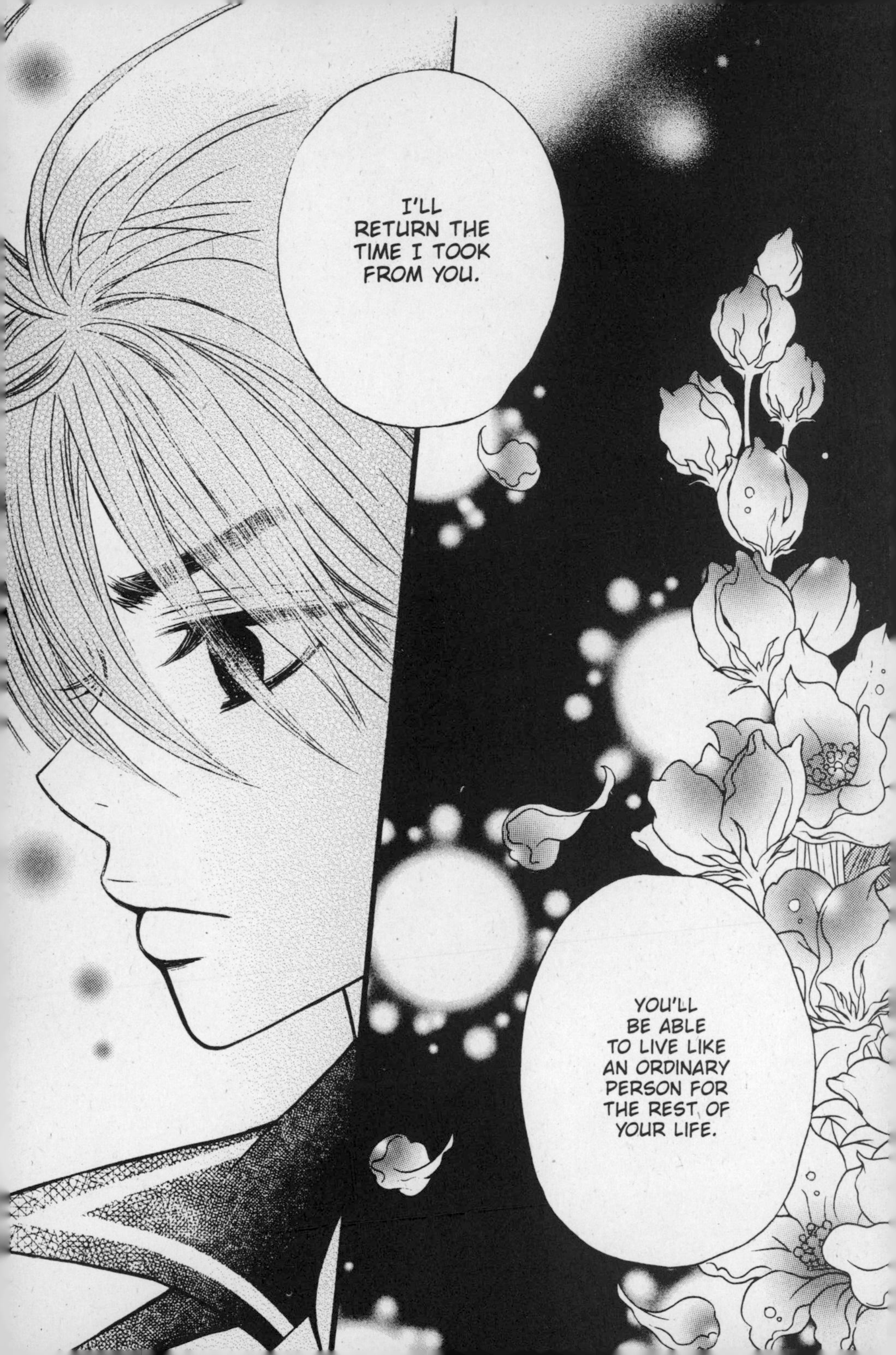
I'LL RETURN THE TIME I TOOK FROM YOU.
YOU'LL BE ABLE TO LIVE LIKE AN ORDINARY PERSON FOR THE REST OF YOUR LIFE.

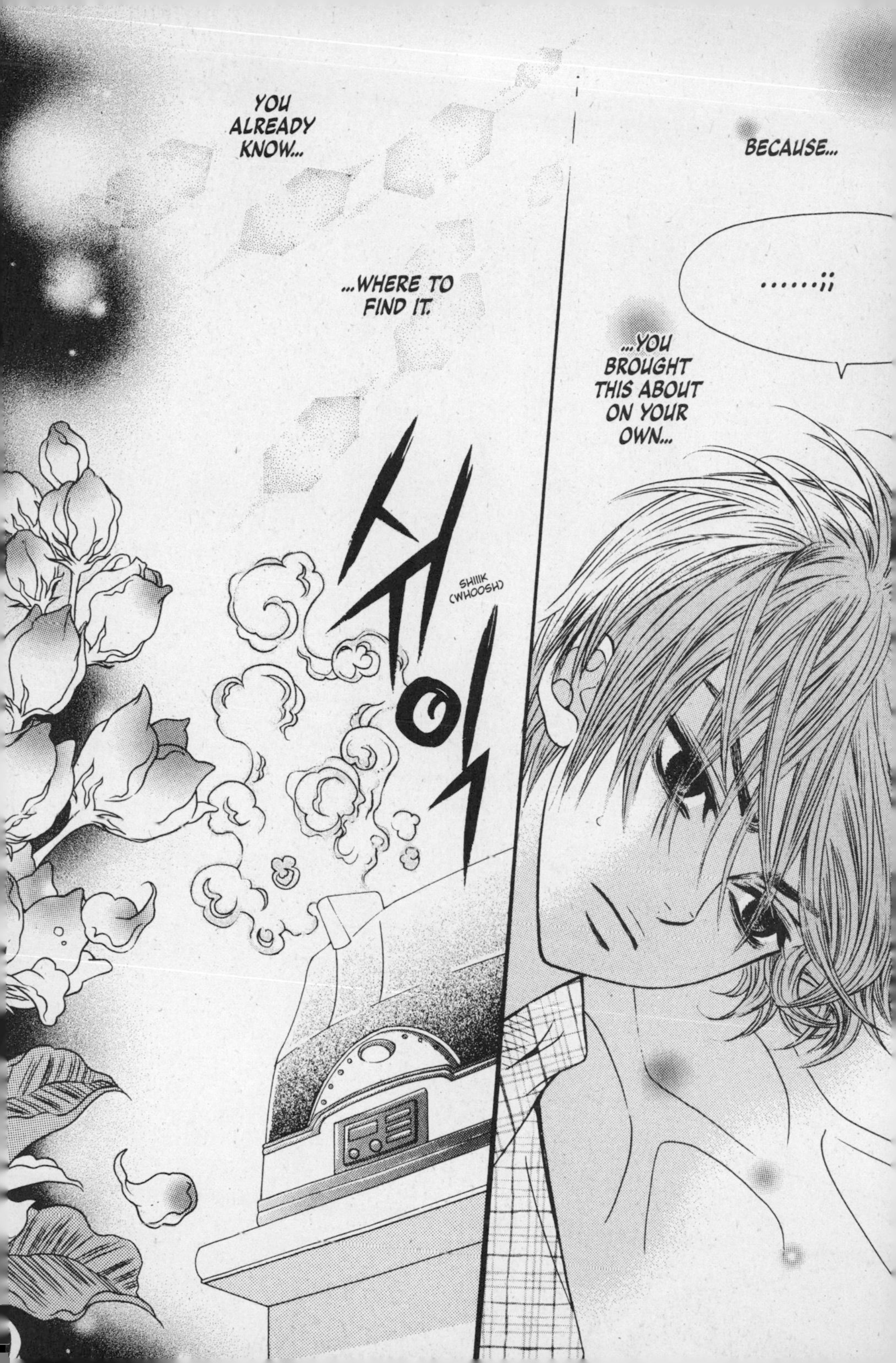
YOU ALREADY KNOW...
...WHERE TO FIND IT.
SHIIK (WHOOSH)
BECAUSE...
......;;
...YOU BROUGHT THIS ABOUT ON YOUR OWN...

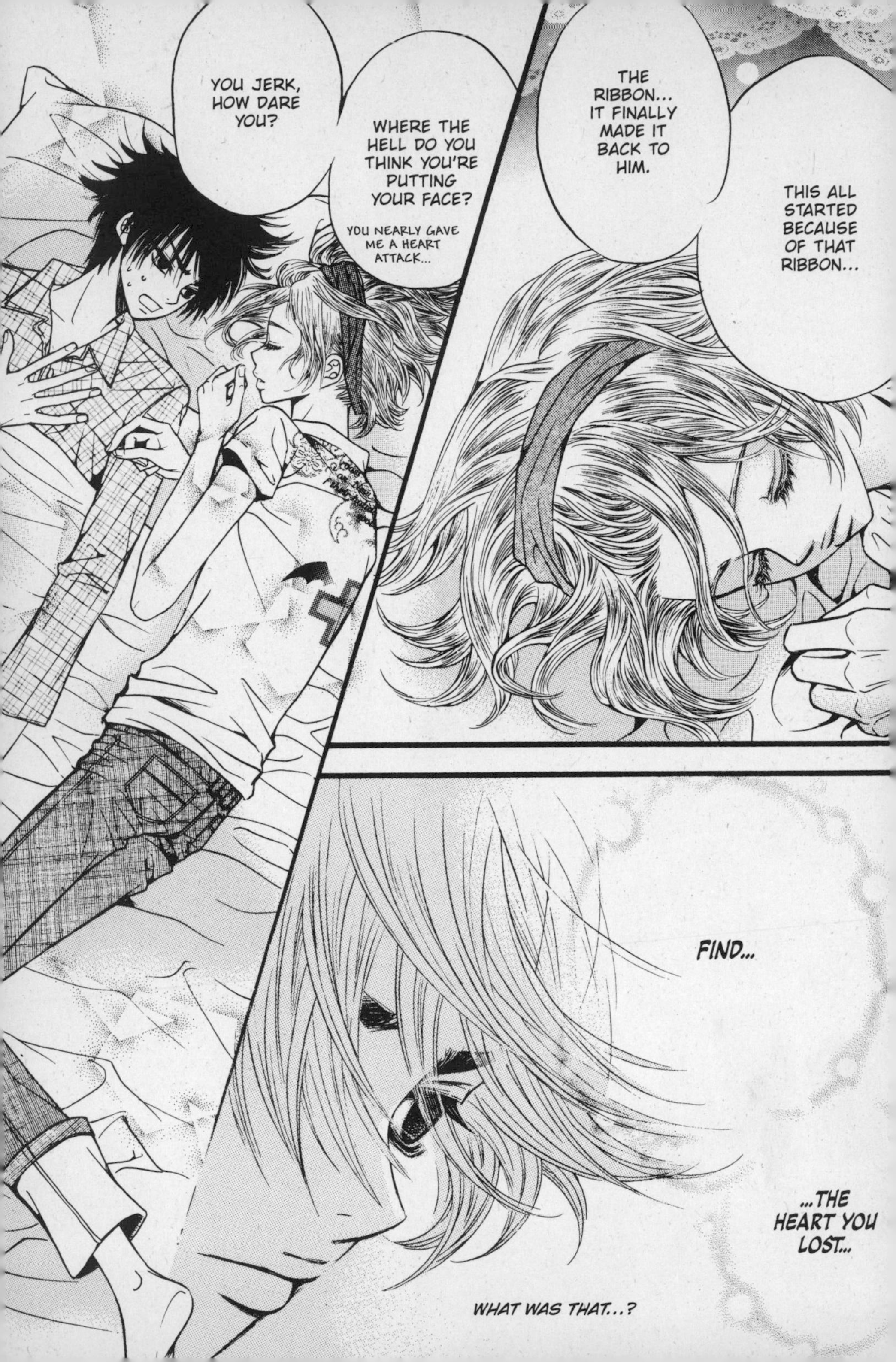
YOU JERK, HOW DARE YOU?
WHERE THE HELL DO YOU THINK YOU'RE PUTTING YOUR FACE?
YOU NEARLY GAVE ME A HEART ATTACK...
THE RIBBON... IT FINALLY MADE IT BACK TO HIM.
THIS ALL STARTED BECAUSE OF THAT RIBBON...
FIND...
...THE HEART YOU LOST...
WHAT WAS THAT...?

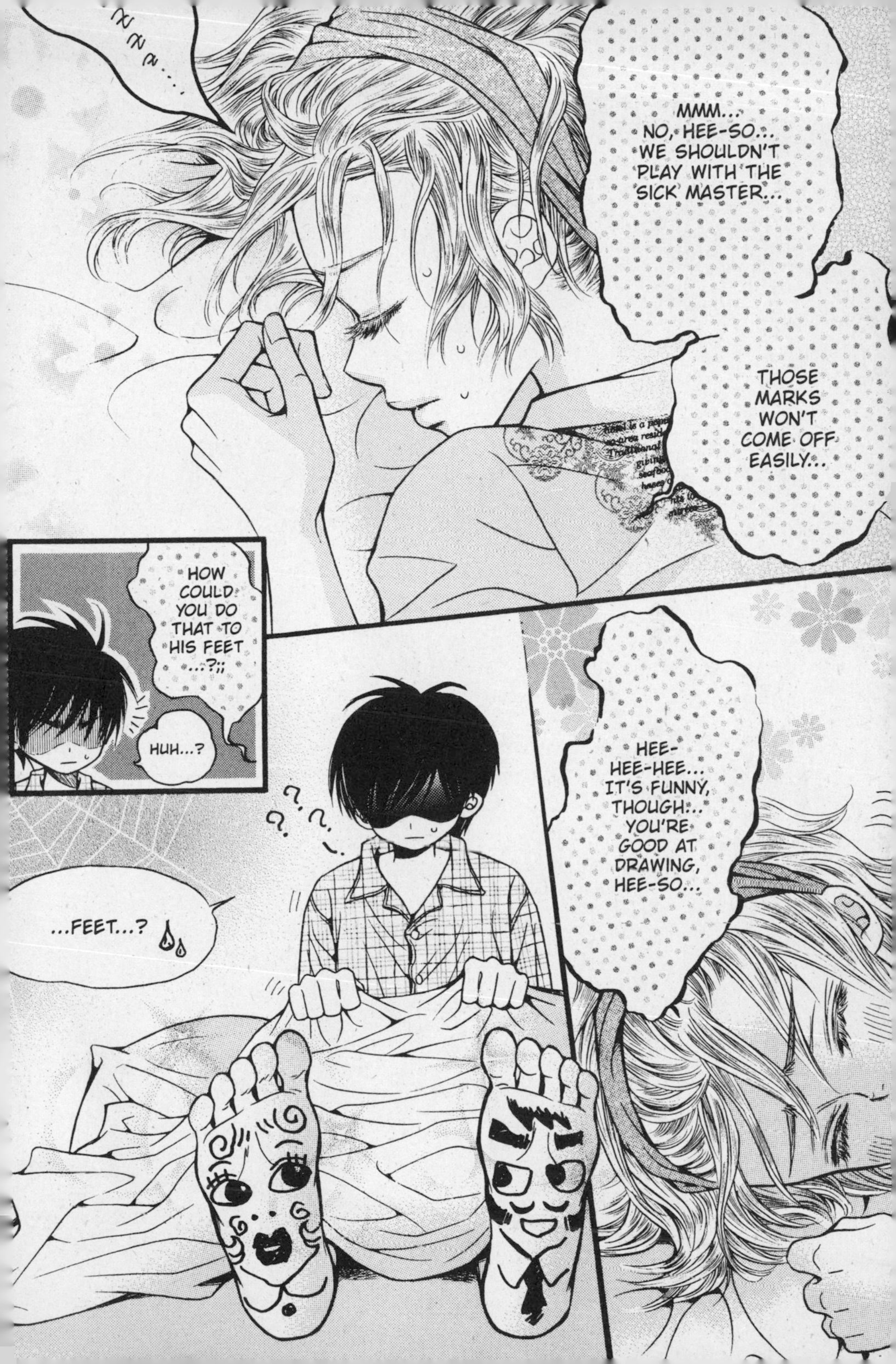
MMM... NO, HEE-SO... WE SHOULDN'T PLAY WITH THE SICK MASTER...
nnn...
THOSE MARKS WON'T COME OFF EASILY...
HEE-HEE-HEE... IT'S FUNNY, THOUGH... YOU'RE GOOD AT DRAWING, HEE-SO...
...FEET...?
HOW COULD YOU DO THAT TO HIS FEET ...?;;
HUH...?

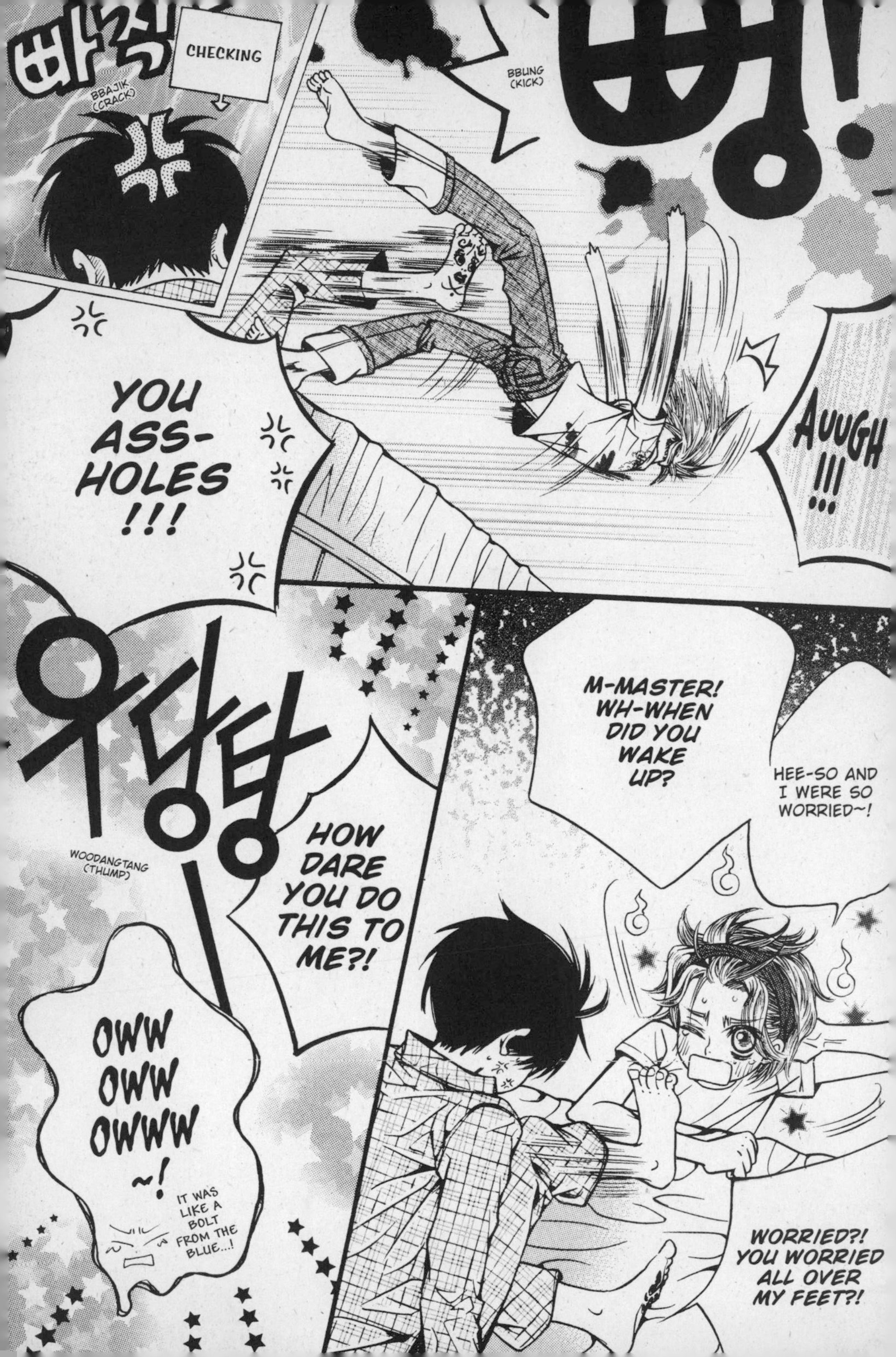
빠직
BBAJIK (CRACK)
CHECKING
BBUNG (KICK)
뻥!
YOU ASS-HOLES !!!
AUUGH !!!
우당탕
WOODANGTANG (THUMP)
HOW DARE YOU DO THIS TO ME?!
OWW OWW OWWW ~!
IT WAS LIKE A BOLT FROM THE BLUE...!
M-MASTER! WH-WHEN DID YOU WAKE UP?
HEE-SO AND I WERE SO WORRIED~!
WORRIED?! YOU WORRIED ALL OVER MY FEET?!

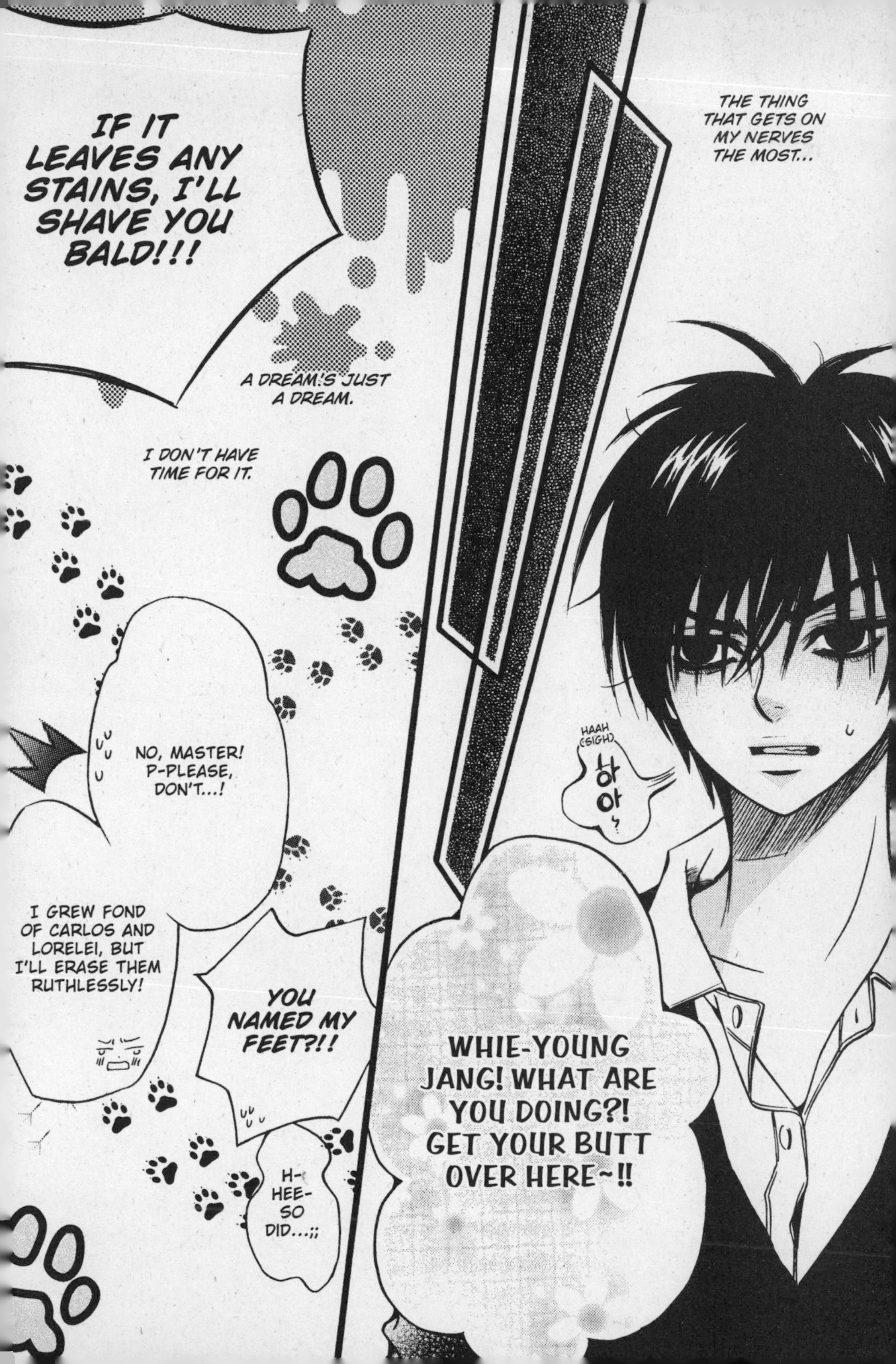
IF IT LEAVES ANY STAINS, I'LL SHAVE YOU BALD!!!
A DREAM'S JUST A DREAM.
I DON'T HAVE TIME FOR IT.
NO, MASTER! P-PLEASE, DON'T...!
I GREW FOND OF CARLOS AND LORELEI, BUT I'LL ERASE THEM RUTHLESSLY!
YOU NAMED MY FEET?!!
H-HEE-SO DID...;;
THE THING THAT GETS ON MY NERVES THE MOST...
HAAH (SIGH)
하아
WHIE-YOUNG JANG! WHAT ARE YOU DOING?! GET YOUR BUTT OVER HERE~!!

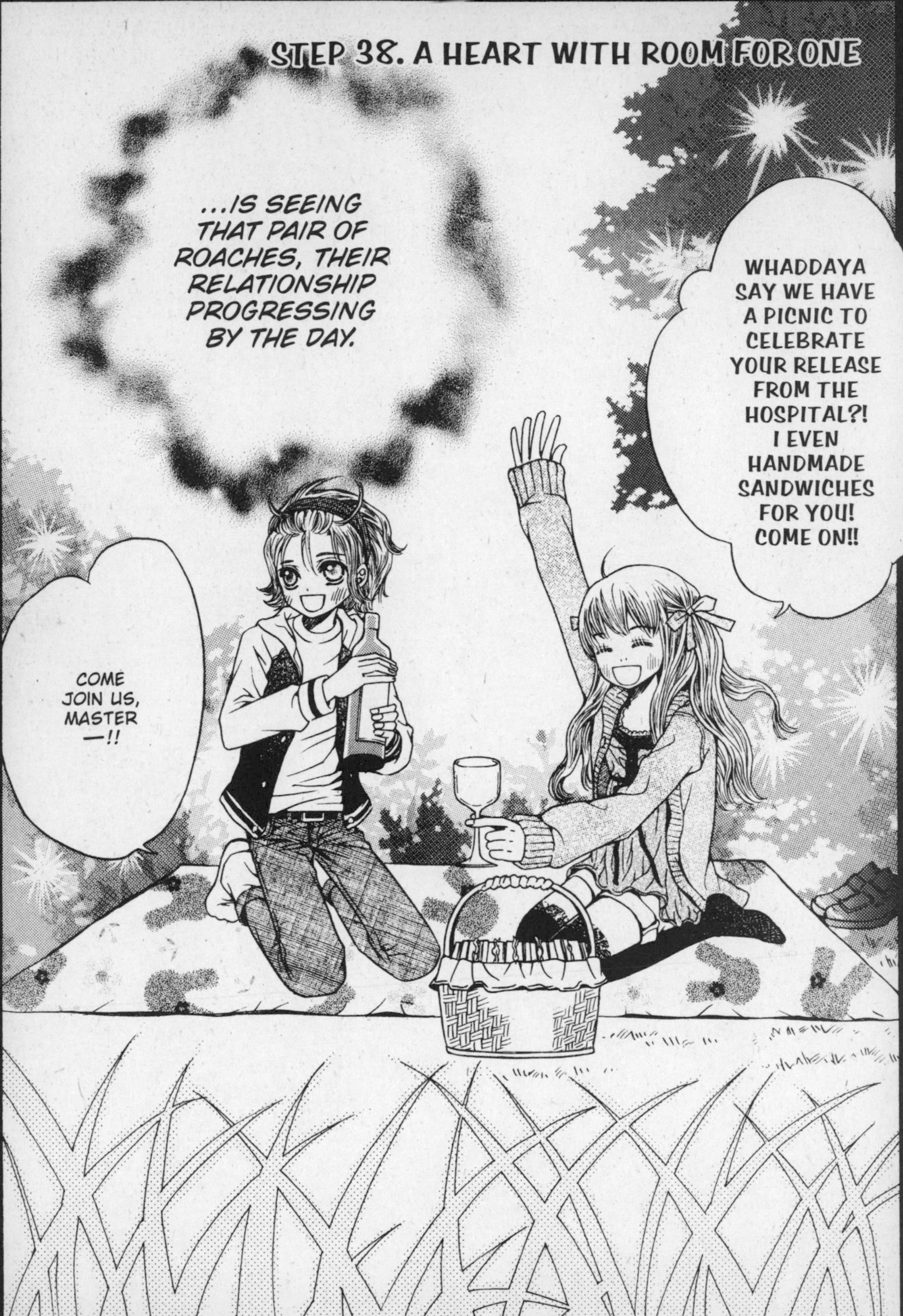
STEP 38. A HEART WITH ROOM FOR ONE
WHADDAYA SAY WE HAVE A PICNIC TO CELEBRATE YOUR RELEASE FROM THE HOSPITAL?! I EVEN HANDMADE SANDWICHES FOR YOU! COME ON!!
...IS SEEING THAT PAIR OF ROACHES, THEIR RELATIONSHIP PROGRESSING BY THE DAY.
COME JOIN US, MASTER —!!

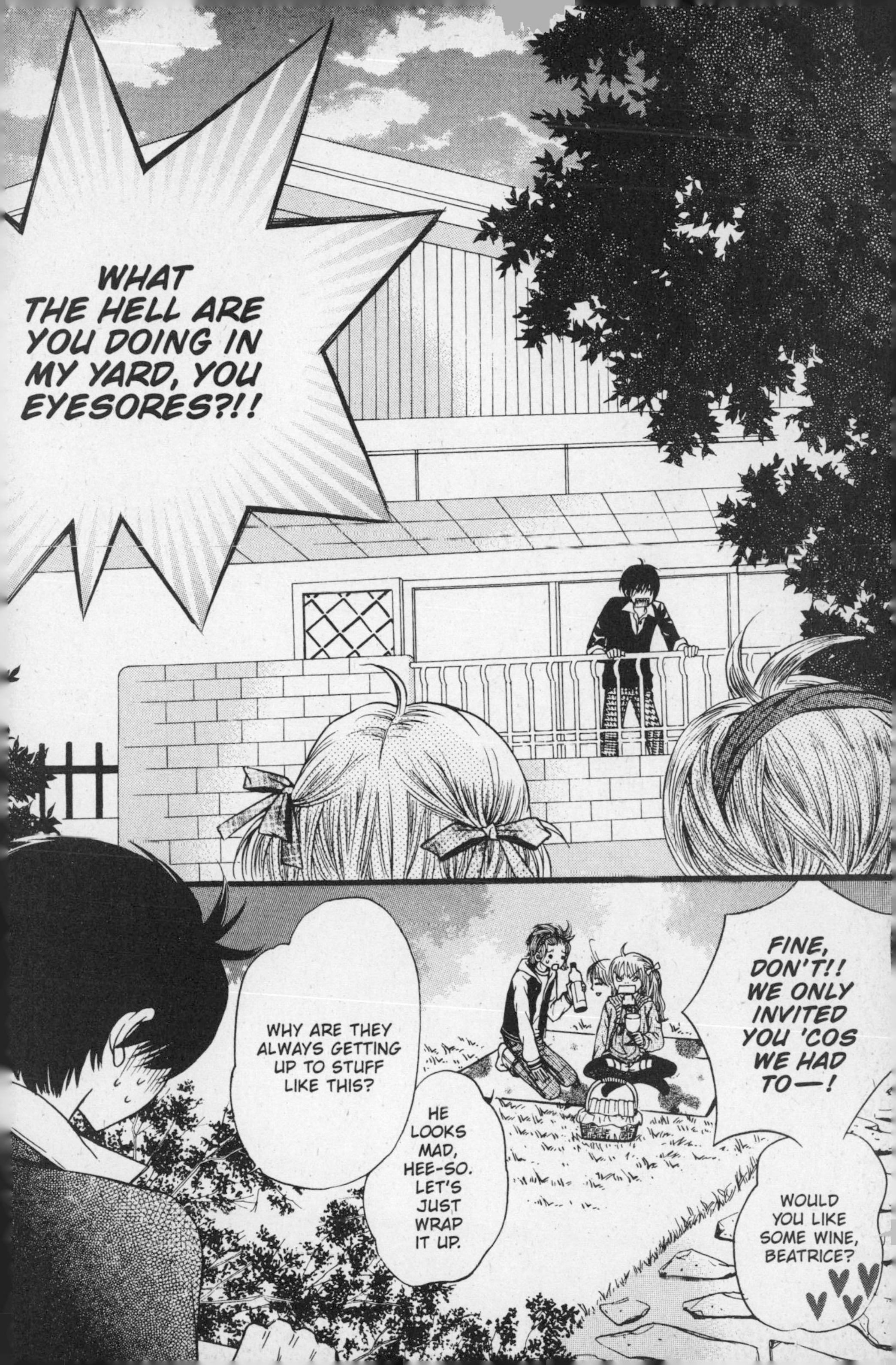
WHAT THE HELL ARE YOU DOING IN MY YARD, YOU EYESORES?!!
FINE, DON'T!! WE ONLY INVITED YOU 'COS WE HAD TO—!
WOULD YOU LIKE SOME WINE, BEATRICE?
HE LOOKS MAD, HEE-SO. LET'S JUST WRAP IT UP.
WHY ARE THEY ALWAYS GETTING UP TO STUFF LIKE THIS?

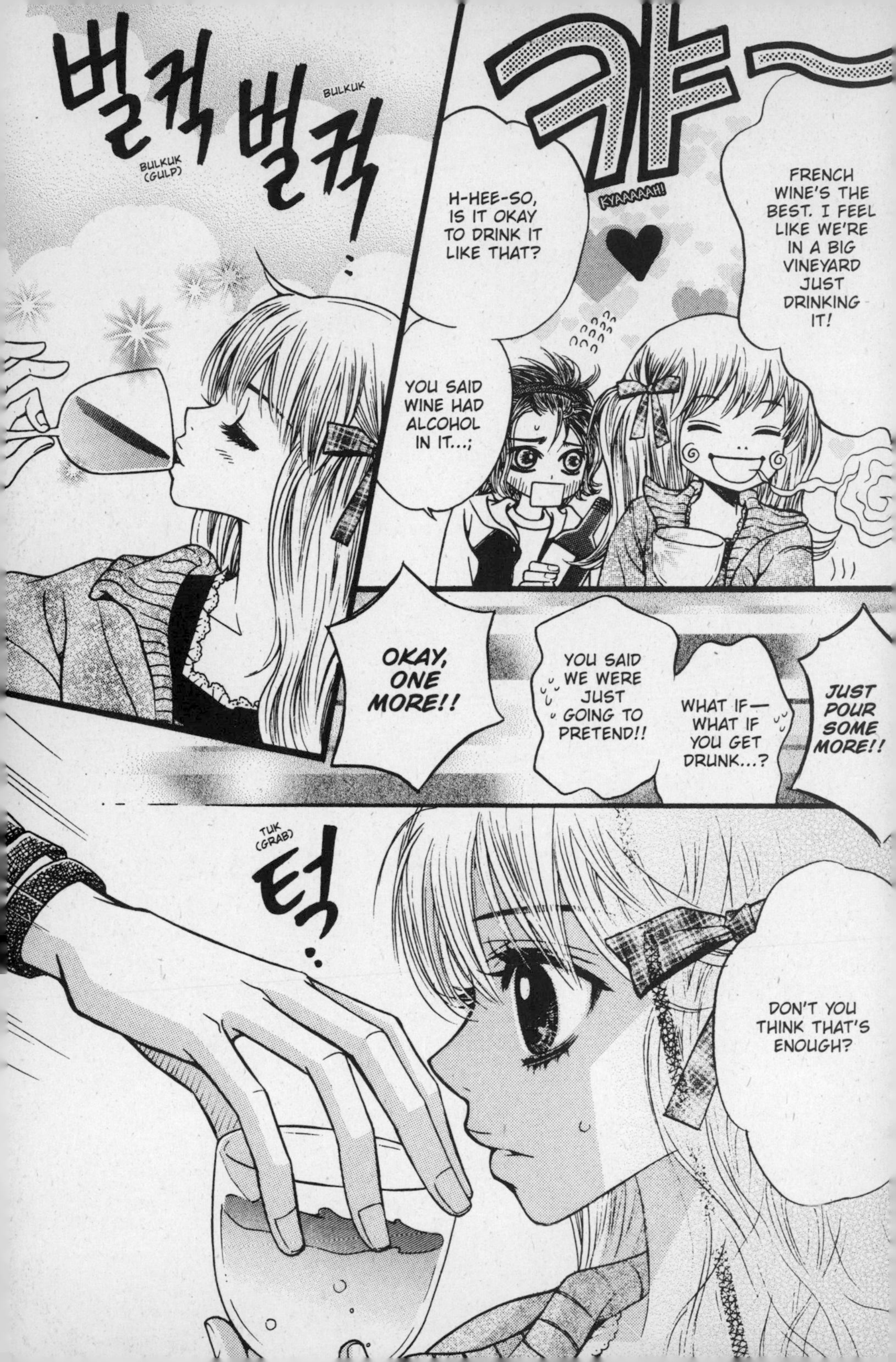

벌컥 벌컥
BULKUK
BULKUK (GULP)
카~
KYAAAAAH!
H-HEE-SO, IS IT OKAY TO DRINK IT LIKE THAT?
FRENCH WINE'S THE BEST. I FEEL LIKE WE'RE IN A BIG VINEYARD JUST DRINKING IT!
YOU SAID WINE HAD ALCOHOL IN IT...;
OKAY, ONE MORE!!
YOU SAID WE WERE JUST GOING TO PRETEND!!
WHAT IF— WHAT IF YOU GET DRUNK...?
JUST POUR SOME MORE!!
턱
TUK (GRAB)
DON'T YOU THINK THAT'S ENOUGH?

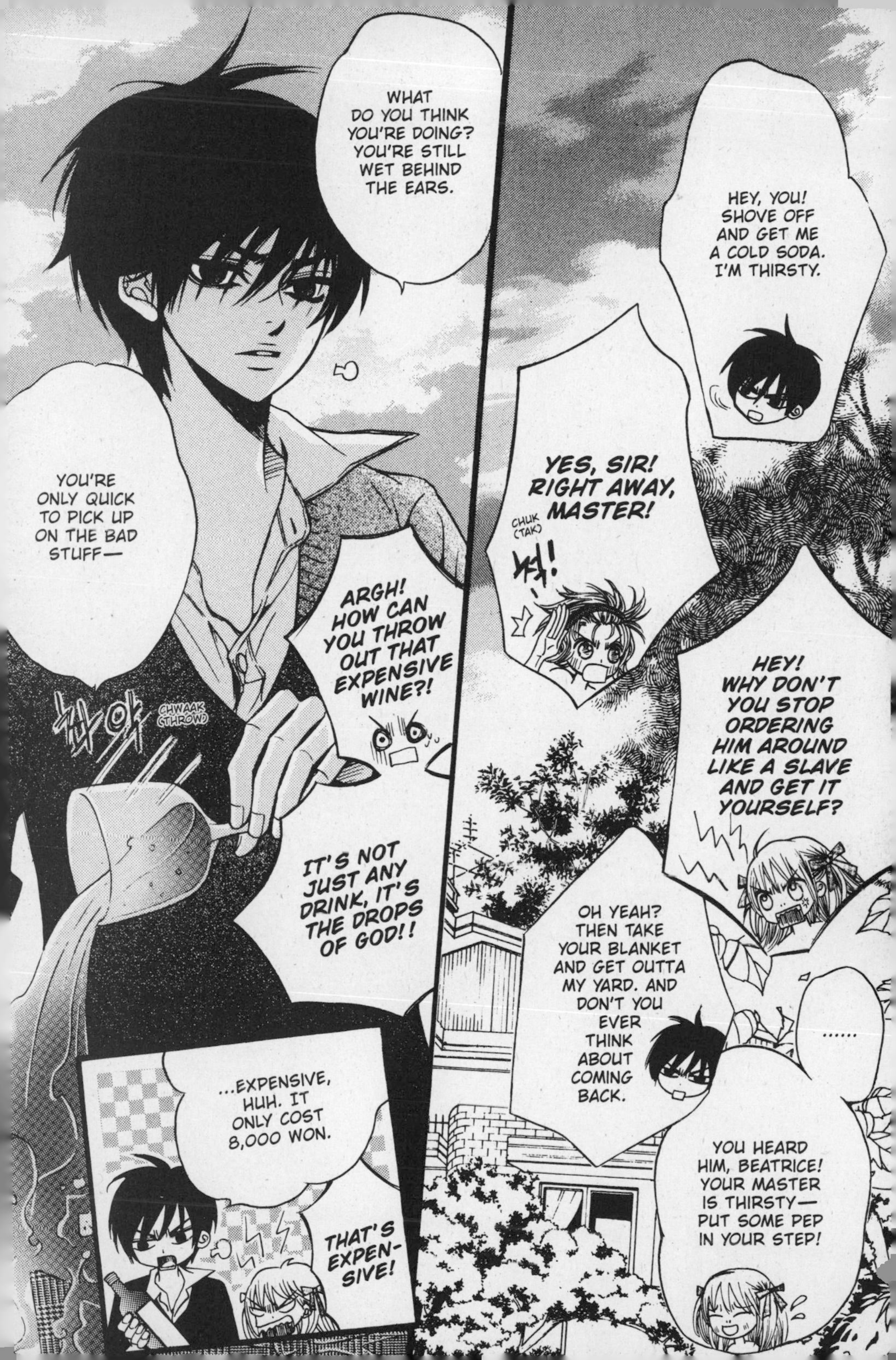
WHAT DO YOU THINK YOU'RE DOING? YOU'RE STILL WET BEHIND THE EARS.
YOU'RE ONLY QUICK TO PICK UP ON THE BAD STUFF—
ARGH! HOW CAN YOU THROW OUT THAT EXPENSIVE WINE?!
CHWAAK (THROW)
IT'S NOT JUST ANY DRINK, IT'S THE DROPS OF GOD!!
...EXPENSIVE, HUH. IT ONLY COST 8,000 WON.
THAT'S EXPEN-SIVE!
HEY, YOU! SHOVE OFF AND GET ME A COLD SODA. I'M THIRSTY.
YES, SIR! RIGHT AWAY, MASTER!
CHUK (TAK)
HEY! WHY DON'T YOU STOP ORDERING HIM AROUND LIKE A SLAVE AND GET IT YOURSELF?
OH YEAH? THEN TAKE YOUR BLANKET AND GET OUTTA MY YARD. AND DON'T YOU EVER THINK ABOUT COMING BACK.
......
YOU HEARD HIM, BEATRICE! YOUR MASTER IS THIRSTY— PUT SOME PEP IN YOUR STEP!

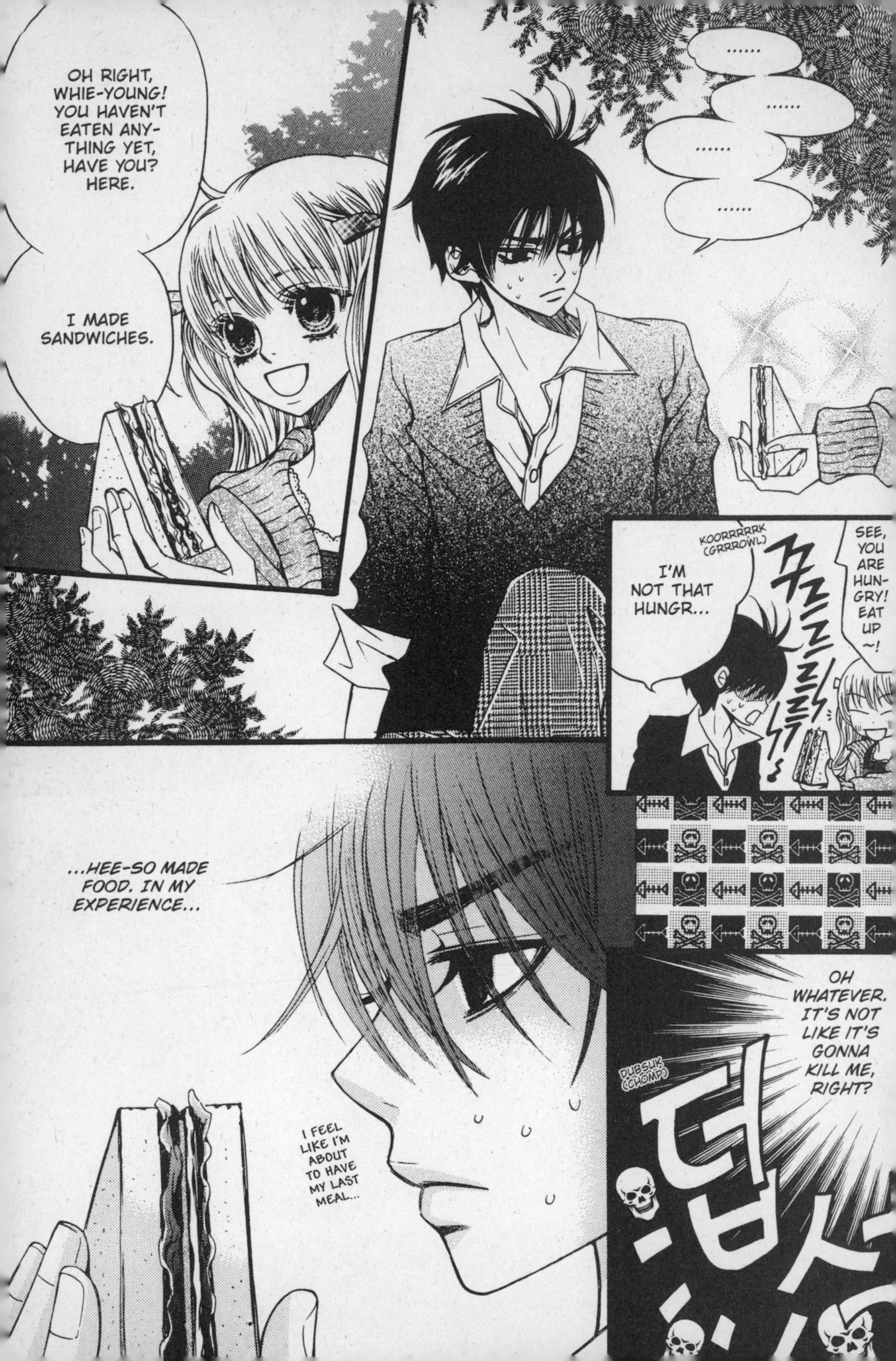
OH RIGHT, WHIE-YOUNG! YOU HAVEN'T EATEN ANY-THING YET, HAVE YOU? HERE.
I MADE SANDWICHES.
......
......
......
......
KOORRRRRK (GRRROWL)
I'M NOT THAT HUNGR...
SEE, YOU ARE HUN-GRY! EAT UP ~!
...HEE-SO MADE FOOD. IN MY EXPERIENCE...
I FEEL LIKE I'M ABOUT TO HAVE MY LAST MEAL...
OH WHATEVER. IT'S NOT LIKE IT'S GONNA KILL ME, RIGHT?
DUBSUK (CHOMP)

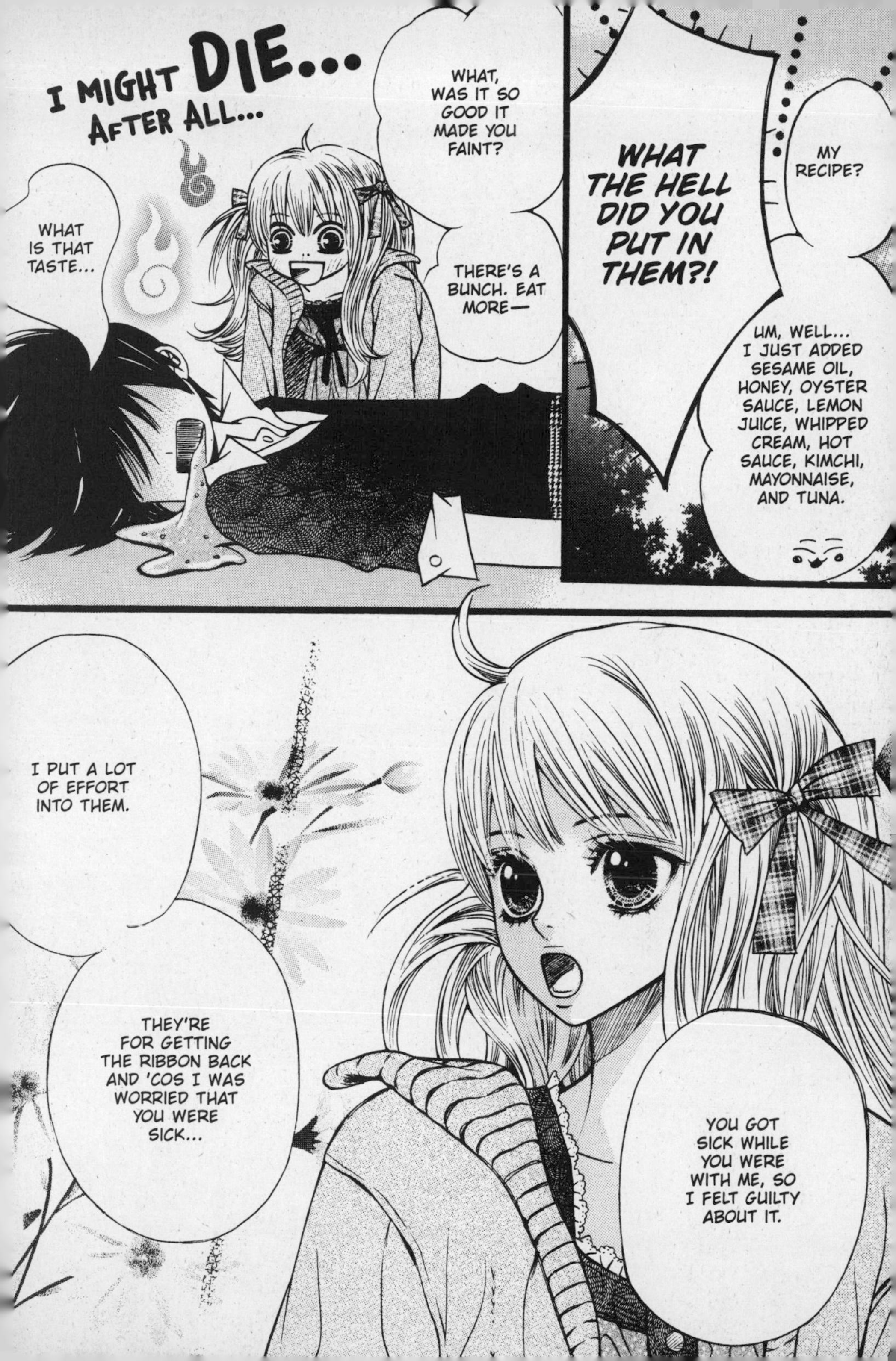
WHAT THE HELL DID YOU PUT IN THEM?!
MY RECIPE?
UM, WELL... I JUST ADDED SESAME OIL, HONEY, OYSTER SAUCE, LEMON JUICE, WHIPPED CREAM, HOT SAUCE, KIMCHI, MAYONNAISE, AND TUNA.
WHAT IS THAT TASTE...
I MIGHT DIE... AFTER ALL...
WHAT, WAS IT SO GOOD IT MADE YOU FAINT?
THERE'S A BUNCH. EAT MORE—
YOU GOT SICK WHILE YOU WERE WITH ME, SO I FELT GUILTY ABOUT IT.
THEY'RE FOR GETTING THE RIBBON BACK AND 'COS I WAS WORRIED THAT YOU WERE SICK...
I PUT A LOT OF EFFORT INTO THEM.

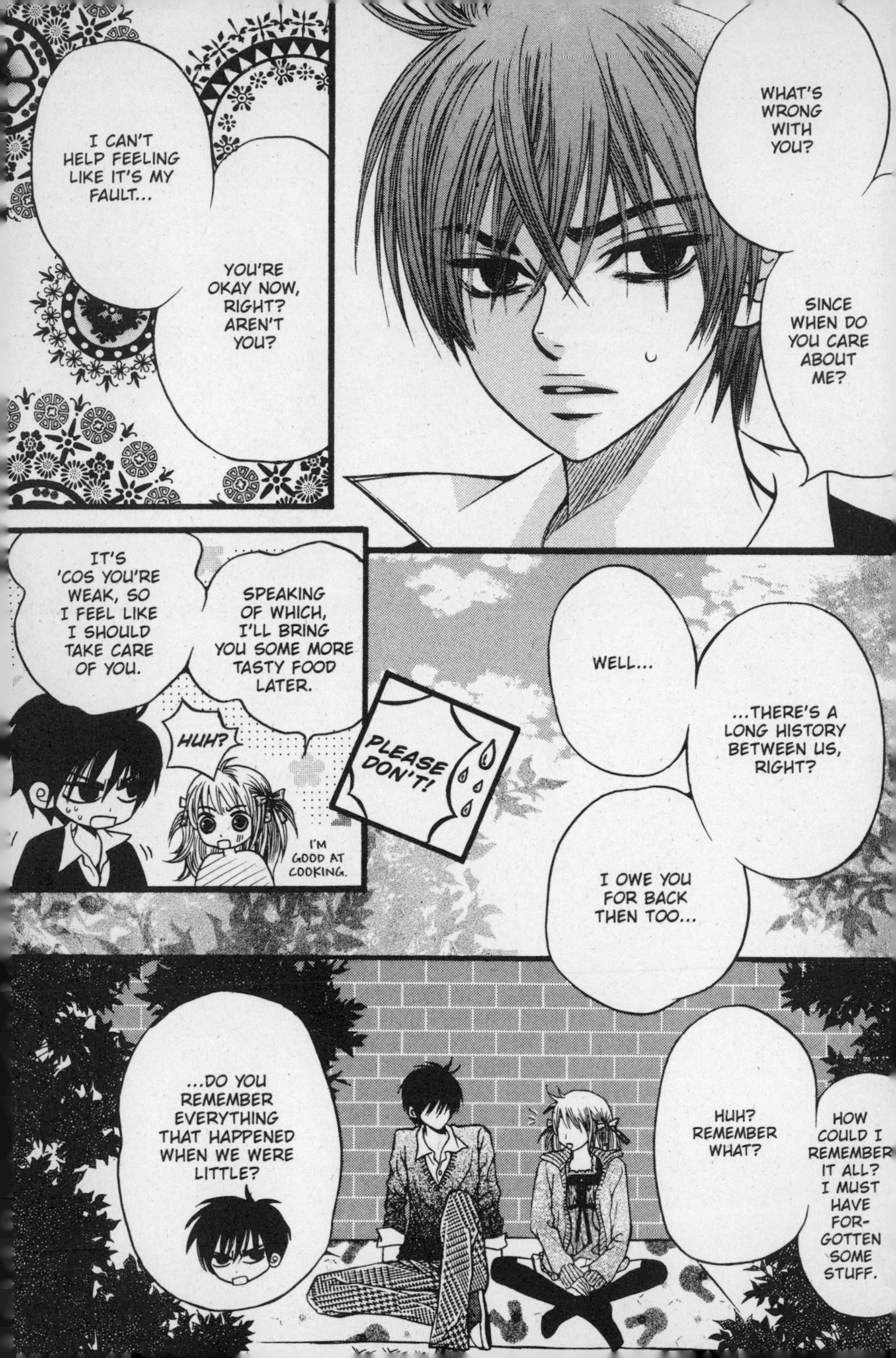
WHAT'S WRONG WITH YOU?
SINCE WHEN DO YOU CARE ABOUT ME?
I CAN'T HELP FEELING LIKE IT'S MY FAULT...
YOU'RE OKAY NOW, RIGHT? AREN'T YOU?
WELL...
...THERE'S A LONG HISTORY BETWEEN US, RIGHT?
IT'S 'COS YOU'RE WEAK, SO I FEEL LIKE I SHOULD TAKE CARE OF YOU.
SPEAKING OF WHICH, I'LL BRING YOU SOME MORE TASTY FOOD LATER.
HUH?
PLEASE DON'T!
I'M GOOD AT COOKING.
I OWE YOU FOR BACK THEN TOO...
...DO YOU REMEMBER EVERYTHING THAT HAPPENED WHEN WE WERE LITTLE?
HUH? REMEMBER WHAT?
HOW COULD I REMEMBER IT ALL? I MUST HAVE FOR-GOTTEN SOME STUFF.

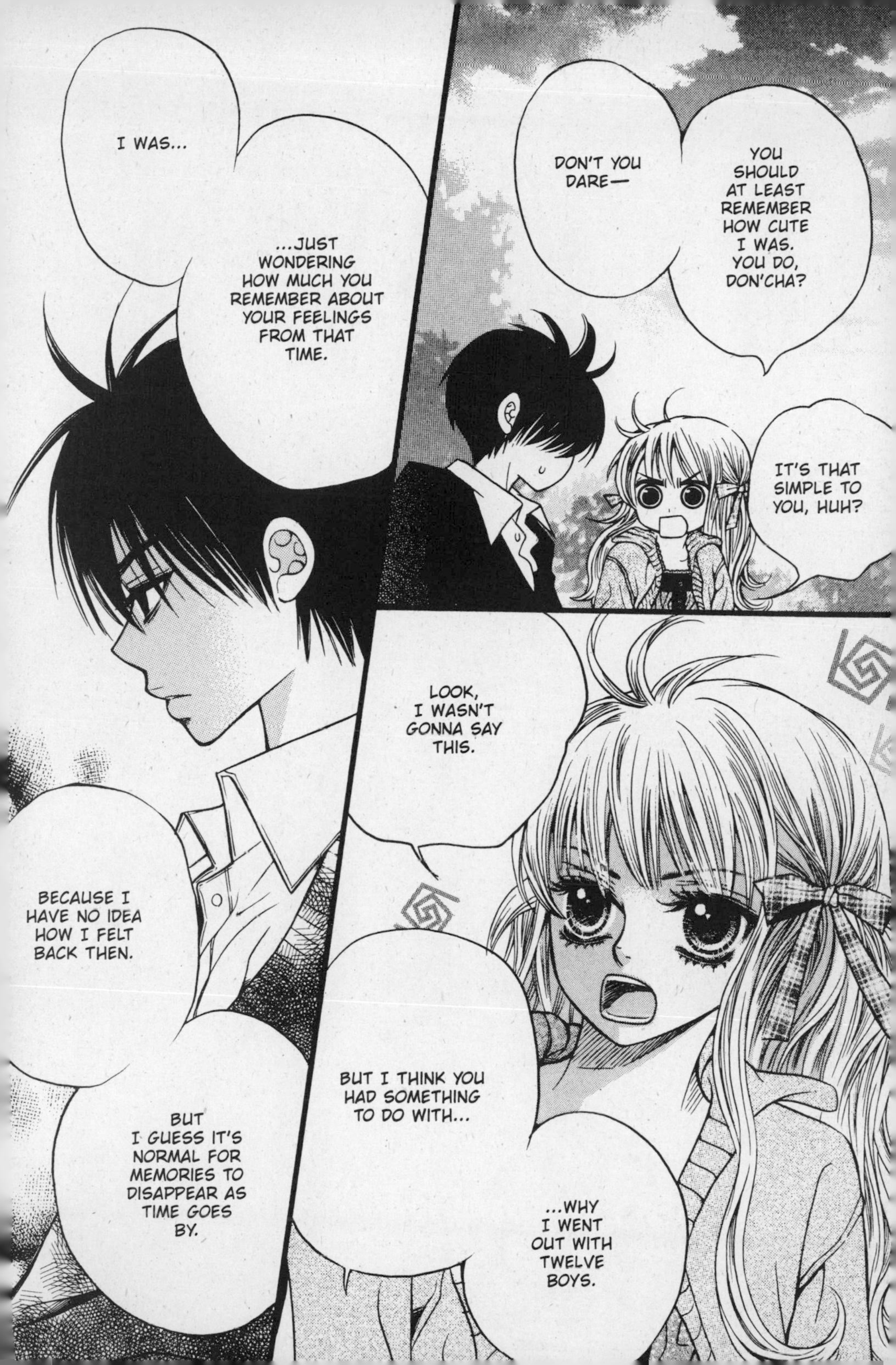
DON'T YOU DARE—
YOU SHOULD AT LEAST REMEMBER HOW CUTE I WAS. YOU DO, DON'CHA?
IT'S THAT SIMPLE TO YOU, HUH?
I WAS...
...JUST WONDERING HOW MUCH YOU REMEMBER ABOUT YOUR FEELINGS FROM THAT TIME.
BECAUSE I HAVE NO IDEA HOW I FELT BACK THEN.
BUT I GUESS IT'S NORMAL FOR MEMORIES TO DISAPPEAR AS TIME GOES BY.
LOOK, I WASN'T GONNA SAY THIS.
BUT I THINK YOU HAD SOMETHING TO DO WITH...
...WHY I WENT OUT WITH TWELVE BOYS.

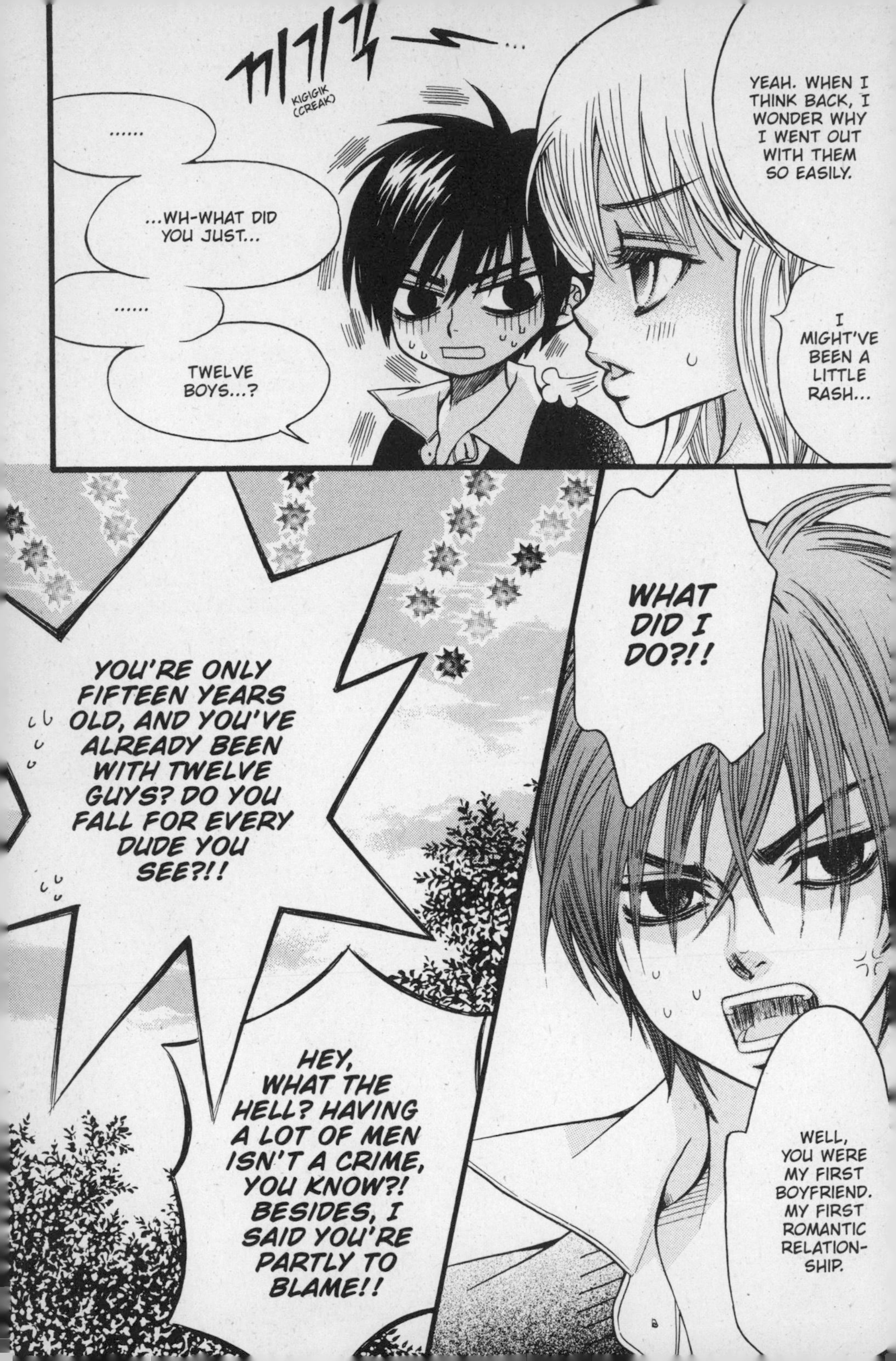
YEAH. WHEN I THINK BACK, I WONDER WHY I WENT OUT WITH THEM SO EASILY.
I MIGHT'VE BEEN A LITTLE RASH...
끼기긱
KIGIGIK (CREAK)
......
...WH-WHAT DID YOU JUST...
......
TWELVE BOYS...?
WHAT DID I DO?!!
YOU'RE ONLY FIFTEEN YEARS OLD, AND YOU'VE ALREADY BEEN WITH TWELVE GUYS? DO YOU FALL FOR EVERY DUDE YOU SEE?!!
HEY, WHAT THE HELL? HAVING A LOT OF MEN ISN'T A CRIME, YOU KNOW?! BESIDES, I SAID YOU'RE PARTLY TO BLAME!!
WELL, YOU WERE MY FIRST BOYFRIEND. MY FIRST ROMANTIC RELATION-SHIP.

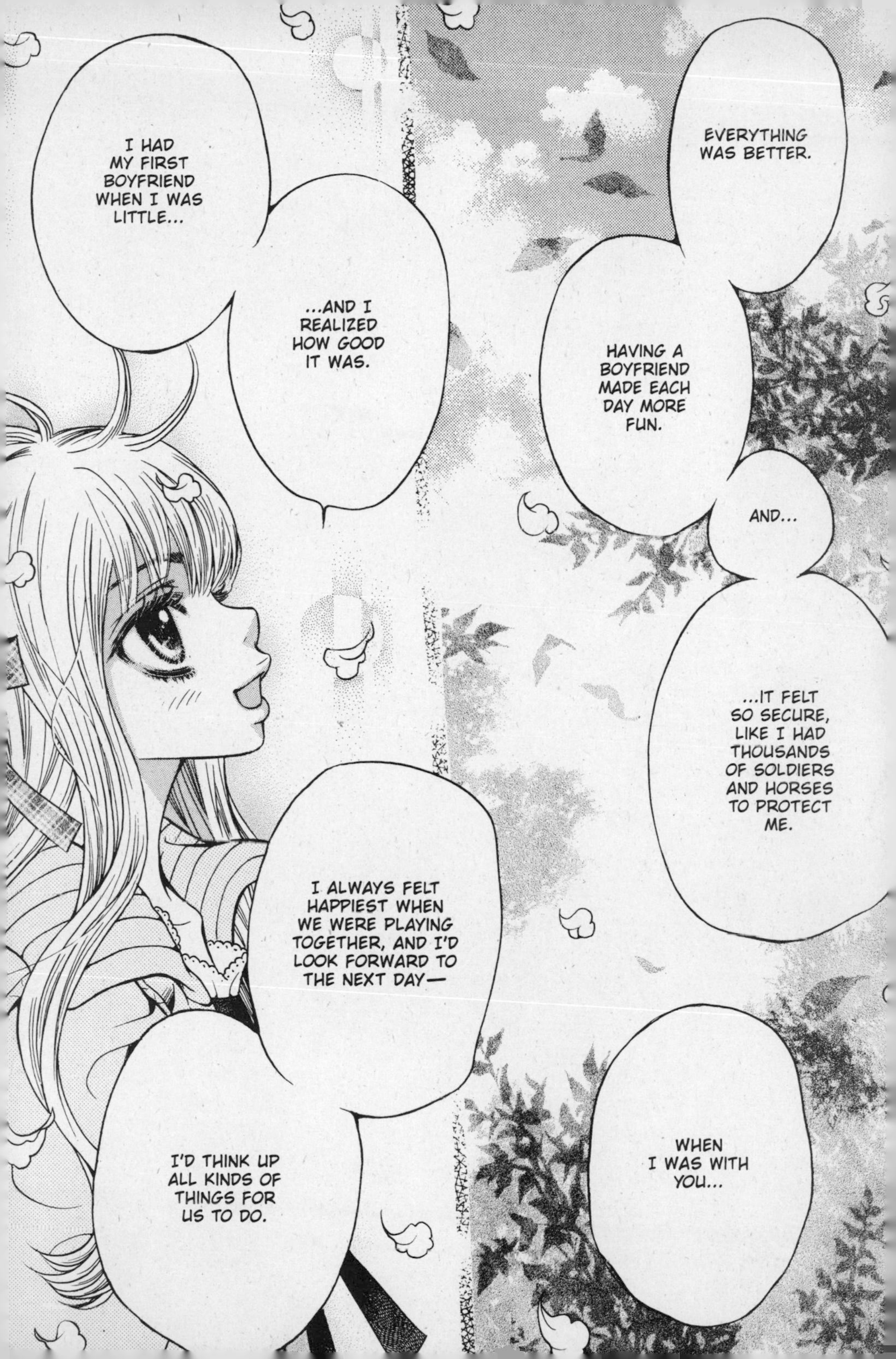
I HAD MY FIRST BOYFRIEND WHEN I WAS LITTLE...
...AND I REALIZED HOW GOOD IT WAS.
EVERYTHING WAS BETTER.
HAVING A BOYFRIEND MADE EACH DAY MORE FUN.
AND...
...IT FELT SO SECURE, LIKE I HAD THOUSANDS OF SOLDIERS AND HORSES TO PROTECT ME.
I ALWAYS FELT HAPPIEST WHEN WE WERE PLAYING TOGETHER, AND I'D LOOK FORWARD TO THE NEXT DAY—
I'D THINK UP ALL KINDS OF THINGS FOR US TO DO.
WHEN I WAS WITH YOU...

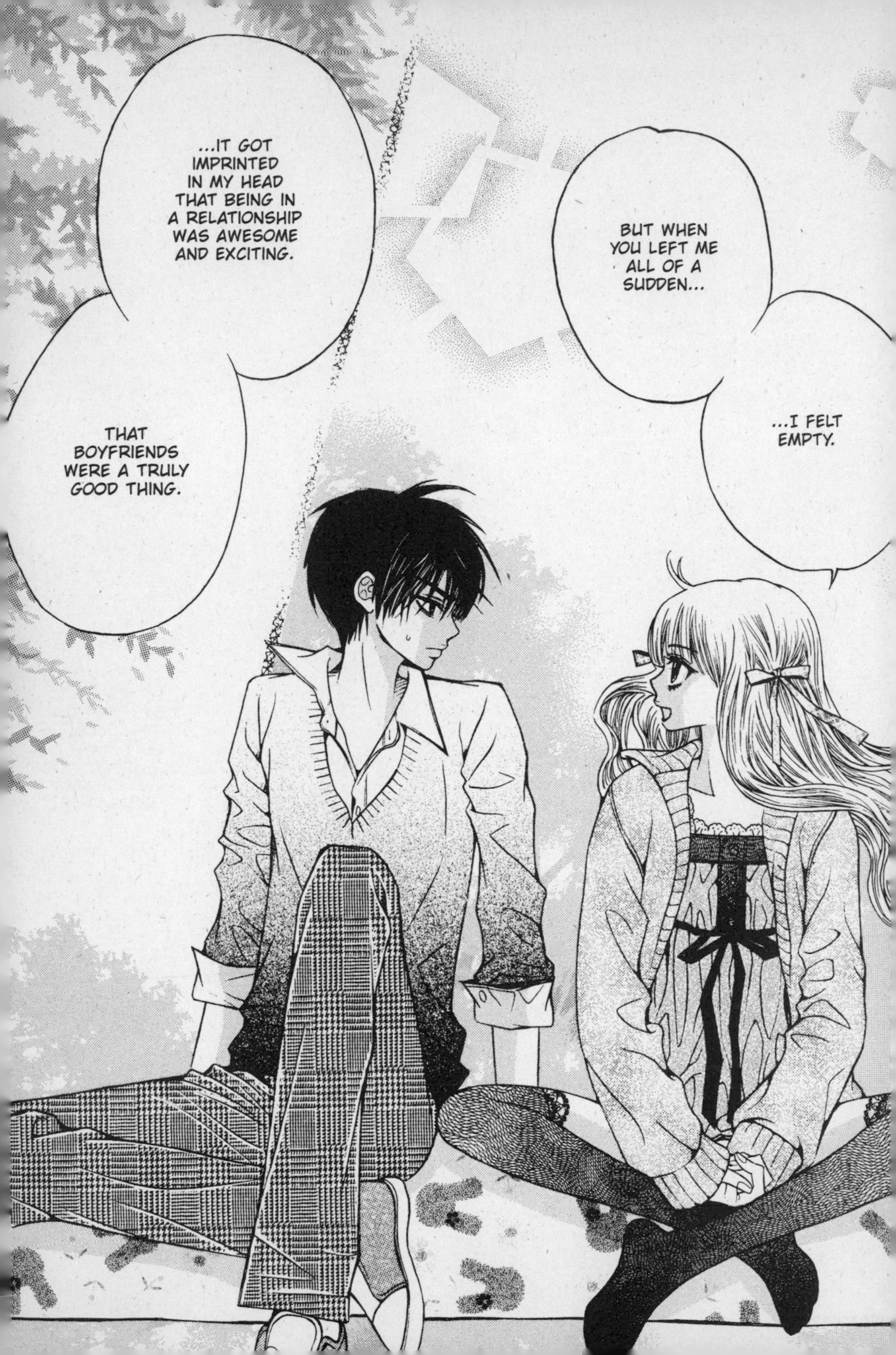
BUT WHEN YOU LEFT ME ALL OF A SUDDEN...
...I FELT EMPTY.
...IT GOT IMPRINTED IN MY HEAD THAT BEING IN A RELATIONSHIP WAS AWESOME AND EXCITING.
THAT BOYFRIENDS WERE A TRULY GOOD THING.

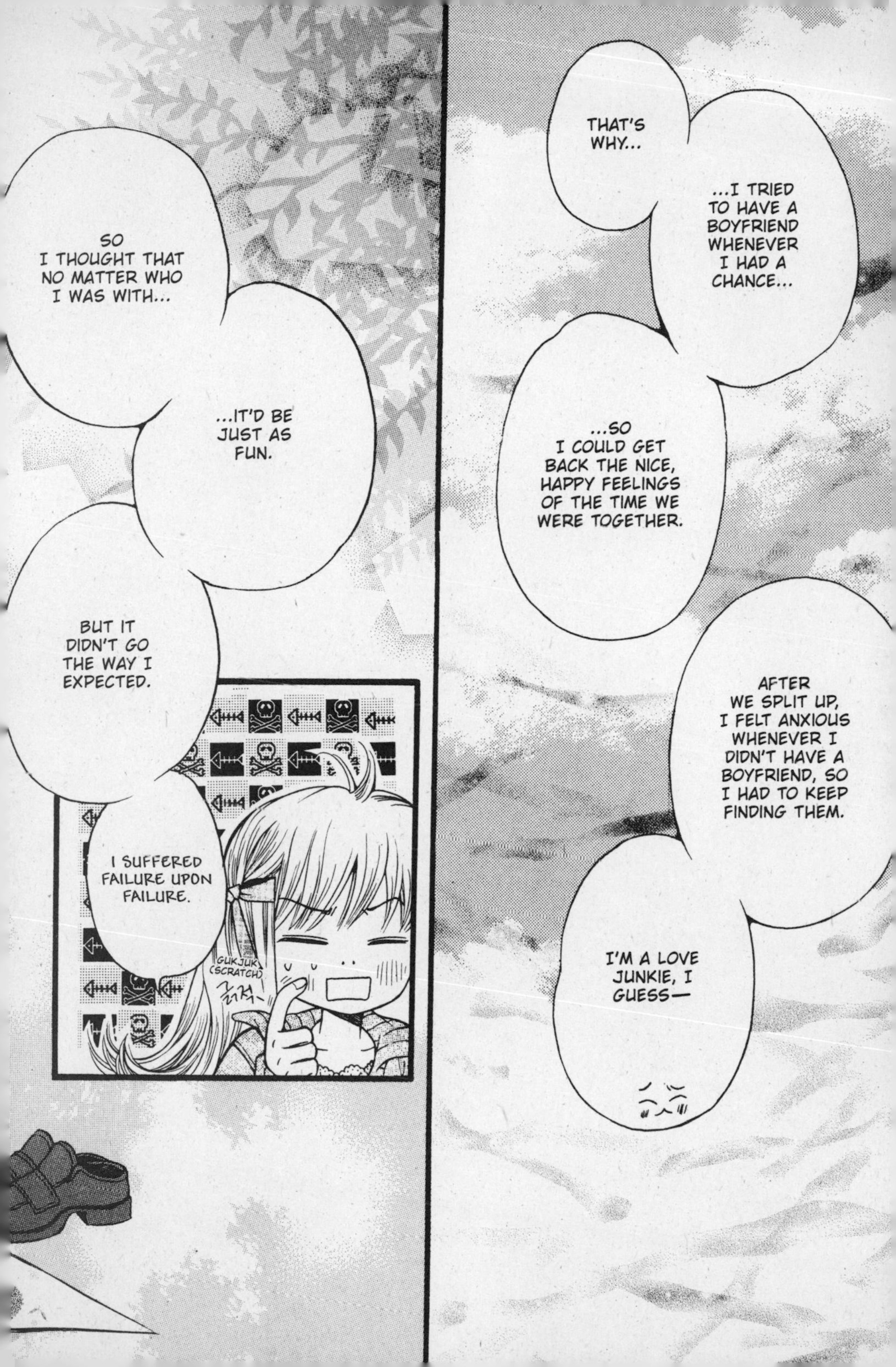

SO I THOUGHT THAT NO MATTER WHO I WAS WITH...
...IT'D BE JUST AS FUN.
BUT IT DIDN'T GO THE WAY I EXPECTED.
I SUFFERED FAILURE UPON FAILURE.
GUKJUK (SCRATCH)
THAT'S WHY...
...I TRIED TO HAVE A BOYFRIEND WHENEVER I HAD A CHANCE...
...SO I COULD GET BACK THE NICE, HAPPY FEELINGS OF THE TIME WE WERE TOGETHER.
AFTER WE SPLIT UP, I FELT ANXIOUS WHENEVER I DIDN'T HAVE A BOYFRIEND, SO I HAD TO KEEP FINDING THEM.
I'M A LOVE JUNKIE, I GUESS—

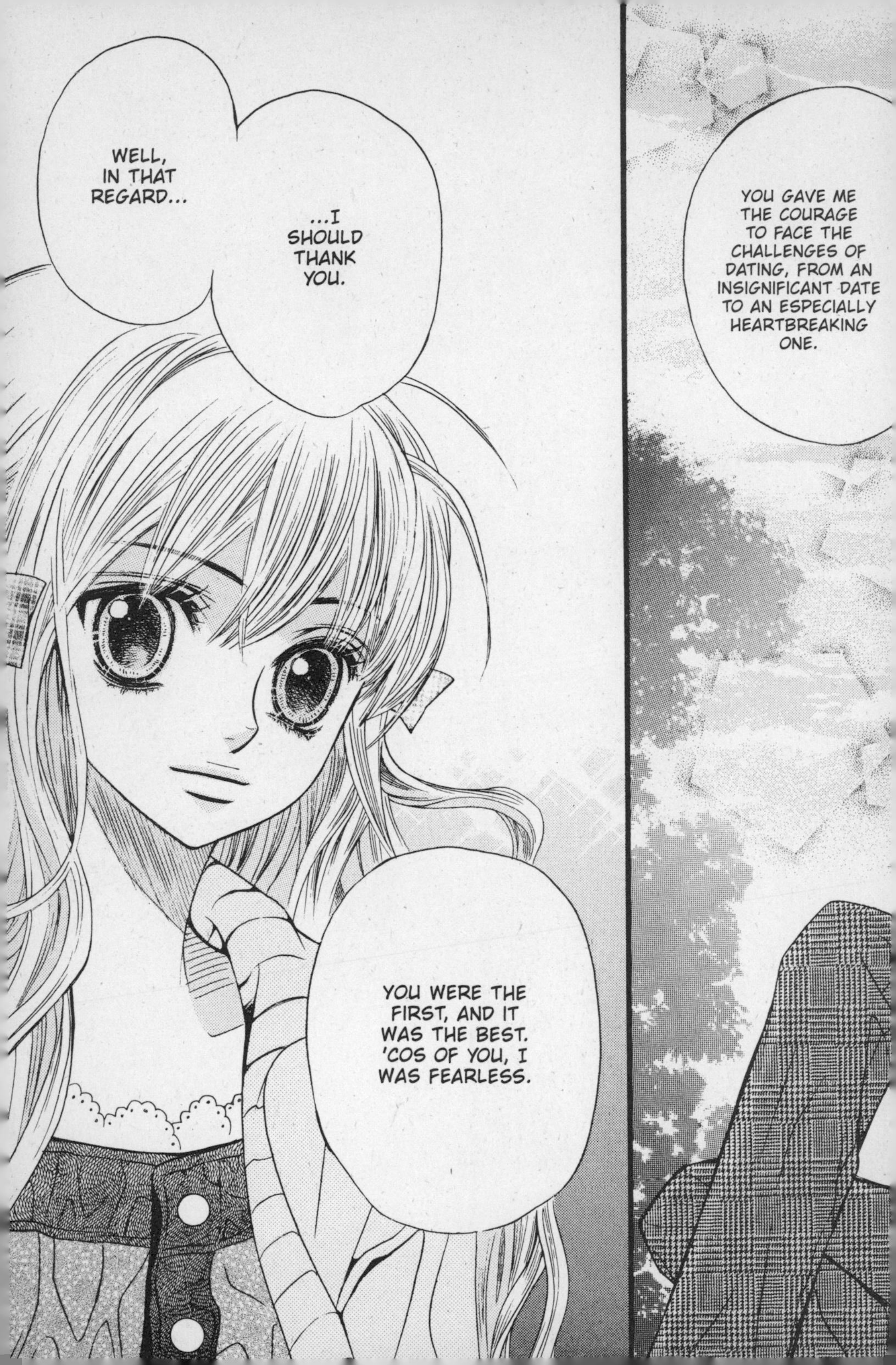
YOU GAVE ME THE COURAGE TO FACE THE CHALLENGES OF DATING, FROM AN INSIGNIFICANT DATE TO AN ESPECIALLY HEARTBREAKING ONE.
WELL, IN THAT REGARD...
...I SHOULD THANK YOU.
YOU WERE THE FIRST, AND IT WAS THE BEST. 'COS OF YOU, I WAS FEARLESS.

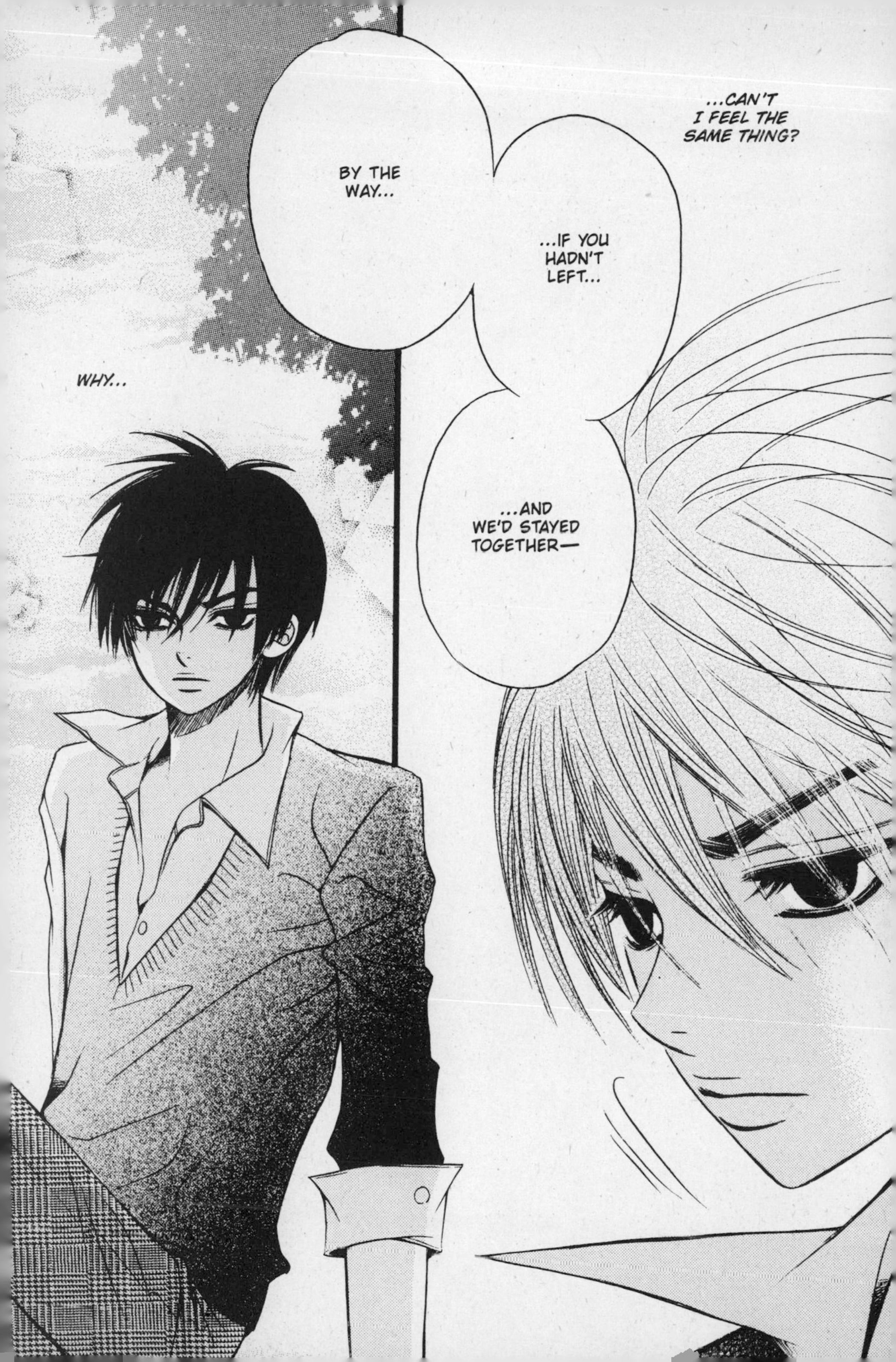
BY THE WAY...
...IF YOU HADN'T LEFT...
...AND WE'D STAYED TOGETHER—
WHY...
...CAN'T I FEEL THE SAME THING?

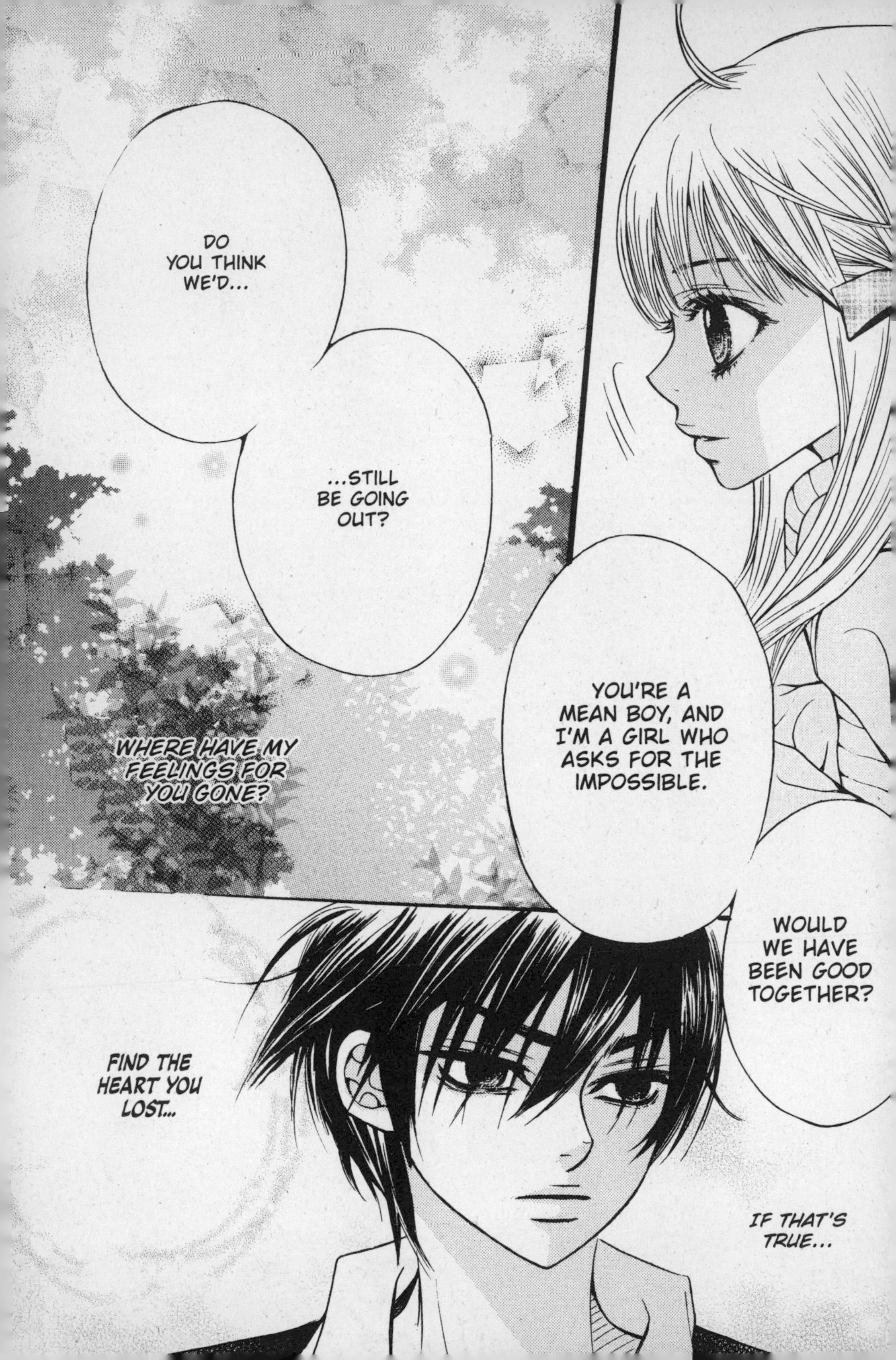
YOU'RE A MEAN BOY, AND I'M A GIRL WHO ASKS FOR THE IMPOSSIBLE.
WOULD WE HAVE BEEN GOOD TOGETHER?
DO YOU THINK WE'D...
...STILL BE GOING OUT?
WHERE HAVE MY FEELINGS FOR YOU GONE?
IF THAT'S TRUE...
FIND THE HEART YOU LOST...

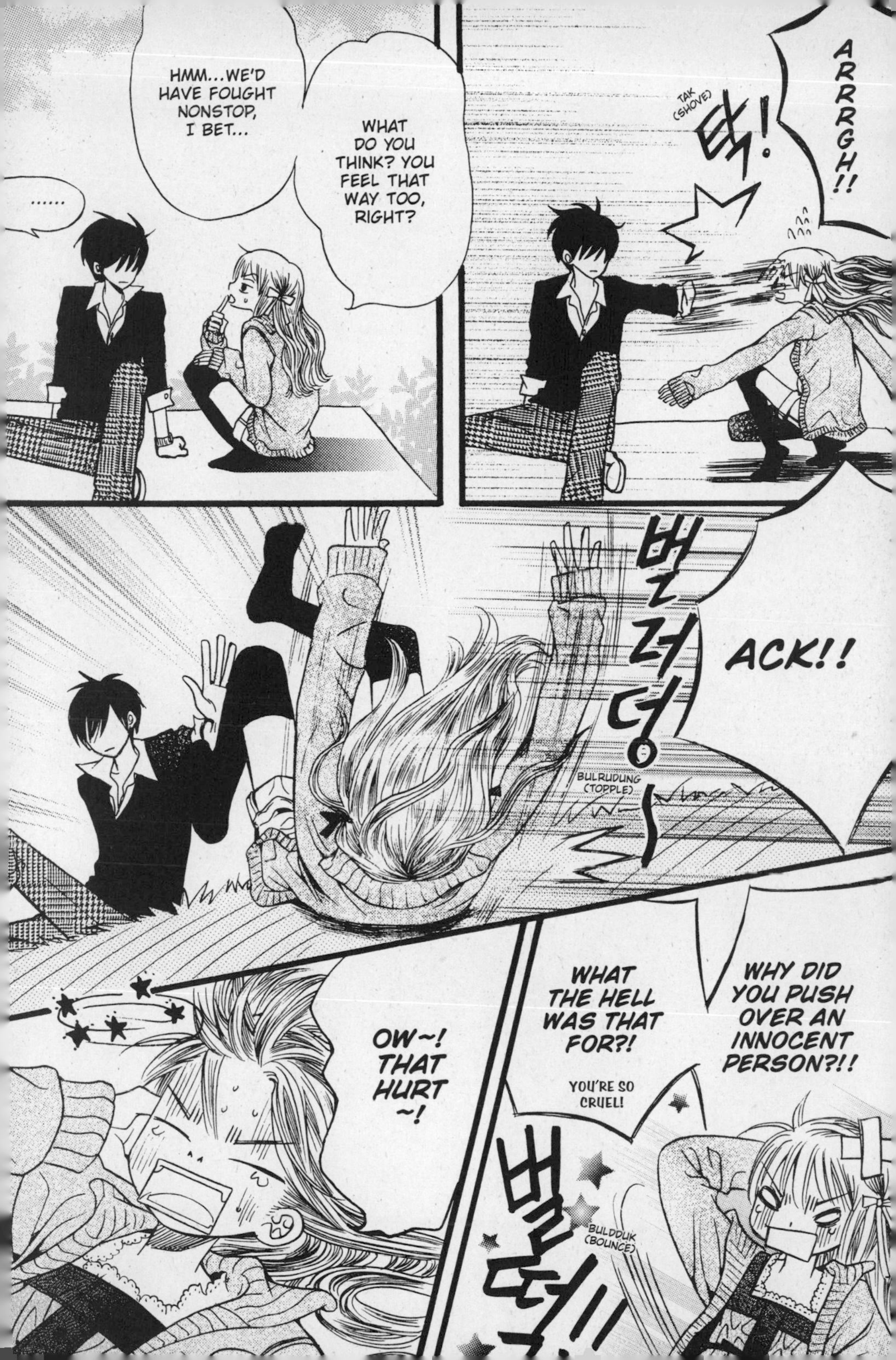
......
HMM...WE'D HAVE FOUGHT NONSTOP, I BET...
WHAT DO YOU THINK? YOU FEEL THAT WAY TOO, RIGHT?
ARRRGH!!
탁!
TAK (SHOVE)
벌러덩~
BULRUDUNG (TOPPLE)
ACK!!
OW~! THAT HURT~!
WHAT THE HELL WAS THAT FOR?!
WHY DID YOU PUSH OVER AN INNOCENT PERSON?!!
YOU'RE SO CRUEL!
벌떡!!
BULDDUK (BOUNCE)

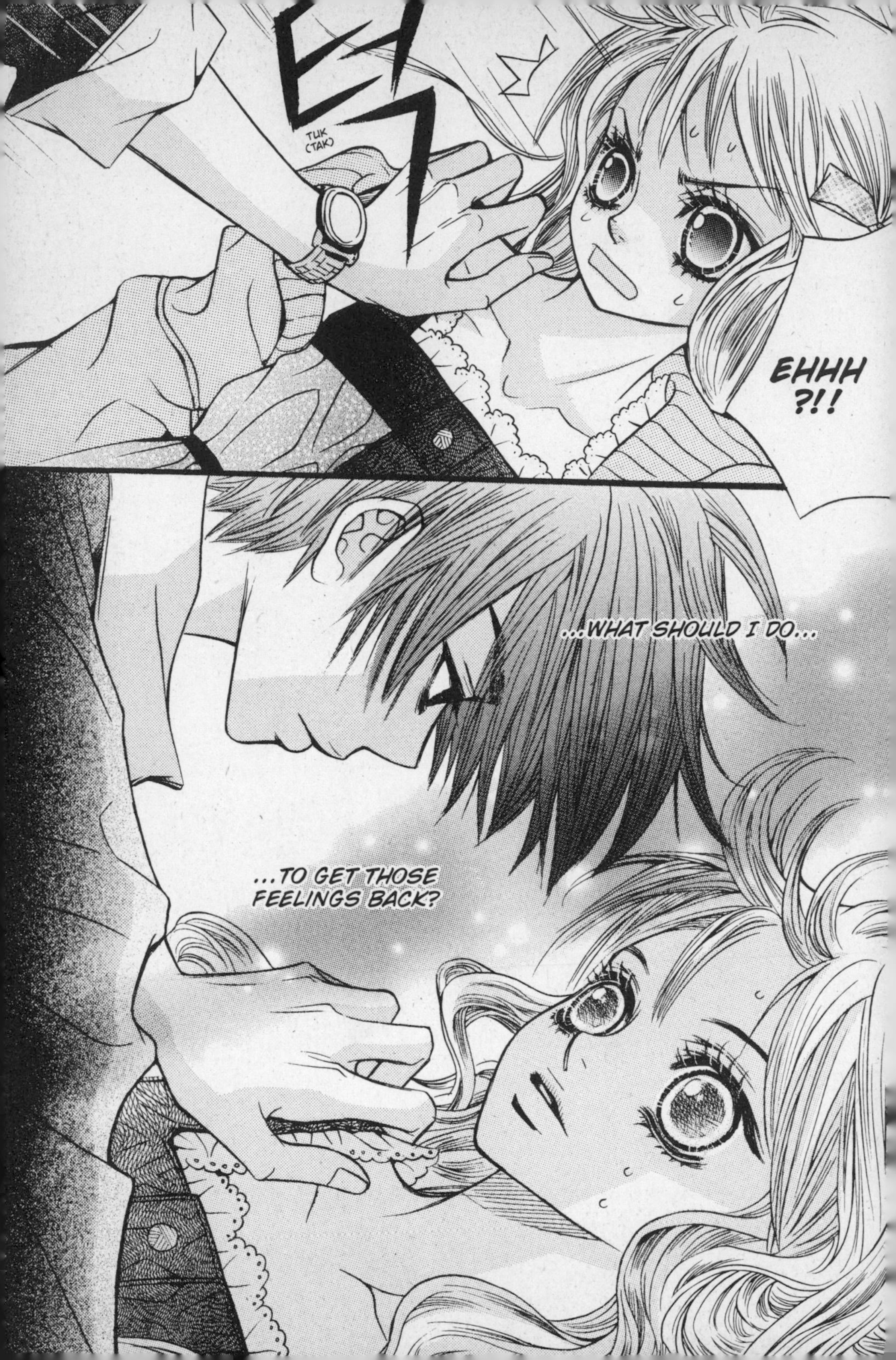

TUK (TAK)
EHHH ?!!
...WHAT SHOULD I DO...
...TO GET THOSE FEELINGS BACK?

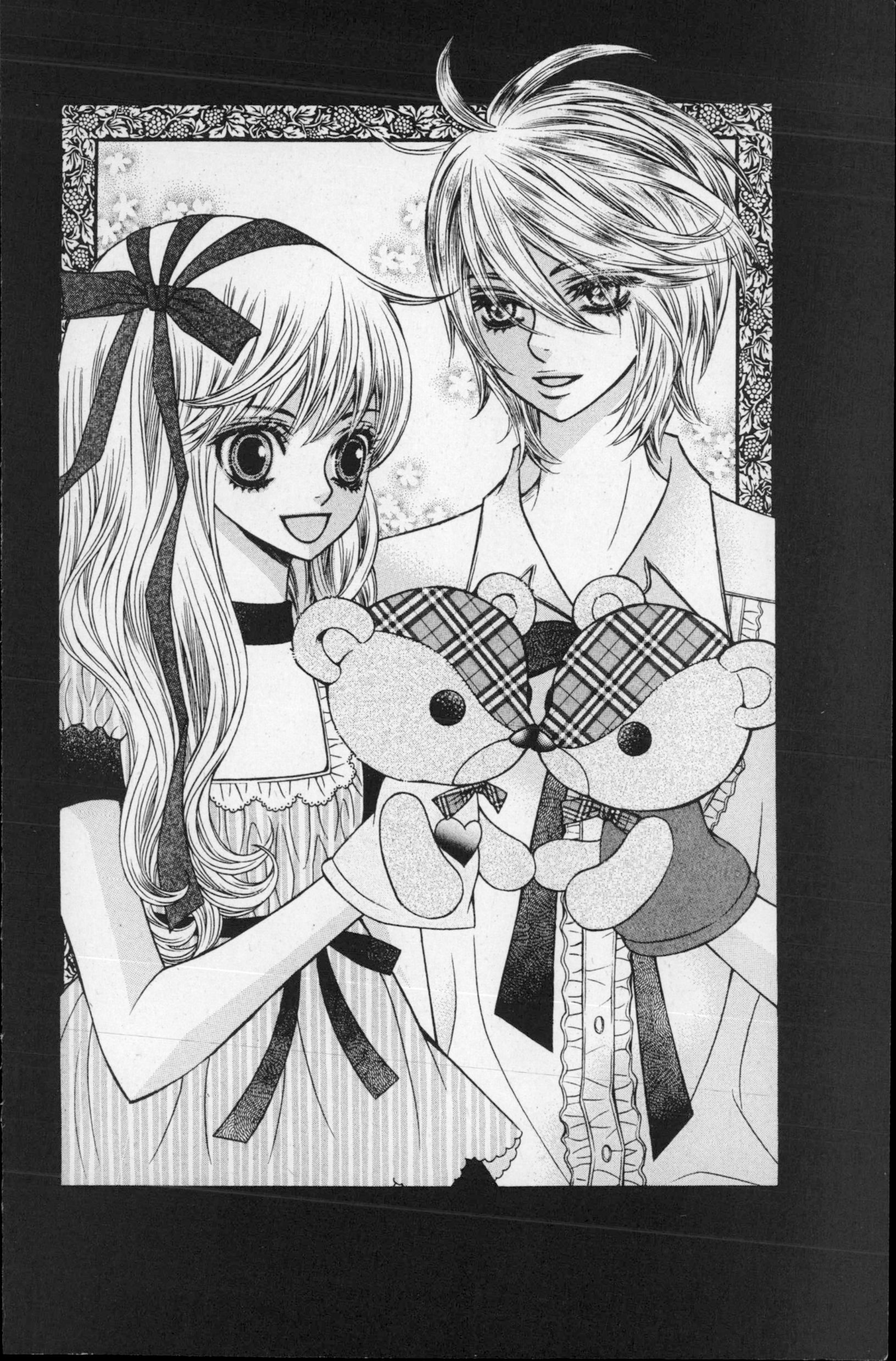

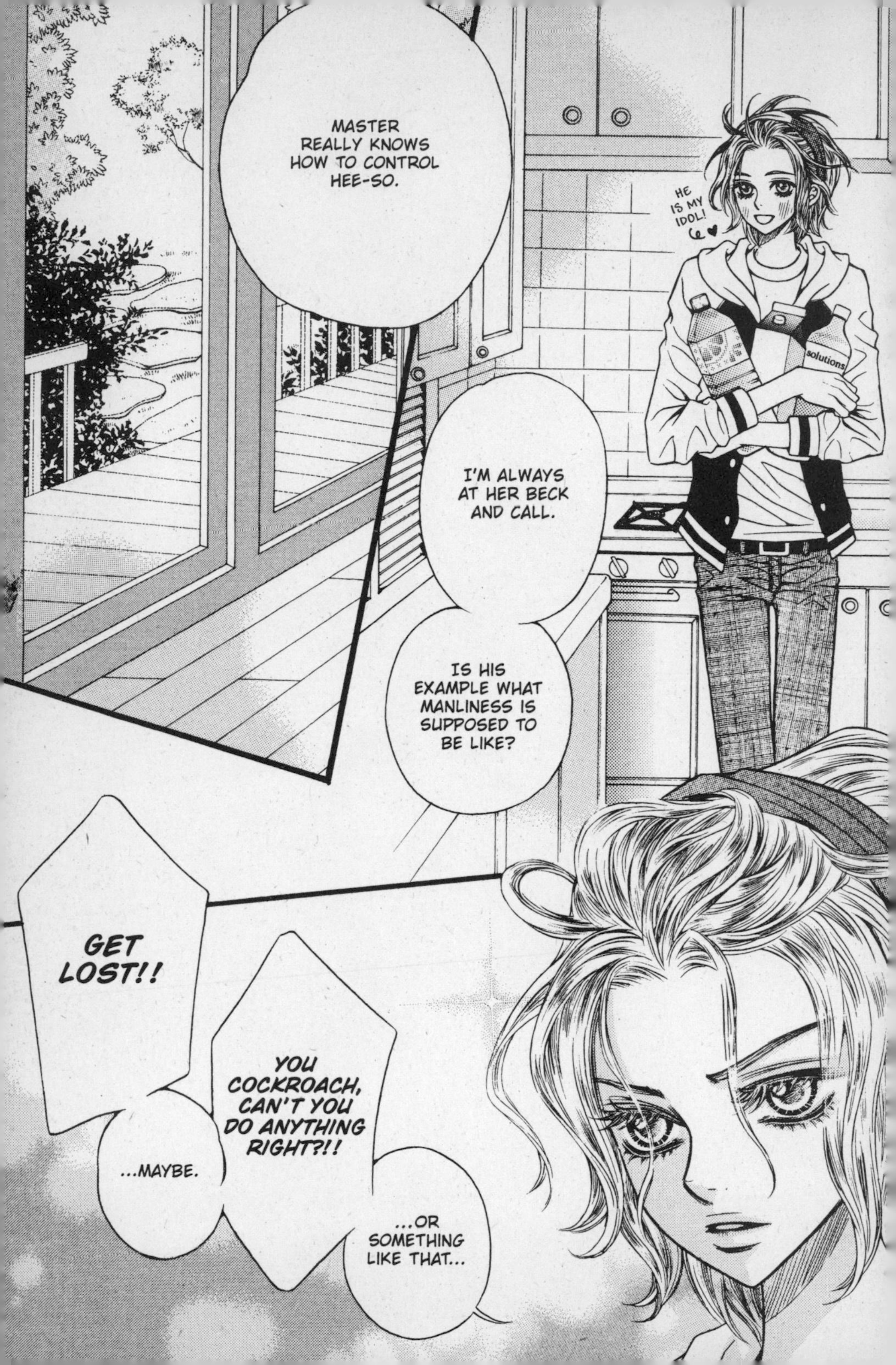
MASTER REALLY KNOWS HOW TO CONTROL HEE-SO.
HE IS MY IDOL!
I'M ALWAYS AT HER BECK AND CALL.
IS HIS EXAMPLE WHAT MANLINESS IS SUPPOSED TO BE LIKE?
solutions
GET LOST!!
YOU COCKROACH, CAN'T YOU DO ANYTHING RIGHT?!!
...MAYBE.
...OR SOMETHING LIKE THAT...

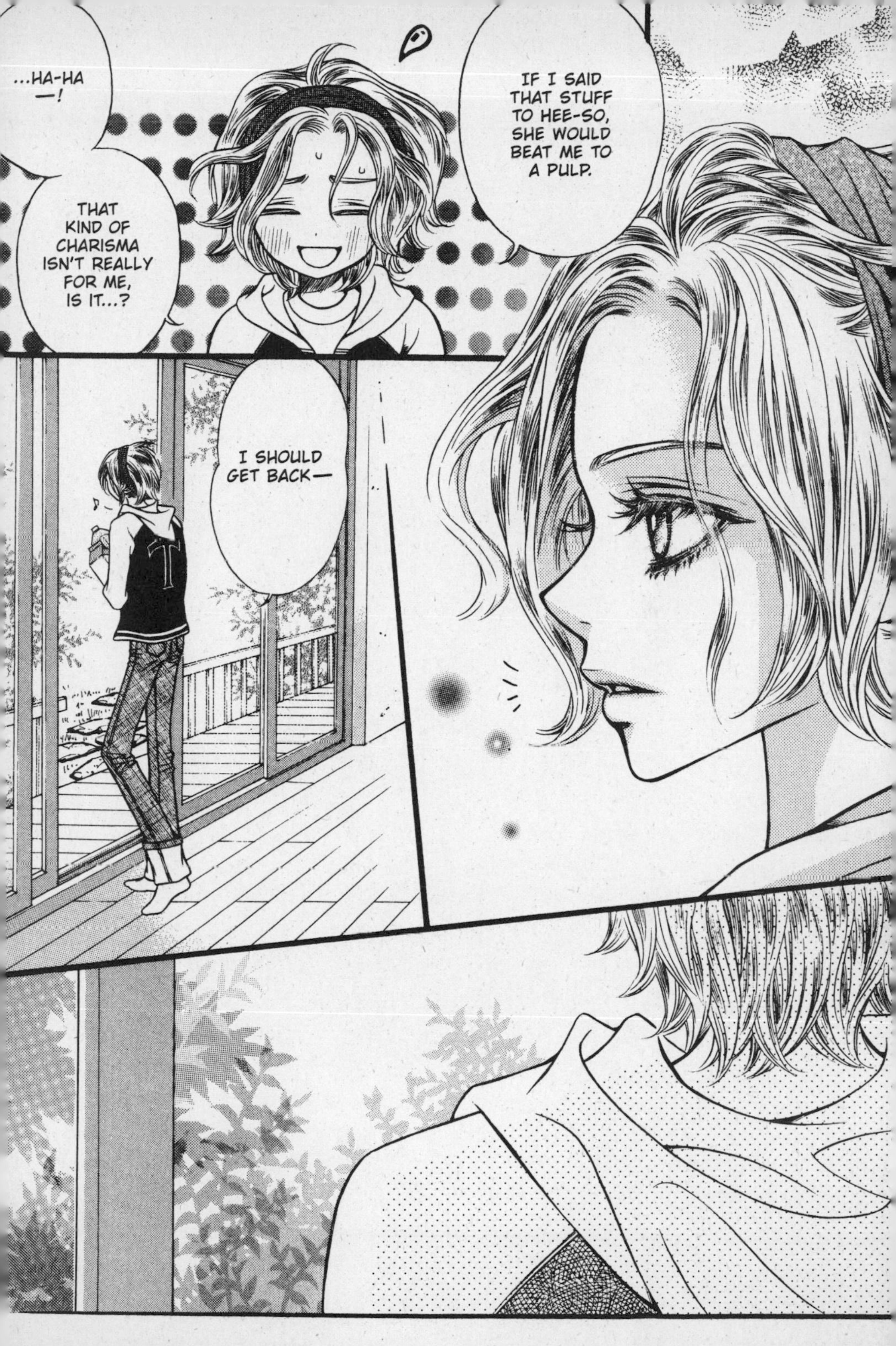
IF I SAID THAT STUFF TO HEE-SO, SHE WOULD BEAT ME TO A PULP.
...HA-HA—!
THAT KIND OF CHARISMA ISN'T REALLY FOR ME, IS IT...?
I SHOULD GET BACK—

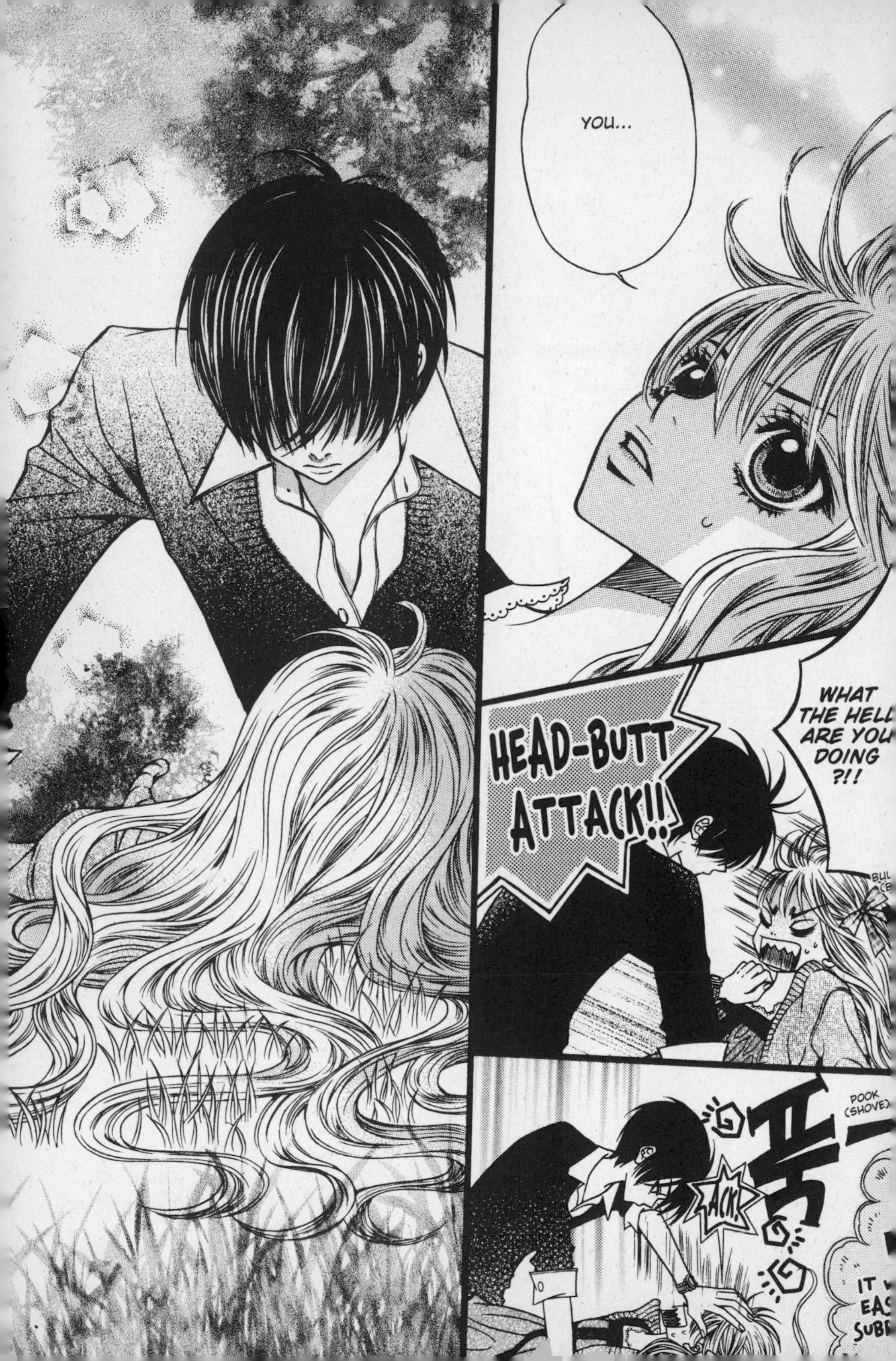
YOU...
WHAT THE HELL ARE YOU DOING ?!!
HEAD-BUTT ATTACK!!
POOK (SHOVE)
ACK!

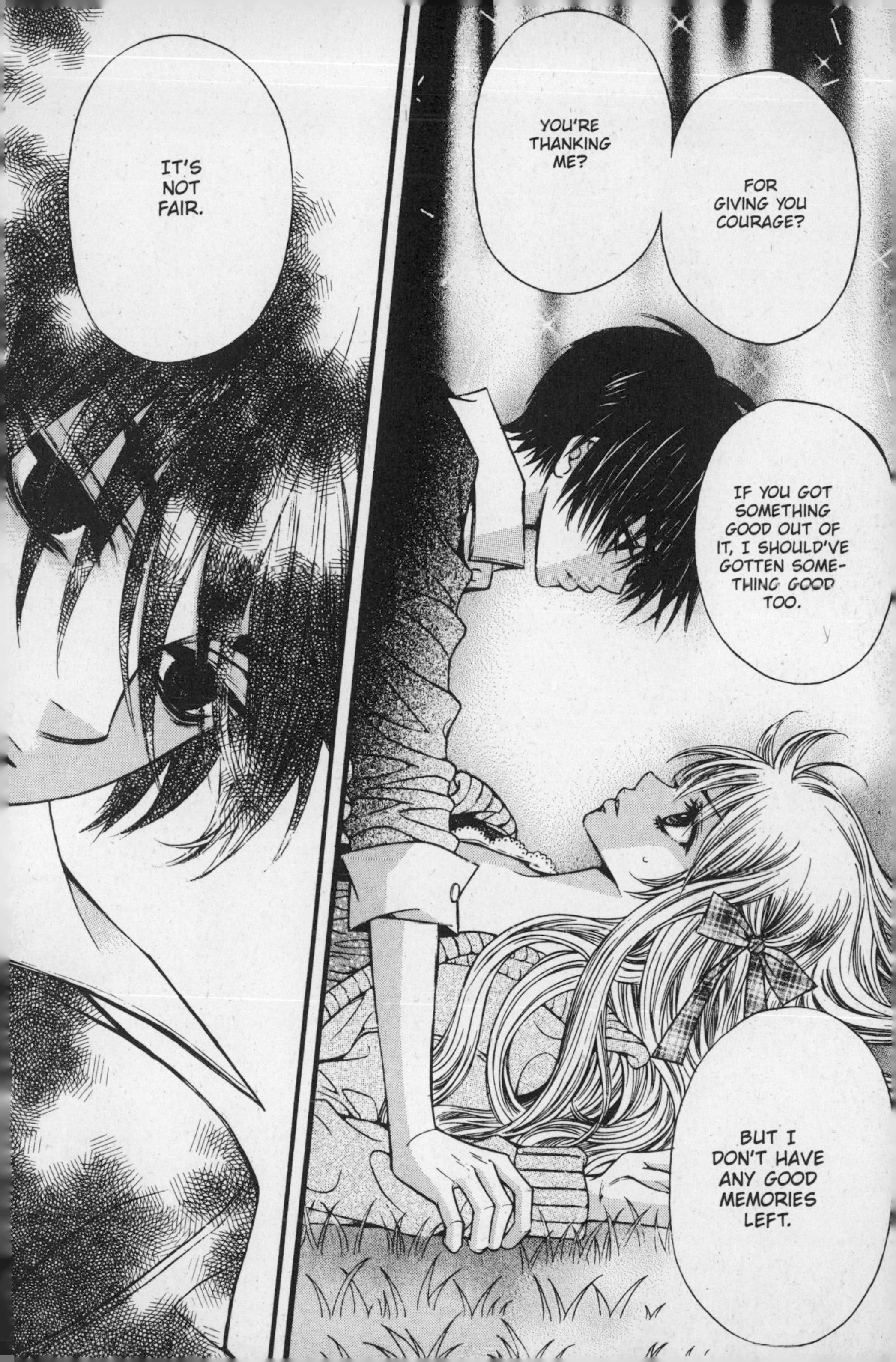
YOU'RE THANKING ME?
FOR GIVING YOU COURAGE?
IF YOU GOT SOMETHING GOOD OUT OF IT, I SHOULD'VE GOTTEN SOME-THING GOOD TOO.
BUT I DON'T HAVE ANY GOOD MEMORIES LEFT.
IT'S NOT FAIR.

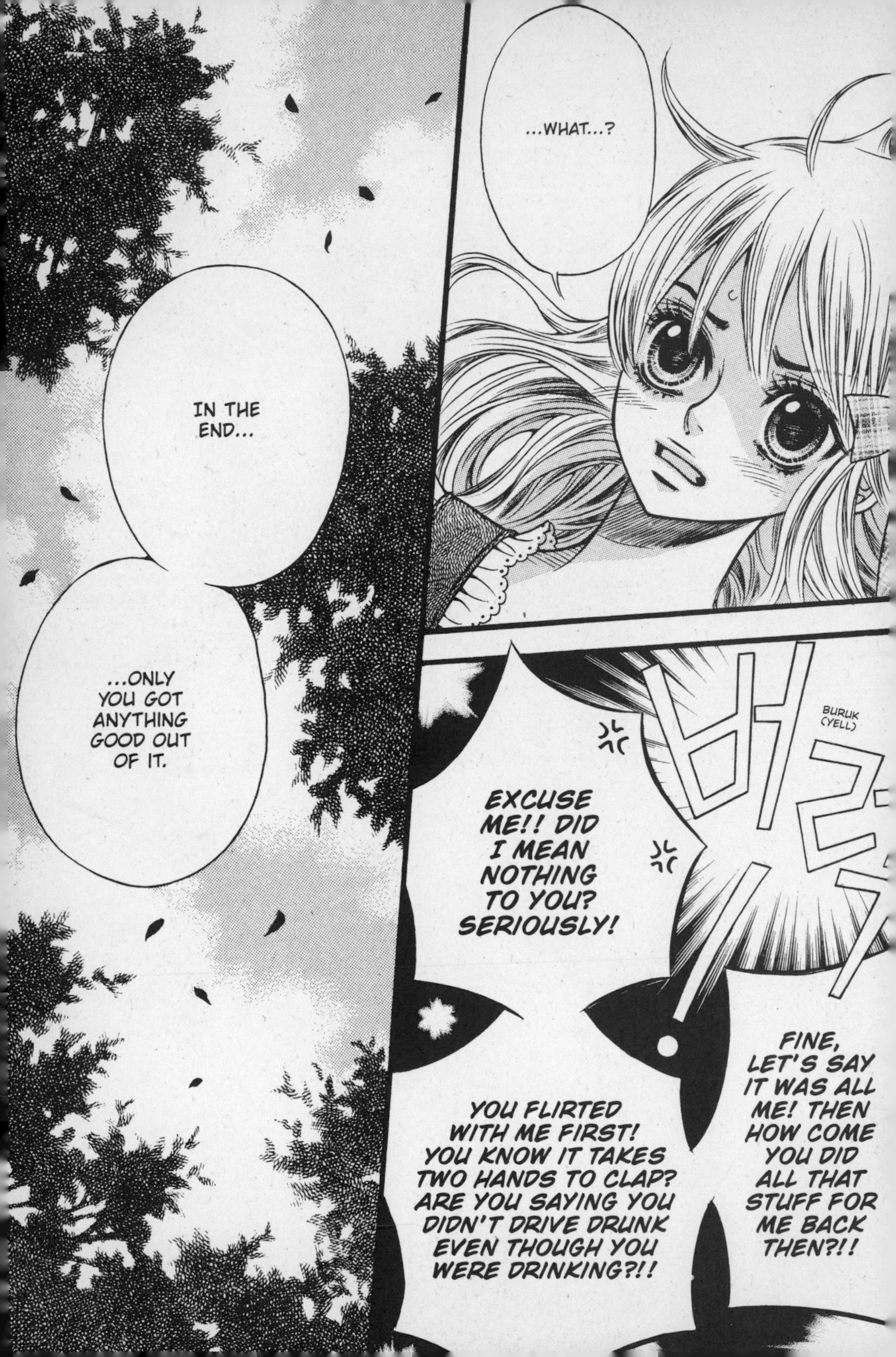
IN THE END...
...ONLY YOU GOT ANYTHING GOOD OUT OF IT.
...WHAT...?
BURUK (YELL)
EXCUSE ME!! DID I MEAN NOTHING TO YOU? SERIOUSLY!
YOU FLIRTED WITH ME FIRST! YOU KNOW IT TAKES TWO HANDS TO CLAP? ARE YOU SAYING YOU DIDN'T DRIVE DRUNK EVEN THOUGH YOU WERE DRINKING?!!
FINE, LET'S SAY IT WAS ALL ME! THEN HOW COME YOU DID ALL THAT STUFF FOR ME BACK THEN?!!

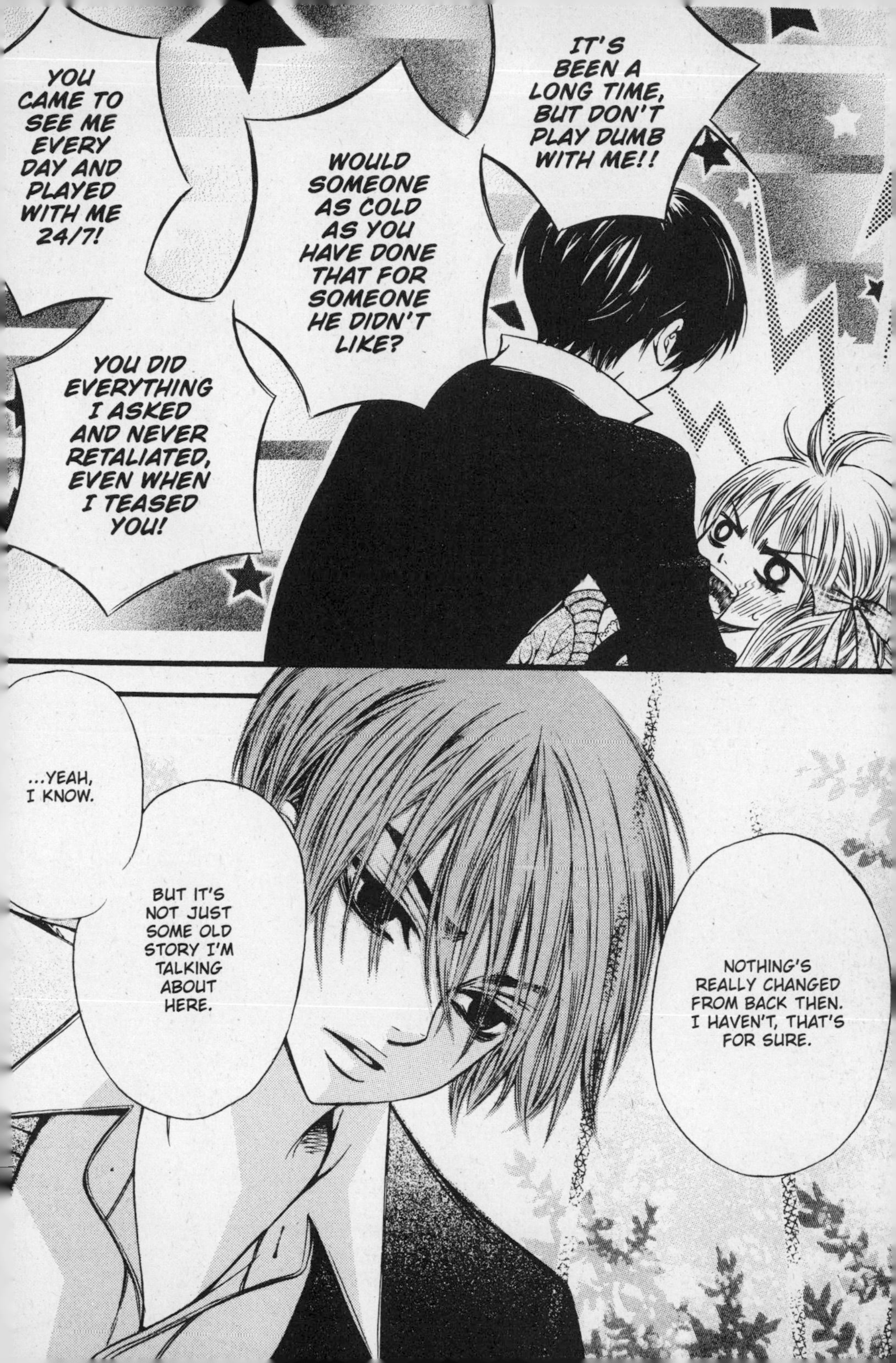
IT'S BEEN A LONG TIME, BUT DON'T PLAY DUMB WITH ME!!
WOULD SOMEONE AS COLD AS YOU HAVE DONE THAT FOR SOMEONE HE DIDN'T LIKE?
YOU CAME TO SEE ME EVERY DAY AND PLAYED WITH ME 24/7!
YOU DID EVERYTHING I ASKED AND NEVER RETALIATED, EVEN WHEN I TEASED YOU!
NOTHING'S REALLY CHANGED FROM BACK THEN. I HAVEN'T, THAT'S FOR SURE.
BUT IT'S NOT JUST SOME OLD STORY I'M TALKING ABOUT HERE.
...YEAH, I KNOW.

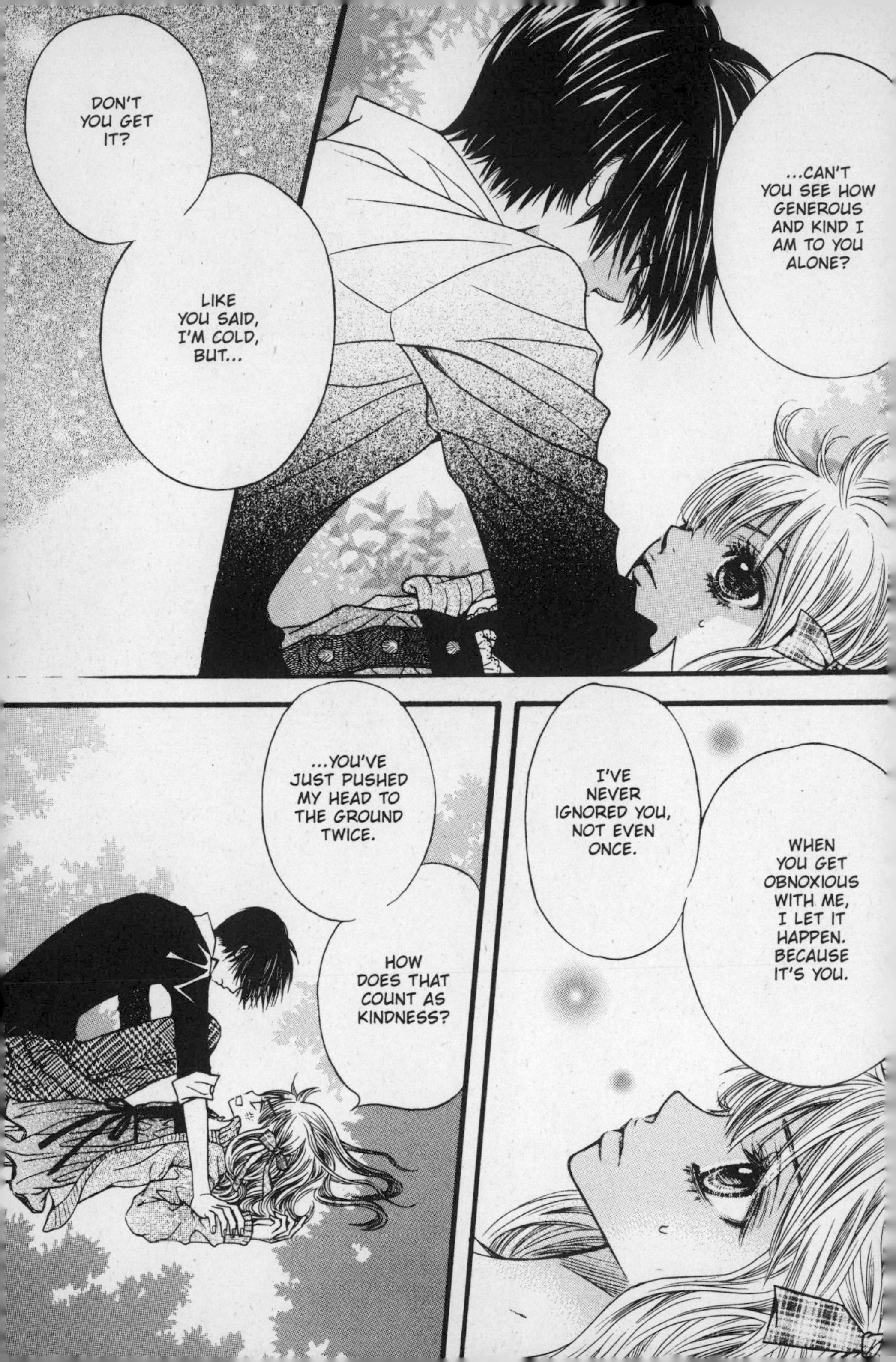
DON'T YOU GET IT?
LIKE YOU SAID, I'M COLD, BUT...
...CAN'T YOU SEE HOW GENEROUS AND KIND I AM TO YOU ALONE?
...YOU'VE JUST PUSHED MY HEAD TO THE GROUND TWICE.
HOW DOES THAT COUNT AS KINDNESS?
I'VE NEVER IGNORED YOU, NOT EVEN ONCE.
WHEN YOU GET OBNOXIOUS WITH ME, I LET IT HAPPEN. BECAUSE IT'S YOU.

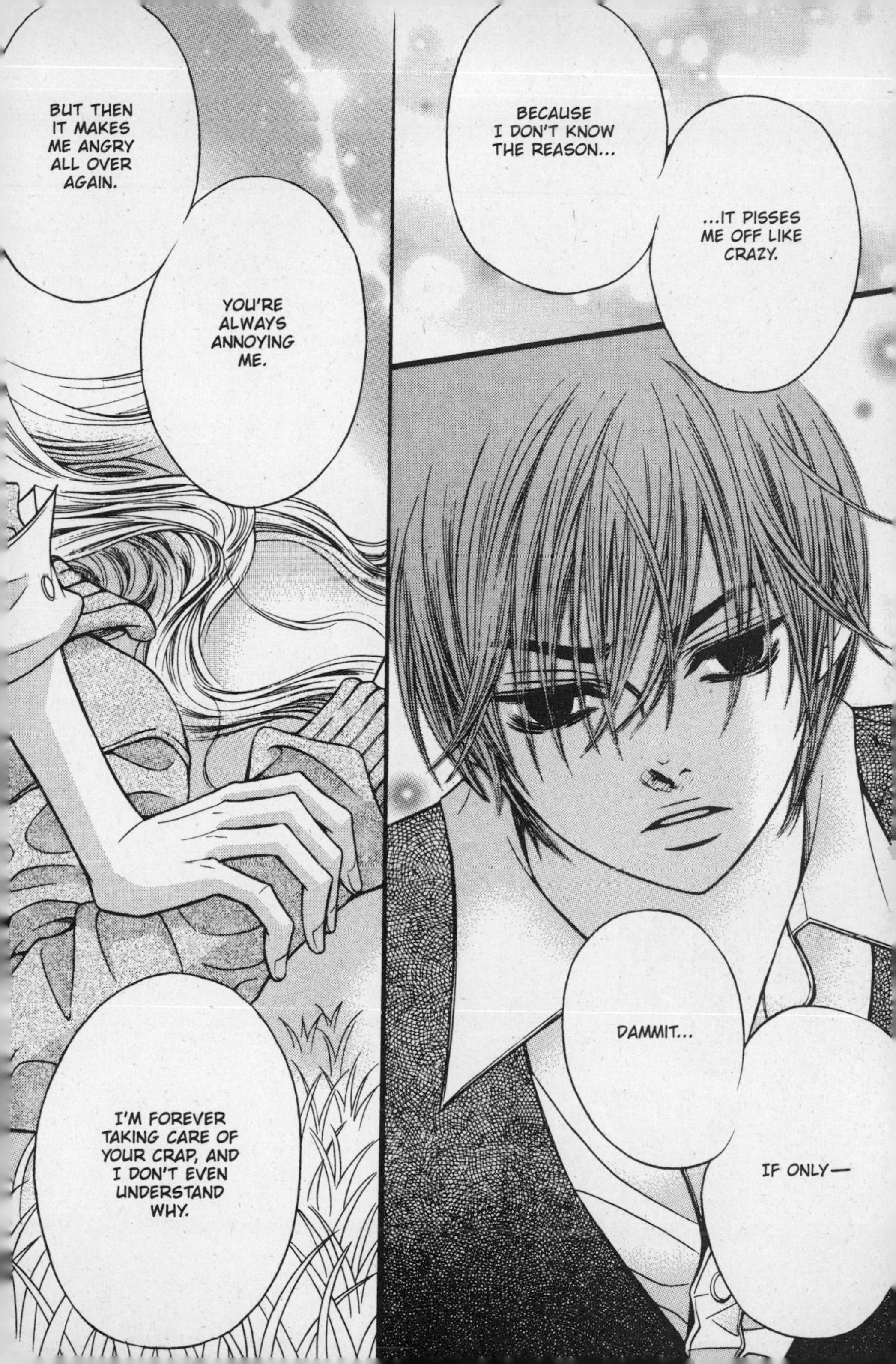
BECAUSE I DON'T KNOW THE REASON...
...IT PISSES ME OFF LIKE CRAZY.
DAMMIT...
IF ONLY—
BUT THEN IT MAKES ME ANGRY ALL OVER AGAIN.
YOU'RE ALWAYS ANNOYING ME.
I'M FOREVER TAKING CARE OF YOUR CRAP, AND I DON'T EVEN UNDERSTAND WHY.

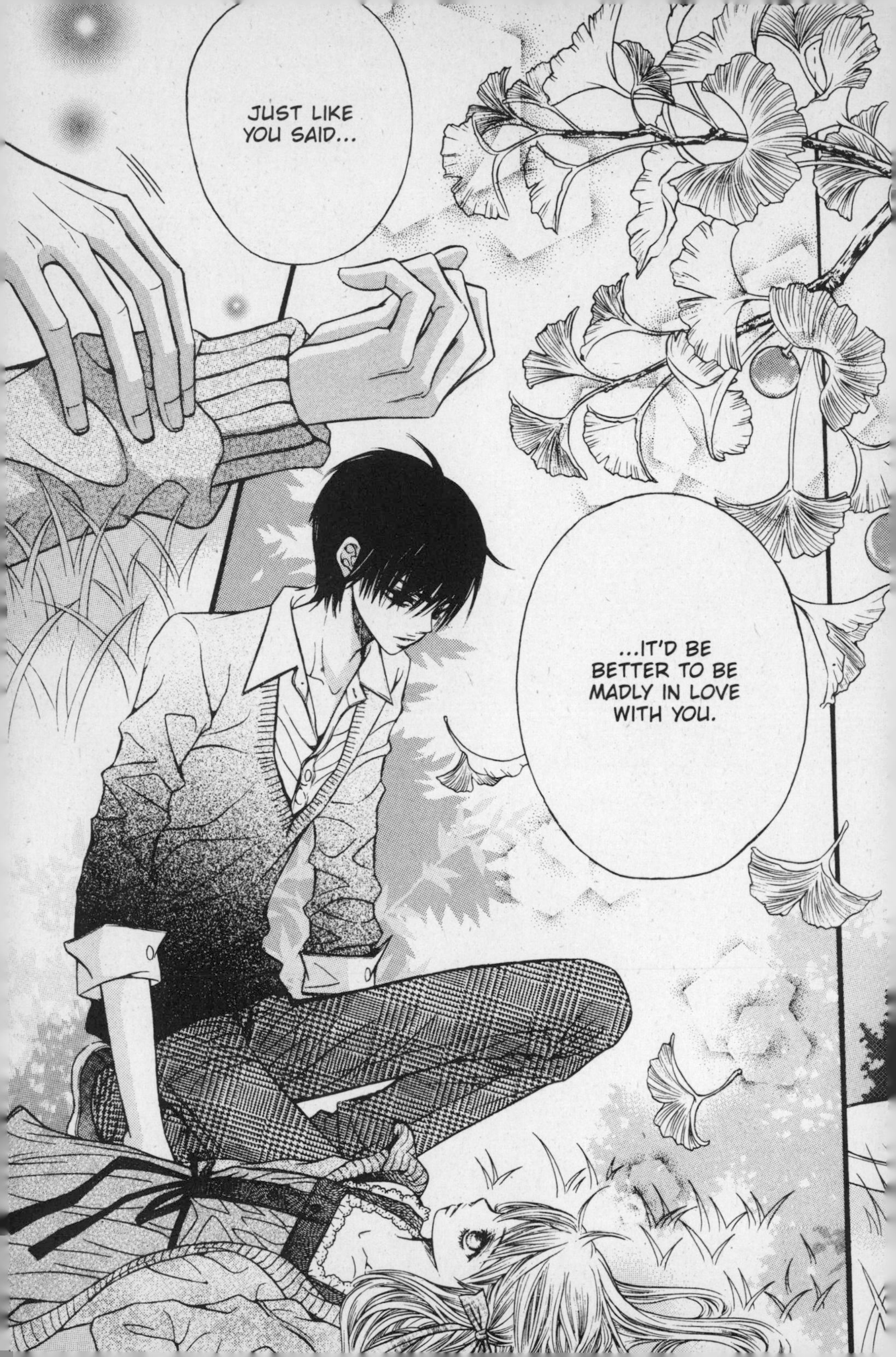

JUST LIKE YOU SAID...
...IT'D BE BETTER TO BE MADLY IN LOVE WITH YOU.

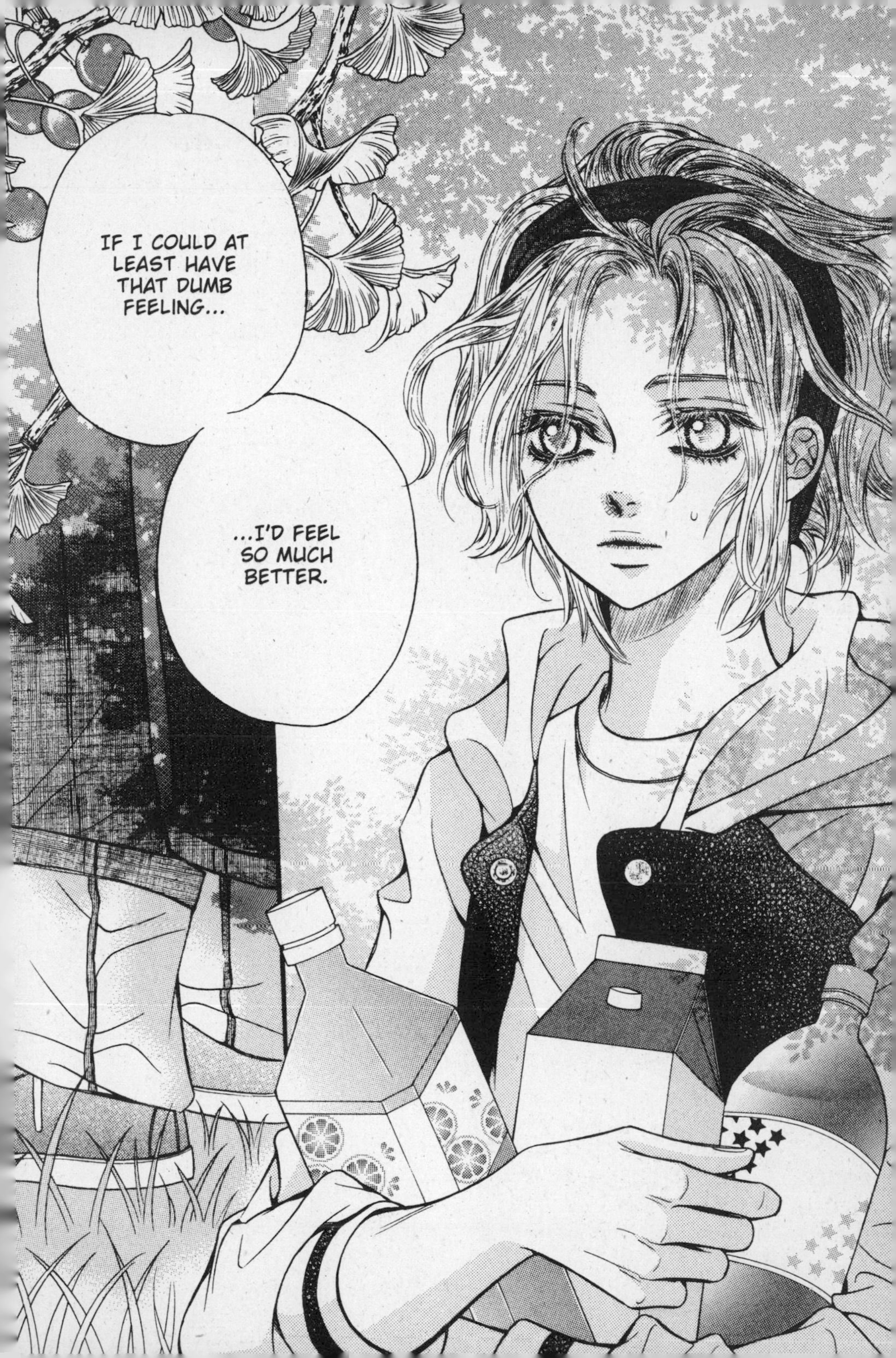
IF I COULD AT LEAST HAVE THAT DUMB FEELING...
...I'D FEEL SO MUCH BETTER.

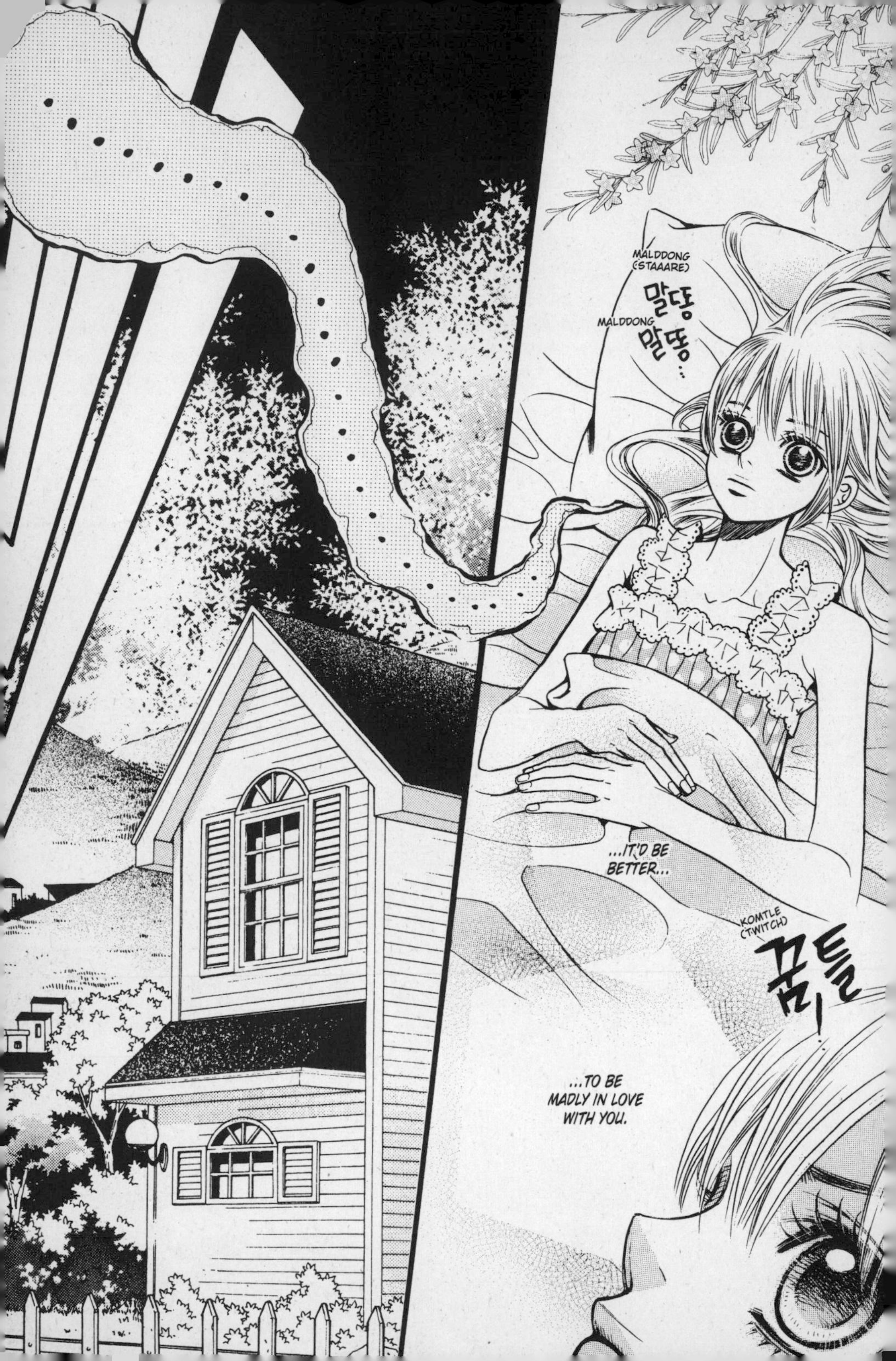
MALDDONG (STAAARE)
말똥
MALDDONG
말똥...
...IT'D BE BETTER...
KOMTLE (TWITCH)
꿈틀
...TO BE MADLY IN LOVE WITH YOU.

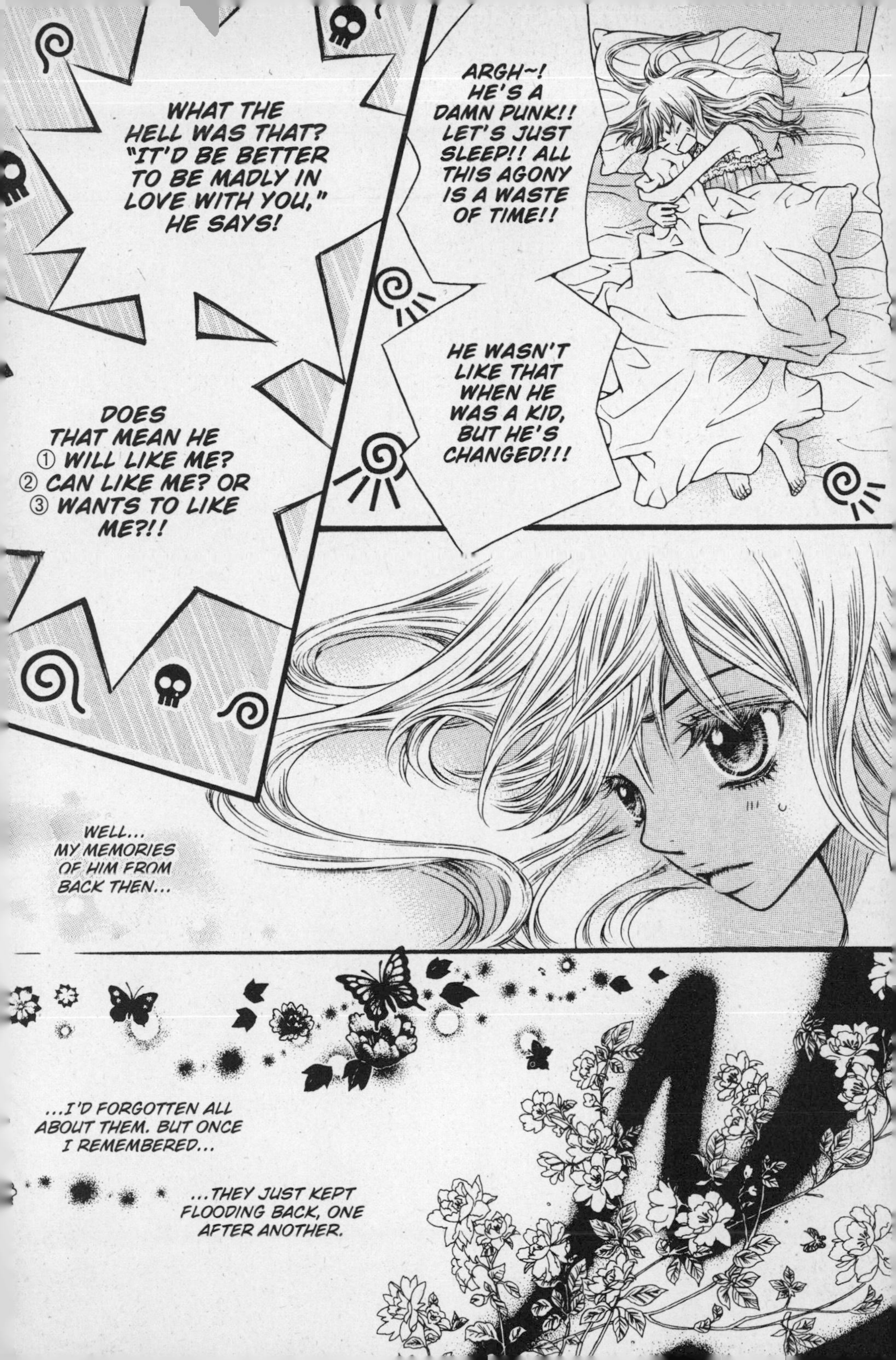

ARGH~! HE'S A DAMN PUNK!! LET'S JUST SLEEP!! ALL THIS AGONY IS A WASTE OF TIME!!
HE WASN'T LIKE THAT WHEN HE WAS A KID, BUT HE'S CHANGED!!!
WHAT THE HELL WAS THAT? "IT'D BE BETTER TO BE MADLY IN LOVE WITH YOU," HE SAYS!
DOES THAT MEAN HE ① WILL LIKE ME? ② CAN LIKE ME? OR ③ WANTS TO LIKE ME?!!
WELL... MY MEMORIES OF HIM FROM BACK THEN...
...I'D FORGOTTEN ALL ABOUT THEM. BUT ONCE I REMEMBERED...
...THEY JUST KEPT FLOODING BACK, ONE AFTER ANOTHER.

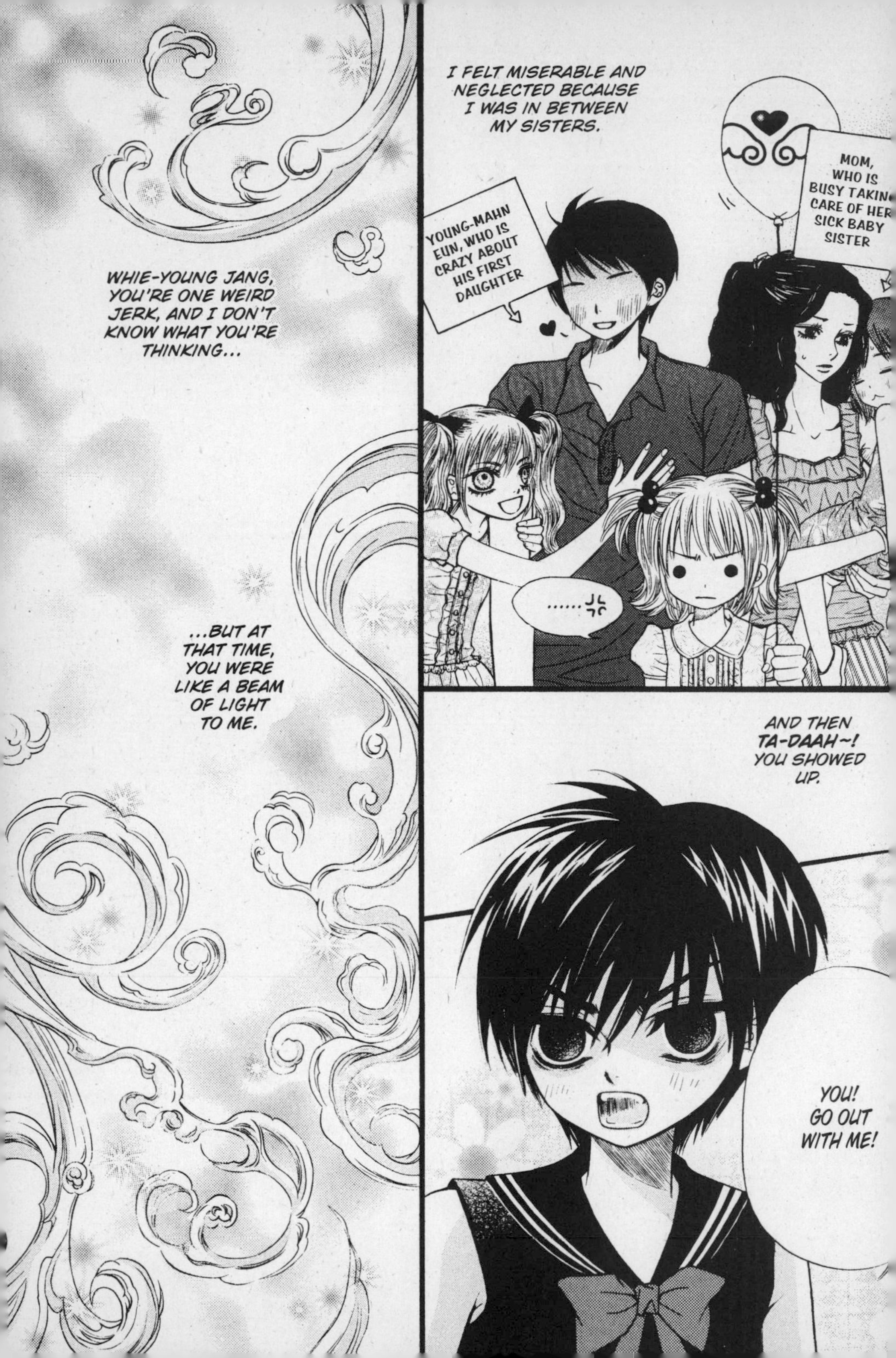
I FELT MISERABLE AND NEGLECTED BECAUSE I WAS IN BETWEEN MY SISTERS.
YOUNG-MAHN EUN, WHO IS CRAZY ABOUT HIS FIRST DAUGHTER
MOM, WHO IS BUSY TAKING CARE OF HER SICK BABY SISTER
......
AND THEN TA-DAAH~! YOU SHOWED UP.
YOU! GO OUT WITH ME!
WHIE-YOUNG JANG, YOU'RE ONE WEIRD JERK, AND I DON'T KNOW WHAT YOU'RE THINKING...
...BUT AT THAT TIME, YOU WERE LIKE A BEAM OF LIGHT TO ME.

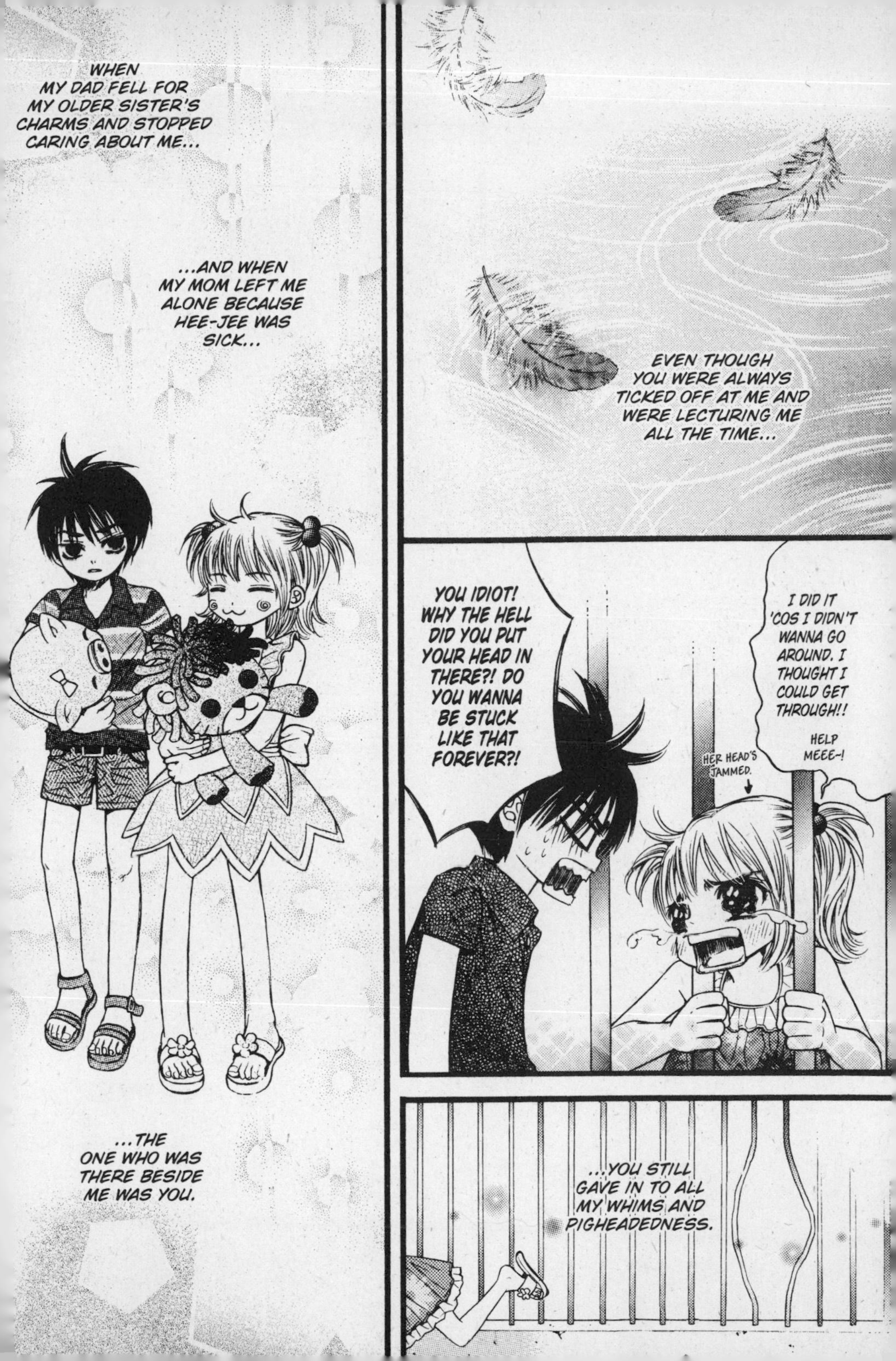
WHEN MY DAD FELL FOR MY OLDER SISTER'S CHARMS AND STOPPED CARING ABOUT ME...
...AND WHEN MY MOM LEFT ME ALONE BECAUSE HEE-JEE WAS SICK...
...THE ONE WHO WAS THERE BESIDE ME WAS YOU.
EVEN THOUGH YOU WERE ALWAYS TICKED OFF AT ME AND WERE LECTURING ME ALL THE TIME...
YOU IDIOT! WHY THE HELL DID YOU PUT YOUR HEAD IN THERE?! DO YOU WANNA BE STUCK LIKE THAT FOREVER?!
I DID IT 'COS I DIDN'T WANNA GO AROUND. I THOUGHT I COULD GET THROUGH!!
HELP MEEE~!
HER HEAD'S JAMMED.
...YOU STILL GAVE IN TO ALL MY WHIMS AND PIGHEADEDNESS.

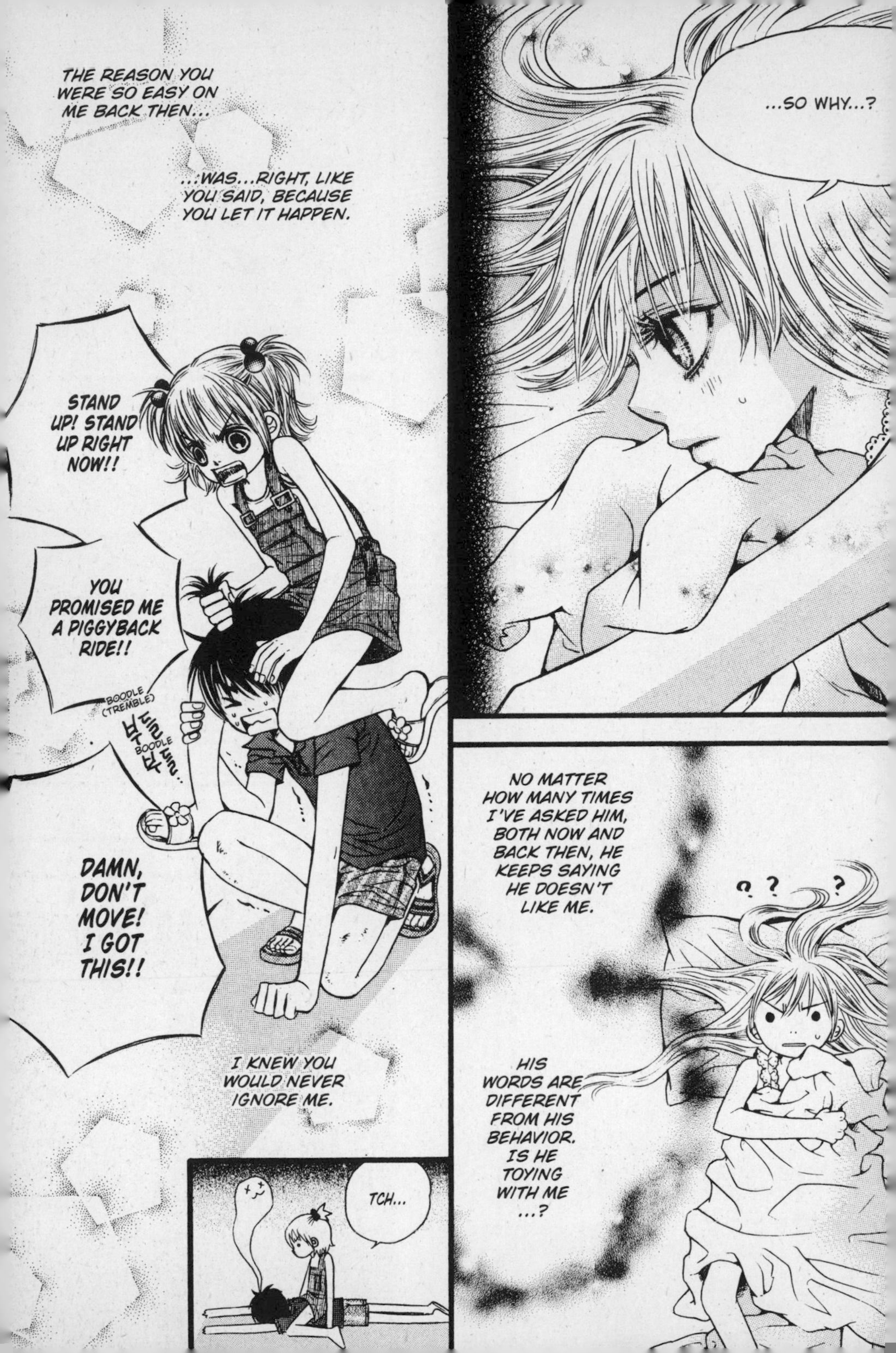
THE REASON YOU WERE SO EASY ON ME BACK THEN...
...WAS...RIGHT, LIKE YOU SAID, BECAUSE YOU LET IT HAPPEN.
STAND UP! STAND UP RIGHT NOW!!
YOU PROMISED ME A PIGGYBACK RIDE!!
BOODLE (TREMBLE)
BOODLE
DAMN, DON'T MOVE! I GOT THIS!!
I KNEW YOU WOULD NEVER IGNORE ME.
TCH...
...SO WHY...?
NO MATTER HOW MANY TIMES I'VE ASKED HIM, BOTH NOW AND BACK THEN, HE KEEPS SAYING HE DOESN'T LIKE ME.
? ? ?
HIS WORDS ARE DIFFERENT FROM HIS BEHAVIOR. IS HE TOYING WITH ME ...?

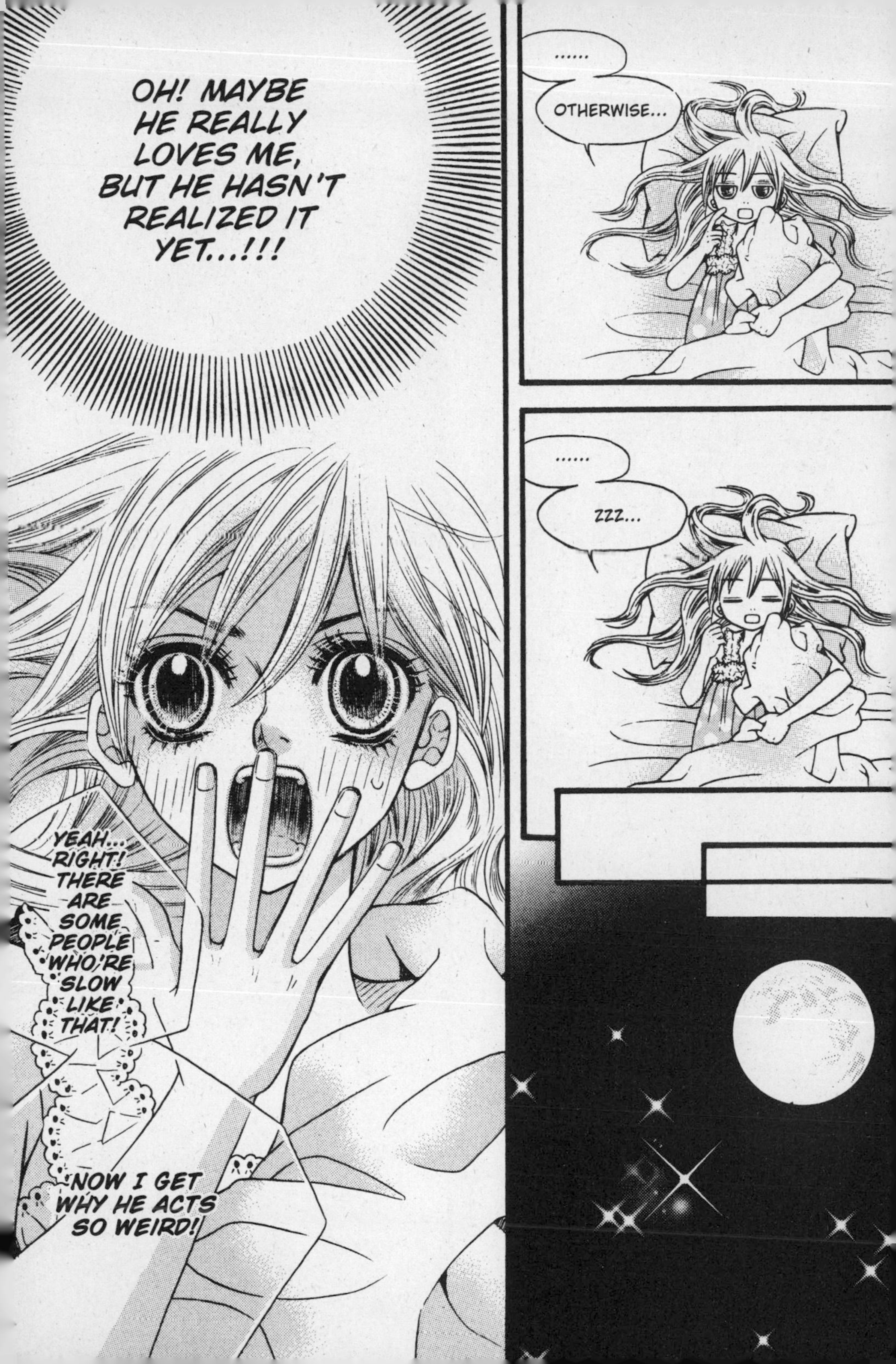
......
OTHERWISE...
......
ZZZ...
OH! MAYBE HE REALLY LOVES ME, BUT HE HASN'T REALIZED IT YET...!!!
YEAH... RIGHT! THERE ARE SOME PEOPLE WHO'RE SLOW LIKE THAT!
NOW I GET WHY HE ACTS SO WEIRD!

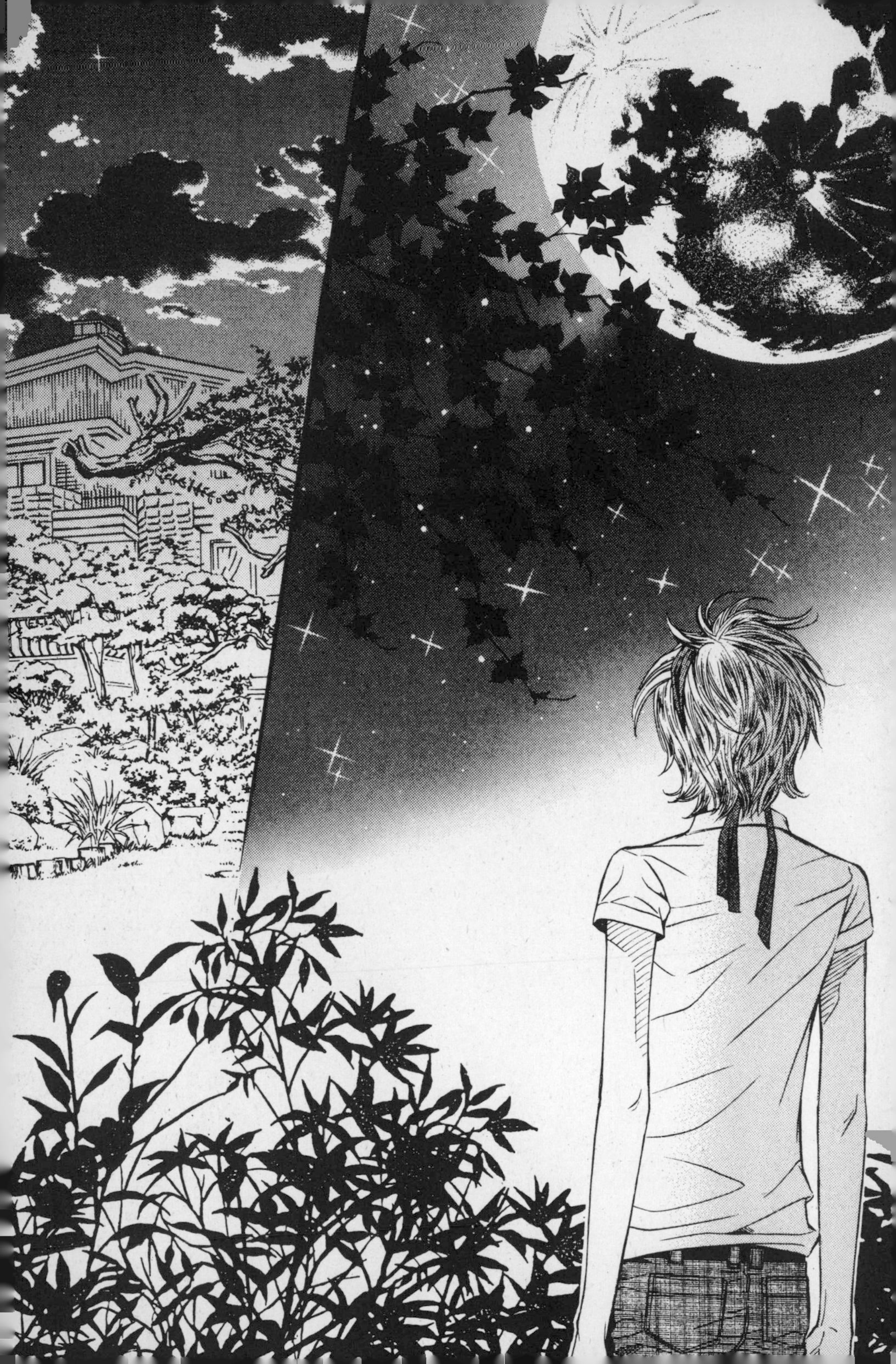

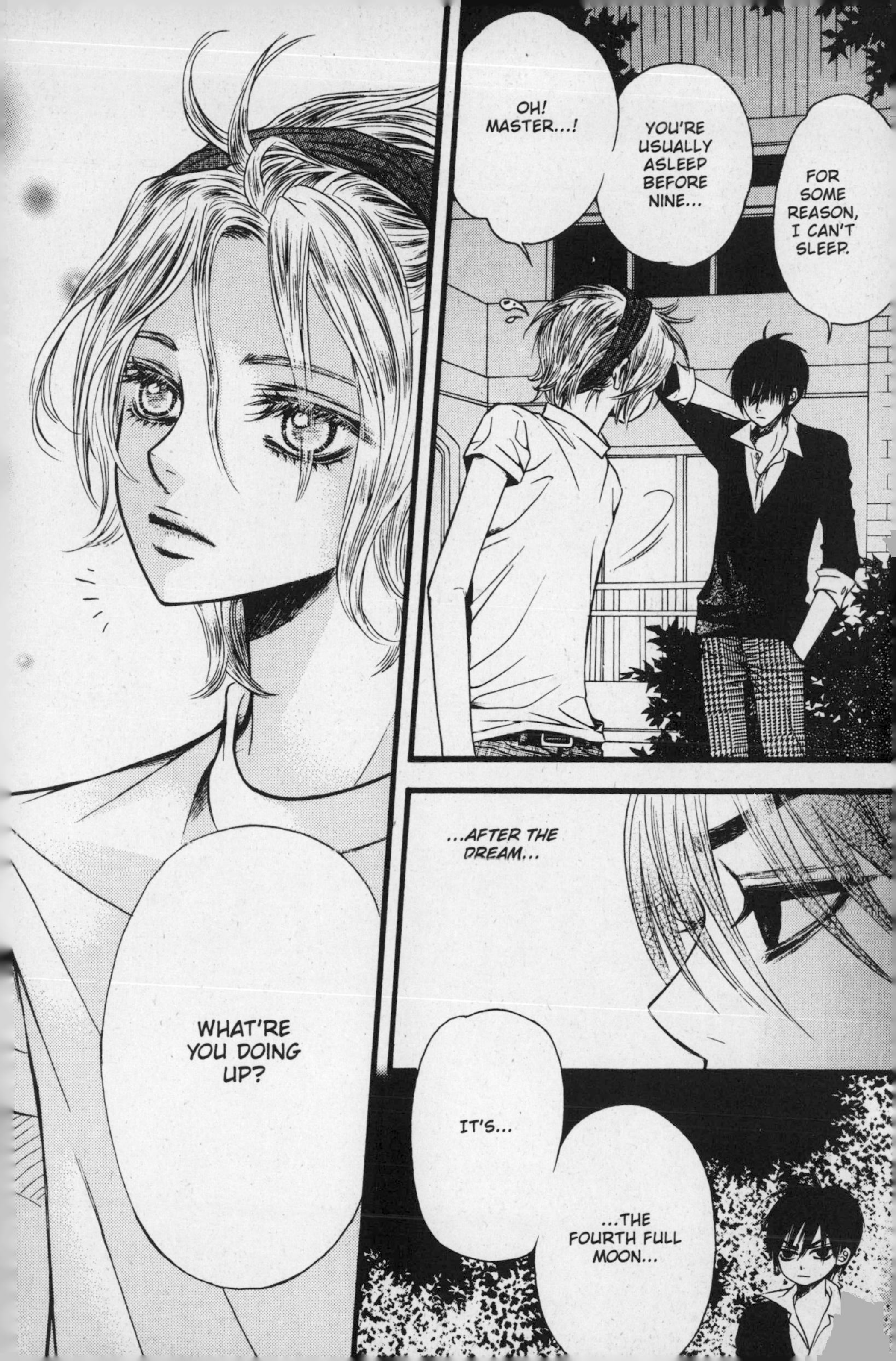
OH! MASTER...!
YOU'RE USUALLY ASLEEP BEFORE NINE...
FOR SOME REASON, I CAN'T SLEEP.
WHAT'RE YOU DOING UP?
...AFTER THE DREAM...
IT'S...
...THE FOURTH FULL MOON...

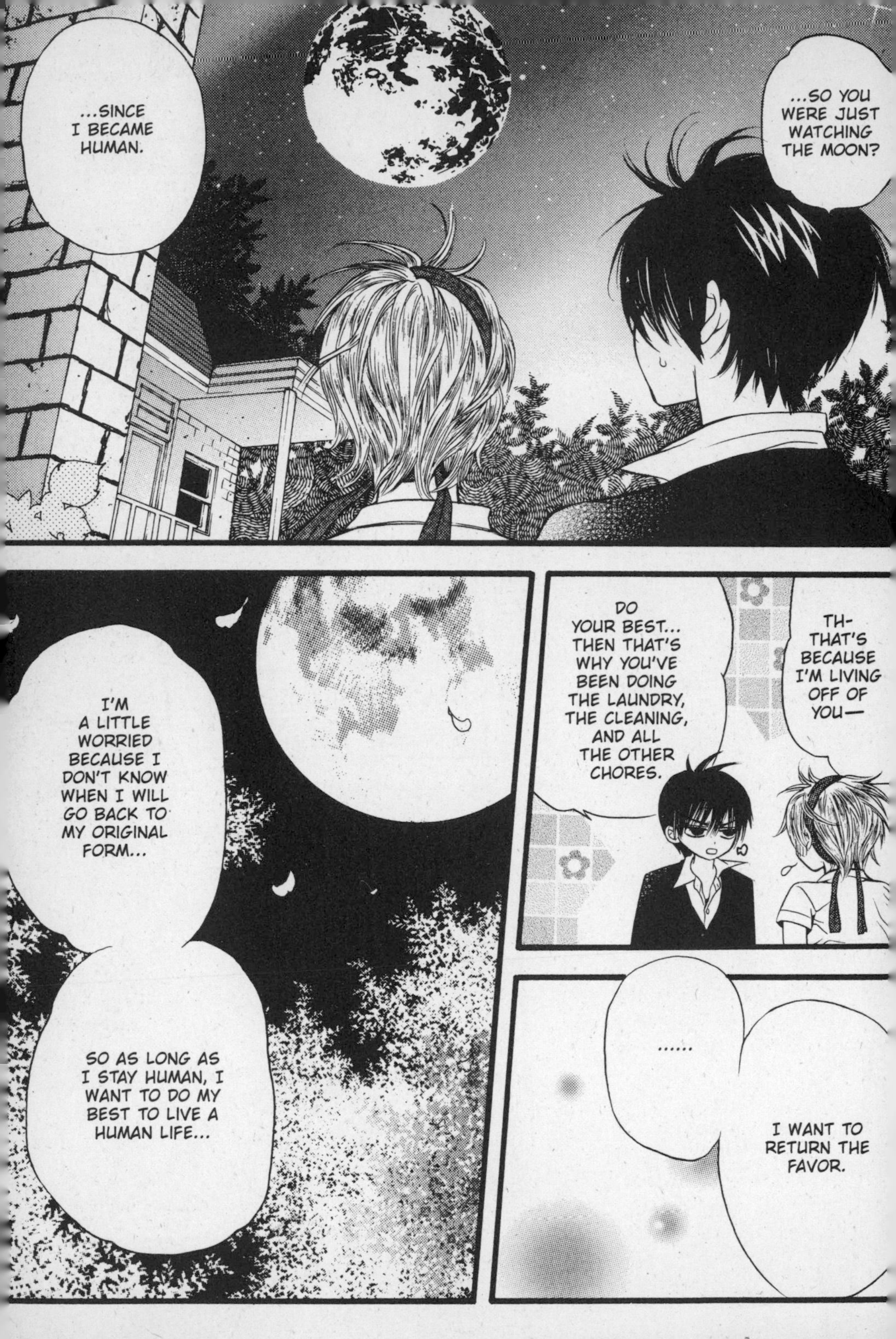
...SO YOU WERE JUST WATCHING THE MOON?
...SINCE I BECAME HUMAN.
I'M A LITTLE WORRIED BECAUSE I DON'T KNOW WHEN I WILL GO BACK TO MY ORIGINAL FORM...
SO AS LONG AS I STAY HUMAN, I WANT TO DO MY BEST TO LIVE A HUMAN LIFE...
DO YOUR BEST... THEN THAT'S WHY YOU'VE BEEN DOING THE LAUNDRY, THE CLEANING, AND ALL THE OTHER CHORES.
TH-THAT'S BECAUSE I'M LIVING OFF OF YOU—
I WANT TO RETURN THE FAVOR.
......

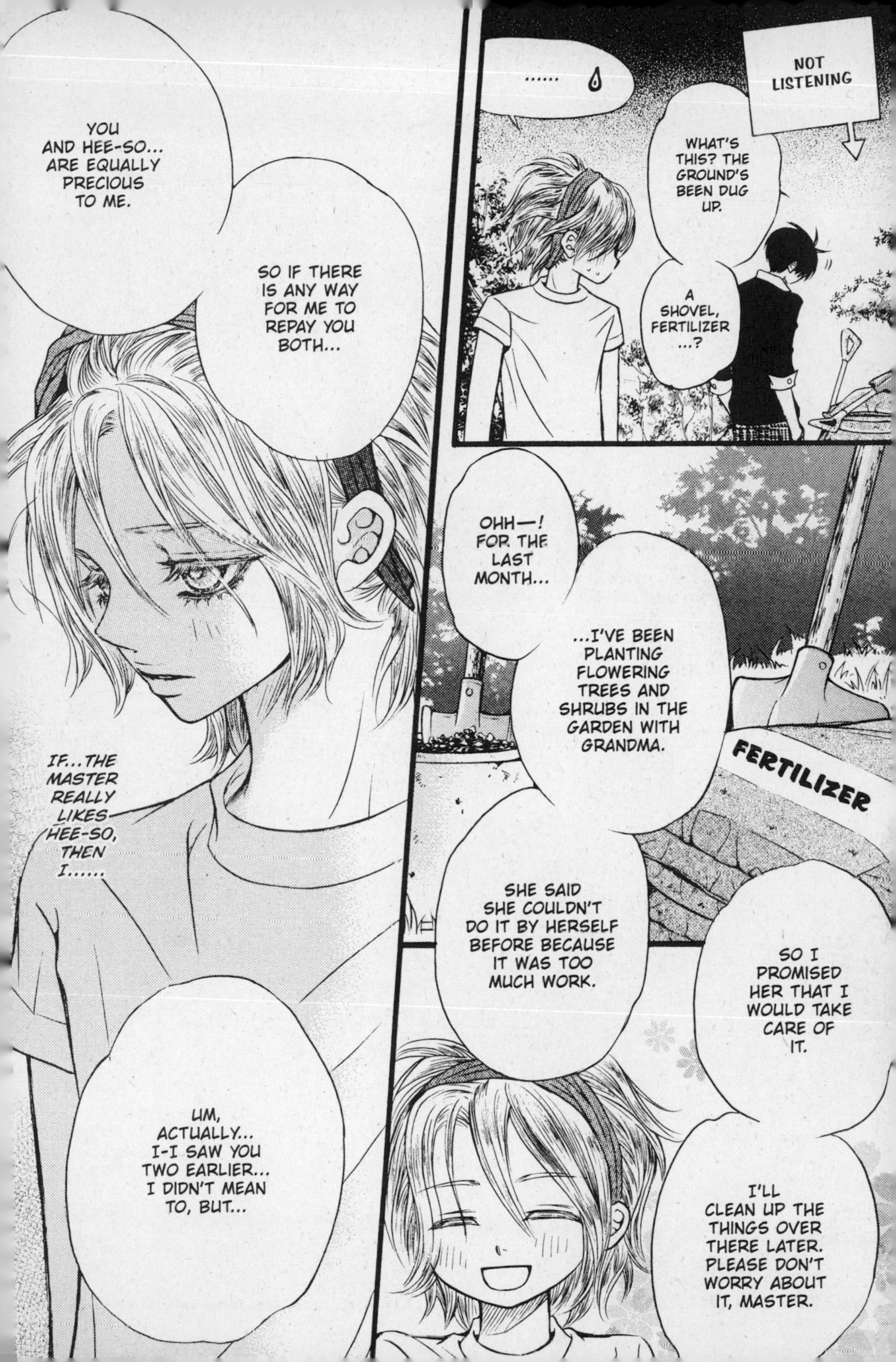
......
NOT LISTENING
WHAT'S THIS? THE GROUND'S BEEN DUG UP.
A SHOVEL, FERTILIZER ...?
OHH—! FOR THE LAST MONTH...
...I'VE BEEN PLANTING FLOWERING TREES AND SHRUBS IN THE GARDEN WITH GRANDMA.
FERTILIZER
SHE SAID SHE COULDN'T DO IT BY HERSELF BEFORE BECAUSE IT WAS TOO MUCH WORK.
SO I PROMISED HER THAT I WOULD TAKE CARE OF IT.
I'LL CLEAN UP THE THINGS OVER THERE LATER. PLEASE DON'T WORRY ABOUT IT, MASTER.
YOU AND HEE-SO... ARE EQUALLY PRECIOUS TO ME.
SO IF THERE IS ANY WAY FOR ME TO REPAY YOU BOTH...
IF...THE MASTER REALLY LIKES HEE-SO, THEN I......
UM, ACTUALLY... I-I SAW YOU TWO EARLIER... I DIDN'T MEAN TO, BUT...

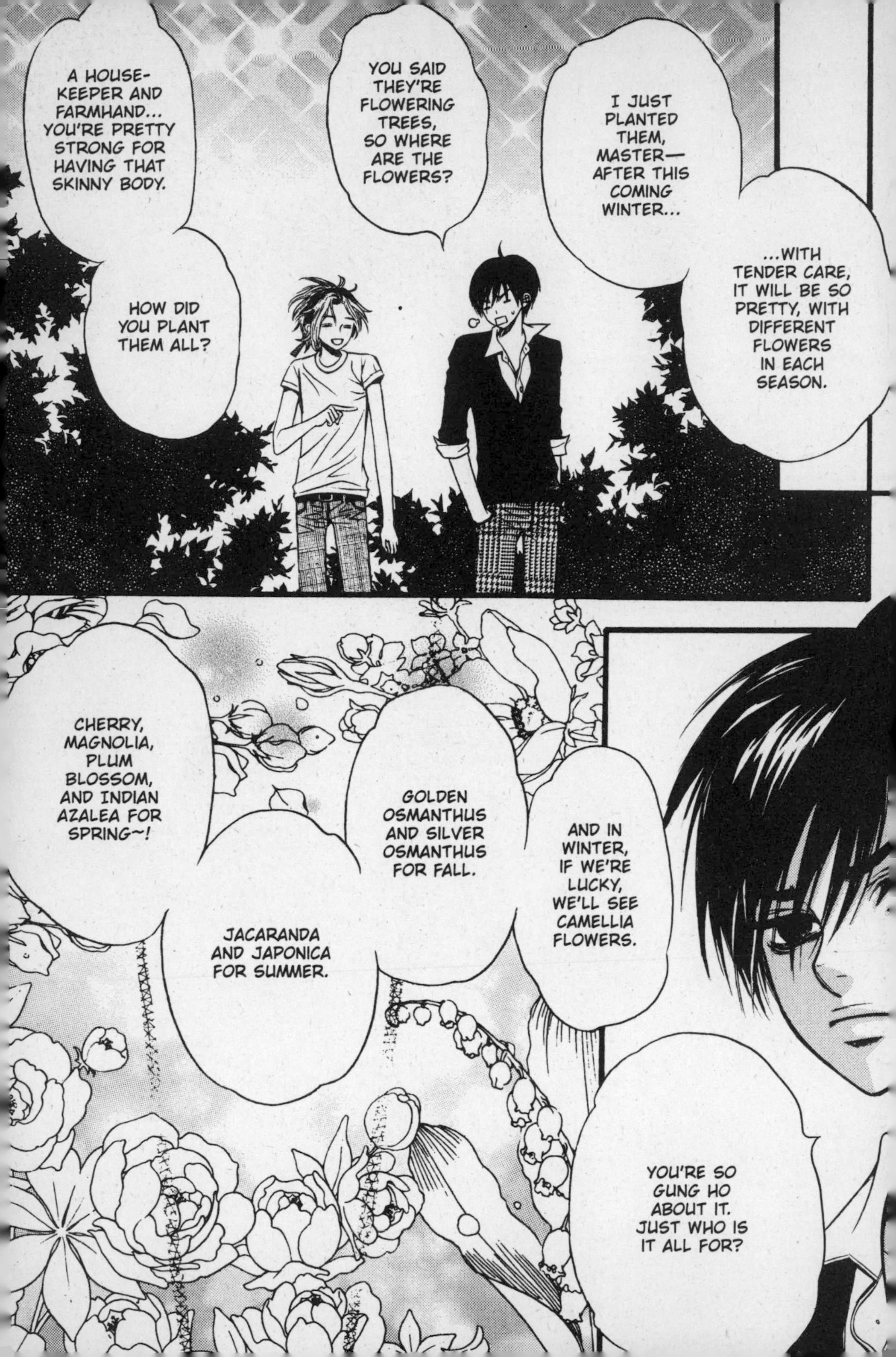
A HOUSE-KEEPER AND FARMHAND... YOU'RE PRETTY STRONG FOR HAVING THAT SKINNY BODY.
HOW DID YOU PLANT THEM ALL?
YOU SAID THEY'RE FLOWERING TREES, SO WHERE ARE THE FLOWERS?
I JUST PLANTED THEM, MASTER— AFTER THIS COMING WINTER...
...WITH TENDER CARE, IT WILL BE SO PRETTY, WITH DIFFERENT FLOWERS IN EACH SEASON.
CHERRY, MAGNOLIA, PLUM BLOSSOM, AND INDIAN AZALEA FOR SPRING~!
JACARANDA AND JAPONICA FOR SUMMER.
GOLDEN OSMANTHUS AND SILVER OSMANTHUS FOR FALL.
AND IN WINTER, IF WE'RE LUCKY, WE'LL SEE CAMELLIA FLOWERS.
YOU'RE SO GUNG HO ABOUT IT. JUST WHO IS IT ALL FOR?

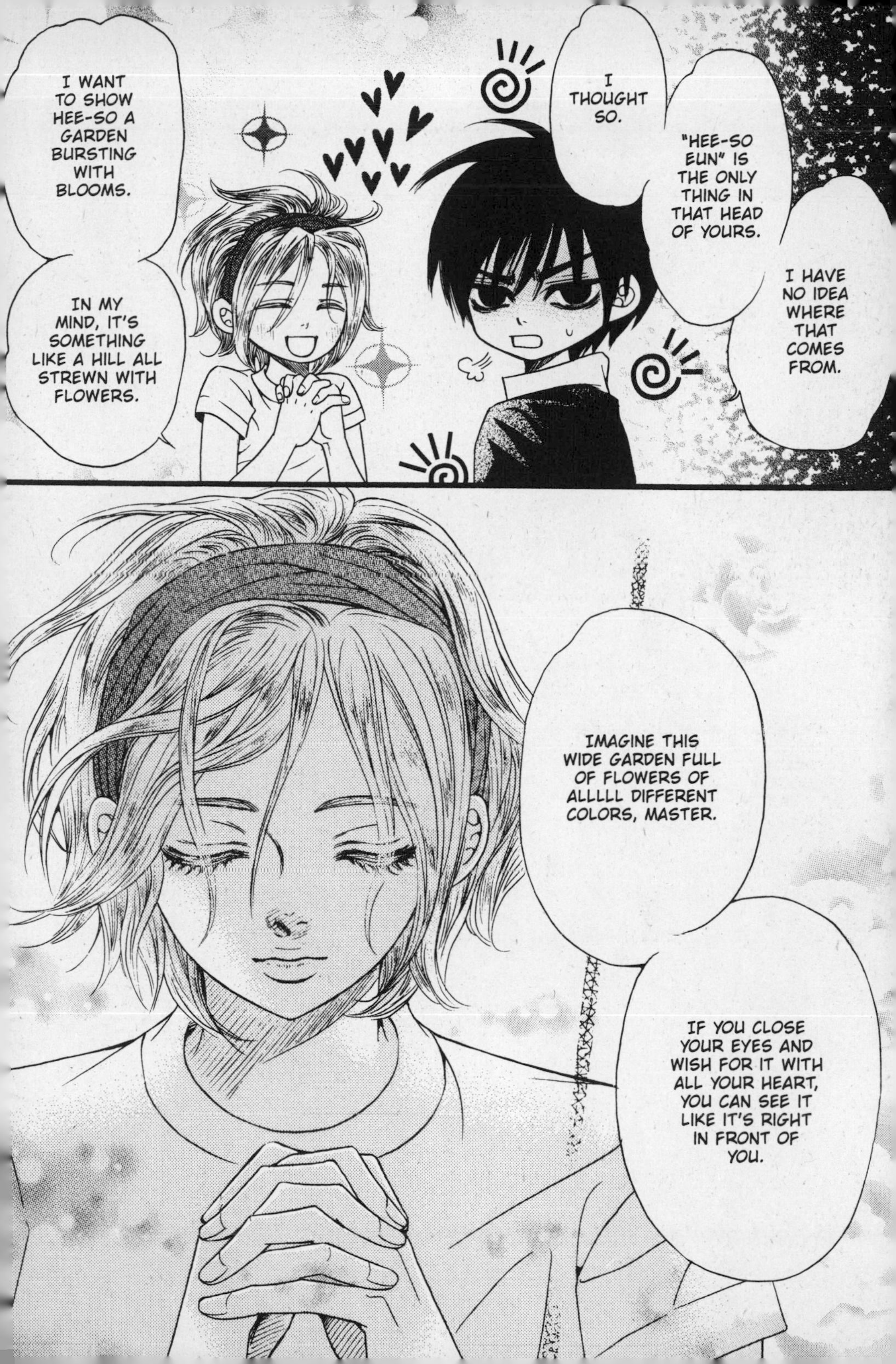
I WANT TO SHOW HEE-SO A GARDEN BURSTING WITH BLOOMS.
IN MY MIND, IT'S SOMETHING LIKE A HILL ALL STREWN WITH FLOWERS.
I THOUGHT SO.
"HEE-SO EUN" IS THE ONLY THING IN THAT HEAD OF YOURS.
I HAVE NO IDEA WHERE THAT COMES FROM.
IMAGINE THIS WIDE GARDEN FULL OF FLOWERS OF ALLLLL DIFFERENT COLORS, MASTER.
IF YOU CLOSE YOUR EYES AND WISH FOR IT WITH ALL YOUR HEART, YOU CAN SEE IT LIKE IT'S RIGHT IN FRONT OF YOU.

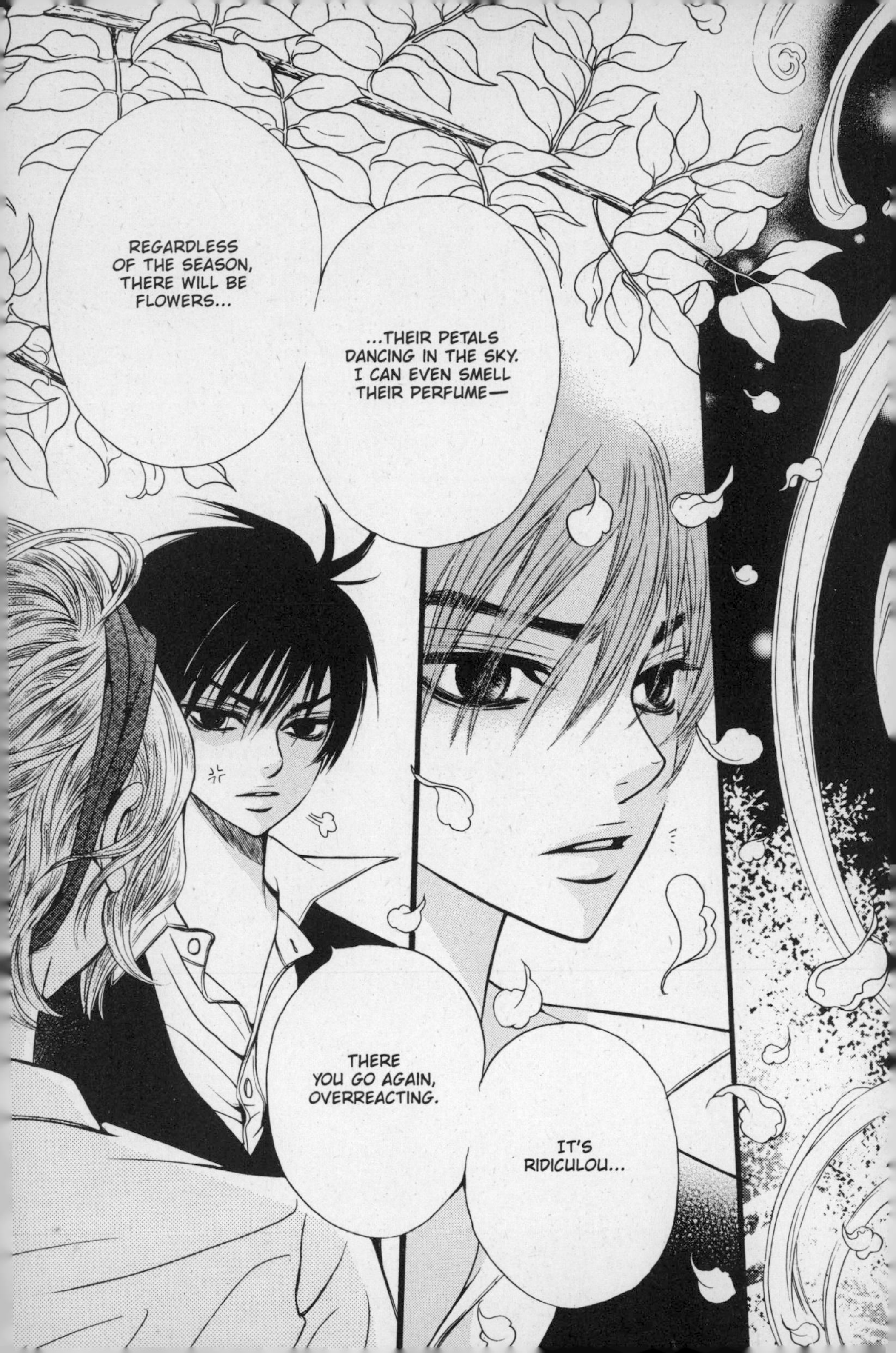
...THEIR PETALS DANCING IN THE SKY. I CAN EVEN SMELL THEIR PERFUME—
REGARDLESS OF THE SEASON, THERE WILL BE FLOWERS...
IT'S RIDICULOU...
THERE YOU GO AGAIN, OVERREACTING.

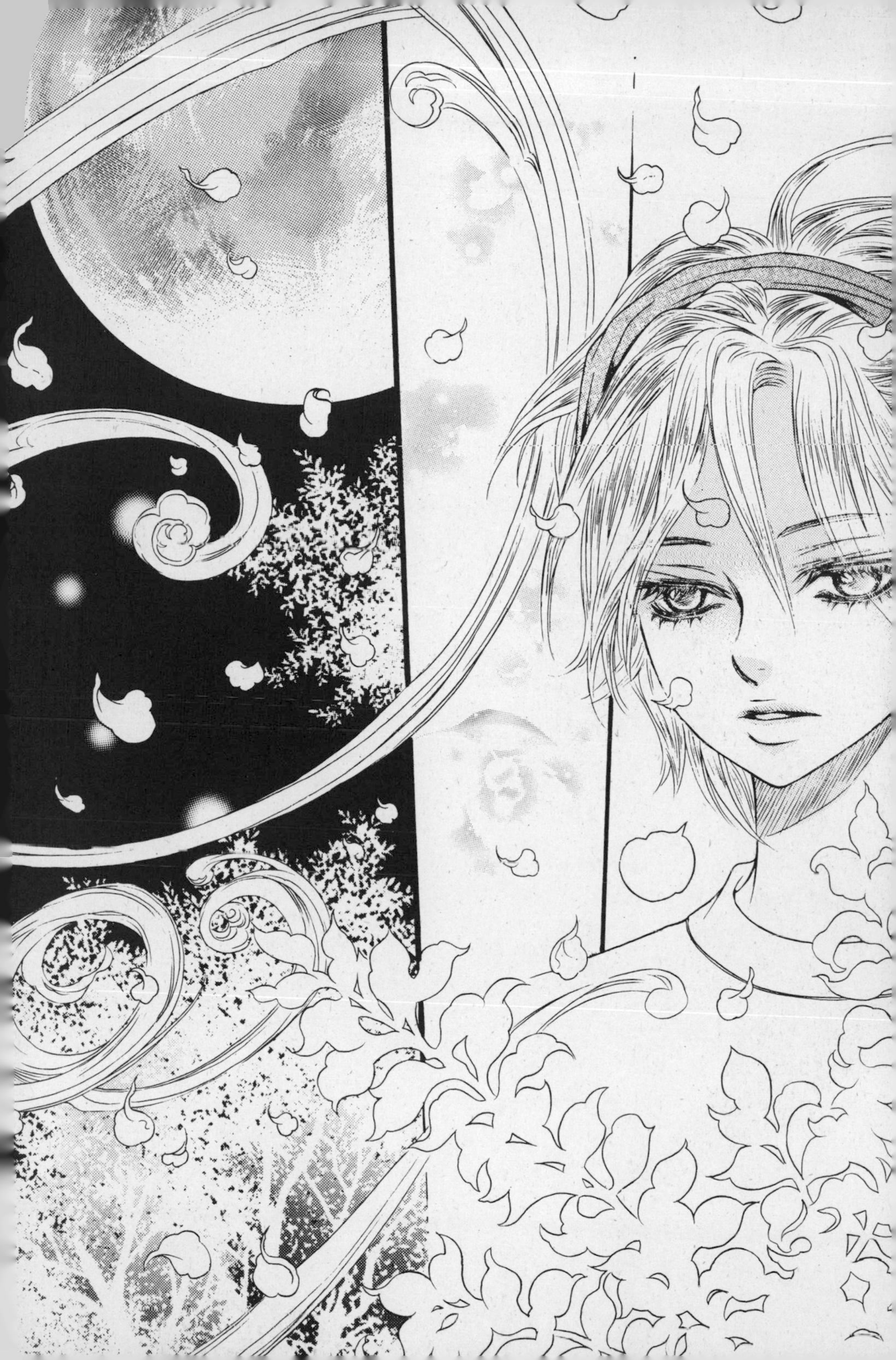

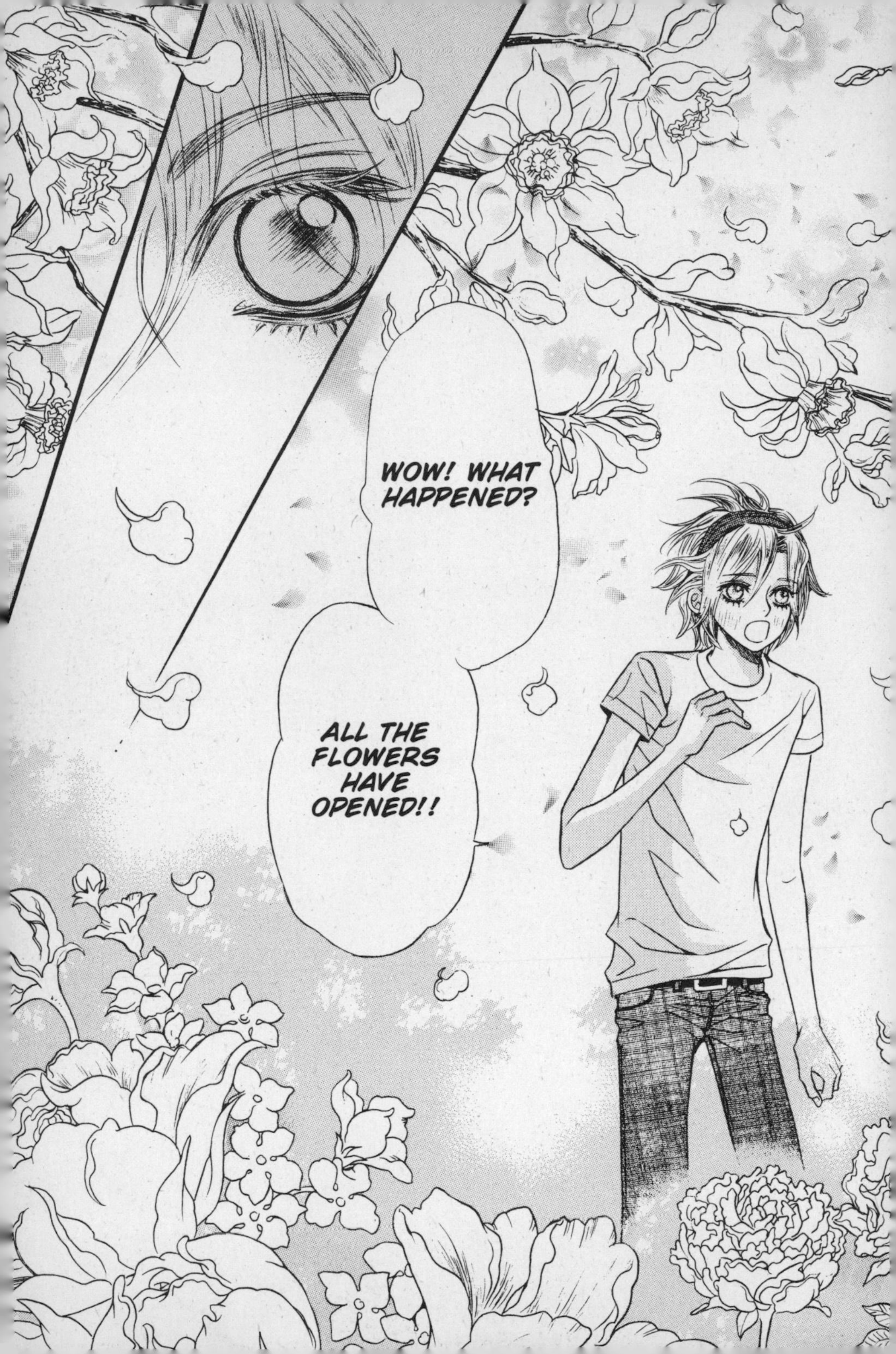
WOW! WHAT HAPPENED?
ALL THE FLOWERS HAVE OPENED!!

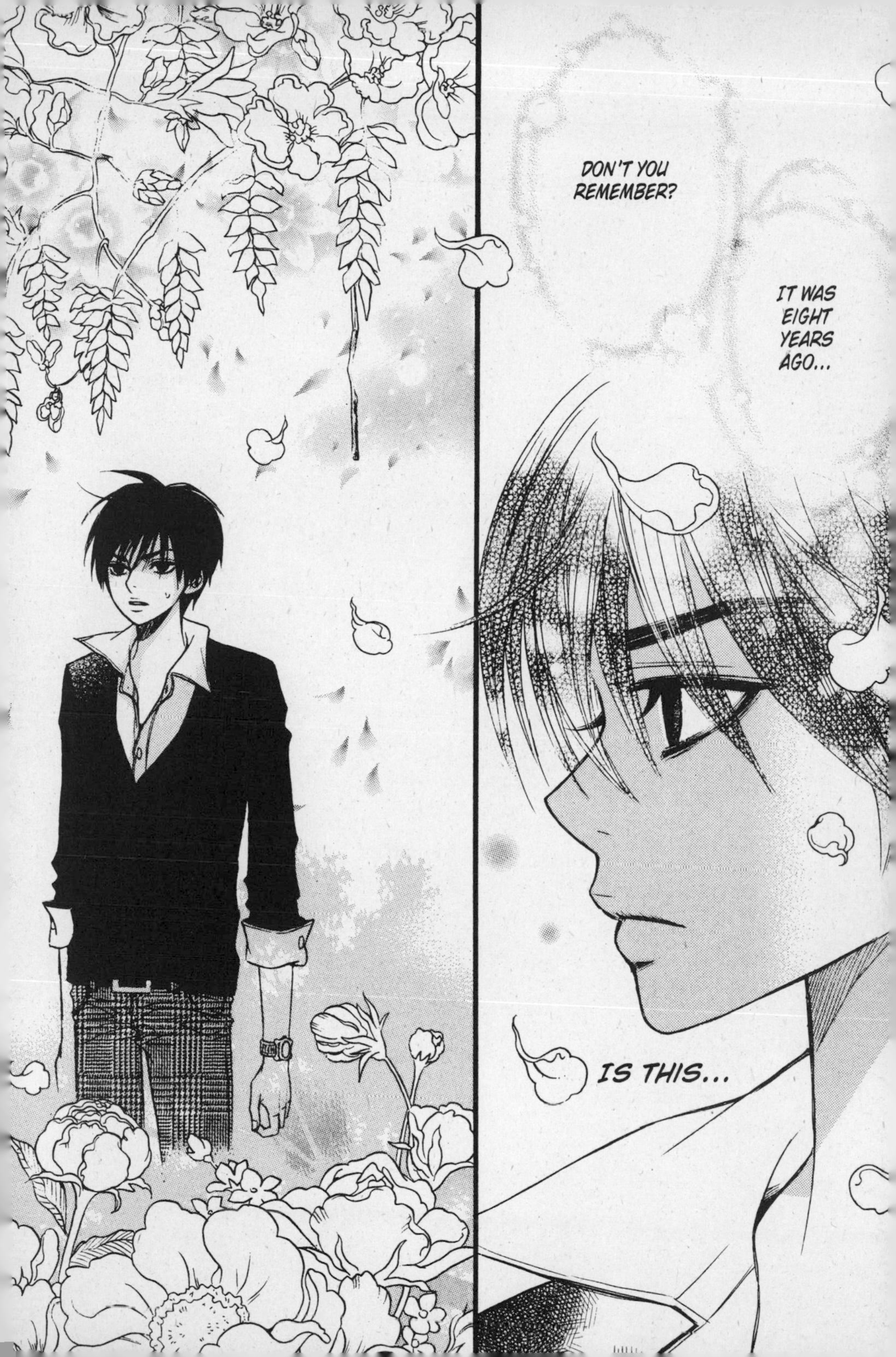
DON'T YOU REMEMBER?
IT WAS EIGHT YEARS AGO...
IS THIS...

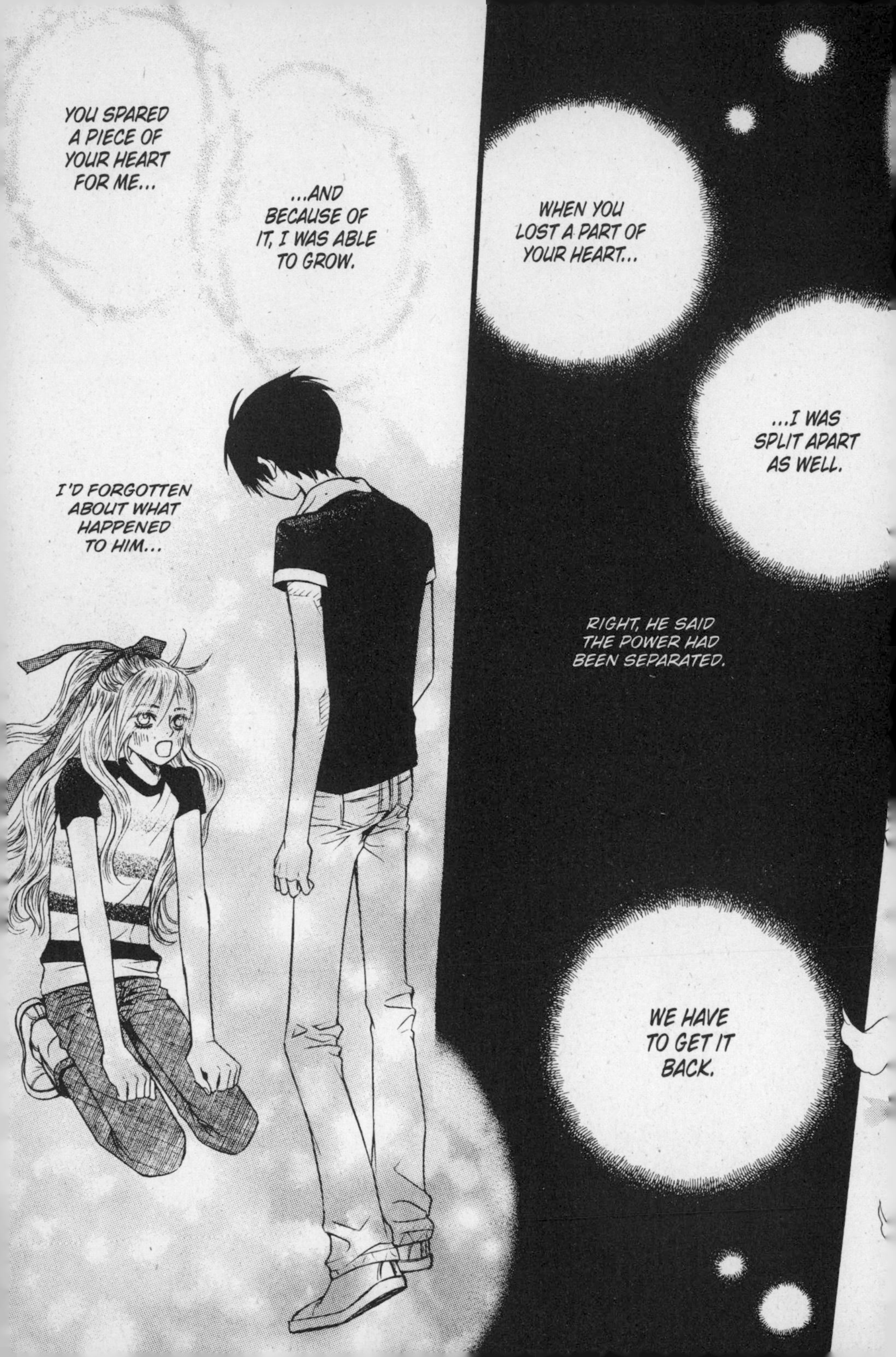
WHEN YOU LOST A PART OF YOUR HEART...
...I WAS SPLIT APART AS WELL.
RIGHT, HE SAID THE POWER HAD BEEN SEPARATED.
WE HAVE TO GET IT BACK.
YOU SPARED A PIECE OF YOUR HEART FOR ME...
...AND BECAUSE OF IT, I WAS ABLE TO GROW.
I'D FORGOTTEN ABOUT WHAT HAPPENED TO HIM...

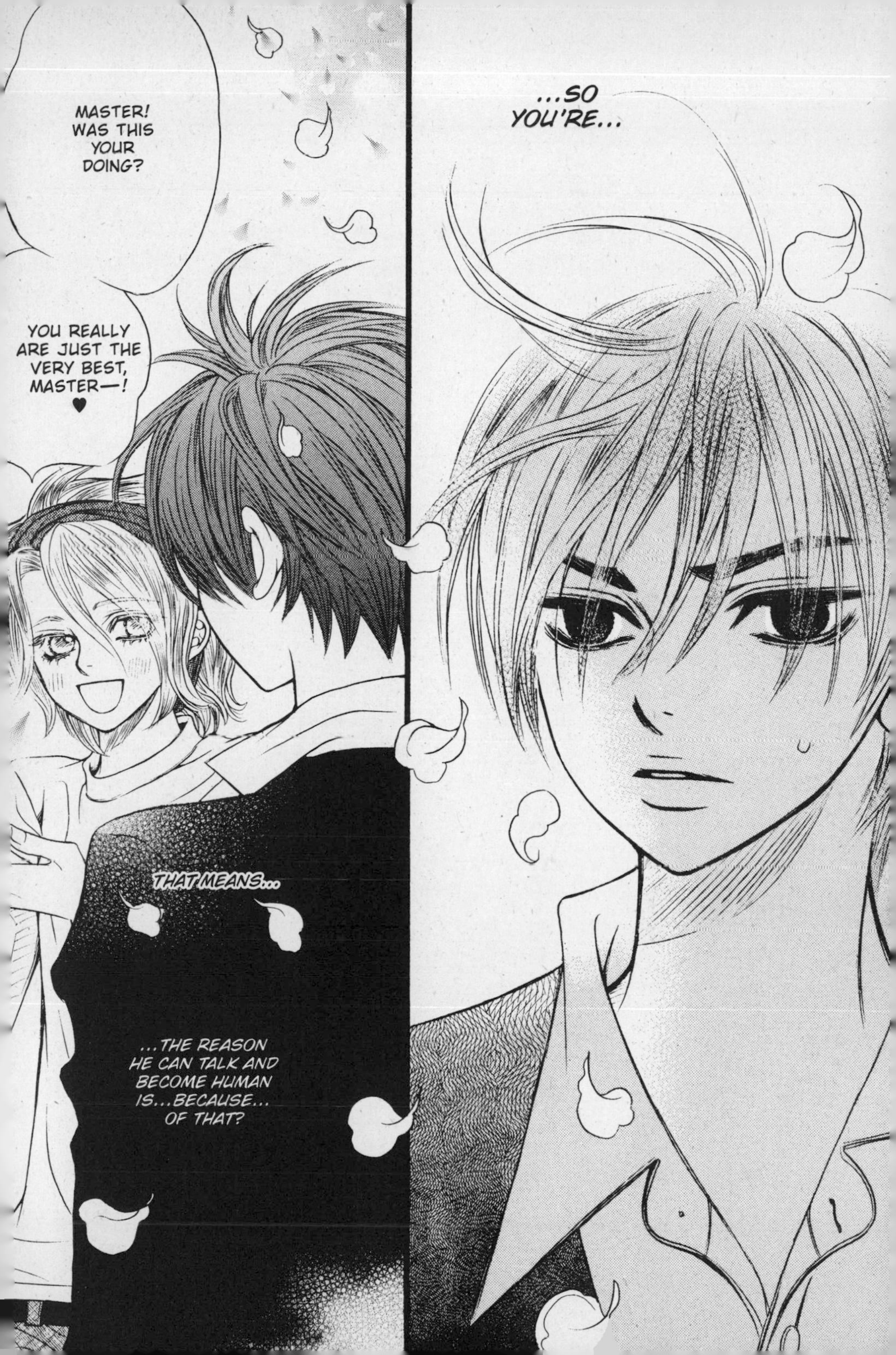
...SO YOU'RE...
MASTER! WAS THIS YOUR DOING?
YOU REALLY ARE JUST THE VERY BEST, MASTER—! ♥
THAT MEANS...
...THE REASON HE CAN TALK AND BECOME HUMAN IS...BECAUSE... OF THAT?

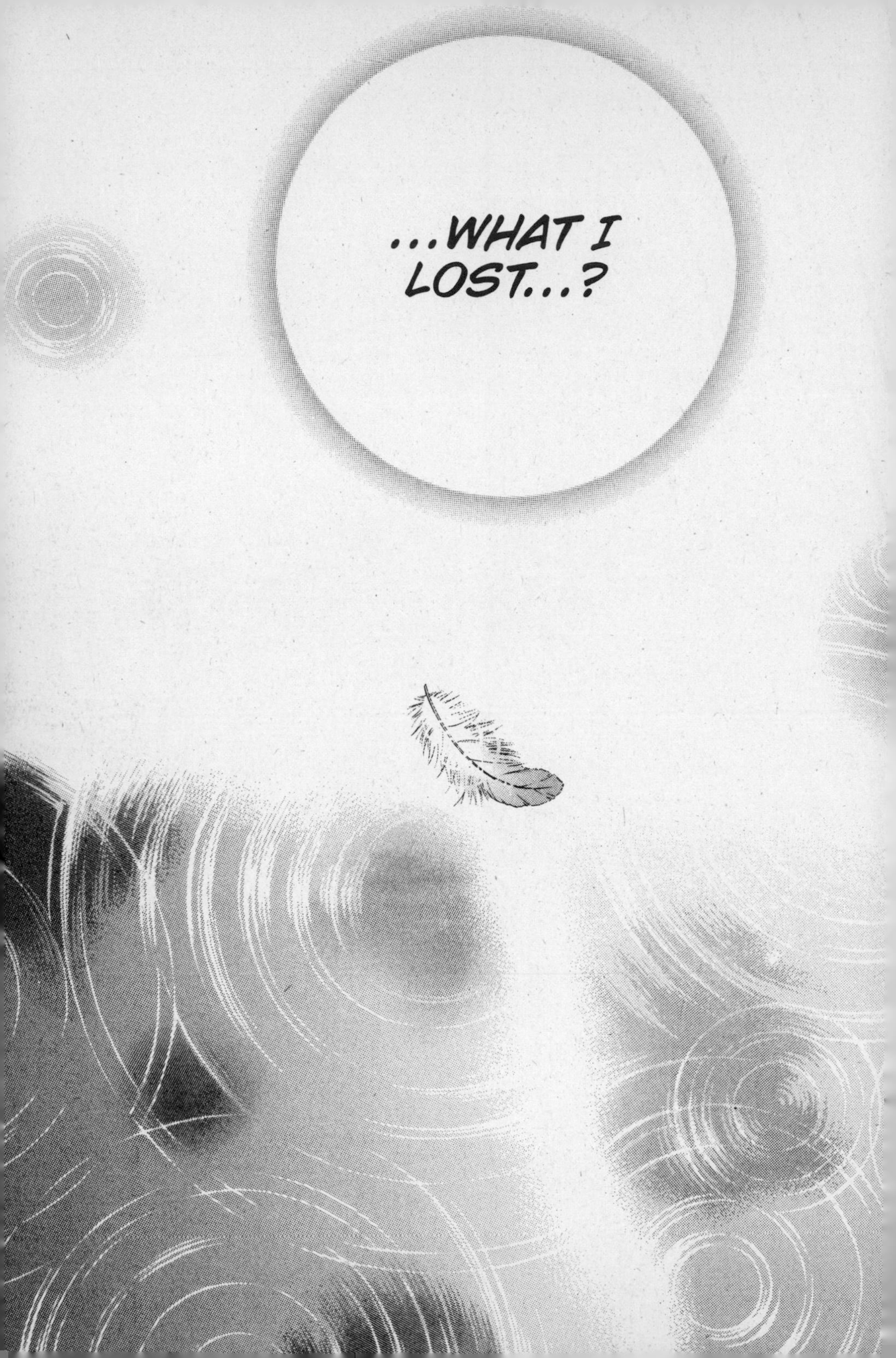
...WHAT I LOST...?

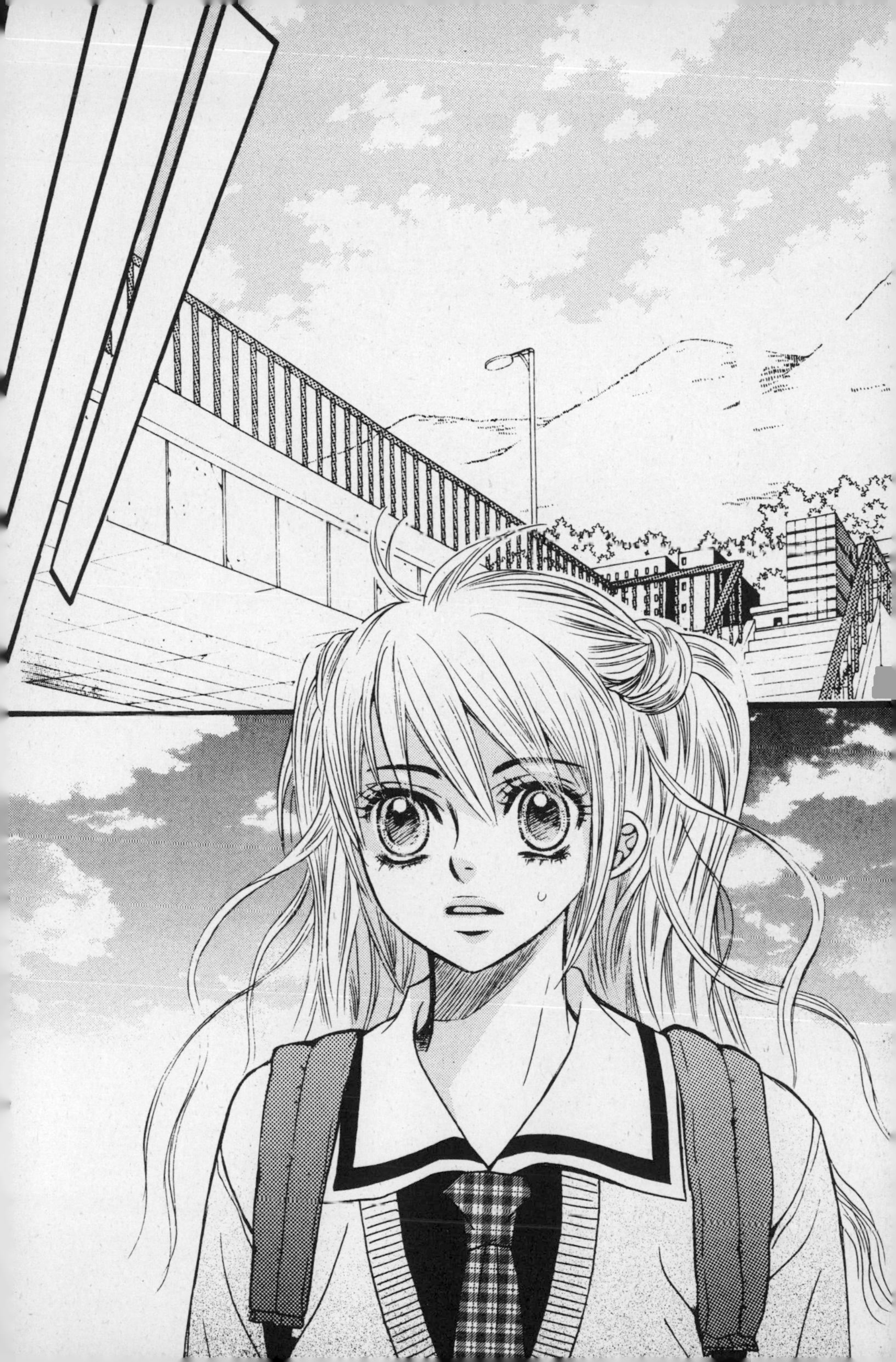

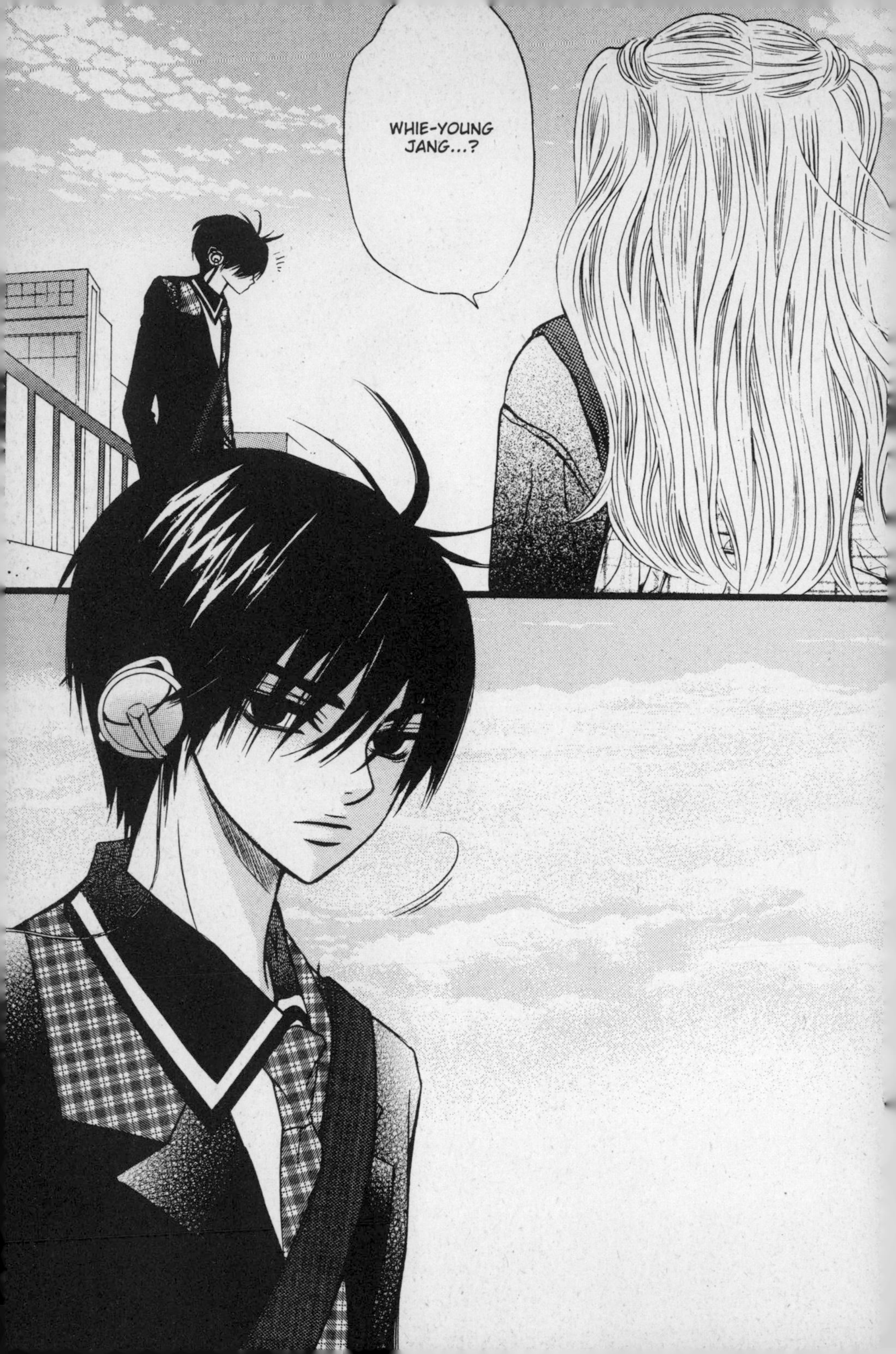
WHIE-YOUNG JANG...?

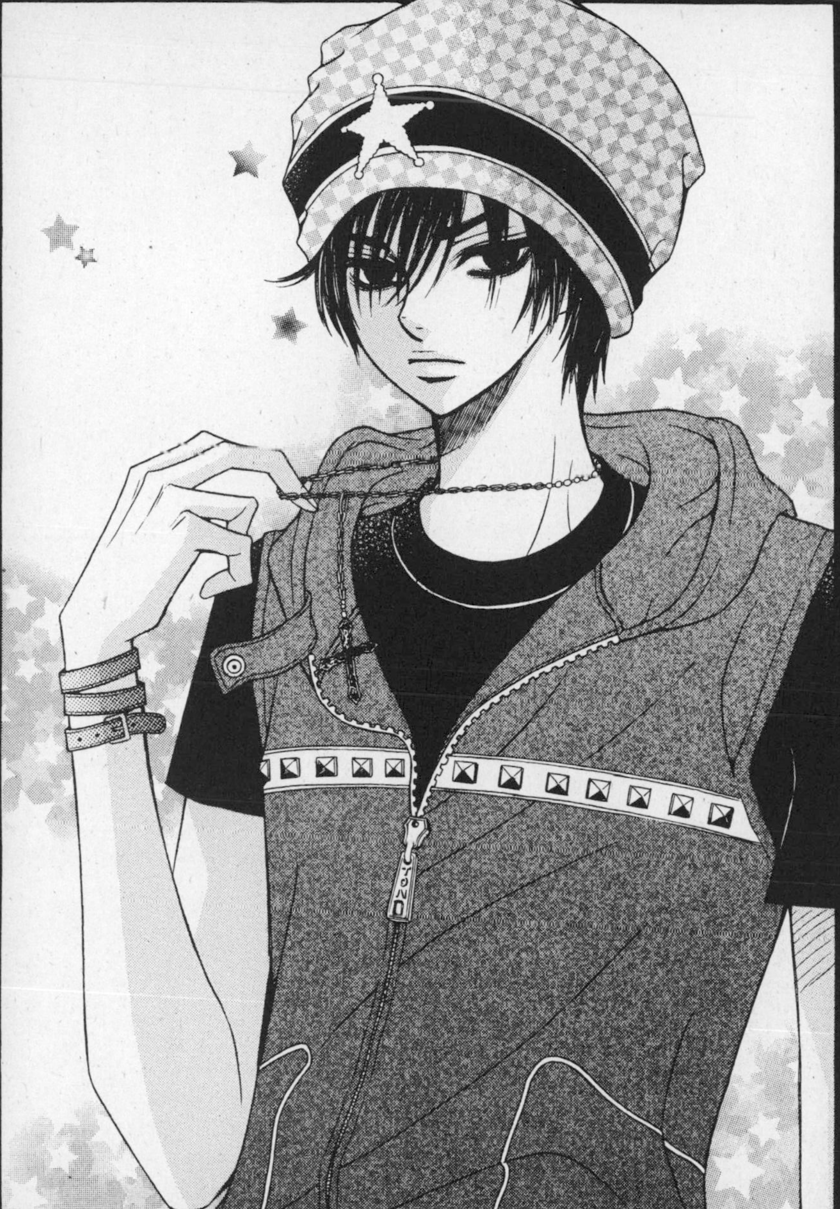

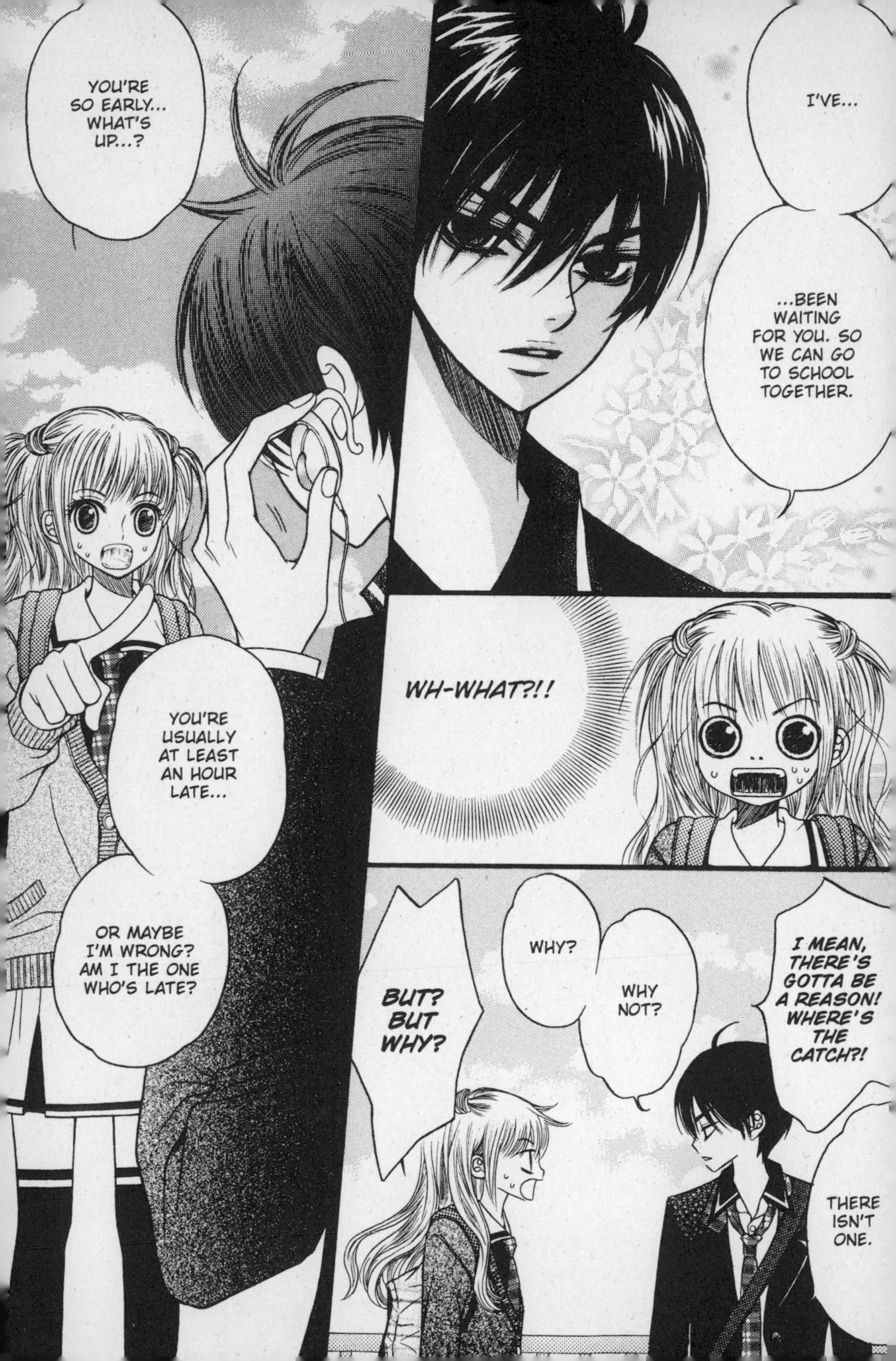
YOU'RE SO EARLY... WHAT'S UP...?
YOU'RE USUALLY AT LEAST AN HOUR LATE...
OR MAYBE I'M WRONG? AM I THE ONE WHO'S LATE?
I'VE...
...BEEN WAITING FOR YOU. SO WE CAN GO TO SCHOOL TOGETHER.
WH-WHAT?!!
BUT? BUT WHY?
WHY?
WHY NOT?
I MEAN, THERE'S GOTTA BE A REASON! WHERE'S THE CATCH?!
THERE ISN'T ONE.

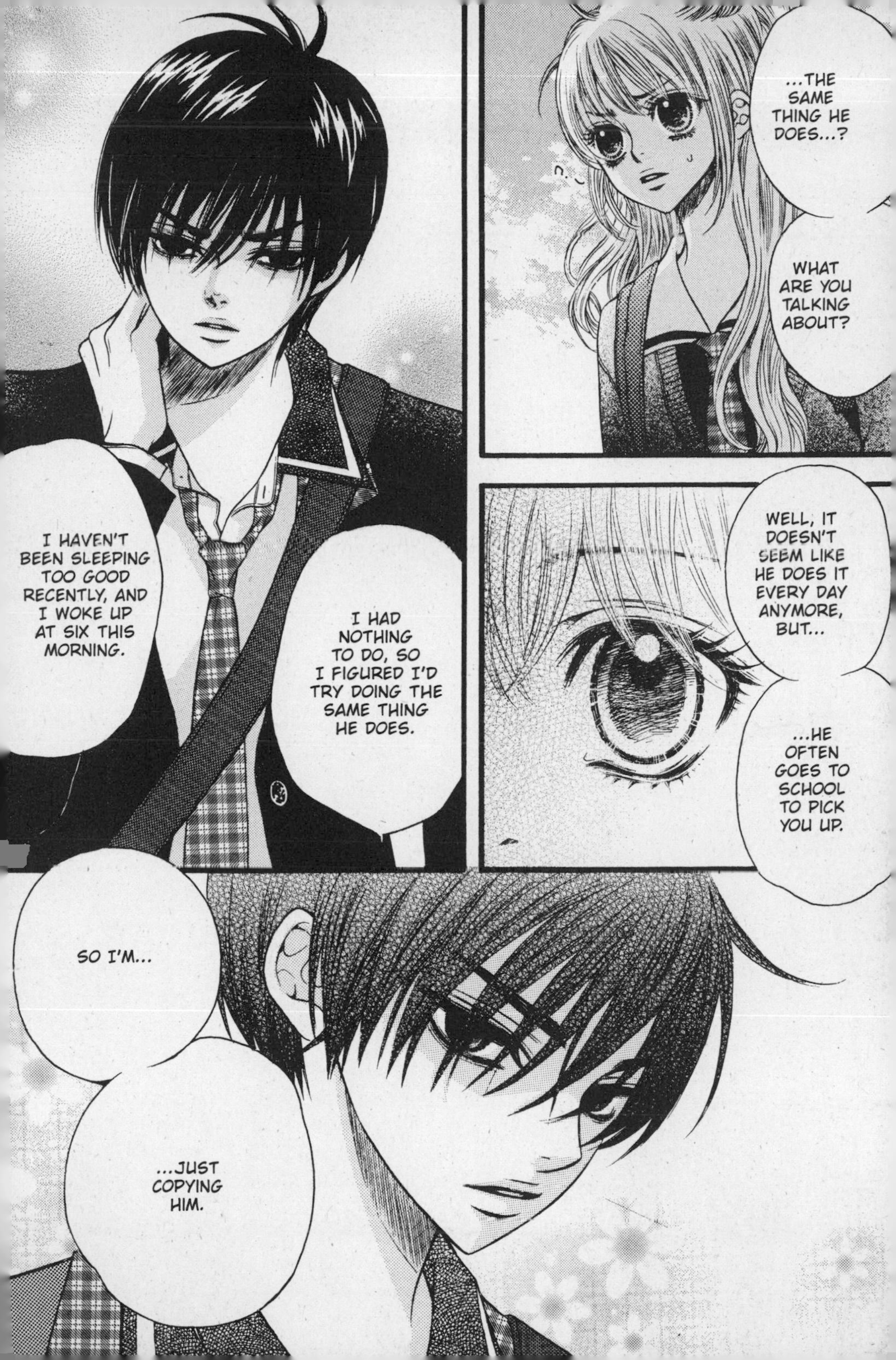

I HAVEN'T BEEN SLEEPING TOO GOOD RECENTLY, AND I WOKE UP AT SIX THIS MORNING.
I HAD NOTHING TO DO, SO I FIGURED I'D TRY DOING THE SAME THING HE DOES.
...THE SAME THING HE DOES...?
WHAT ARE YOU TALKING ABOUT?
WELL, IT DOESN'T SEEM LIKE HE DOES IT EVERY DAY ANYMORE, BUT...
...HE OFTEN GOES TO SCHOOL TO PICK YOU UP.
SO I'M...
...JUST COPYING HIM.

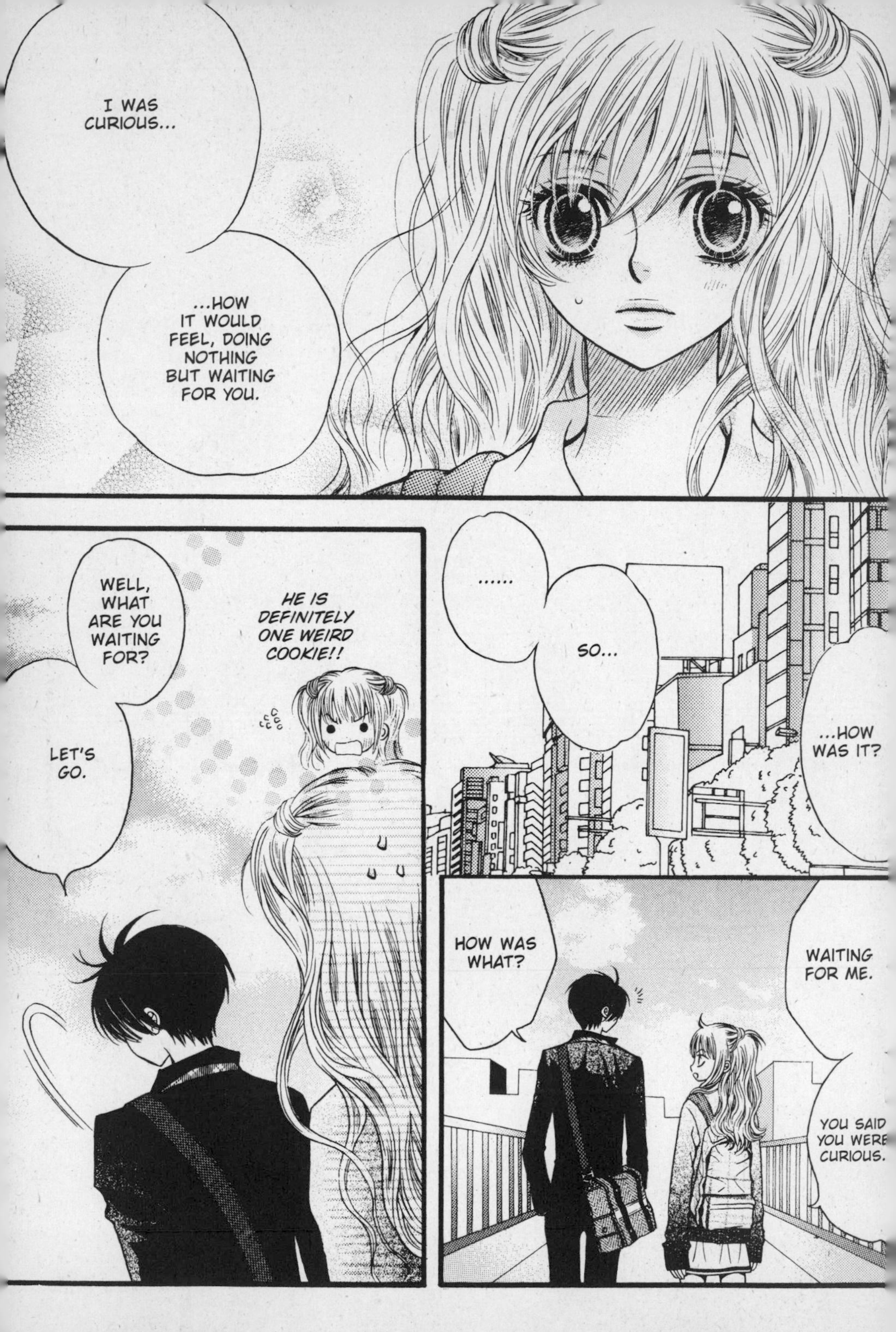
I WAS CURIOUS...
...HOW IT WOULD FEEL, DOING NOTHING BUT WAITING FOR YOU.
......
SO...
...HOW WAS IT?
HOW WAS WHAT?
WAITING FOR ME.
YOU SAID YOU WERE CURIOUS.
WELL, WHAT ARE YOU WAITING FOR?
LET'S GO.
HE IS DEFINITELY ONE WEIRD COOKIE!!

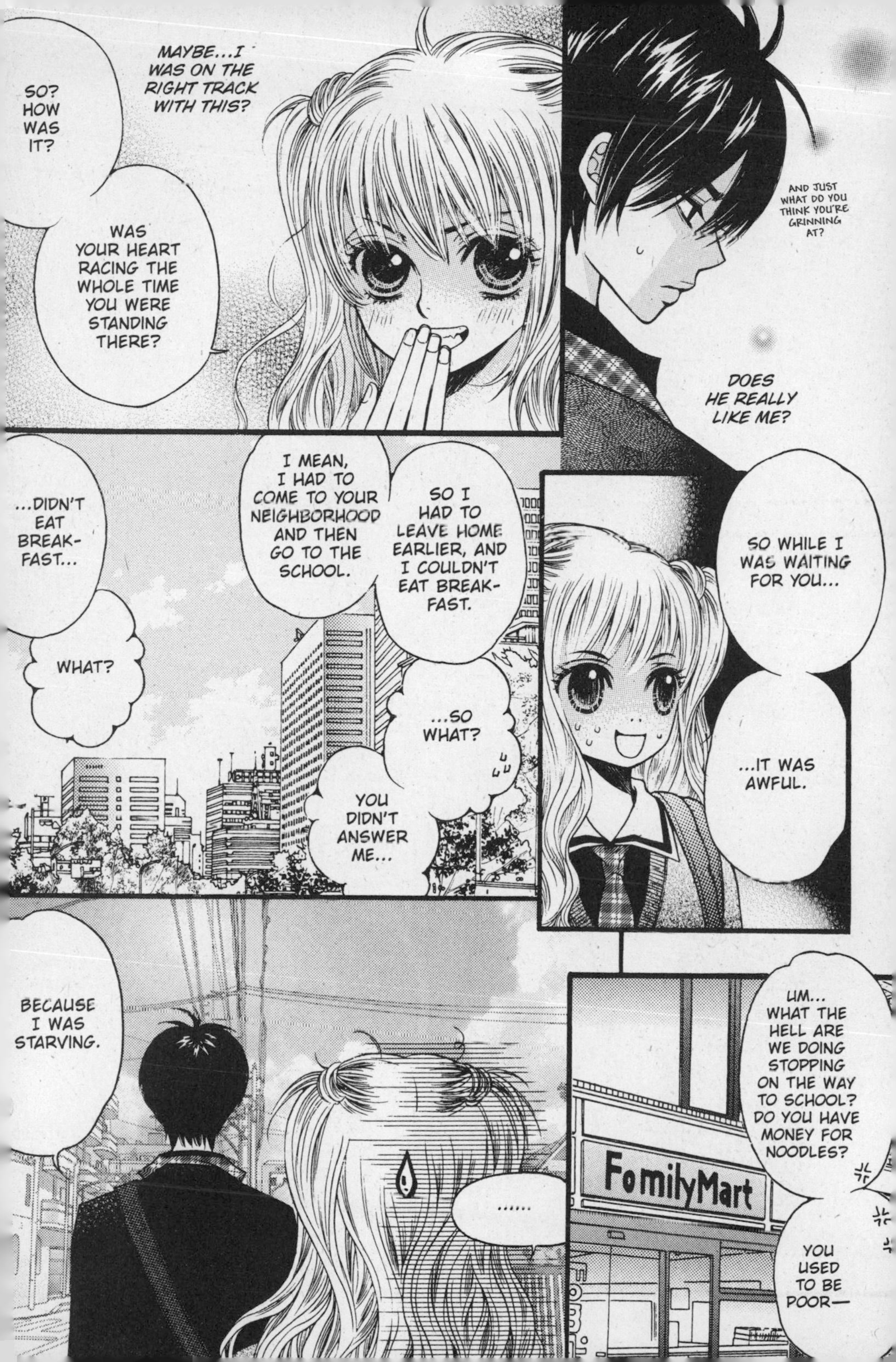
SO? HOW WAS IT?
WAS YOUR HEART RACING THE WHOLE TIME YOU WERE STANDING THERE?
MAYBE...I WAS ON THE RIGHT TRACK WITH THIS?
AND JUST WHAT DO YOU THINK YOU'RE GRINNING AT?
DOES HE REALLY LIKE ME?
SO WHILE I WAS WAITING FOR YOU...
...IT WAS AWFUL.
I MEAN, I HAD TO COME TO YOUR NEIGHBORHOOD AND THEN GO TO THE SCHOOL.
SO I HAD TO LEAVE HOME EARLIER, AND I COULDN'T EAT BREAK-FAST.
...DIDN'T EAT BREAK-FAST...
WHAT?
...SO WHAT?
YOU DIDN'T ANSWER ME...
UM... WHAT THE HELL ARE WE DOING STOPPING ON THE WAY TO SCHOOL? DO YOU HAVE MONEY FOR NOODLES?
YOU USED TO BE POOR—
FamilyMart
BECAUSE I WAS STARVING.
......

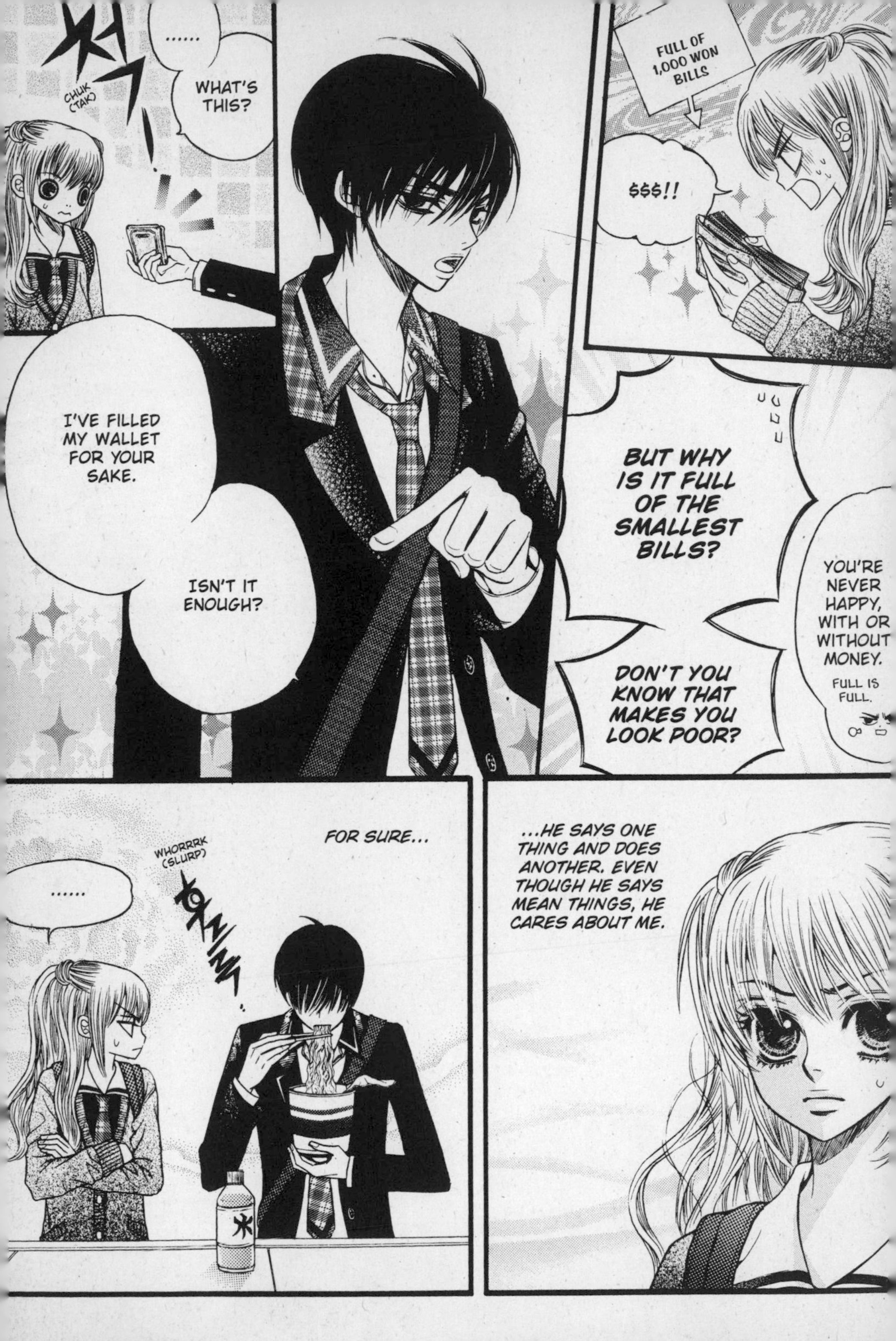

CHUK (TAK)
......
WHAT'S THIS?
FULL OF 1,000 WON BILLS
$$$!!
I'VE FILLED MY WALLET FOR YOUR SAKE.
ISN'T IT ENOUGH?
BUT WHY IS IT FULL OF THE SMALLEST BILLS?
DON'T YOU KNOW THAT MAKES YOU LOOK POOR?
YOU'RE NEVER HAPPY, WITH OR WITHOUT MONEY.
FULL IS FULL.
......
WHORRRK (SLURP)
FOR SURE...
...HE SAYS ONE THING AND DOES ANOTHER. EVEN THOUGH HE SAYS MEAN THINGS, HE CARES ABOUT ME.

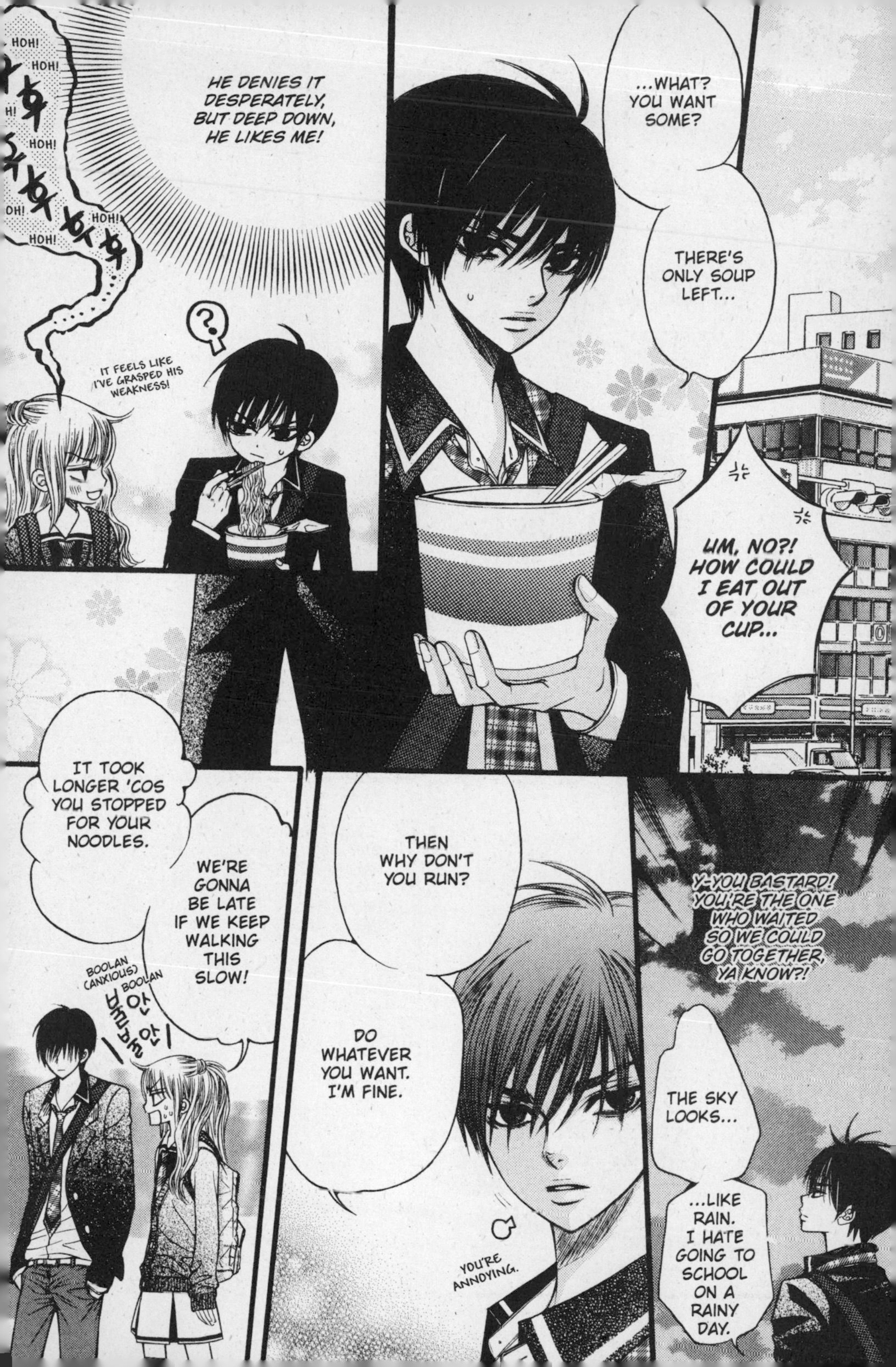

...WHAT? YOU WANT SOME?
THERE'S ONLY SOUP LEFT...
UM, NO?! HOW COULD I EAT OUT OF YOUR CUP...
HE DENIES IT DESPERATELY, BUT DEEP DOWN, HE LIKES ME!
HOH! HOH! HOH! HOH!
IT FEELS LIKE I'VE GRASPED HIS WEAKNESS!
THE SKY LOOKS...
...LIKE RAIN. I HATE GOING TO SCHOOL ON A RAINY DAY.
Y-YOU BASTARD! YOU'RE THE ONE WHO WAITED SO WE COULD GO TOGETHER, YA KNOW?!
THEN WHY DON'T YOU RUN?
DO WHATEVER YOU WANT. I'M FINE.
YOU'RE ANNOYING.
IT TOOK LONGER 'COS YOU STOPPED FOR YOUR NOODLES.
WE'RE GONNA BE LATE IF WE KEEP WALKING THIS SLOW!
BOOLAN (ANXIOUS) BOOLAN

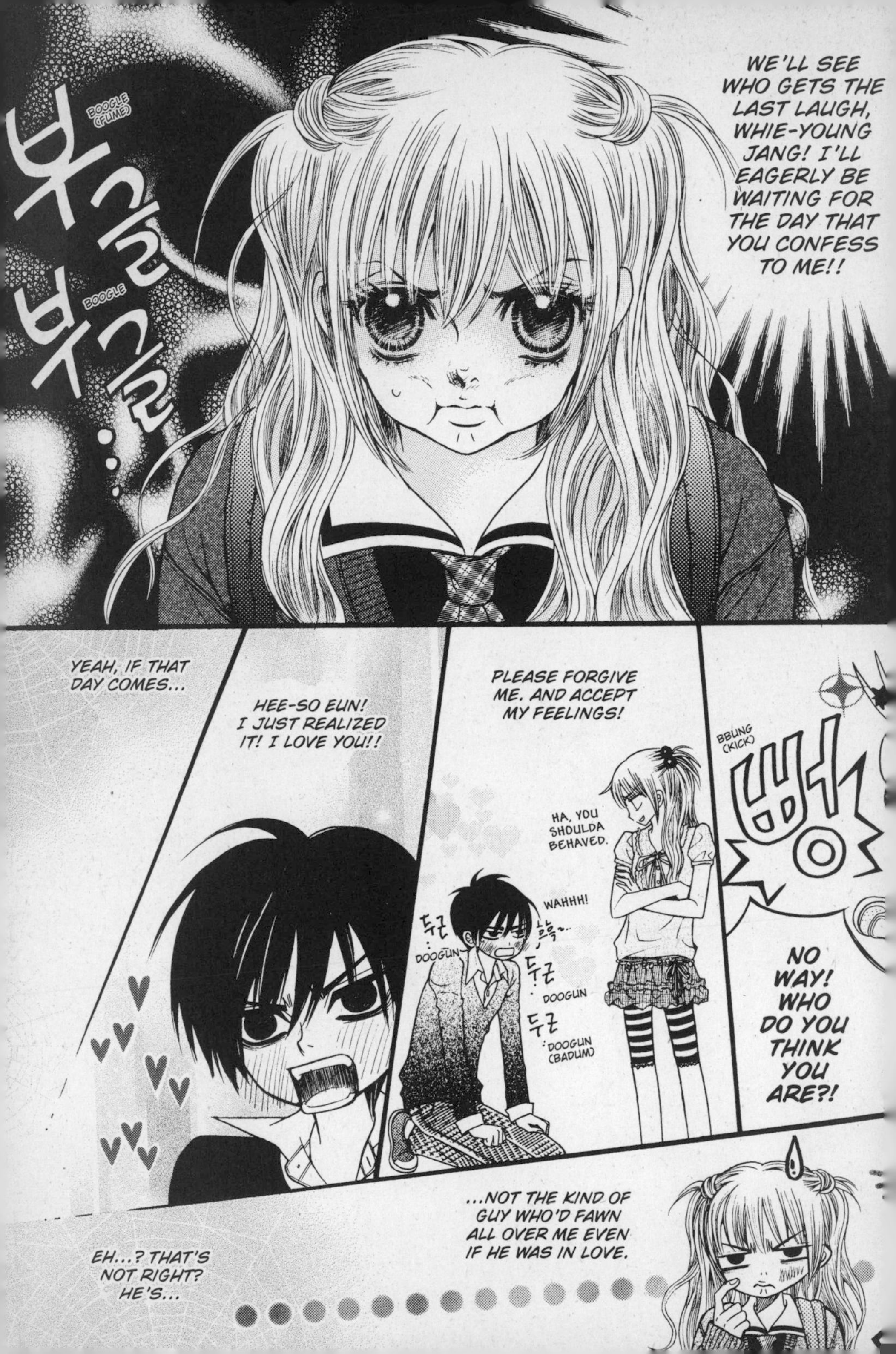

부글
BOOGLE (FUME)
부글...
BOOGLE
WE'LL SEE WHO GETS THE LAST LAUGH, WHIE-YOUNG JANG! I'LL EAGERLY BE WAITING FOR THE DAY THAT YOU CONFESS TO ME!!
YEAH, IF THAT DAY COMES...
HEE-SO EUN! I JUST REALIZED IT! I LOVE YOU!!
PLEASE FORGIVE ME. AND ACCEPT MY FEELINGS!
HA, YOU SHOULDA BEHAVED.
WAHHH!
두근
DOOGUN
두근
DOOGUN
두근
DOOGUN (BADUM)
뻥
BBUNG (KICK)
NO WAY! WHO DO YOU THINK YOU ARE?!
EH...? THAT'S NOT RIGHT? HE'S...
...NOT THE KIND OF GUY WHO'D FAWN ALL OVER ME EVEN IF HE WAS IN LOVE.

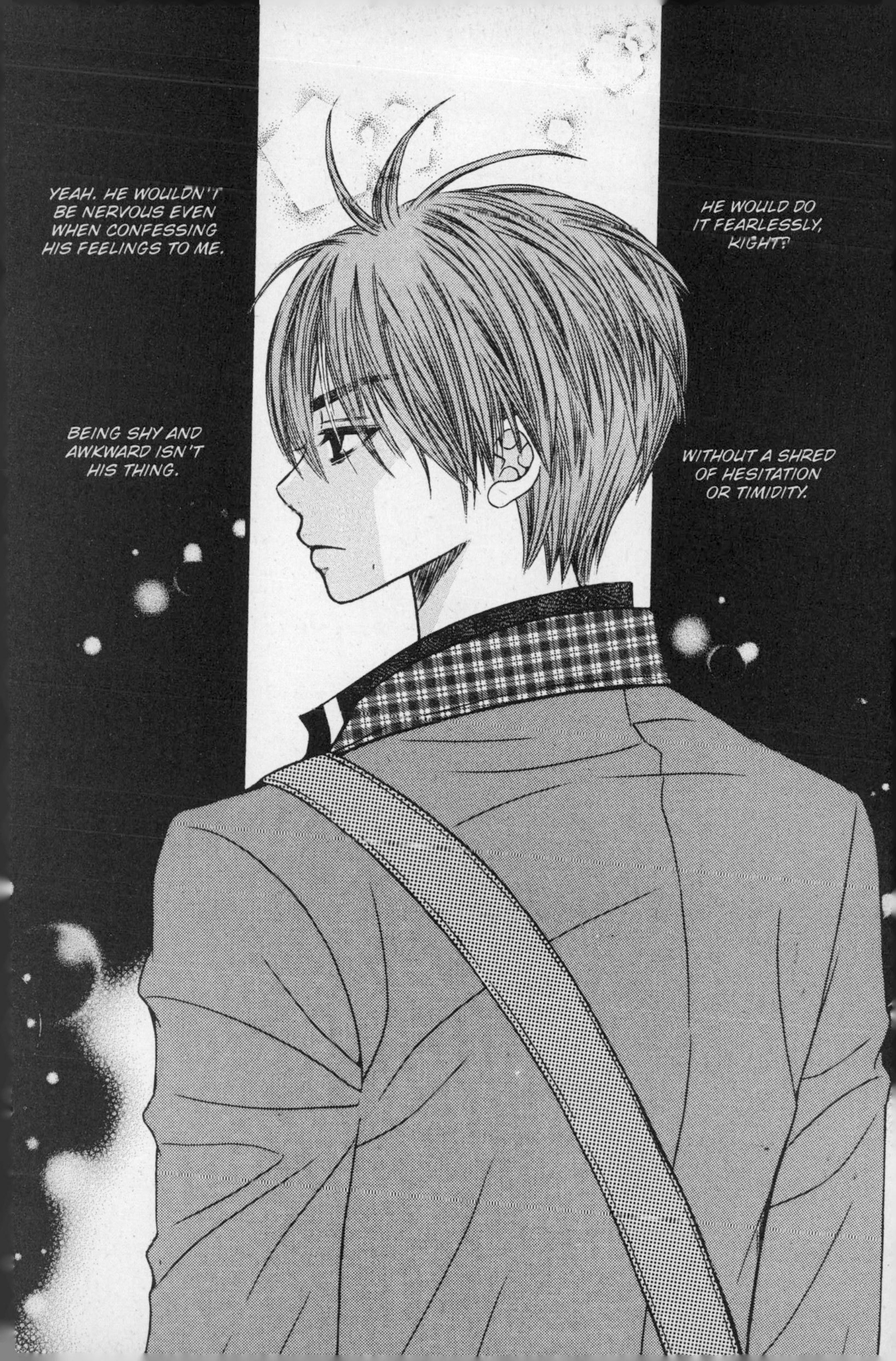
YEAH. HE WOULDN'T BE NERVOUS EVEN WHEN CONFESSING HIS FEELINGS TO ME.
HE WOULD DO IT FEARLESSLY, RIGHT?
BEING SHY AND AWKWARD ISN'T HIS THING.
WITHOUT A SHRED OF HESITATION OR TIMIDITY.

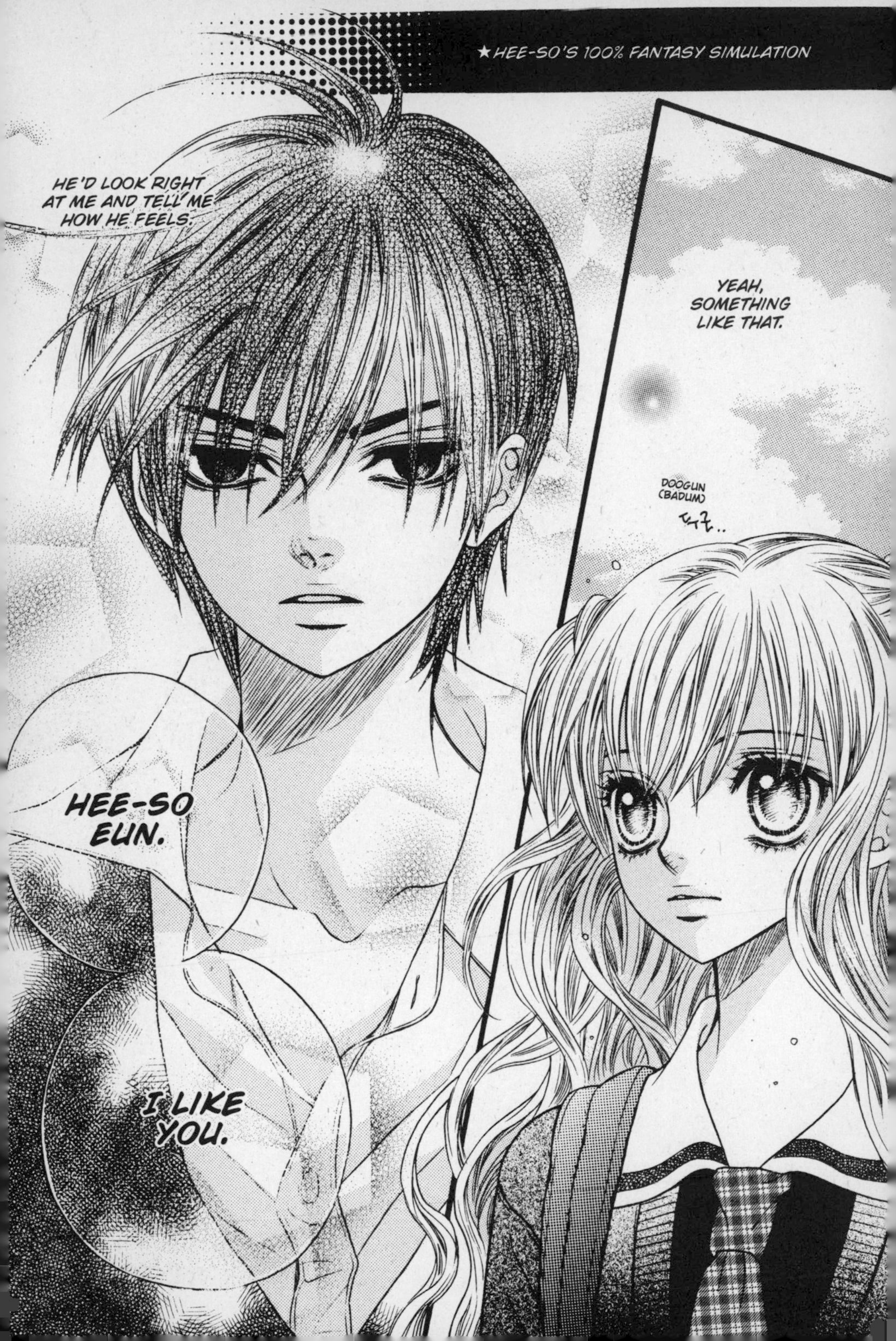
★HEE-SO'S 100% FANTASY SIMULATION
HE'D LOOK RIGHT AT ME AND TELL ME HOW HE FEELS.
YEAH, SOMETHING LIKE THAT.
DOOGUN (BADUM)
HEE-SO EUN.
I LIKE YOU.

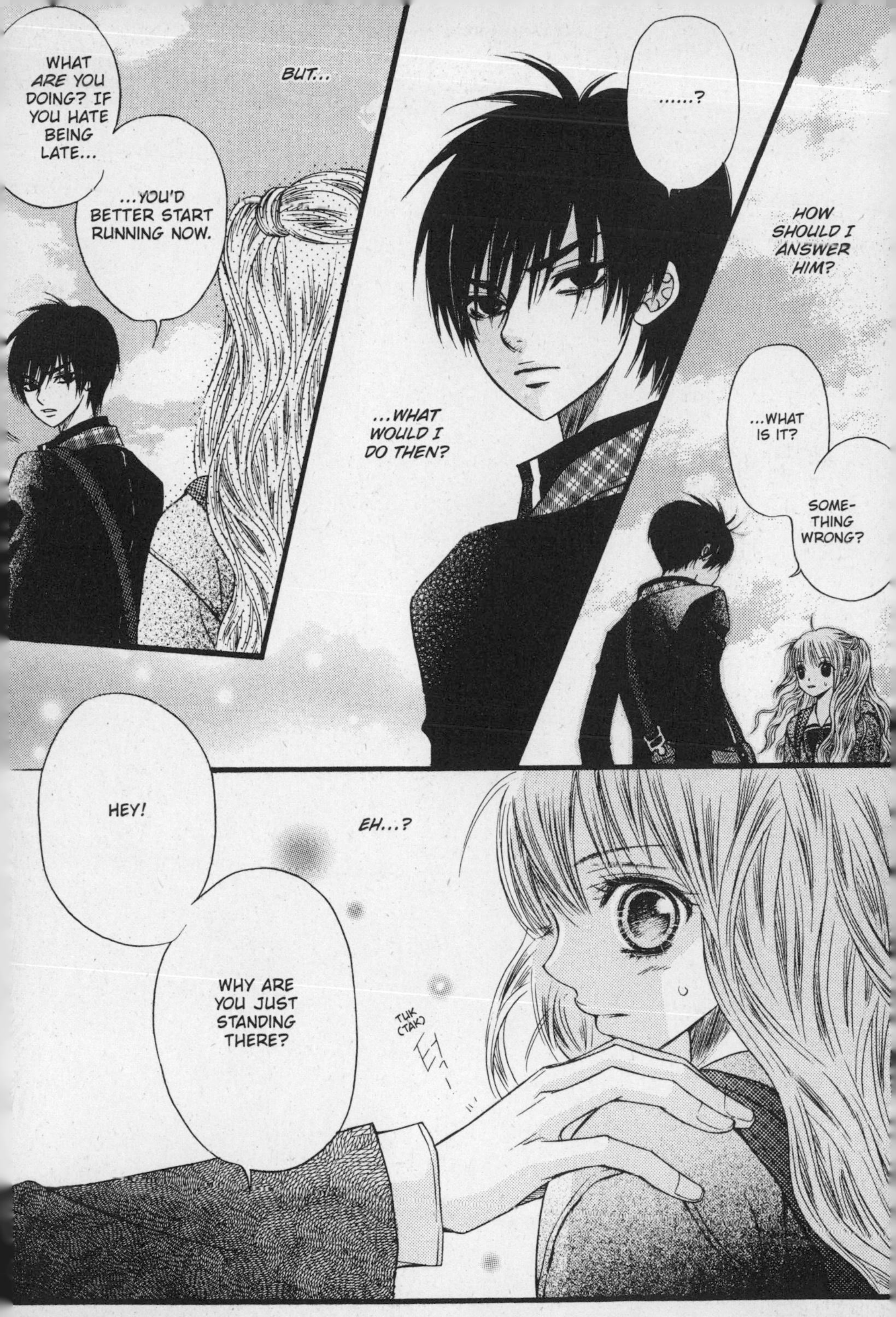
HOW SHOULD I ANSWER HIM?
...WHAT IS IT?
SOME-THING WRONG?
......?
...WHAT WOULD I DO THEN?
WHAT ARE YOU DOING? IF YOU HATE BEING LATE...
...YOU'D BETTER START RUNNING NOW.
BUT...
EH...?
HEY!
WHY ARE YOU JUST STANDING THERE?
TUK (TAK)

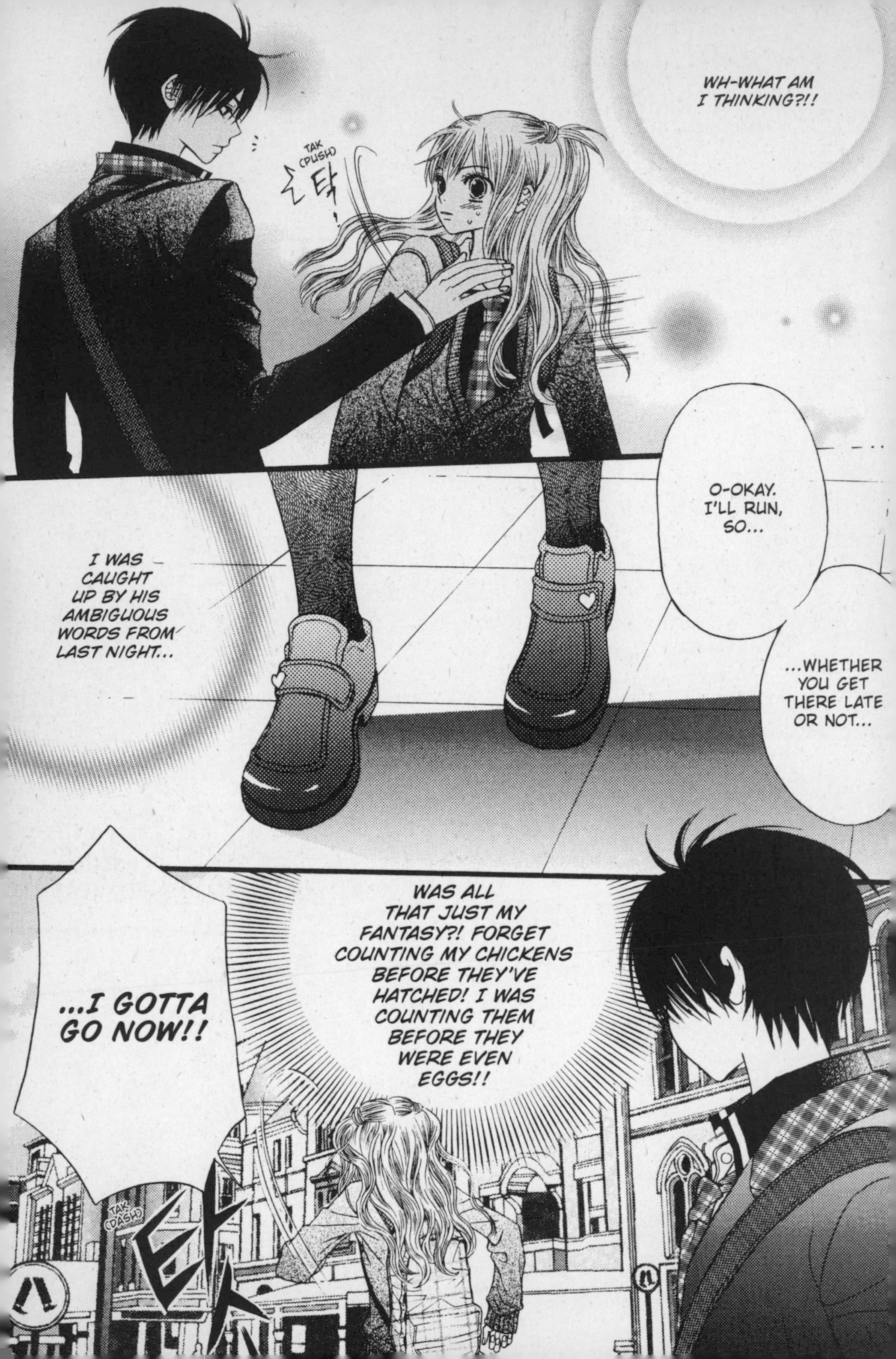
TAK (PUSH)
탁
WH-WHAT AM I THINKING?!!
O-OKAY. I'LL RUN, SO...
I WAS CAUGHT UP BY HIS AMBIGUOUS WORDS FROM LAST NIGHT...
...WHETHER YOU GET THERE LATE OR NOT...
...I GOTTA GO NOW!!
WAS ALL THAT JUST MY FANTASY?! FORGET COUNTING MY CHICKENS BEFORE THEY'VE HATCHED! I WAS COUNTING THEM BEFORE THEY WERE EVEN EGGS!!
TAK (DASH)

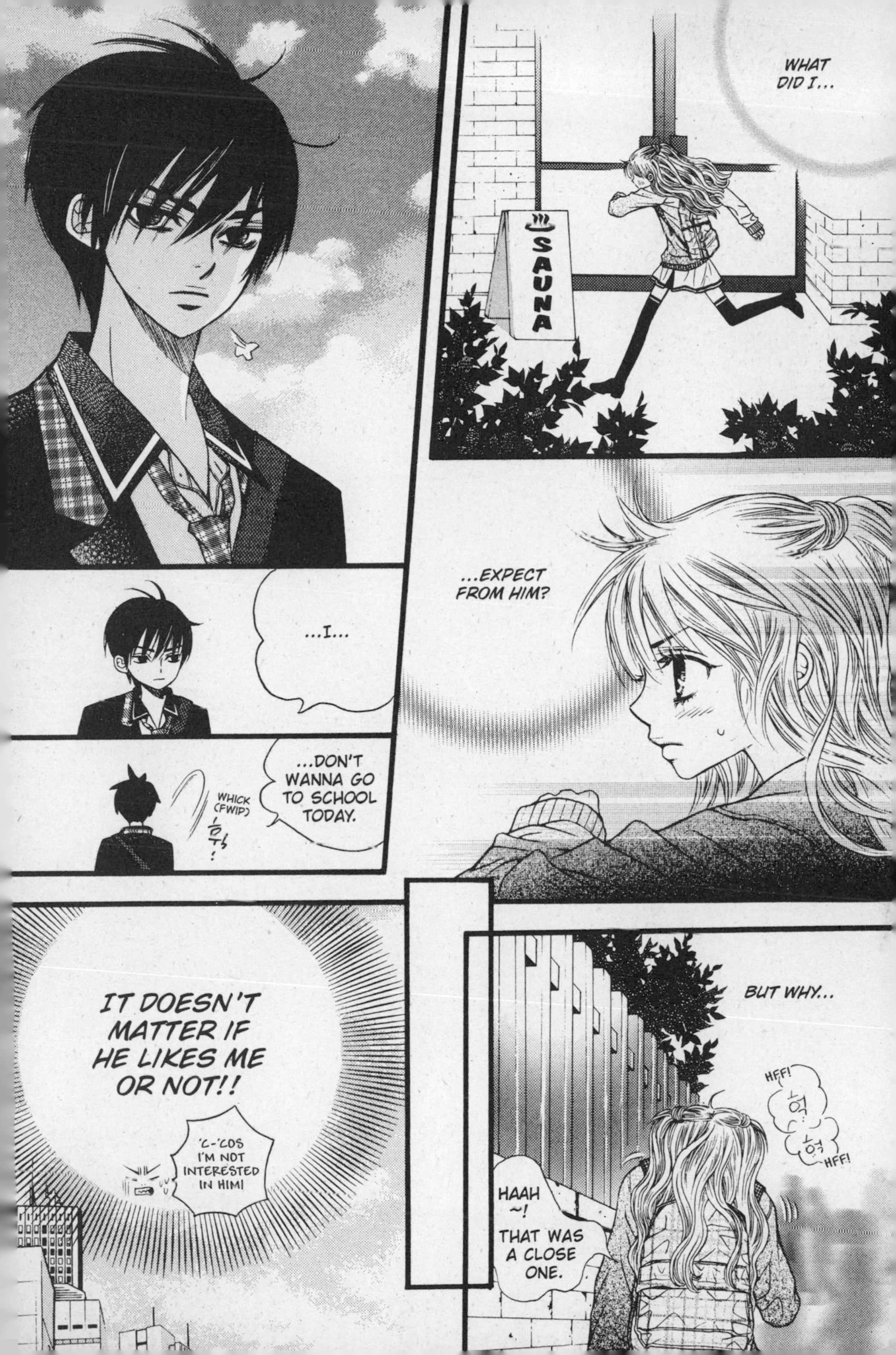
...I...
...DON'T WANNA GO TO SCHOOL TODAY.
WHICK (FWIP)
휙!
WHAT DID I...
SAUNA
...EXPECT FROM HIM?
IT DOESN'T MATTER IF HE LIKES ME OR NOT!!
'C-'COS I'M NOT INTERESTED IN HIM!
BUT WHY...
HFF!
헉
헉
HFF!
HAAH~! THAT WAS A CLOSE ONE.

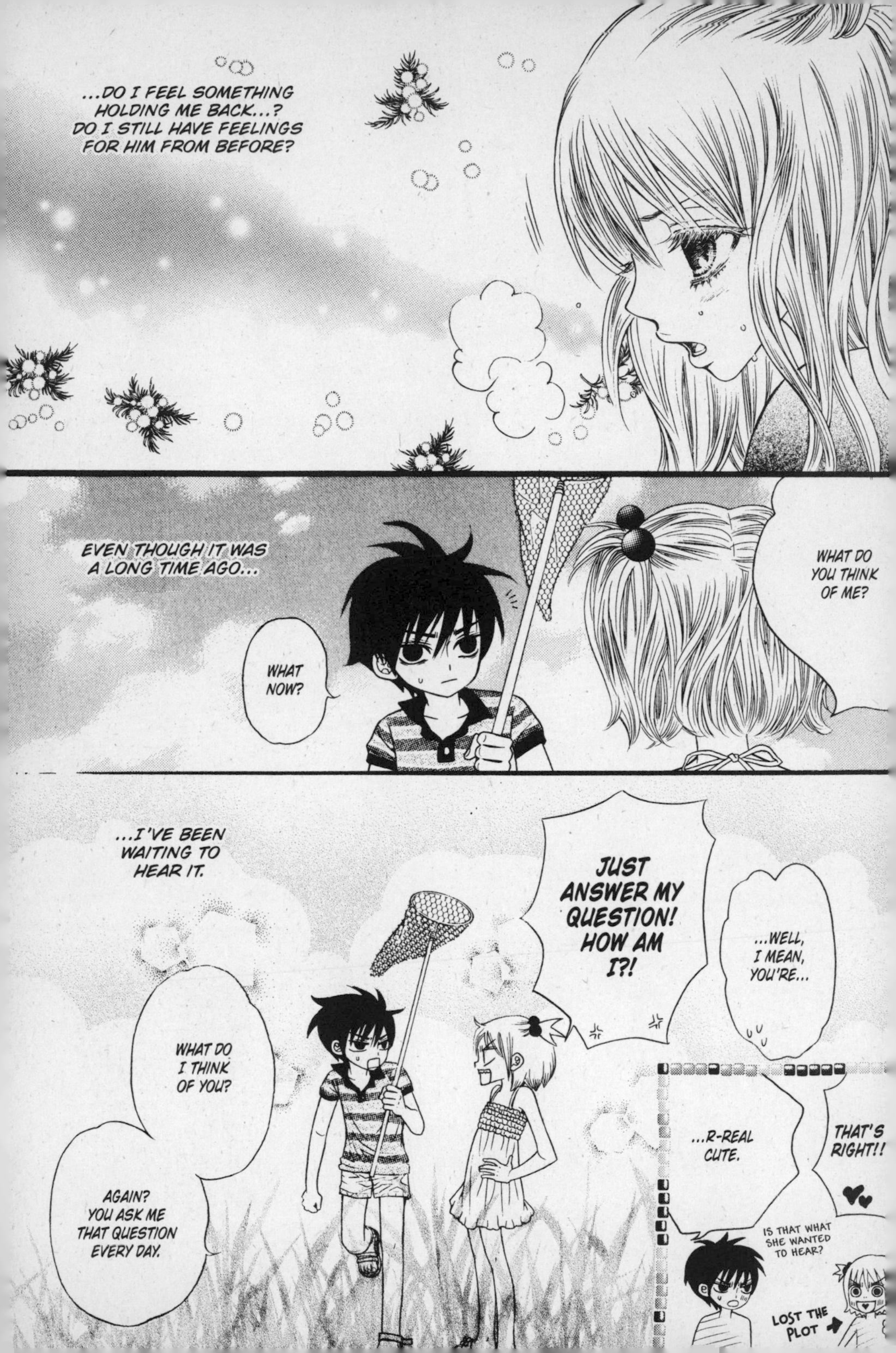
...DO I FEEL SOMETHING HOLDING ME BACK...? DO I STILL HAVE FEELINGS FOR HIM FROM BEFORE?
WHAT DO YOU THINK OF ME?
EVEN THOUGH IT WAS A LONG TIME AGO...
WHAT NOW?
...I'VE BEEN WAITING TO HEAR IT.
...WELL, I MEAN, YOU'RE...
JUST ANSWER MY QUESTION! HOW AM I?!
WHAT DO I THINK OF YOU?
AGAIN? YOU ASK ME THAT QUESTION EVERY DAY.
THAT'S RIGHT!!
...R-REAL CUTE.
IS THAT WHAT SHE WANTED TO HEAR?
LOST THE PLOT

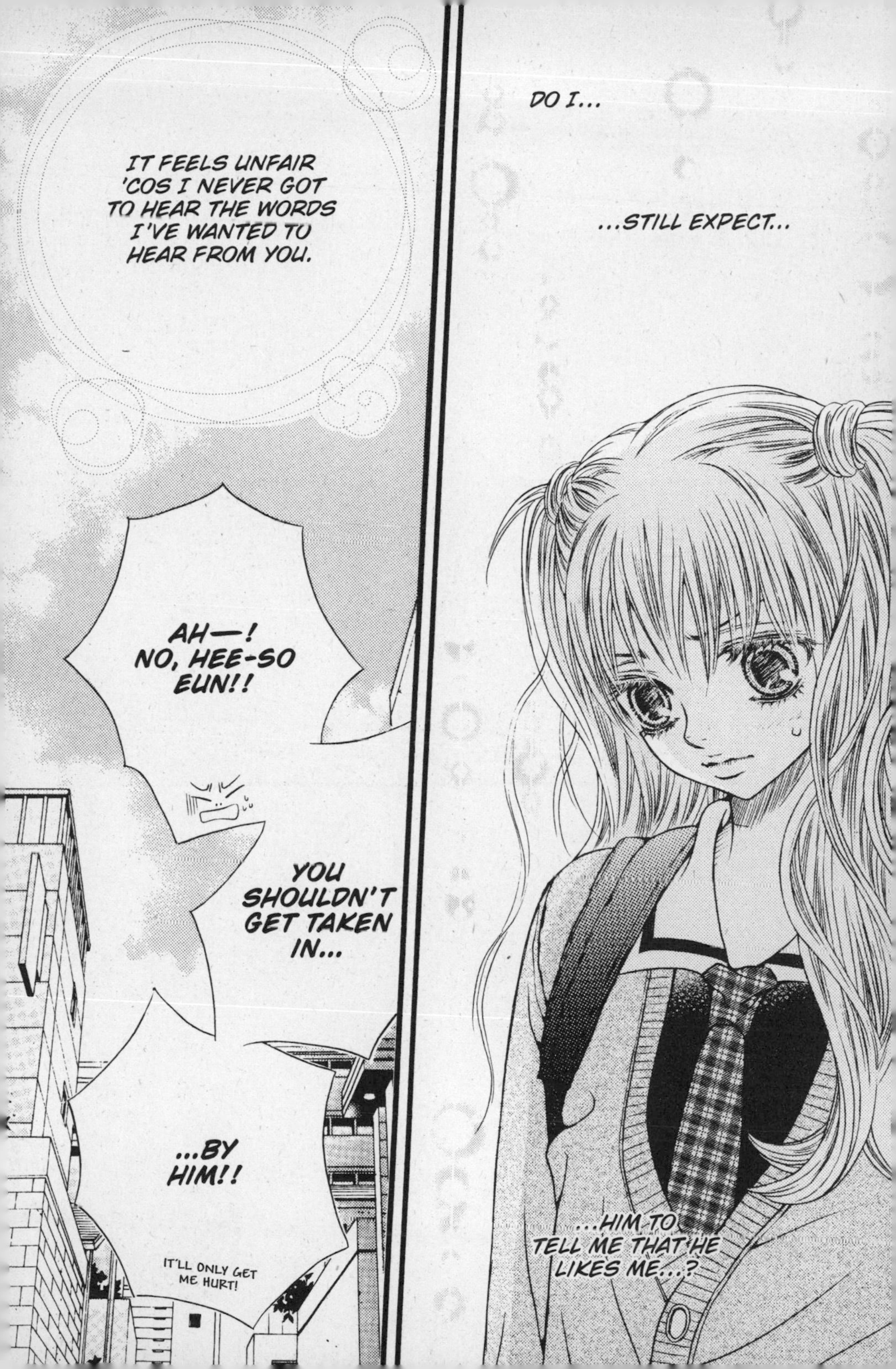
DO I...
...STILL EXPECT...
...HIM TO TELL ME THAT HE LIKES ME...?
IT FEELS UNFAIR 'COS I NEVER GOT TO HEAR THE WORDS I'VE WANTED TO HEAR FROM YOU.
AH—! NO, HEE-SO EUN!!
YOU SHOULDN'T GET TAKEN IN...
...BY HIM!!
IT'LL ONLY GET ME HURT!

STEP 39. MY MASTER

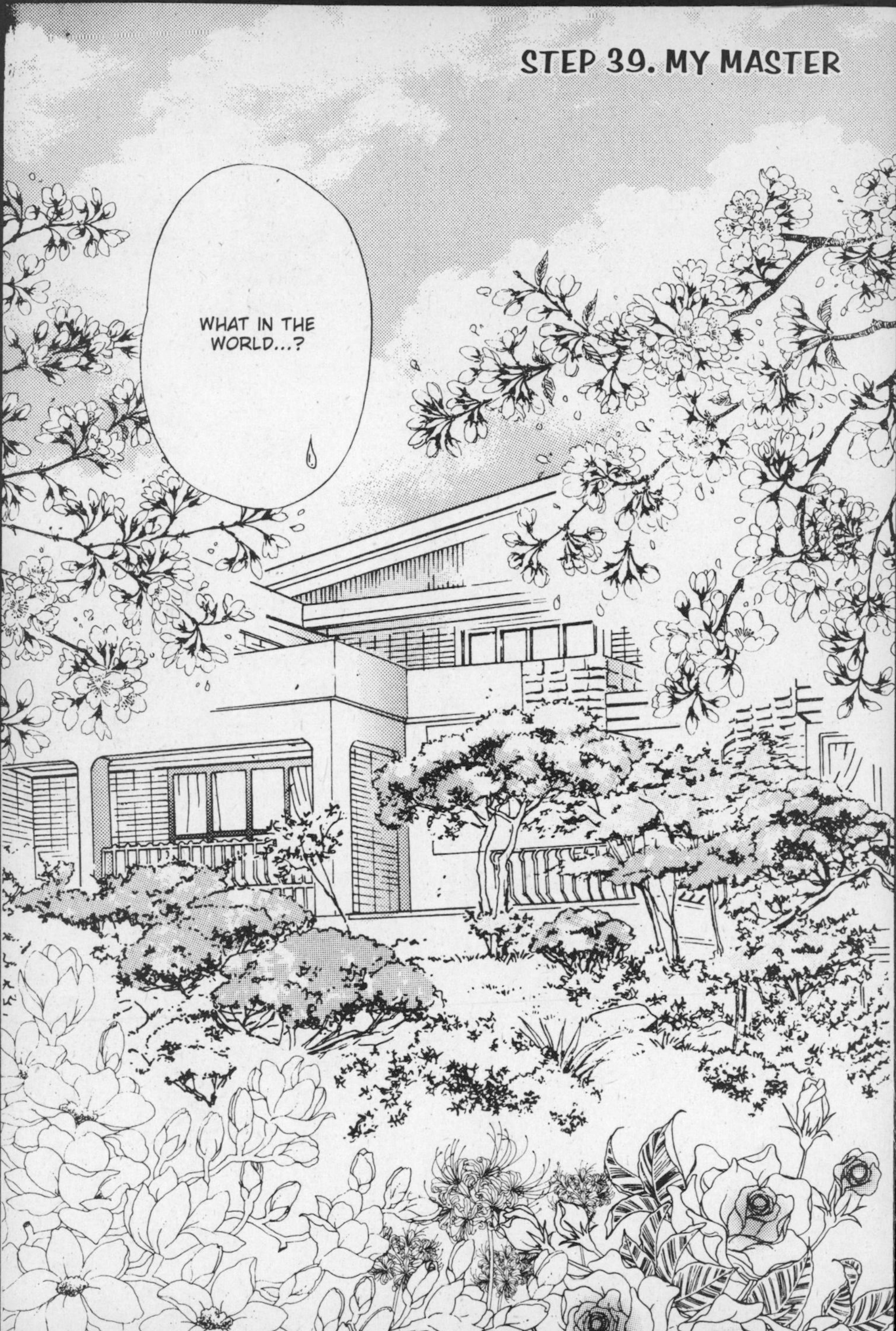

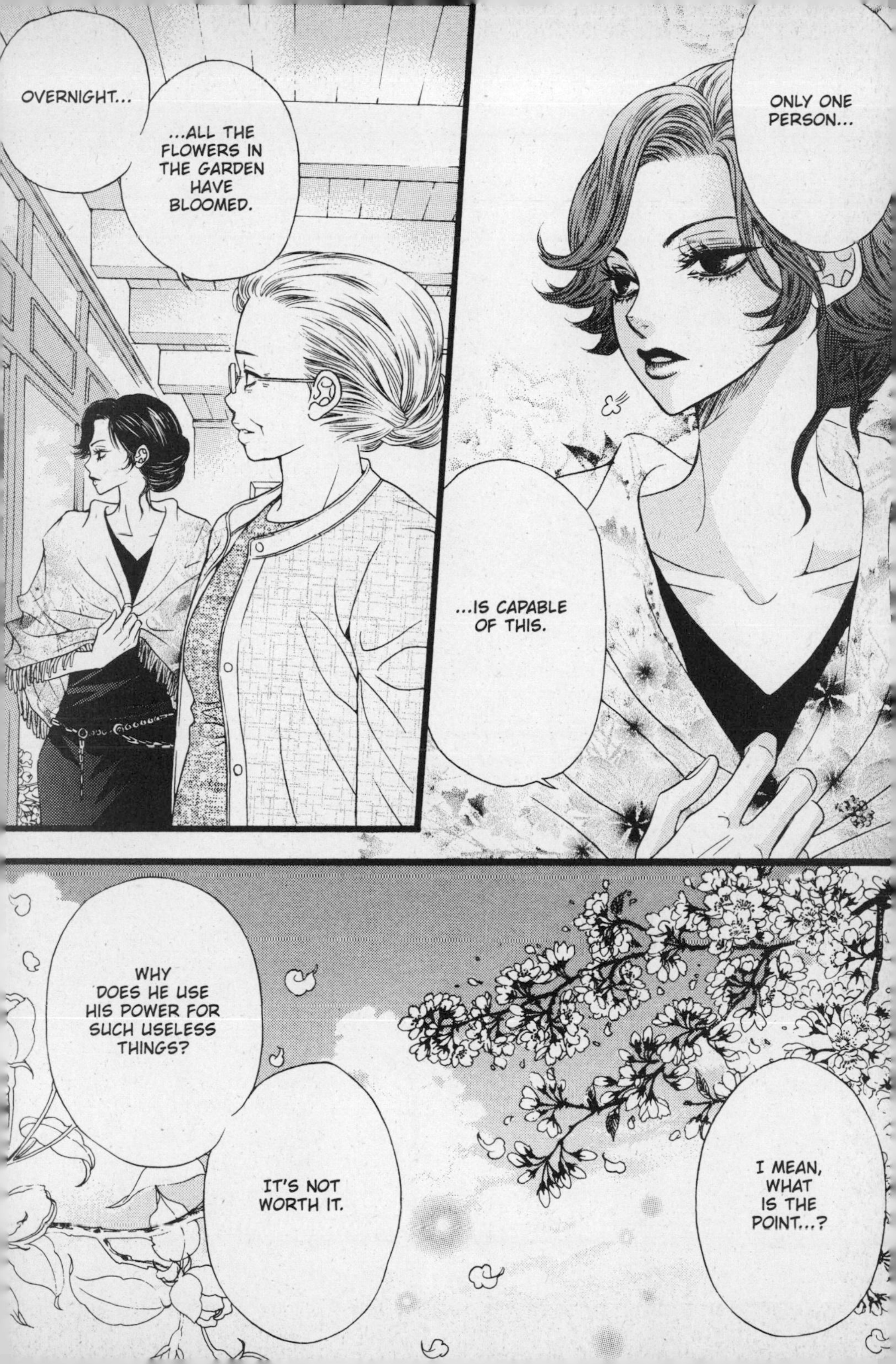
OVERNIGHT...
...ALL THE FLOWERS IN THE GARDEN HAVE BLOOMED.
ONLY ONE PERSON...
...IS CAPABLE OF THIS.
WHY DOES HE USE HIS POWER FOR SUCH USELESS THINGS?
IT'S NOT WORTH IT.
I MEAN, WHAT IS THE POINT...?

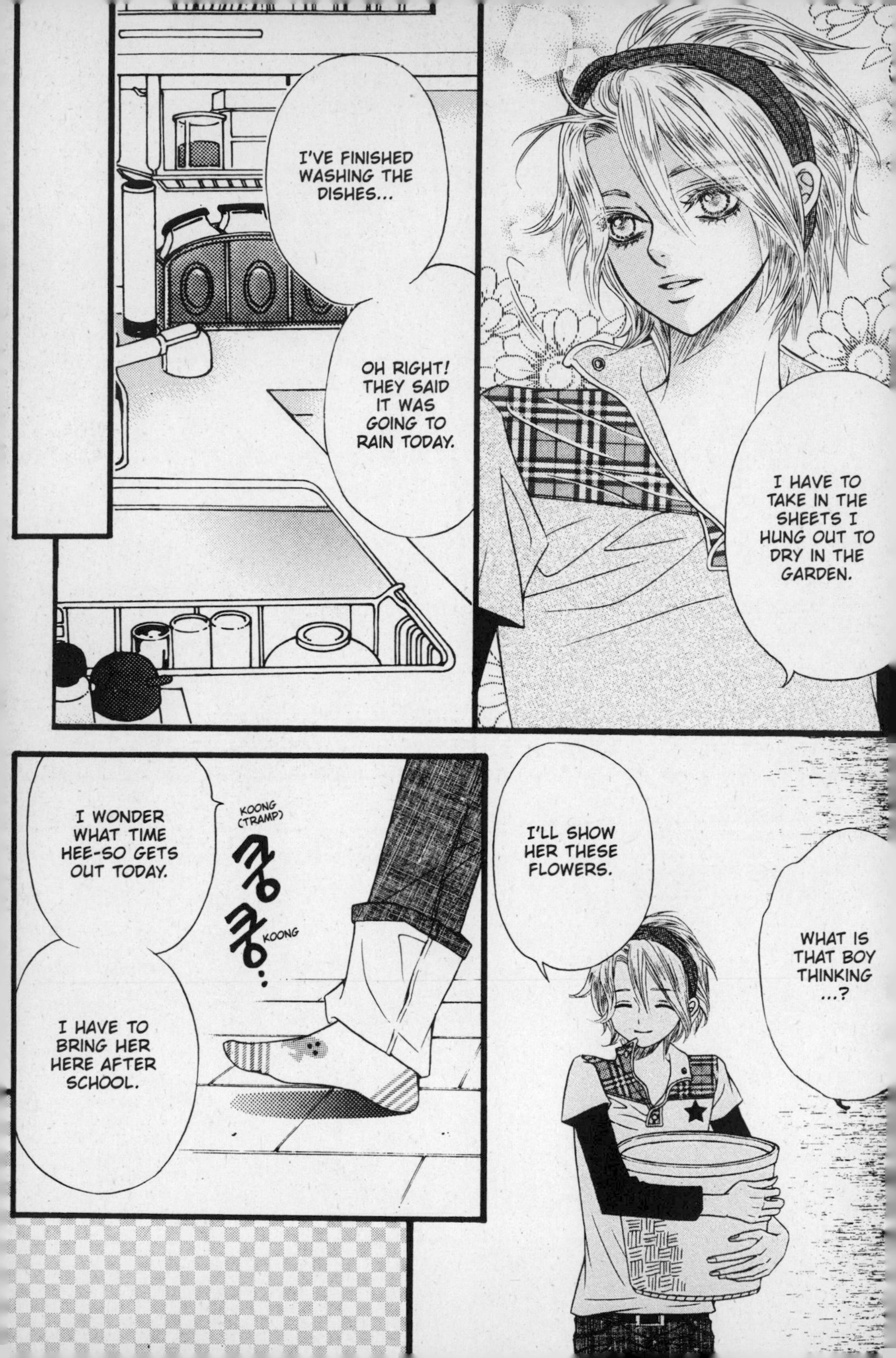
I'VE FINISHED WASHING THE DISHES...
OH RIGHT! THEY SAID IT WAS GOING TO RAIN TODAY.
I HAVE TO TAKE IN THE SHEETS I HUNG OUT TO DRY IN THE GARDEN.
I WONDER WHAT TIME HEE-SO GETS OUT TODAY.
I HAVE TO BRING HER HERE AFTER SCHOOL.
KOONG (TRAMP)
쿵
쿵..
KOONG
I'LL SHOW HER THESE FLOWERS.
WHAT IS THAT BOY THINKING ...?

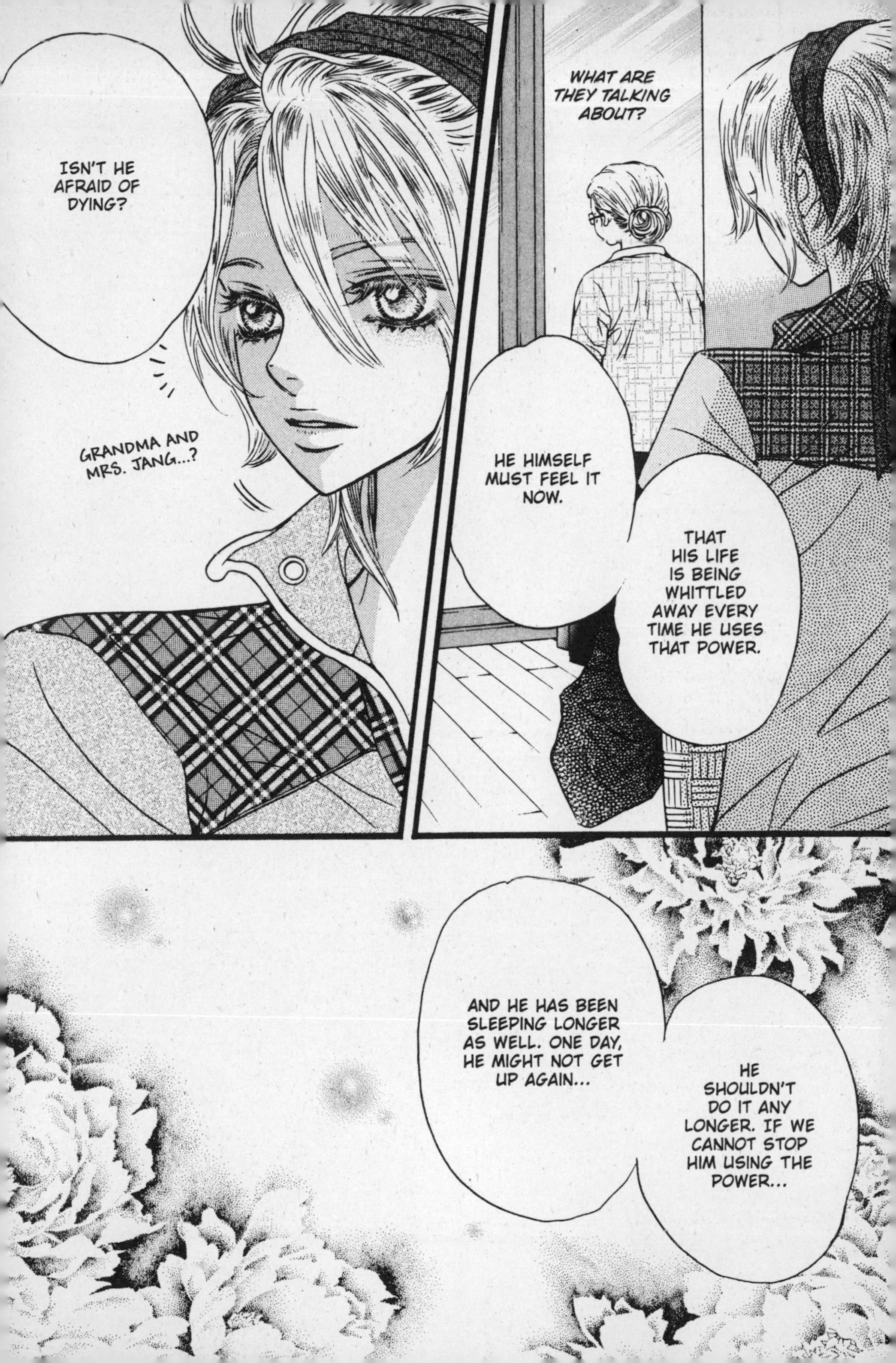
ISN'T HE AFRAID OF DYING?
GRANDMA AND MRS. JANG...?
WHAT ARE THEY TALKING ABOUT?
HE HIMSELF MUST FEEL IT NOW.
THAT HIS LIFE IS BEING WHITTLED AWAY EVERY TIME HE USES THAT POWER.
AND HE HAS BEEN SLEEPING LONGER AS WELL. ONE DAY, HE MIGHT NOT GET UP AGAIN...
HE SHOULDN'T DO IT ANY LONGER. IF WE CANNOT STOP HIM USING THE POWER...

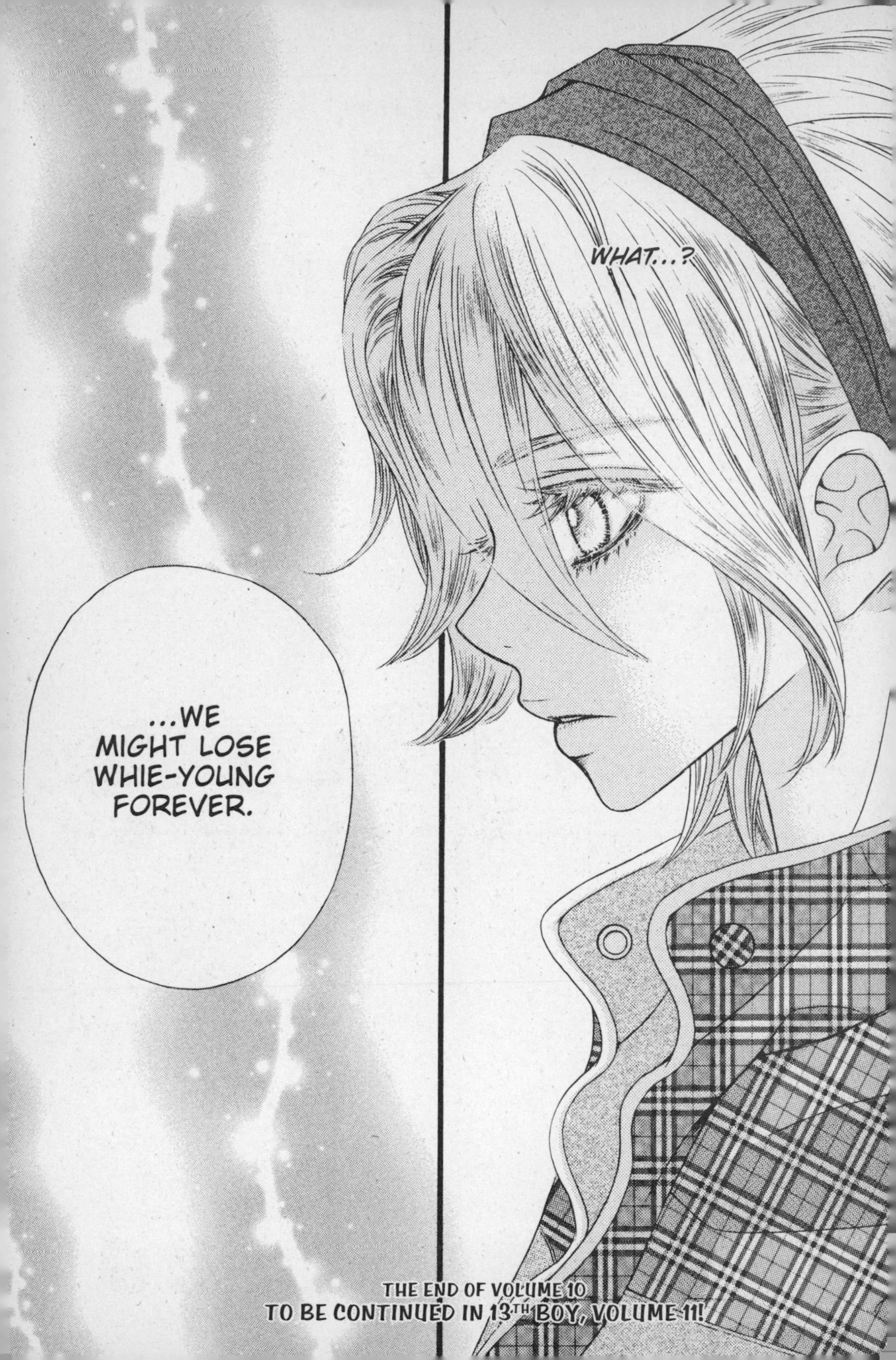
WHAT...?
...WE MIGHT LOSE WHIE-YOUNG FOREVER.
THE END OF VOLUME 10
TO BE CONTINUED IN 13TH BOY, VOLUME 11!

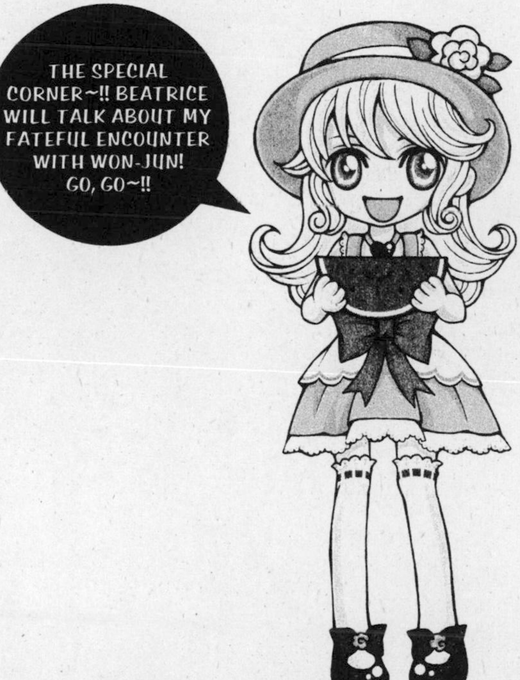
THE SPECIAL CORNER~!! BEATRICE WILL TALK ABOUT MY FATEFUL ENCOUNTER WITH WON-JUN! GO, GO~!!

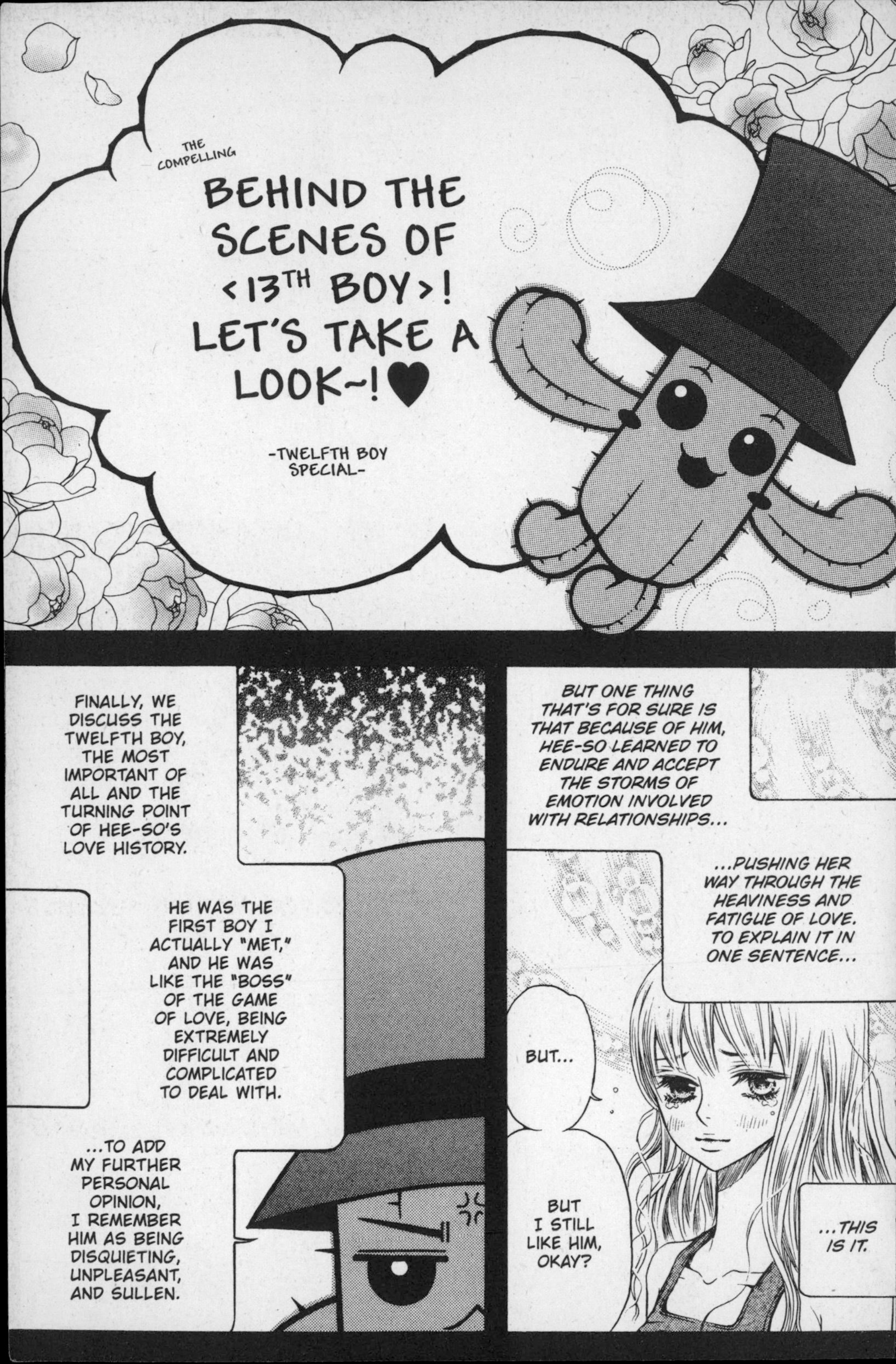

THE COMPELLING
BEHIND THE SCENES OF <13TH BOY>! LET'S TAKE A LOOK~!♥
-TWELFTH BOY SPECIAL-
FINALLY, WE DISCUSS THE TWELFTH BOY, THE MOST IMPORTANT OF ALL AND THE TURNING POINT OF HEE-SO'S LOVE HISTORY.
HE WAS THE FIRST BOY I ACTUALLY "MET," AND HE WAS LIKE THE "BOSS" OF THE GAME OF LOVE, BEING EXTREMELY DIFFICULT AND COMPLICATED TO DEAL WITH.
...TO ADD MY FURTHER PERSONAL OPINION, I REMEMBER HIM AS BEING DISQUIETING, UNPLEASANT, AND SULLEN.
BUT ONE THING THAT'S FOR SURE IS THAT BECAUSE OF HIM, HEE-SO LEARNED TO ENDURE AND ACCEPT THE STORMS OF EMOTION INVOLVED WITH RELATIONSHIPS...
...PUSHING HER WAY THROUGH THE HEAVINESS AND FATIGUE OF LOVE. TO EXPLAIN IT IN ONE SENTENCE...
BUT...
BUT I STILL LIKE HIM, OKAY?
...THIS IS IT.

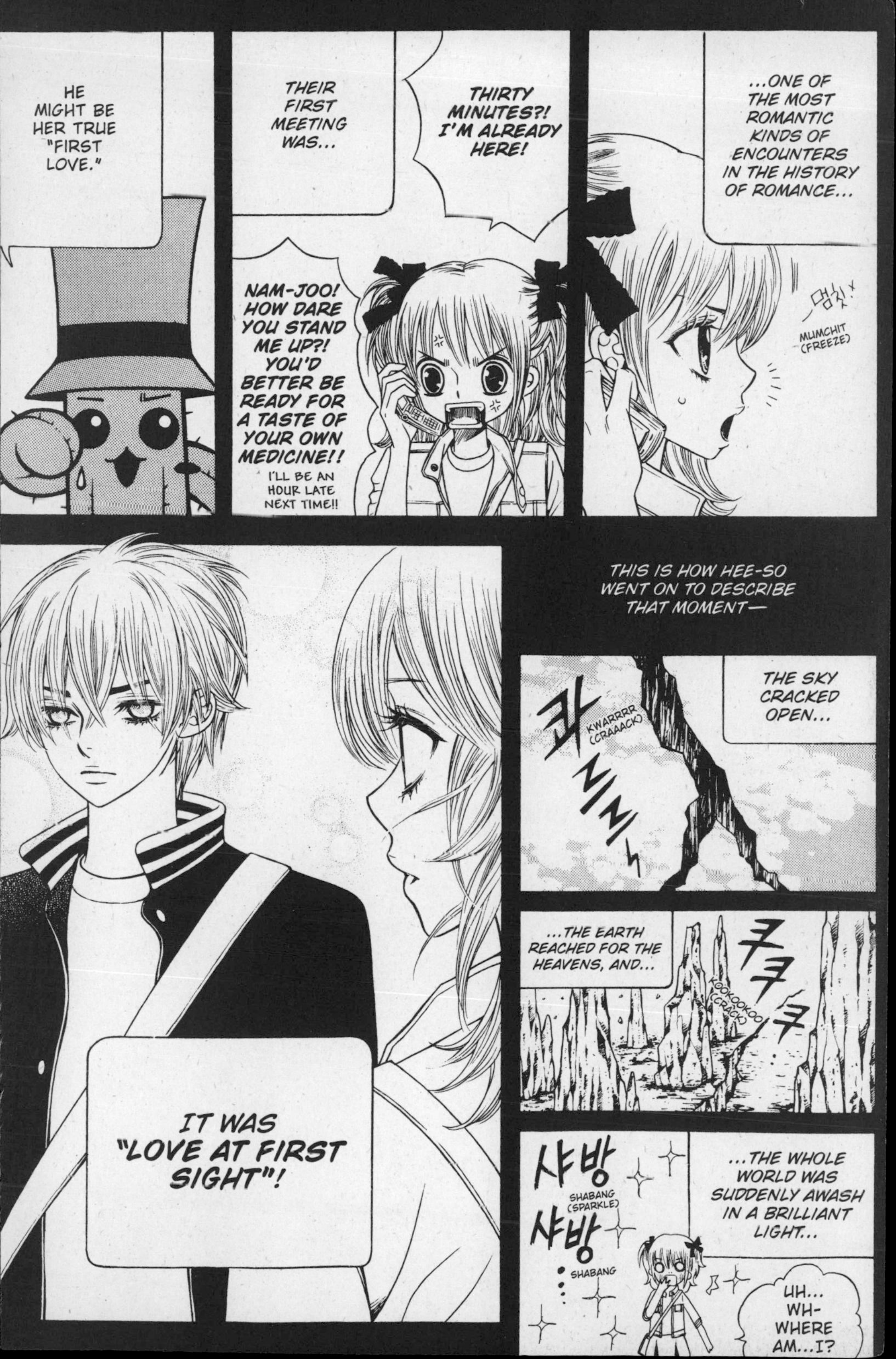
HE MIGHT BE HER TRUE "FIRST LOVE."
THEIR FIRST MEETING WAS...
THIRTY MINUTES?! I'M ALREADY HERE!
NAM-JOO! HOW DARE YOU STAND ME UP?! YOU'D BETTER BE READY FOR A TASTE OF YOUR OWN MEDICINE!!
I'LL BE AN HOUR LATE NEXT TIME!!
...ONE OF THE MOST ROMANTIC KINDS OF ENCOUNTERS IN THE HISTORY OF ROMANCE...
멈칫
MUMCHIT (FREEZE)
IT WAS "LOVE AT FIRST SIGHT"!
THIS IS HOW HEE-SO WENT ON TO DESCRIBE THAT MOMENT—
THE SKY CRACKED OPEN...
KWARRRR (CRAAACK)
...THE EARTH REACHED FOR THE HEAVENS, AND...
쿠쿠쿠
KOOKOOKOO (CRACK)
...THE WHOLE WORLD WAS SUDDENLY AWASH IN A BRILLIANT LIGHT...
샤방
SHABANG (SPARKLE)
샤방
SHABANG
UH... WH-WHERE AM...I?

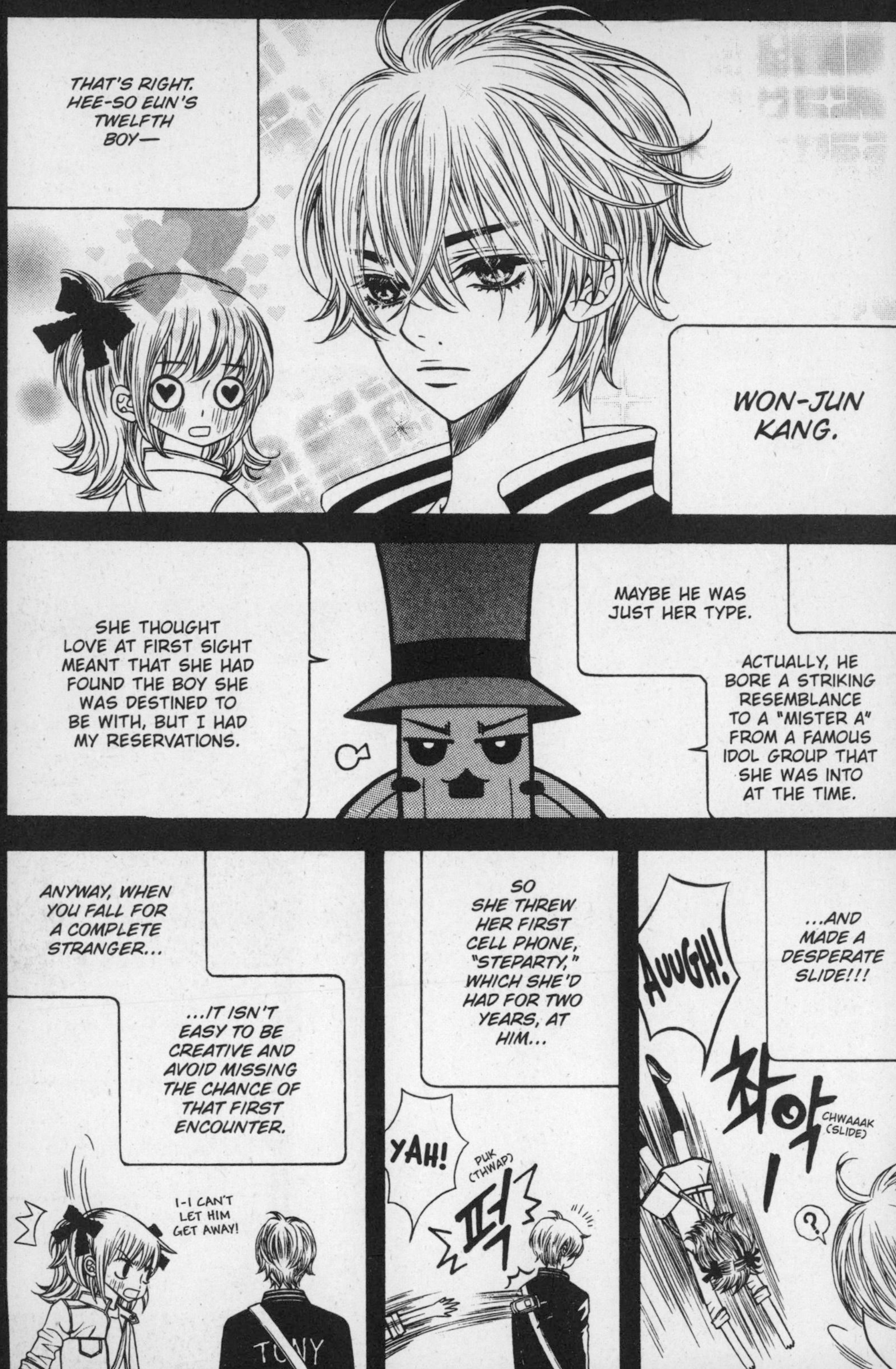
THAT'S RIGHT. HEE-SO EUN'S TWELFTH BOY—
WON-JUN KANG.
SHE THOUGHT LOVE AT FIRST SIGHT MEANT THAT SHE HAD FOUND THE BOY SHE WAS DESTINED TO BE WITH, BUT I HAD MY RESERVATIONS.
MAYBE HE WAS JUST HER TYPE.
ACTUALLY, HE BORE A STRIKING RESEMBLANCE TO A "MISTER A" FROM A FAMOUS IDOL GROUP THAT SHE WAS INTO AT THE TIME.
ANYWAY, WHEN YOU FALL FOR A COMPLETE STRANGER...
...IT ISN'T EASY TO BE CREATIVE AND AVOID MISSING THE CHANCE OF THAT FIRST ENCOUNTER.
I-I CAN'T LET HIM GET AWAY!
TONY
SO SHE THREW HER FIRST CELL PHONE, "STEPARTY," WHICH SHE'D HAD FOR TWO YEARS, AT HIM...
YAH!
PUK (THWAP)
...AND MADE A DESPERATE SLIDE!!!
AUUGH!
CHWAAAK (SLIDE)
?

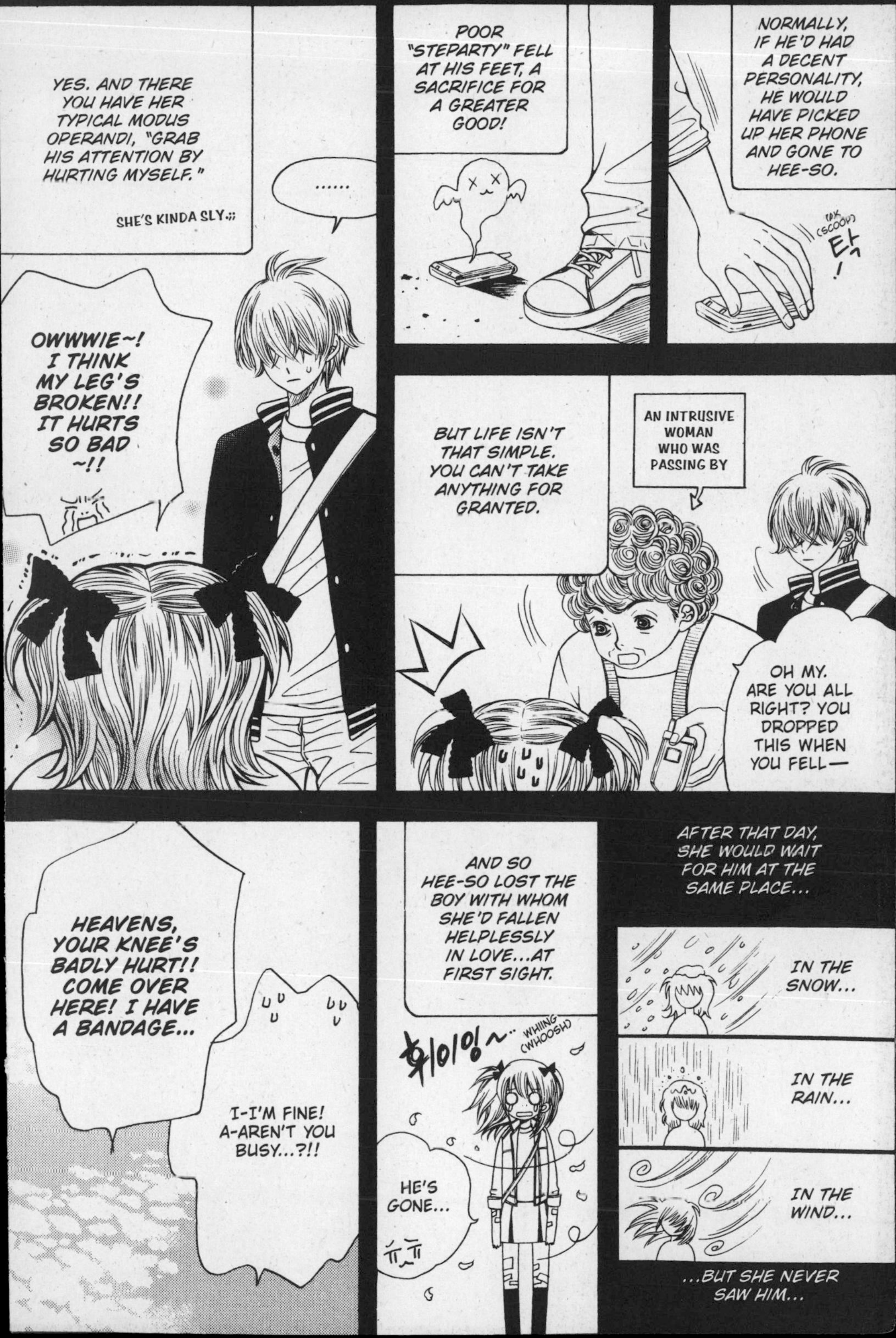
YES. AND THERE YOU HAVE HER TYPICAL MODUS OPERANDI, "GRAB HIS ATTENTION BY HURTING MYSELF."
SHE'S KINDA SLY.;;
......
OWWWIE~! I THINK MY LEG'S BROKEN!! IT HURTS SO BAD ~!!
POOR "STEPARTY" FELL AT HIS FEET, A SACRIFICE FOR A GREATER GOOD!
NORMALLY, IF HE'D HAD A DECENT PERSONALITY, HE WOULD HAVE PICKED UP HER PHONE AND GONE TO HEE-SO.
탁
(TAK (SCOOP))
BUT LIFE ISN'T THAT SIMPLE. YOU CAN'T TAKE ANYTHING FOR GRANTED.
AN INTRUSIVE WOMAN WHO WAS PASSING BY
OH MY. ARE YOU ALL RIGHT? YOU DROPPED THIS WHEN YOU FELL—
HEAVENS, YOUR KNEE'S BADLY HURT!! COME OVER HERE! I HAVE A BANDAGE...
I-I'M FINE! A-AREN'T YOU BUSY...?!!
AND SO HEE-SO LOST THE BOY WITH WHOM SHE'D FALLEN HELPLESSLY IN LOVE...AT FIRST SIGHT.
휘이잉~
WHIIING (WHOOSH)
HE'S GONE...
AFTER THAT DAY, SHE WOULD WAIT FOR HIM AT THE SAME PLACE...
IN THE SNOW...
IN THE RAIN...
IN THE WIND...
...BUT SHE NEVER SAW HIM...

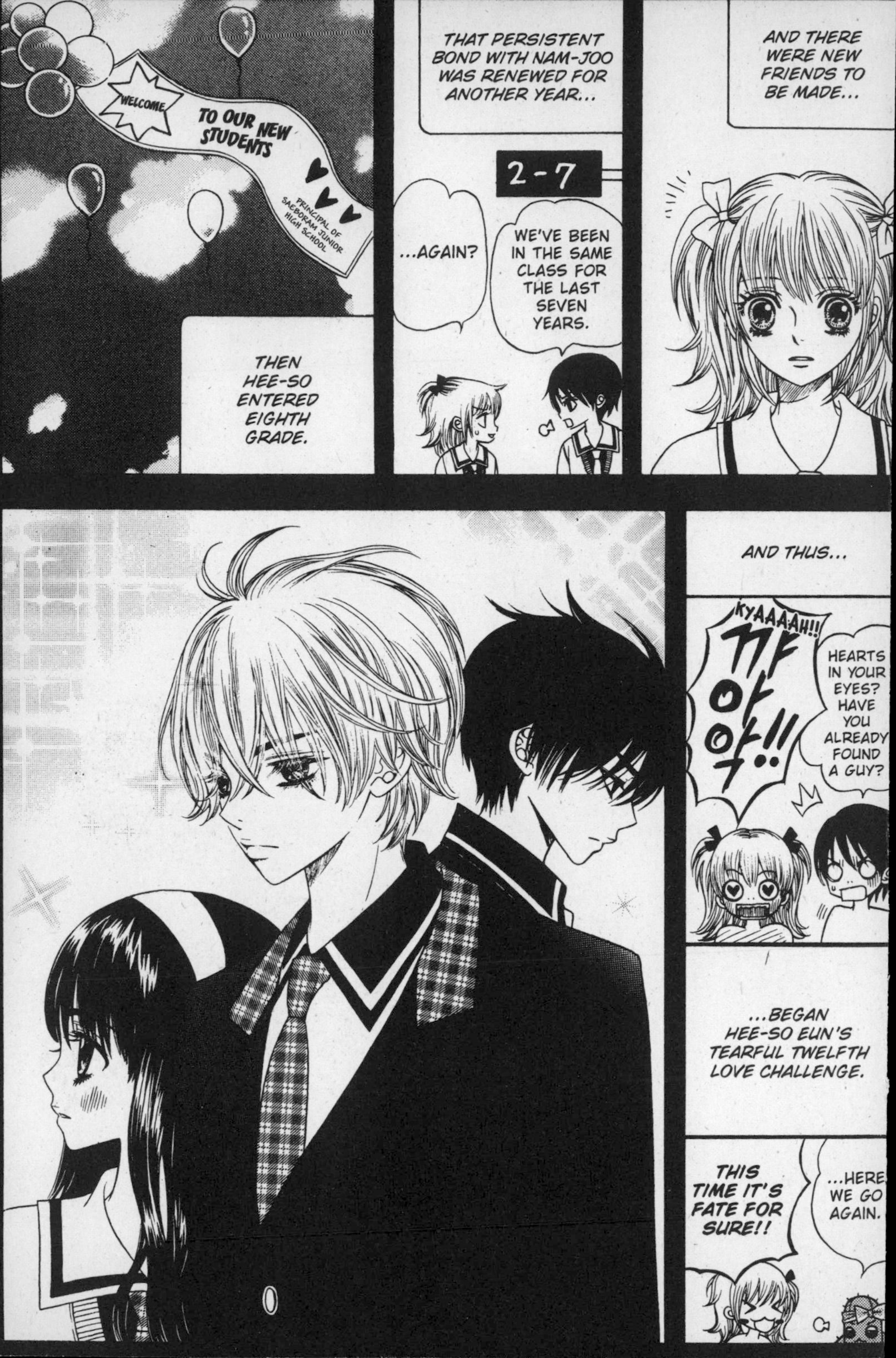
WELCOME
TO OUR NEW STUDENTS
PRINCIPAL OF SAEBORAM JUNIOR HIGH SCHOOL
THEN HEE-SO ENTERED EIGHTH GRADE.
THAT PERSISTENT BOND WITH NAM-JOO WAS RENEWED FOR ANOTHER YEAR...
2-7
...AGAIN?
WE'VE BEEN IN THE SAME CLASS FOR THE LAST SEVEN YEARS.
AND THERE WERE NEW FRIENDS TO BE MADE...
AND THUS...
KYAAAAH!!!
꺄아악!!
HEARTS IN YOUR EYES? HAVE YOU ALREADY FOUND A GUY?
...BEGAN HEE-SO EUN'S TEARFUL TWELFTH LOVE CHALLENGE.
THIS TIME IT'S FATE FOR SURE!!
...HERE WE GO AGAIN.

Page 30
Won: Korean monetary unit. It's worth about US$0.90.

Kim-bab: Korean sushi roll.

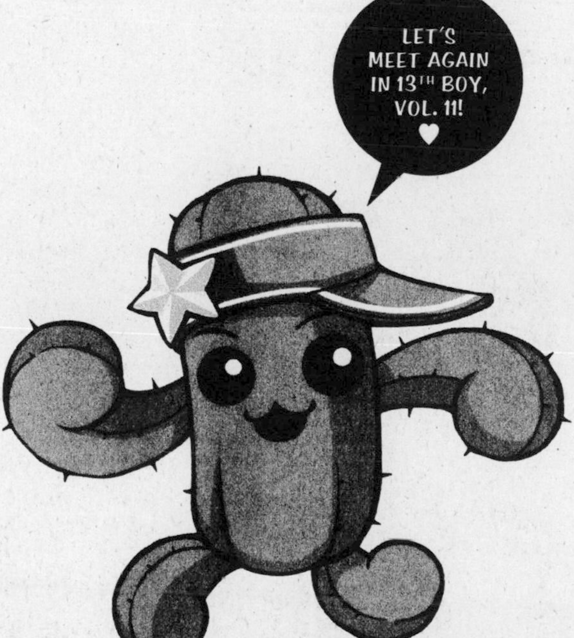
LET'S MEET AGAIN IN 13TH BOY, VOL. 11! ♥

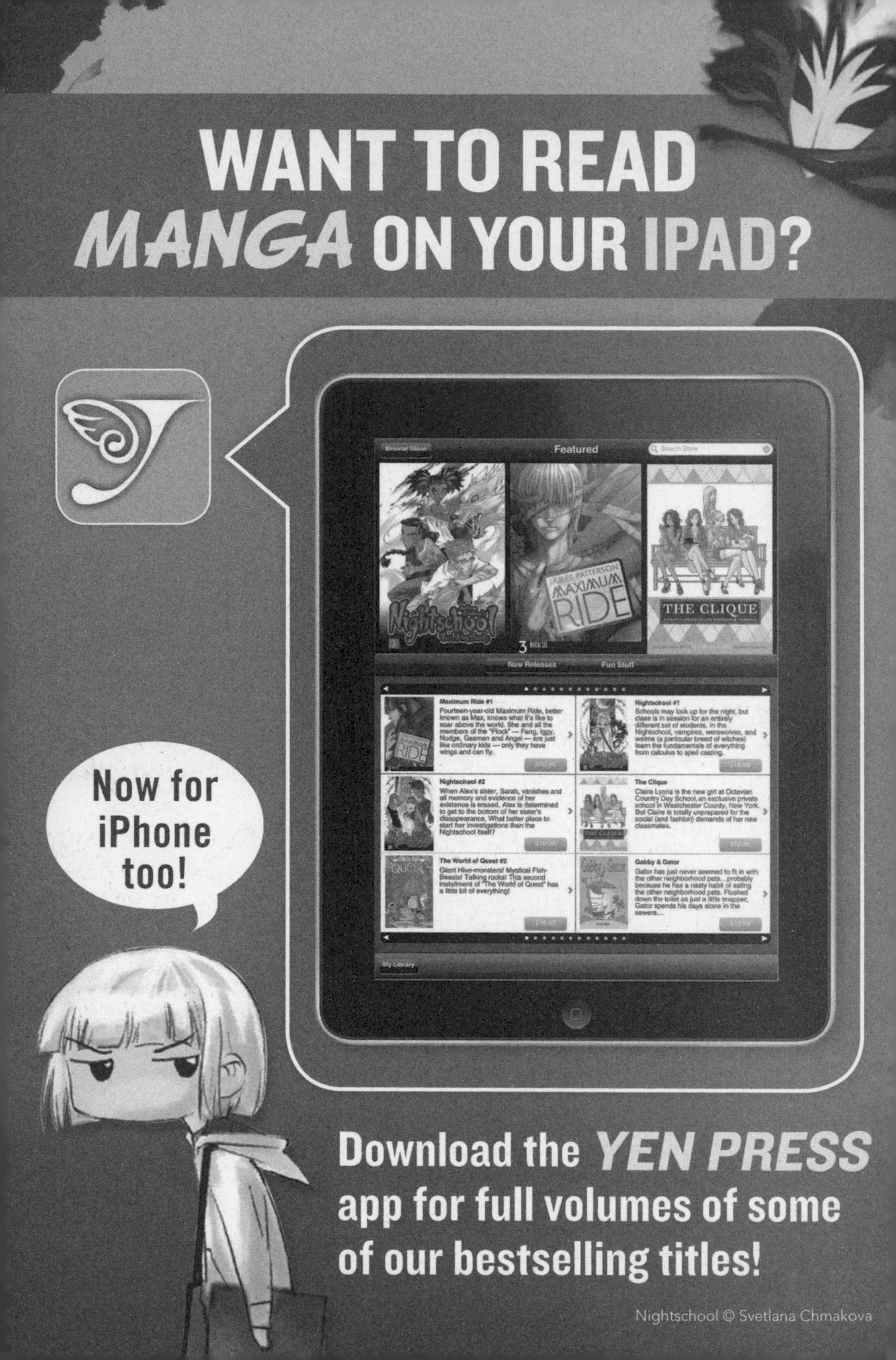
WANT TO READ
MANGA ON YOUR IPAD?
Now for iPhone too!
Featured
New Releases
Fun Stuff
Download the YEN PRESS app for full volumes of some of our bestselling titles!
Nightschool © Svetlana Chmakova

Can't wait for the next volume? You don't have to!

Keep up with the latest chapters of some of your favorite manga every month online in the pages of YEN PLUS!

WITCH & WIZARD

MAXIMUM RIDE

DANIEL X

SOULLESS

K-ON!

Visit us at
www.yenplus.com
for details!

YEN+ Plus

Yen
Press
www.yenpress.com

Becoming the princess... Isn't that every girl's dream?!

Monarchy rule ended long ago in Korea, but there are still other countries with kings, queens, princes and princesses. What if Korea had continued monarchism? What if all the beautiful palaces, which are now only historical relics, were actually filled with people? What if the glamorous royal family still maintained the palace customs? Welcome to a world where Korea still has the royal family living in their everyday lives! Only for this one high school girl, Chae-Kyung, is this a tragedy, since she has to marry the prince — who apparently is a total bastard!

THE ROYAL PALACE
Goong
vol.1~12

Park SoHee

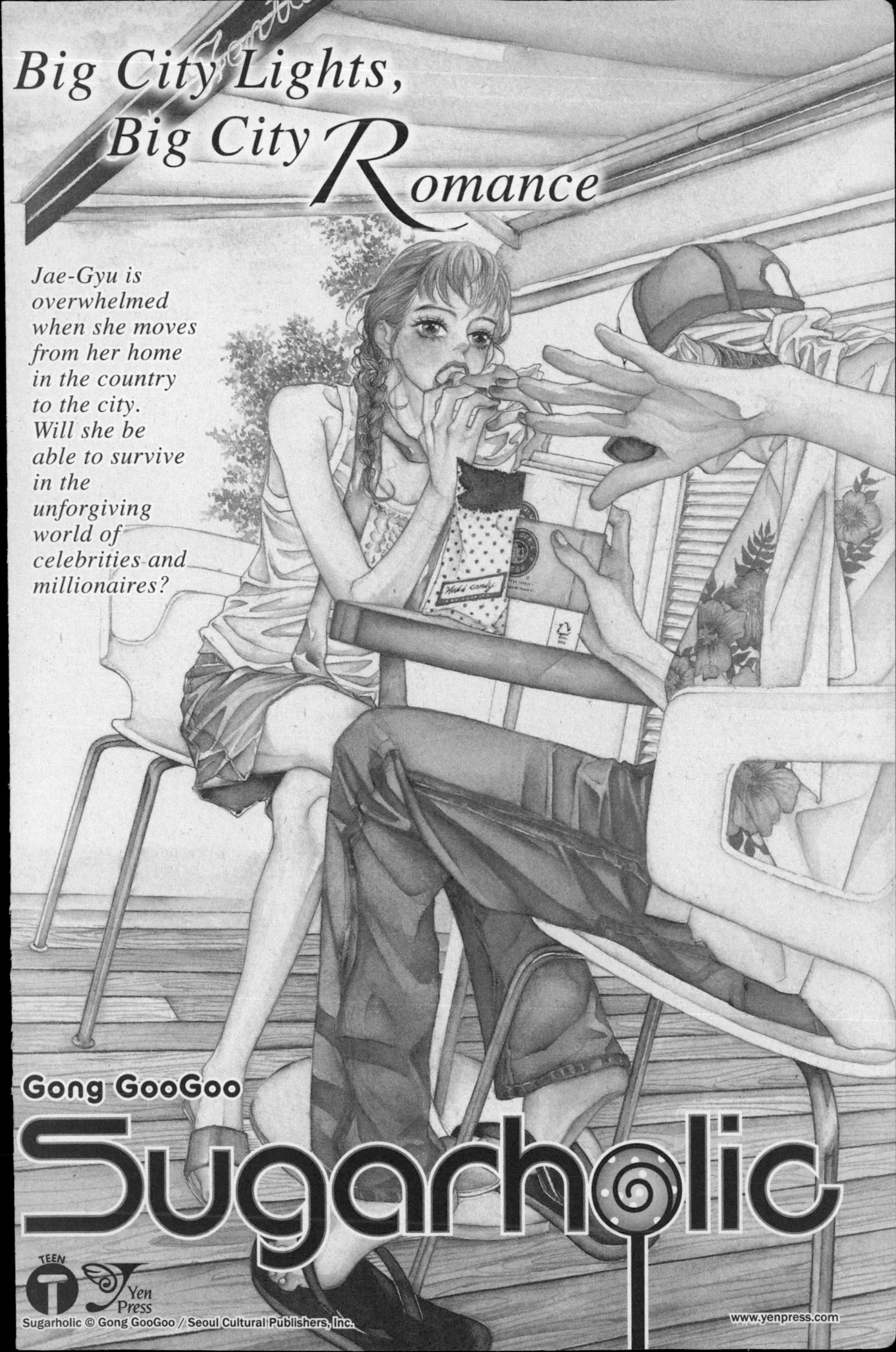
Big City Lights,
Big City Romance
Jae-Gyu is overwhelmed when she moves from her home in the country to the city. Will she be able to survive in the unforgiving world of celebrities and millionaires?
Gong GooGoo
Sugarholic
TEEN
Yen Press
Sugarholic © Gong GooGoo / Seoul Cultural Publishers, Inc.
www.yenpress.com

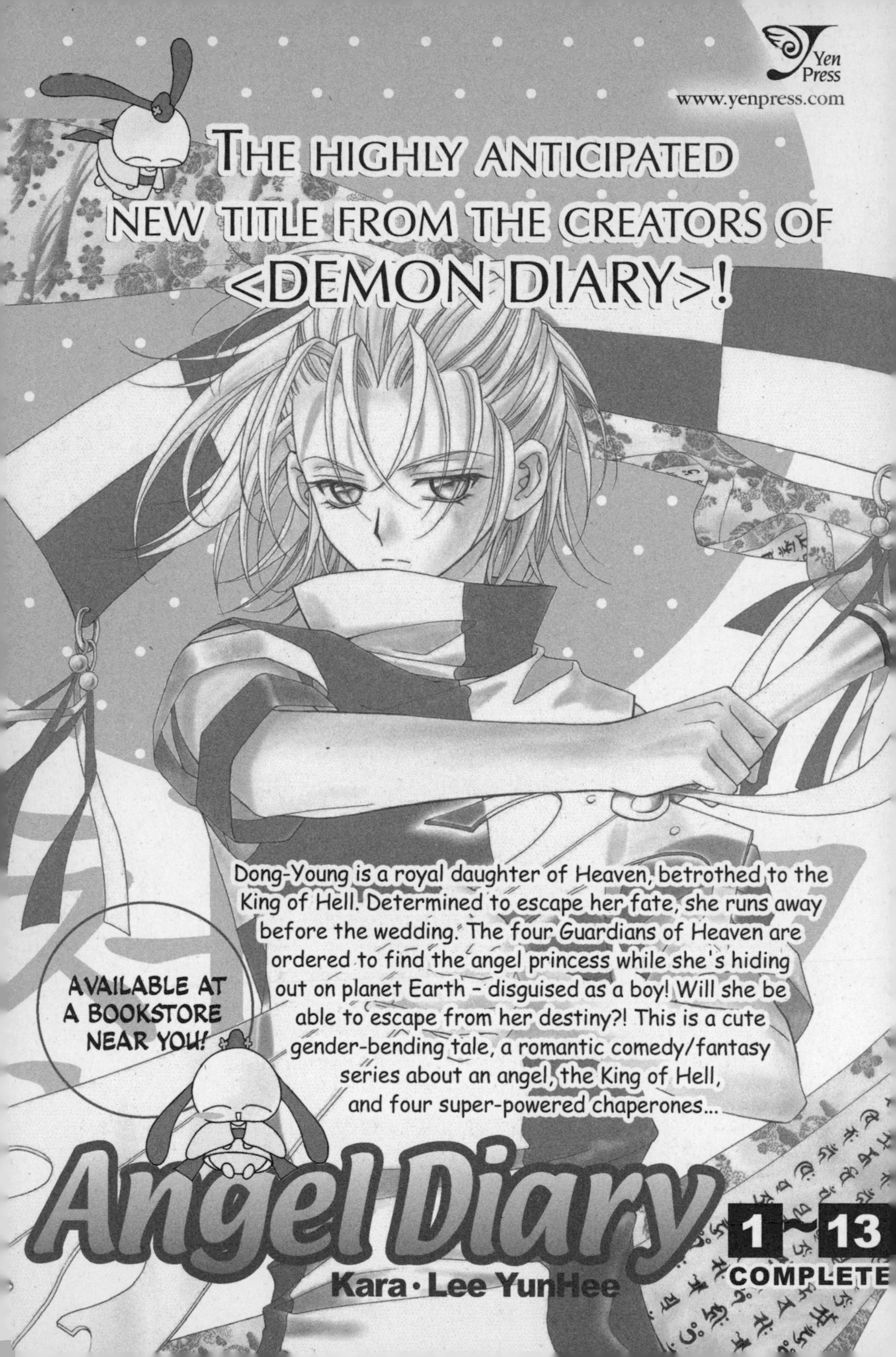
Yen Press
www.yenpress.com
THE HIGHLY ANTICIPATED
NEW TITLE FROM THE CREATORS OF
<DEMON DIARY>!
Dong-Young is a royal daughter of Heaven, betrothed to the King of Hell. Determined to escape her fate, she runs away before the wedding. The four Guardians of Heaven are ordered to find the angel princess while she's hiding out on planet Earth – disguised as a boy! Will she be able to escape from her destiny?! This is a cute gender-bending tale, a romantic comedy/fantasy series about an angel, the King of Hell, and four super-powered chaperones...
AVAILABLE AT A BOOKSTORE NEAR YOU!
Angel Diary
1~13
COMPLETE
Kara · Lee YunHee

Y Yen
Press
www.yenpress.com

The newest title from the creators of <Demon Diary> and <Angel Diary>!

Once upon a time, a selfish king summoned the monstrous Bulkirin into the real world. The monster killed half of all human beings, leaving the rest helpless as to what to do. That is, until one day when a hero appeared and defeated the Bulkirin with the legendary "Seven Blade Sword." But···what does all this have to do with 8th grader Eun-Gyo Sung?! First, she gets suspended from school for fighting. Then, she runs away from home. The last thing she needed was to be kidnapped—and whisked into the past by a mysterious stranger named No-Ah!

Legend

Available at bookstores near you!

1-10 COMPLETE

K a r a · W o o   S o o J u n g

13th BOY ⑩

SANGEUN LEE

Translation: JiEun Park
English Adaptation: Natalie Baan

Lettering: Terri Delgado

13th Boy, Vol. 10 © 2008 SangEun Lee. All rights reserved. First published in Korea in 2008 by Haksan Publishing Co., Ltd. English translation rights in U.S.A., Canada, UK, and Republic of Ireland arranged with Haksan Publishing Co., Ltd.

English translation © 2012 Hachette Book Group, Inc.

Yen Press
Hachette Book Group
237 Park Avenue, New York, NY 10017

www.HachetteBookGroup.com
www.YenPress.com

Yen Press is an imprint of Hachette Book Group, Inc.
The Yen Press name and logo are trademarks of Hachette Book Group, Inc.

First Yen Press Edition: January 2012

ISBN: 978-0-316-19081-7

10 9 8 7 6 5 4 3 2 1

BVG

Printed in the United States of America